LAȝAMON'S *ARTHUR*

The Arthurian section of Laȝamon's *Brut*

LAȝAMON'S 𝔄𝔯𝔱𝔥𝔲𝔯

The Arthurian section of Laȝamon's *Brut*

(Lines 9229 — 14297)

Edition and Translation

with Introduction, Textual Notes and Commentary

W. R. J. Barron and S. C. Weinberg

UNIVERSITY OF TEXAS PRESS, AUSTIN

International Standard Book Number 0-292-74660-1
Library of Congress Catalog Card Number 88-51676

First University of Texas Press Edition, 1989

Produced by Longman Singapore Publishers (Pte) Ltd.
Printed in Singapore

CONTENTS

CONTENTS

PREFACE

A glance at any bibliography of English medieval literature will suggest that critical appreciation of Laȝamon's *Brut*, represented by a handful of items, has been hindered by lack of an accessible text. The text of both Sir Frederic Madden's edition of 1847 and the Early English Text Society edition, still incomplete, is unpunctuated and presents difficulties for the non-specialist. Yet merely in terms of cultural history, its literary quality apart, the *Brut* is a work of major importance: proof that the English language was fit to be a literary medium after some century and a half of virtual silence, the first clear indication that the native poetic tradition had survived the Norman Conquest, the earliest vernacular version of the Arthurian legend which was to be a recurrent theme across the centuries to come.

This book is intended to supply a text of the Arthurian section, most frequently studied in relation to other versions, and a parallel translation as an aid to understanding its somewhat difficult language and diction. The text is based on that of the British Library manuscript, Cotton Caligula A.ix as edited by G. L. Brook and R. F. Leslie for the Early English Text Society, and made available to us by the Oxford University Computing Service from its text archive. The EETS edition closely reproduces the manuscript, with the minimum of emendation but carefully indicating textual imperfections and scribal alterations. In order to present a clear and readable text, we have omitted the various types of bracket by which these are indicated, the sign showing unnecessary reduplication of letters (together with the reduplicated letter), and the scribal indication of mid-line caesura and end of verse line. The caesura itself has been retained since it often provides a helpful guide to meaning by marking sense units within a sentence. Where a line seems metrically deficient but there is no break in sense, we have not felt it necessary to emend; where it has been necessary to fill an obvious lacuna from the other *Brut* text, BL, Cotton Otho C.xiii, printed in parallel by Brook and Leslie, the words supplied are enclosed in square brackets. We have also supplied modern punctuation and capitalisation, and divided the text into paragraphs. We have simplified the editorial system of hyphenation, retaining the hyphen only where it is a useful guide to the meaning of compound formations. The line-numbering of the EETS edition has been retained to facilitate reference both to it and the studies based upon it.

The text has been checked throughout against the Madden edition, justly praised for the accuracy of its transcription, in part against a photocopy of the Caligula manuscript and, in cases of doubt, against the manuscript itself. Where we have rejected the reading of Brook and Leslie, as with other textual issues, an asterisk directs attention to a comment in the Textual Notes. In the translation, the symbol # indicates a point of clarification in the Commentary. In both Textual Notes and Commentary we have confined ourselves to matters essential for the understanding of the text and translation without pre-empting the detailed critical apparatus to be supplied by the final volume of the EETS edition.

We acknowledge with gratitude our indebtedness to the original editors and to the Council of the Early English Text Society for permission to base our text upon their transcription, to the Oxford University Computing Service for supplying the computer tape of the text, and to the trustees of the British Library for access to the Caligula manuscript. Our thanks are also due to the friends and colleagues who have read and commented helpfully upon portions of the translation: John Anderson, John Eadie, Peter Field, Marion Glasscoe, Maldwyn Mills, Ron Waldron, Joy Watkin. It has greatly benefited from their perception and critical skill; for the defects which remain we must take responsibility. We owe a particular debt to our colleague David Denison, not only for assistance in understanding Laȝamon's syntax, but for his patient guidance in all aspects of computer word-processing, which greatly facilitated the production of this book at every stage of the work.

W. R. J. Barron, S. C. Weinberg
Manchester, March 1988

INTRODUCTION

All that we know with any certainty of the authorship and sources of Laȝamon's *Brut* is given in the opening lines of the poem:

An preost wes on leoden,   Laȝamon wes ihoten;

he wes Leouenaðes sone   —liðe him beo Drihten!

He wonede at Ernleȝe   at æðelen are chirechen

vppen Seuarne staþe   —sel þar him þuhte—

onfest Radestone;   þer he bock radde.   5

    Hit com him on mode   and on his mern þonke

þet he wolde of Engle   þa æðelæn tellen,

wat heo ihoten weoren   and wonene heo comen

þa Englene londe   ærest ahten

æfter þan flode   þe from Drihtene com,   10

þe al her aquelde   quic þat he funde,

buten Noe and Sem,   Iaphet and Cham,

and heore four wiues   þe mid heom weren on archen.

    Laȝamon gon liðen   wide ȝond þas leode

and biwon þa æðela boc   þa he to bisne nom.   15

He nom þa Englisca boc   þa makede Seint Beda.

Anoþer he nom on Latin   þe makede Seinte Albin

and þe feire Austin   þe fulluht broute hider in.

Boc he nom þe þridde,   leide þer amidden,

þa makede a Frenchis clerc   20

Wace wes ihoten,   þe wel couþe writen,

and he hoe ȝef þare æðelen   Ælienor

þe wes Henries quene   þes heȝes kinges.

    Laȝamon leide þeos boc   and þa leaf wende;

he heom leofliche biheold   —liþe him beo Drihten!   25

Feþeren he nom mid fingren   and fiede on boc-felle

and þa soþere word   sette togadere,

and þa þre boc   þrumde to are.

    Nu biddeð Laȝamon   alcne æðele mon,

for þene almiten Godd,   30

þet þeos boc rede   and leornia þeos runan,

þet he þeos soðfeste word   segge tosumne

for his fader saule   þa hine forðbrouhte,

and for his moder saule   þa hine to monne iber,

and for his awene saule   þat hire þe selre beo. Amen.   35

There is no counterpart in any of Laȝamon's supposed sources to this introductory passage which raises many problems of interpretation and even of translation. In general terms it may be translated as follows:

There was a priest in the land who was called Laȝamon;
he was the son of Leovenath —God be merciful to him!
He lived at Areley by a noble church
on the bank of the Severn —he thought it pleasant there—
5 close to Redstone; there he read books.
    It came into his mind, an excellent intention of his,
that he would relate the noble origins of the English,
what they were called and whence they came
who first possessed the land of England
10 after the flood sent by God,
which here on earth destroyed all living things it came upon,
save Noah and Shem, Japhet and Ham,
and their four wives who were with them in the ark.
    Laȝamon travelled far and wide throughout this land,
15 and collected the excellent books which he took as a model.
He chose the English book which St Bede composed.
He chose another in Latin composed by St Albin
and the good Austin who introduced baptism here.
He chose a third book and placed it with the others,
20 a book which a French cleric
called Wace, who could write well, had composed
and presented to the noble Eleanor
who was the great King Henry's queen.
    Laȝamon laid these books down and turned the pages;
25 he looked on them with pleasure —God be gracious to him!
He took quill pens in his hand and wrote on parchment
and set down together the most truthful words,
and compressed the three books into one.
    Now Laȝamon begs every good man,
30 for the sake of almighty God,
that he should read this book and study these writings,
that he should repeat in full these truthful words
for the soul of his father who begot him,
and for the soul of his mother who gave birth to him,
35 and for his own soul that it may be the better for it. Amen.

In outline this is the conventional literary prologue which often introduced a major medieval poem, announcing author, subject and source, and calling for the prayers of the audience — normally the only return the poet could expect from his work. But in detail it is unusually personal, precise, and in some respects puzzling. The poet's name is of Scandinavian origin, meaning Law-man, his patronymic is Anglo-Saxon; together they reflect the fusion of earlier settler cultures in the England for which he wrote some century and a half after the Norman Conquest. His home village of Areley Kings, about ten miles upstream from Worcester at a point where the Severn runs between red sandstone cliffs, looks east to the rolling green hills of England and west to the Black Mountains of the Welsh borders. Its fifteenth-century church incorporates some traces — three Norman arches, bits of moulding and lettering — of its predecessor where Laȝamon served. But it is his status as a scholar, rather than his office as parish priest, which he proclaims in declaring that 'þer he bock radde' (5). If he could read all the books he names as his sources, he had more learning than most country priests at that time.

Sources, manuscripts and date

Of the books Laȝamon mentions (16-21), the third must be the *Roman de Brut*, a verse chronicle by the Jerseyman Robert Wace. The 'Englisca boc þa makede Seint Beda' suggests the anonymous Anglo-Saxon translation of the *Historia Ecclesiastica* originally written by the Venerable Bede in Latin prose early in the eighth century. The book 'þe makede Seinte Albin and þe feire Austin' is a mystery, unless it is a confused reference to Bede's Latin original whose opening mention of Albinus, Abbot of St Augustine's, Canterbury (708-32), might be misunderstood as calling him the author, while later in the first book Augustine himself figures prominently. The assumption is that Laȝamon, glancing through the opening pages of the Latin Bede, mistook the two as joint authors, though they lived a century apart. If so, it says something about the Latinity of a country priest that he did not recognise he was dealing with two versions of the same book. But the famous names, like those of Bede and Wace, would lend prestige to a historical work by a backwoods cleric. Such claims to learned sources were conventional and there need have been no conscious deceit; Laȝamon may have assembled prestigious sources without knowing in advance which could be of use to him. In the event, the massive work he produced, over 16,000 lines in length, shows little sign of direct dependence on anything other than Wace's *Brut*.

Laȝamon's poem survives in two British Library manuscripts, Cotton Caligula A.ix and Cotton Otho C.xiii, the latter radically altered in language and abbreviated in content. The indications are that both texts are independently derived from a common version which cannot have been the author's original; both, in varying degrees, show sufficient traces of the south-west Midlands dialect to suggest that the original was written in Worcestershire. So at least three copies of this vast work must once have existed. Who can have paid for the quantities of expensive parchment needed to make them, not to mention the bookskin on which the poem was originally composed? The Otho proem refers to the poet living 'wid þan gode cniþte' (3), possibly as the chaplain of some local landowner; but it is difficult to imagine what kind of patron can have supported such an ambitious enterprise in an age when English was barely the language of books at all.

In forming an impression of the cultural circumstances in which the work was produced, an initial difficulty is presented by problems of dating. The use of the past tense in the reference to Eleanor as Henry's queen (23) suggests that it was written after the death of Henry II in 1189, possibly after Eleanor's own death in 1204. How long after involves a judgement on the fidelity with which Laȝamon's work is represented in the two surviving texts. The contrast between the two has suggested a difference of date and in the immediacy of their relationship to the original. The Caligula text, archaic in language, largely devoid of French loan-words, rich in compound terms, some familiar from Old English, others apparently newly formed on traditional patterns, has been dated c.1250; the Otho, simplified in syntax and vocabulary, French borrowings replacing many of the compound words, c.1275. Recently, however, palaeographical examination has assigned the Caligula manuscript to the second half of the thirteenth century, effectively eliminating the distinction of date between the two texts.[1]

This poses the apparent paradox that the *Brut* was equally viable in two contemporary versions radically different in expression. If the language of the Otho text reflects the usage of the second half of the thirteenth century, the Caligula version must have seemed strangely outdated, a literary curiosity, to contemporary readers. The high quality of the Caligula text, presenting comparatively few textual problems, does not suggest a complicated manuscript tradition involving repeated recopying. If it faithfully reproduces the idiom of the original, what evidence does that idiom offer for the date of composition? It has been suggested that the antique diction it preserves was deliberately contrived by the poet, consciously imprinting upon his work an archaic character which he felt appropriate to its subject.[2] But a personal stylistic fantasy could not have ensured the success of the poem unless the original audience shared at least something of the linguistic and stylistic tradition in which it was rooted.

The roots of that tradition can be traced to the literature of the pre-Conquest period. But the Conquest, by sweeping away the old ruling class, doomed to eventual extinction the secular literature in which its codes and values were expressed. How long elements of the Old English secular tradition can have persisted after the Conquest is impossible to estimate. The conservative influence of the Worcester scriptoria under the long-lived Bishop Wulfstan (*ob.*1095) ensured the continuity of the homiletic tradition in Laȝamon's neighbourhood. The homiletic prose tradition might have supplied elements of style and syntax to Laȝamon's idiom, but not the many features reminiscent of Old English poetry. The corpus of secular texts preserved is too limited to register the process of decline and change in that tradition; no doubt it proceeded at different rates in different parts of the country. Laȝamon, living in the remote west, may have been as much influenced by oral as by textual tradition; but it is impossible to estimate what elements of the formal literary idiom could have entered popular tradition. The persistence of pre-Conquest poetic traditions, literary or oral, into the second half of the thirteenth century is difficult to credit. Whatever its sources, Laȝamon's idiom does not suggest a literary pastiche; it is sustained, variable, self-consistent, a natural if highly idiosyncratic medium. To have incorporated in it so many elements of Old English tradition, Laȝamon can scarcely have been born much more than a century after the Conquest. He might have written in old age, but the evident success of the *Brut* presupposes an audience sufficiently familiar with the components of its style to find the idiom effective. Passive copying by a conservative scribe might explain the archaic character of the Caligula text, but the original composition can hardly have been written later than the opening decades of the thirteenth century.[3]

The cultural context

Whether the *Brut* was written ten years before the turn of the century or twenty years after will have made little difference to the cultural context at the level of English life familiar to a country priest. In his western backwater social circumstances changed slowly, and everywhere in England the political conditions established by the Norman Conquest had long been accepted and absorbed. Those who understood such matters recognised that the Conqueror had had some claim to the throne; simpler men regarded his victory at Hastings as God's judgement in his favour, and he legitimised it by exacting the formality of election by the Witan, the old royal council. The bitterness of the Anglo-Saxon aristocracy, robbed of its patrimony, did not outlive the generation decimated at Hastings, proscribed for their resistance to the Conqueror there or in the regional rebellions of the early years, deprived of their lands and so of their rank, power and prosperity. All passed to the Conqueror's kinsmen and followers, Normans, Bretons, Flemings, who had supported him in his military adventure. Their numbers were small; by the end of William's reign (1087) some fifteen hundred held estates in England, representing between one and two per cent of the population. But they were widely dispersed and, under the king, their power was absolute.

The power of the Church passed, with its lands and treasures, out of English hands. Odo of Bayeux, the Conqueror's brother, distributed benefices to Norman churchmen and by the end of the reign, when only two Englishmen held estates directly from the king, only one native bishop, Wulfstan of Worcester, still retained his see. Lesser men had less to lose; what shocked them was not the replacement of one ruling class by another, but the thoroughness with which the new masters exploited their conquest, the ruthless efficiency with which the Domesday survey (1086) listed every acre, every ox in the kingdom, the rapacity which carried off crucifixes, shrines, altar plate and embroideries to adorn continental churches or Norman dinner-tables.

As memories of the Conquest faded in the course of the twelfth century, it was not the illegal actions of foreigners of which all classes complained, but the punctiliousness with which their new masters enforced English law for their own advantage. Absolute monarchical rule was imitated at local level in the new stone castles whose holders administered justice to the tenants they armed and mounted as their followers in war. The social relationship was familiar to Englishmen accustomed to group themselves in peace and war about a chieftain who was often their kinsman as well as lawgiver. But the new feudal system formalised what had been a voluntary association of social equals; lesser thanes who might once have headed a war-band of their own were forced into dependence by the high costs of mounted warfare, and many yeomen farmers, deprived of their lands, sank into serfdom.

Socially dominant and widely dispersed, the seigneurs exerted an influence out of all proportion to their numbers, their Norman entourage living closely and working daily with their English sub-tenants, village reeves, childrens' nurses and other domestic servants. The age was one of comparative peace, after centuries of Islamic and Viking threat to Europe, when an unprecedented rise in population facilitated forest clearances, marsh drainage, the use of heavier ploughs and the foundation of thousands of new villages. The consequent increase in trade and the flourishing of the towns allowed some Englishmen to rise in the world and achieve a degree of social independence: skilled craftsmen, merchants, goldsmiths who were bankers to the barons, the minters of coin who continued to come from traditional English families. As their wealth increased, their daughters married into Norman families; English women of good family had made such marriages since the Conquest. Slowly the two peoples began to mingle, to share common values, to forget their different racial origins.

The social situation was mirrored in the linguistic, evolving slowly from age to age, area to area, with a complexity too great to be recorded in detail. The conquerors had no nationalistic bias against English; though William abandoned his personal effort to learn the language, he continued its administrative use in the first generation. But with the displacement of the old ruling class, the spoken language diversified into the dialects of a land-bound peasantry which the new rulers had no incentive to learn. Their Norman French assumed any administrative function for which Latin was inappropriate: pleading in the lawcourts, the keeping of estate records and household accounts, the education of nuns. It was also the language of polite society which any Englishman hoping to rise in the world — surviving thanes anxious for assimilation with their peers, native clergy seeking preferment, the higher servants on baronial estates — had to master as perfectly as possible. For some two centuries it retained its dominance as an island-wide vernacular, spoken by all who aspired to power in any sphere, increasingly cut off from its continental roots, slowly evolving into Anglo-Norman.

But the great mass of Englishmen knew no more of it than the occasional word of command thrown at them or a snatch of song picked up from the castle servants. Gradually their weight of numbers told and their masters became increasingly, if at first casually, bilingual. The children of mixed marriages carried into adult life a smattering of the mother-tongue learnt in the nursery. Conscientious Norman clerics, if they hoped to be effective at parish level, needed English as administrators even if they left preaching to the ill-educated native clergy. Great churchmen, civil servants as much as priests, and the great nobles, crown officers as much as landed magnates, with whom they did formal business in Latin, might use French and English at other levels of their complex lives.

The early thirteenth century, when Laʒamon seems most likely to have been parish priest of Areley Kings, was a turning point in the shifting balance between the three languages. In 1204 Normandy was lost to the English crown in a dispute with the king of France as nominal overlord, forcing those with feudal holdings in both countries to decide where their allegiance lay and abandon their estates in one or the other to younger brothers. England had meanwhile acquired, through marriage or conquest, vast territories in south-west France which kept her in constant conflict with the emergent nation-state whose dialect, Francien, was increasingly the medium of French cultural dominance in western Europe. Anglo-Norman, in its insular isolation, seemed increasingly a provincial dialect to be replaced in the education of the nobility, whose children now had to be taught the class idiom, by continental French. Though its social prestige had begun to wane, Anglo-Norman relinquished its administrative function reluctantly, sphere by sphere, over the centuries as English again became the language of government, lawcourts, schools and eventually, in the age of Chaucer, of courtly literature. Its eventual triumph was still far off in the age of Laʒamon; to his contemporaries its literary renaissance would have seemed highly improbable.

With the hindsight of our modern perspective, the future of English literature seems no more in doubt than that of the language. Since the mass of the people continued to speak English, their need for entertainment and instruction would ensure its ultimate return to literary use. But whatever form it took in the post-Conquest centuries, the literature of an under-class was unlikely to find more than accidental and fugitive record in written form. Some scriptoria at least went on copying those forms of pre-Conquest literature whose social function remained valid: the *Anglo-Saxon Chronicle*, a historical record given national status by Alfred the Great (871-99), was continued at local level, surviving until 1154 at Peterborough Abbey; the homilies which Ælfric, Abbot of Eynsham (*c*.955-*c*.1020), wrote for the spiritual instruction of laymen and uneducated clerics, lived on in the south-west well into the twelfth century. From the west too came the *Katherine*-group of religious texts (lives of Katherine and other female saints, a treatise on virginity, devotional pieces to the Virgin and Christ — in highly wrought prose full of the rhythmical and alliterative effects of Old English verse), and the *Ancrene Wisse*, a practical and devotional guide for anchoresses revised for use by a wider community of female recluses. The practical function of such texts in the education of female religious was to keep their influence alive for centuries to come; the Old English prose tradition had survived the Conquest. Poetry, when it was again recorded in any quantity, wore the metrical dress of the French tradition — chiefly the octosyllabic couplet — ornamented with features of Anglo-Saxon verse, but showing a native wit, some learning and an English idiom, enriched with borrowed terms, wholly at home in the new forms. It was polite, the product of minor monastic houses or the grammar schools attached to them, but not courtly.

The court of the Normans and Angevins spoke the language and shared the tastes of the French-dominated courts of western Europe. The oldest surviving copy of the national epic, *La Chanson de Roland*, said to have been sung on the battlefield at Hastings, was made in England. For a century and more there was little to distinguish continental and insular literature; the same patrons employed writers on both sides of the Channel and the literary traffic in a revolutionary age was not all one-way. The court of Henry I (1100-35) produced, under the patronage of his queens, a novel amalgam of saint's life, adventure story and spiritual vision in the *Voyage of St Brendan*, the oldest *Bestiaire* in the French language, and a verse history of the reign. Henry II's queen, Eleanor of Aquitaine, dedicatee of Wace's *Brut*, was also patroness of Benoit de Sainte-Maure's *Roman de Troie*; her husband was most probably the king to whom Marie de France dedicated her *Lais*, some, if not all, written in England. Of the earliest versions of the Tristan story, precursors of the full-blown *roman courtois*, one was certainly, the other most probably composed there. To the end of the Middle Ages French was to remain an acceptable literary language at the English court.

Both vernacular traditions drew freely upon Latin, the medium of the common intellectual culture of western Christendom. England had had its place in that tradition as beneficiary and contributor ever since the establishment of the Christian missions in Kent in the last years of the sixth century and in Northumbria early in the seventh. In the monastic schools of Canterbury and at Wearmouth, Jarrow and

York, Latin and Greek were taught as well as anywhere in the western world. From them missionaries and scholars went out to spread the faith in Germany and teach in the palace-schools of Charlemagne's empire. The northern tradition faded after the Danish invasions and the destruction at York of the largest library in Europe; the southern contributed to Alfred's revival of English culture in resistance to Danish barbarism.

The Conquest was to involve England in the intellectual revival of the twelfth century, by which time men of native stock had returned to leadership of the Church and English clerics moved freely between cathedral schools and nascent continental universities. Their learning, intended for the service of religion, also served the needs of the state, and their Latinity, shaped in the schoolroom by models drawn from classical antiquity, inevitably absorbed and reflected some of the associated values. A typical example, John of Salisbury (c.1115-80), educated under Abelard at Paris and later Bishop of Chartres, believed the ethical teaching of Horace and Cicero compatible with the Christian faith and regarded Virgil as expressing, in allegorical form, the truth of all philosophy. Others might warn about the insidious influence of pagan authors, but their style was redolent of the very works they warned against. And style as well as learning could bring advancement at court; men like Walter Map (c.1140-1210) and Giraldus Cambrensis (1147-1223) served Henry II as civil servants but also as entertainers writing history, pseudo-history, anecdote and folklore with wit and elegance. Others wrote poetry with the epic pretensions of their classical models, such as Joseph of Exeter's *De Bello Troiano* in which ancient history is strongly coloured with medieval romance. It was this sphere of clerical learning in the service of courtly entertainment, remote from the world of a provincial parish priest, which, somewhat improbably, saw the genesis of Laȝamon's *Brut*.

Geoffrey of Monmouth's *Historia Regum Britanniae*

The inspiration came from a provincial cleric ambitious to rise in the world but who, as far as we know, was never directly associated with the court. Geoffrey's cognomen, presumably derived from his birthplace, suggests that he was Welsh, or possibly Breton since many immigrants from Brittany settled in the Welsh borders. A number of documents witnessed by him between 1129 and 1151 show him in association with Walter, Archdeacon of Oxford and Provost of the secular College of St George. Geoffrey may well have been a teacher there, since he twice styled himself *magister*, though the university of Oxford had not yet been formally constituted. The various dedications to his writings suggest a man in search of patronage, but when he was eventually rewarded with the bishopric of St Asaph in 1151, Welsh rebellion against central rule probably prevented him entering his see before his death in 1155.

Whatever his standing as churchman and scholar, he had a shrewd instinct in literary matters. In his *Prophetie Merlini* he wove a collection of political prophecies, supposedly translated from early Welsh verse, round Myrddin, the half-crazed seer whom legend credited with asserting that the Celts would ultimately drive the Anglo-Saxon invaders from their land. Though apparently completed about 1135 and in independent circulation thereafter, they were also incorporated in his masterwork, the *Historia Regum Britanniae* (§111-117)[4] with the original dedication to his clerical superior, Alexander, Bishop of Lincoln, and an introduction (§109) explaining that friends had urged him to release material of whose importance rumours had reached them. The Prophecies, relating to events included in the *Historia*, to Geoffrey's own age and onwards — with increasing vagueness allowing the maximum of interpretative ingenuity — to doomsday, were cleverly calculated to appeal to a society which knew little of the past, and viewed the future with an apprehension fired by its troubled present. Within a few months of their appearance, they were being cited by serious historians; and they were still in circulation centuries later, each age seeing in them something relevant to its own circumstances. Geoffrey later capitalised upon their success with a life of Merlin in Latin verse dedicated to another canon of the College of St George, Alexander's successor as Bishop of Lincoln.

The same sound instinct for useful patrons and contemporary tastes marked his *History of the Kings of Britain*, completed in 1138 and variously dedicated to King Stephen (1135-54) and to two great nobles representing rival factions in the civil war of his reign, as if to catch the shifting currents of favour in a troubled age. To an age in need of historical precedents which might resolve current constitutional issues, yet conscious of the darkness cutting it off from a past only fitfully illuminated by Bede's account of ecclesiastical history and the increasingly incomprehensible record of the *Anglo-Saxon Chronicle*, Geoffrey's *Historia* furnished a link with the ancient, honourable, seemingly stable world of its schoolroom texts. Beginning with the fall of Troy, a society of heroes in defeat, the *Historia* follows Aeneas to the west, where nations were to trace their inheritance of heroic values from those descendants of his whom they claimed as their founders. His great-grandson Brutus gives his name to the new colony he plants in the island of Albion whose capital city on the Thames is to be Trinovantum, 'New Troy'. Among the kings said to be his successors are Bladud, founder of Bath, Leir and Cymbeline, later to be Shakespeare's heroes, and Belin who, with his brother Brenne, is said to have sacked Rome.

This is fantasy; with the coming of Julius Caesar it is challenged by a reality which Geoffrey only reluctantly admits, the eventual success of the Roman conquest in the face of stubborn British resistance. The epoch ends when the half-British Maximian,[5] hoping to use his native backing to seize imperial power, undertakes the conquest of Gaul, leaving the now Christian island vulnerable to attack by the barbarian Picts and Huns. When the Romans finally abandon Britain, the royal line established from among followers of Maximian settled in Brittany is displaced by the usurper Vortigern who enlists the help of the pagan Saxons Hengest and Horsa against the incursions of the Picts. His new allies, seeing the vulnerability of the kingdom, invite their Germanic kinsmen to join them; they treacherously massacre many of the leading Britons, and Vortigern takes refuge in Snowdonia.

Summoned to his aid, Merlin prophesies Britain's long-term future, Vortigern's imminent fate, and the return of the royal line he had displaced. Two sons of the assassinated Constantine II, Aurelius and Uther, come from Brittany, defeat and kill Hengest and, on Merlin's advice, transport the Giants' Ring from Ireland to build Stonehenge as a monument to the Britons massacred by him. Both in turn are poisoned by their Saxon enemies, but not before Uther has fathered the greatest of British heroes illicitly upon another man's wife. At a feast to celebrate his defeat of Hengest's successors, he is seized with a passion for Ygerne, wife of Gorlois, Duke of Cornwall, ravages his lands and, transformed by Merlin into the likeness of the duke, enters Tintagel and sires the future King Arthur at the moment when Gorlois meets his death in battle, allowing the boy to be born in wedlock. Later the Saxon leaders escape to Germany and return with reinforcements to besiege St Albans; Uther defeats and kills them before being himself poisoned by some of their followers.

Arthur, aged fifteen, is recognised as Uther's successor and immediately marches against the Saxons under Colgrim and overcomes him and his Pictish and Scottish allies on the river Douglas, besieges him in York and eventually, with the help of Howel, King of Brittany, defeats him at Lincoln and finally at Bath. Turning upon the Picts and Scots, he corners them at Loch Lomond and forces their surrender. Having restored his northern allies to their Scottish fiefdoms and rebuilt the ruined churches of York, he marries Guenevere, descendant of a noble Roman family. To punish the Irish for their aid to the Scots, he conquers their country, then Iceland, the Orkneys, and Norway. Invading Gaul, he kills the Roman Tribune Frolle in single combat, captures Paris, then the entire province. While he is celebrating at a plenary court in the City of the Legions (Caerleon-upon-Usk), envoys arrive from Lucius, Procurator of the Roman Republic, summoning him to Rome to be tried for crimes against the state; Arthur sends a message of defiance and gathers his forces. Leaving Britain in the care of his nephew Modred, he crosses to Barfleur, kills the giant of Mont St Michel single-handed, defeats the Roman army at Saussy, subdues Burgundy and is about to march on Rome when news comes that Modred has seized the throne and taken the queen adulterously. Returning in haste to Britain, Arthur drives Modred into Cornwall, kills him in a final battle on the river Camlann, is himself mortally wounded and carried off to the Isle of Avalon, leaving the kingdom to the care of his cousin Constantin.

After Arthur's departure, the twin forces of foreign enmity and internal treason combine to overwhelm the nation; Modred's two sons join in revolt with the Saxons recruited as allies by their father. Constantin corners and kills the two young men, but the Saxons continue to harass his successors, allying themselves with Gormund, King of the Africans, who has established himself in Ireland. Together they drive the Britons to the west, into Wales and Cornwall where they maintain their Christian faith until Augustine is sent by Pope Gregory to convert the pagan invaders. Eventually a friendship grows up between the British ruler and the King of the Northumbrians whose son, Edwin, is brought up in Brittany with Cadwallo, heir to the British throne. When Cadwallo succeeds, Edwin asks for a crown of his own, but the British king, reminded of the repeated treachery of the Saxons, refuses and, in the ensuing war, is driven out of his kingdom. Returning, with the help of his Breton kinsmen, he kills Edwin, and is widely successful against the Saxons, allying himself with the Mercians to defeat the Northumbrians, and against the ever-troublesome Scots. But under his son Cadwallader, God turns against the Britons, famine and plague overwhelm the country, and the king takes refuge in Brittany. When he thinks of returning to his kingdom, an angelic voice forbids it, though prophesying that, at the appointed time, the faithful British should once again hold the island as their own. Cadwallader goes as a penitent to Rome and dies there in the year AD 689.

This closing date, one of only three in the whole *Historia*, is uncharacteristic in its preciseness; but the air of historical precision is intentional. Elsewhere Geoffrey maintains the historical fiction by relating events in Britain to others in world history: the reigns of native kings are correlated with those of Old Testament kings and prophets; Cordelia's brief reign after the death of Leir is followed by the founding of Rome by Romulus and Remus; that of Cymbeline falls during the long reign of the Emperor Augustus. This synchronic dating contributes to structure as well as verisimilitude, marking the passage of time over almost two thousand years. Some periods are covered in schematic outline, a hundred years passing in as many words; others are detailed at length, the narrative pausing while Geoffrey paints landscapes, marshals divisions, details battle tactics, and records the formal speeches of wheedling suppliants, defiant rebels, triumphant victors and magnanimous monarchs. The air of authenticity is maintained by concrete detail, precise numbers in military divisions, names of divisional commanders, lists of those attending ceremonies or killed in battles — some, such as the improbable Her, son of Hider, showing signs of inventive strain — lending conviction to what is basically fiction.

History requires authentification by learned, preferably Latin, sources. Geoffrey makes his claim for respectability by the statement (§2) that he is merely translating a very ancient book written in the British language, given him by Walter, Archdeacon of Oxford, who, he adds in a final paragraph (§208), brought it 'ex Britannia'. Scholarly opinion is divided as to whether the language was intended to be Welsh or Breton, and whether the geographical term refers to Wales or Brittany. But on the 'very ancient book' itself the present consensus is that no such source ever existed: among other anachronisms, the *Historia's* references to Norman allies in Arthur's Roman wars would be impossible in a truly ancient book. Geoffrey's work suggests a wide-ranging and consciously contrived composite from a variety of sources. The confidence with which he boasts of the uniqueness of his source, warning his contemporaries William of Malmesbury and Henry of Huntingdon to confine themselves to the history of the Saxon kings since they do not have Archdeacon Walter's book in the British language (§208), may reflect his conscious superiority in treating a subject on which available historical sources were largely silent.

The work of identifying the materials upon which Geoffrey drew in filling the silence in British history is still at a fairly rudimentary stage, but the complexity of the compositional process is already apparent. As general models for what the history of a race in search of its identity as a nation should be, he had the Old Testament, Livy, and other Roman historians, and, for the heroic manner in which such a subject should be treated, Virgil's *Aeneid*. Among earlier historians of the island he acknowledges (§1) Gildas (*c.*516-70) whose lament for the internecine strife and moral decline among the British, *De Excidio et Conquestu Britanniae*, provided the dark undercurrent of his national epic, and Bede (673-735) whose *Historia Ecclesiastica* supplied details of the Anglo-Saxon invaders and their eventual conversion by the Augustine mission. Geoffrey's reworking of Gildas is radical both in structure and style, selecting and reordering passages to harmonise with other materials in his overall interpretation, and simplifying the rhetorical language of complaint and lamentation while retaining vivid phrases which suited his taste for the vigorous and concrete. Thematically, too, he has been highly selective: modifying the superiority of the Saxon invaders by transferring their sack of British cities to the army of the African king Gormund summoned by them from Ireland (§§184-6); postponing a characteristic lamentation for the moral decline of the British until he can put it into the mouth of Cadwallo as the final collapse approaches (§195); conflating a plague and a famine in the catastrophe which ultimately overwhelms the nation (§203). These alterations bring Gildas's tragic view of British history to bear upon Geoffrey's vision of national greatness with all the greater effect after the glory of Arthur's reign.[6]

The compositional process is less clear in the Arthurian section, about a fifth of the whole, since Geoffrey's sources for a figure unknown to history are less clear. The Arthur of legend is a charismatic figure whose shadowy career may reflect that of some British war-leader who, for a period towards the end of the fifth century, temporarily delayed the Anglo-Saxon conquest. Celtic literature gives various fleeting glimpses of him: a battle-epic of the Edinburgh Celts evokes his name as a touchstone of valour; the Welsh Annals refer to him as victor in the battle of Mount Badon, then as victim of the battle of Camlann; late-recorded folk-tales show him and his wonder-working companions as assistants in the test imposed upon some folklore hero; Latin lives of Welsh saints cast him as a rumbustious pagan subdued by their spiritual powers. How much of this material — no doubt a fragment of what once existed — was known to Geoffrey, born and bred in the Welsh borders, we cannot tell.

One form in which material relevant to his purpose might have reached him with some gloss of historical respectability is exemplified by a manuscript in the British Library, Harley 3859, containing texts of the Welsh Annals, medieval Welsh king-lists and genealogies, and the *Historia Britonum* traditionally attributed to the eighth-century Welsh historian Nennius. From the last of these Geoffrey apparently took the story of a youthful prodigy, the boy Ambrosius, who comes to Vortigern's aid, adding that he was also called Merlin and attaching to him elements of oral tradition, such as the building of Stonehenge, as well as much matter of his own invention. From Nennius's list of battles against the Saxons he took the sites of several of Arthur's victories, including Loch Lomond with its natural wonders and Mount Badon, arbitrarily located near Bath. Though the Welsh Annals may have supplied the basis for the battle of Camlann, it was apparently Geoffrey who made Modred Arthur's opponent, an embodiment of the discord and treachery among the Britons lamented by Gildas. From the lists of British cities given in Nennius, Geoffrey contrived both a concrete setting and a sense of national history, often accounting for a place-name by inventing a story about the supposed founder, just as he recruited Arthur's lieutenants from the Welsh genealogies and his opponents from classical texts and stories of the Muslim East. The concept of a court of faithful lieutenants gathered about a warrior king is already present in the wonder-working companions, heroes of lost epics and gods of dead religions, found in the Welsh folk-tales, as are the names of many of Arthur's weapons.

Further research may fill in other parts of the jigsaw from Welsh sources, but is unlikely to find a model for the whole. The *Historia*, created on organic rather than jigsaw principles, is unique: a fictitious chronicle disguised with the trappings of history and informed by the spirit of national epic. A nation rooted in antiquity through its Trojan inheritance, fit rival of other European nations claiming similar descent, is early brought into conflict with Rome through the legendary feats of the brothers Belin and Brenne who, reunited after civil strife, conquer Gaul and sack Rome. Britain's stature as the equal of great empires is reaffirmed when the invasion of Julius Caesar is twice repulsed and finally succeeds only through treachery among the British commanders. Weakened by the imperial ambitions of Maximian and the treachery of the usurping Vortigern, the spirit of the nation is renewed from its Breton colony in a royal line which battles valiantly against the new Germanic enemy introduced by the usurper. Arthur comes as the triumphant climax of that struggle, expels the Saxons, unites the Britons under just laws and firm leadership, and goes on to surpass the imperial feats of his ancestors by conquering all western Europe. But, just when Rome seems at his mercy, the treason of Modred, kinsman and trusted lieutenant, brings it all to nothing and once more exposes Britain to the ravages of the Saxons. Thereafter, the limited success of Cadwallo provides only a faint echo of ancestral triumphs in the midst of national decline until the land is abandoned to the degenerate Welsh in their western wilderness and to the conquering English, legend at last yielding reluctantly to the facts of history. The form may be chronicle but the spirit is that of romance, projecting upon historical reality, reluctantly admitted, a golden age of national triumph. Inevitably, as must be the case when wish-fulfilment is contradicted by brute fact, it ends in tragedy, a tragedy carefully prepared in repeated patterns of national triumph against external powers undermined by internal treachery, leaving only the hope of eventual regeneration offered by the prophetic element in the *Historia*.

The lingering hope, like the imaginary triumph, was no doubt consoling to the humiliated spirit of a defeated people. But who in 1138 cared about the feelings of the long-displaced British? The appeal of the *Historia* is, however, much wider and the dispossessed Welsh were not Geoffrey's primary audience. To his scholar contemporaries he offered a new historiography, replacing the predominately Christian and moral interpretation of Gildas and Bede (who saw history as the operation of divine providence) with a secular one dominated by repetitive patterns of individual behaviour and national destiny. The twelfth-century revival of classical knowledge had induced a pre-Christian perspective which viewed human affairs as shaped by heroic personalities and by the operation of fortune. The achievements of Norman rulers impressed contemporaries both with the power of dominant personalities and the disasters brought by their ambition and rapacity. Historians influenced by the old Christian historiography saw the Normans as operating under divine providence for the punishment of sinful nations; Henry of Huntingdon drew parallels between the Norman conquest of the English and the English conquest of the Britons in a way reminiscent of Gildas. But they saw them also as imperial repressors of English liberty whose internecine squabbles undermined national greatness and presented them, in the classical perspective, as individuals subject to the vagaries of fortune.

The inherent tension in their work between the classical and the Christian perspective is resolved in the *Historia* by Geoffrey's primarily secular account of the rise and fall of a nation in recurring cycles of personal ambition and human failure. Like them, he gives a schematic record of the distant past broadening in detail and intimacy of presentation as it approaches the 'present' — for him the age of Arthur — then tailing away in less circumstantial chronicle form. But Geoffrey, freed from the restraint of historical fact, pauses to elaborate an individual career or explore a society in crisis as his thematic purpose requires. The career of Brutus, moral heir of a noble society overwhelmed by alien forces, of whom both triumph and disaster are foretold, liberator of fellow Trojans enslaved by the Greeks, founder of a new society, giant-slayer, and giver of just laws, foreshadows that of Arthur. Intermediate figures illustrate parts of the same pattern: Cassivelaunus defying Caesar, twice driving him back to Gaul, ultimately betrayed into surrender by an embittered Briton; the brothers Brenne and Belin, rivals embroiled in civil war, reconciled by their mother and united in the conquest of Rome; the brothers Aurelius and Uther, each repeating in turn a pattern of resistance to the usurper Vortigern, struggling against the Saxons with the advice and encouragement of Merlin, unifying the British under just laws, and dying by poison at the hands of their enemies, their ultimate failure preparing for Arthur's success. But the repeated patterns also emphasise the vulnerability of greatness, personal and national, to fate and human folly, culminating again in Arthur, product of an illicit union, imperious, ambitious, his empire ultimately brought to ruin through his fatal trust in the treacherous Modred. And the enmity of uncle and nephew, surviving their deaths, ensures the final destruction of imperial Britain, just as Merlin's prophecy, having validated Geoffrey's account of the past, ends in an apocalypse of universal chaos.[7]

Though most readers of the *Historia* might be no more aware of the secular bias underlying its startling account of national history shaped by dominant, often deviant, personalities than of its highly fictional basis, it had multiple appeal for the mingled races of post-Conquest England. For the Celts it furnished an impressive racial history culminating in the apotheosis of a national hero still potent in folk memory and the assurance of Merlin's prophecy that the seed of Brutus shall return to rule the land known by his name. To the English it offered sublimation of their recent humiliation through identification with ancient national tradition rather than Anglo-Saxon history, repeating the process by which the Celts they once defeated had turned that brutal fact into romantic fiction. For the Normans it provided legitimation of their conquest by putting it into historical perspective, showing Brutus as an invader bringing a superior culture, Cadwallader accepting the end of British rule as God-ordained, the Saxons as perfidious and brutal, unfit to rule.

The politically conscious may have been aware of issues of their own age reflected in recurrent themes of the *Historia*: the seizure of thrones legitimised by an invitation to take power, much as the Conqueror's usurpation was by the vote of the Witan; numerous instances of disputed inheritance as among William's sons, and much stress on the rights of younger sons such as his eventual successor Henry I; constant concern over dynastic continuity perhaps reflecting the loss of Henry's heir in the White Ship. Consciously or unconsciously, Geoffrey reproduced the ideology of an age hovering between tyranny and anarchy, when the Conqueror's own example invited others to imitate him and the self-interested treachery of his feudal dependants threatened his *arriviste* regime from within. The hopes and fears of his contemporaries seem mirrored in a repeated pattern of realism tinged with optimism: traitors murder the ruler and turn on the deserving younger brother among his heirs, but he gains help from allies overseas or wins national support by his inherent qualities. Arthur provides the climactic example, justifying Norman rule by the rigour with which he imposes his will on domestic foes, foreshadowing Angevin imperial ambitions by his continental conquests and freeing his supposed successors from contemporary claims that, as dukes of Normandy, they were vassals of the kings of France. But even he is not proof against what the age most dreaded: betrayal from within, civil war, and national collapse. There remains only the hope of the British that Arthur may one day return from Avalon, only vaguely expressed by Geoffrey since it was not likely to please the Norman magnates to whom he dedicated the *Historia*.[8]

Whatever the precise appeal of its components, the *Historia* took the Anglo-Norman world by storm. In January 1139, the chronicler Henry of Huntingdon, visiting the abbey of Bec in Normandy, was shown a copy of the *Historia*, completed perhaps only a few months earlier. He was amazed by its detailed coverage of a past about which so little had previously been known and, though doubtful of its authenticity, drew upon it in revising his own *Historia Anglorum*. Fellow historians were equally ambivalent: William of Newburgh, though he denounced it as full of falsehoods, accepted the Prophecies as genuine translations from the Welsh; Giraldus Cambrensis, though he told scabrous stories of how the *Historia* attracted crowds of evil spirits which could distinguish false passages in a book, cited it in his own work. Their ambivalence, patriotic imagination in conflict with academic rectitude, is perfectly typified by William of Malmesbury:

> He is that Arthur about whom the trifles of the Bretons (*nugae Britonum*)
> rave even today, a man worthy not to be dreamed about in false fables
> but proclaimed in veracious histories, for he long upheld his sinking
> fatherland and quickened the failing spirits of his countrymen to war.[9]

Though many historians were to remain sceptical, popular chroniclers gratefully filled the blanks in their records by incorporating material which so perfectly matched their idea of what British history ought to have been. The poets were equally willing to be convinced, and in the centuries ahead the *Historia* and its vernacular derivatives served as source books for Spenser, Shakespeare, Milton, Dryden, Wordsworth and Tennyson. The authors of romance, rapidly evolving on both sides of the Channel in the following decades, found the ambivalence inherent in the *Historia* entirely in keeping with the spirit of the new literary form, allowing them to project upon an Arthurian society, whose historicity now seemed guaranteed, the idealised values they wished to express. Though their story-matter derived largely from legend, knowledge of the *Historia*, widely diffused among their audience, lent it a truth and conviction which have lingered down the ages. It is the underlying historical structure of the *Historia* which gives Malory's *Morte Darthur* the sense of a cosmic tragedy, of a great society destroyed by conflicting ideals, a sense which lingers still in Tennyson's *Idylls of the King.*

Robert Wace's *Roman de Brut*

Geoffrey's *Historia* survives in more than two hundred manuscripts; its widespread influence was extended by adaptations of the Latin text, and as far afield as Poland its format was imitated and some of its material incorporated in national chronicles. Vernacular versions quickly made it available to popular audiences; Wales alone produced at least five, of which some sixty texts still survive. But its most profound and long-lasting influence was to be through imaginative literature for which, in the twelfth century, French was the most viable medium and women in Angevin England the most likely patrons. It was Constance, wife of Ralph Fitz-Gilbert, a Lincolnshire magnate, who gave the *Historia* copy which he had borrowed from a Yorkshire nobleman to her chaplain Geoffrey Gaimar to translate. The version which he produced between 1147 and 1151 was to form the first part of a trilogy constituting a history of the country from Trojan to contemporary times: the *Brut* was to be followed by an *Estorie des Engleis* based on the Anglo-Saxon Chronicle, and the whole to end with a sketch of the reign of Henry I. It set the pattern of popular history for some three centuries and its medium, the octosyllabic rhyming couplet, became that of romance and other courtly literature in French and Anglo-Norman. However influential it may have been, the trilogy as a whole has not survived; though we know its content from the linking passage introducing the *Estorie des Engleis*, in the four surviving manuscripts Gaimar's *Brut* has been replaced by a version of the *Historia* made by Robert Wace. The *Estorie* suggests that Gaimar lacked the stylistic ease and narrative vivacity of Wace, but the displacement of his *Brut* may equally well have been due to his provincial status and the more powerful patronage of his rival.

Wace, a Jerseyman educated at Caen and Paris, scholar and teacher (to judge from his title, *Maistre*), was the author of saints' lives and other works in the vernacular intended, he says, for 'rich folks who possess revenues and silver, since for them books are made and good words are composed and well set forth'. With the instinct of the professional author, he presented his *Roman de Brut*, completed in 1155, to Queen Eleanor, or so La3amon says (22). If so, the instinct was sound, since it brought him the patronage of her husband, Henry II, for a continuation of the national record in a *Roman de Rou*, a history of his Norman ancestors from the eponymous Rollo onwards. If he planned a trilogy modelled on Gaimar, it was cut short, still incomplete after fourteen years, when the king transferred the commission to another poet, evoking dry comments from Wace on the nature of royal promises. The long-term success of the *Roman de Brut*, which survives in twenty-eight manuscripts, vindicated him, even if it came too late to console him. Its influence upon contemporary courtly literature appears to have been profound, though it is not always easy to distinguish from that of the *Historia* itself, of Gaimar's version, or of other French adaptations which survive in fragmentary form.

At almost 15,000 lines Wace's *Brut* represents a considerable expansion of Geoffrey's original, yet he has added only two significant incidents, both in the Arthurian section. To Geoffrey's account of the twelve years of peace between Arthur's conquest of Orkney and his invasion of Norway (§153), Wace adds a few lines on how the Round Table was made to prevent quarrels over precedence among the royal retainers (9747-60). And to Geoffrey's statement that after the battle of Camlann, Arthur, mortally wounded, was carried off to the Isle of Avalon so that his wounds might be attended to (§178), he adds:

> Encore i est, Bretun l'atendent,
> Si cum il dient e entendent;
> De la vendra, encor puet vivre.
> Maistre Wace, ki fist cest livre,
> Ne volt plus dire de sa fin
> Qu'en dist li prophetes Merlin;
> Merlin dist d'Arthur, si ot dreit,
> Que sa mort dutuse serreit.
> Li prophetes dist verité;
> Tut tens en ad l'um puis duté,
> E dutera, ço crei, tut dis,
> Se il est morz u il est vis.   (13279-90)[10]

> (*He is there still, awaited by the Britons, for, as they say and believe, he will return from thence and live again. Master Wace, who made this book, wishes to say no more about his end than was said by Merlin the prophet; Merlin said of Arthur — and rightly so — that his death would remain in doubt. The prophet spoke truth; men have always doubted and, as I believe, always will doubt whether he is dead or whether he lives.*)

For the Round Table it seems likely that he had a source in Celtic tradition, though its origin and significance there have not been precisely established; the idea of making it a symbol of Arthur's chivalric fellowship, as other brief references treat it (10285, 13269-70), was probably his own.

Had he been interested in such material, he might have drawn much more freely on the *contes*, brief prose synopses of the lyric performances of Celtic story-tellers currently wandering western Europe, from which most possibly these details were taken. He may have feared to dilute the serious 'historical' character of the work with fabulous material, to judge from his sceptical comment on the truth of such stories:

> They are not all lies nor all true, not all nonsense nor all good sense. The minstrel has recited his tale and the storyteller retold his story so often, to improve upon their narratives, that they have made them all seem fables. (9793-8)

He may, indeed, have been temperamentally averse to the atmosphere of fantasy and mystery which such matter bred in Arthurian romance, since he comments in the *Roman de Rou* on his visit to the magic fountain of Barenton in the forest of

Broceliande (near Rennes), the setting for many chivalric adventures: 'I went there to seek marvels; I saw the forest, I saw the land; I looked for marvels, but I did not find them; a fool I went and a fool I returned.' These limited additions are offset by his omission of Merlin's prophecies, leaving the supernatural element in the work reduced rather than heightened.

In all essentials of narrative, proportion, thematic content and historical colouring, Wace's *Brut* remains what the *Historia* is.[11] But there is a self-consciousness in Wace's poetic art which has altered its literary character. The influence of the manuals of composition in which the Schoolmen of the age were currently codifying what they believed to be the rhetorical principles of the classical poets is evident in his tendency to introduce brief portraits among Geoffrey's catalogues of names — characterising one as a mighty hunter, another as a great drinker, short descriptions rhetorically organised but enlivened with concrete detail, and occasional summations of meaning or situation in proverbs and epigrams. But these rhetorical embellishments are few and brief: to Geoffrey's conventional description of Guenevere as the most beautiful woman in Britain, Wace adds a single line on her generous nature and elegance of speech; at the council where war against Rome is determined, he gives Gawain a speech on the merits of peace, characteristic of the poet in its stylistic parallelism and verbal repetition:

> 'Bone est la pais emprés la guerre,
> Plus bele e mieldre en est la terre;
> Mult sunt bones les gaberies
> E bones sunt les drueries.
> Pur amistié e pur amies
> Funt chevaliers chevaleries.'   (10767-72)

('Peace is pleasant after war, the earth is fairer and better. The gallant boasts and amorous exchanges are pleasant. It is through love and for the sake of their ladies that knights do knightly deeds.')

The traits mentioned were to be characteristic of the courteous queen and the amorous Gawain in *roman courtois*, significant precursors of new social and literary currents, but trifling in themselves.

Some of Wace's descriptive elaborations have been seen as contributing to the new courtliness, particularly the scene of Arthur's Whitsun feast at Caerleon (10244-620) with its assembly of vassals from every part of his empire, separate processions of the king and queen, their ceremonious service at separate tables, the crowds of splendidly dressed women, the sports, music and tale-telling which follow. But all this is in the *Historia* (§§156-7), including the details most suggestive of the age of chivalry and courtly love:

> Indeed, every knight in Britain who was famed for his bravery wore livery and arms of one particular colour. Women of fashion also wore similar garments, scorning to have the love of any man who had not proved himself three times in battle. In this way the women became chaste and more virtuous, and for the sake of their love the knights became more daring.
> . . . the knights then planned a mock battle, competing together on horseback; the women watched from the top of the city walls and by their

encouraging manner aroused in them passions of ardent love. (§157)
This is the pure doctrine of the age of romance, which had scarcely declared itself
when Geoffrey wrote: the mutual relationship of chivalry and courtly love, each
inspiring and honouring the other. Wace thoroughly appreciates it but does not
significantly add to it; instead he extends the association between Arthur's court and
those of contemporary feudal monarchs by elaborating with concrete details the
ceremonial element, the numbers, standing and piety of the clerics, the dicing and
gaming among the festive sports. Geoffrey makes no mention of board games; Wace
builds a dramatic picture of the players swearing and cheating, drinking and
quarrelling, wagering their clothes when they have lost everything else: 'Many sat
down to dice richly clothed, who rose to leave stark naked' (10587-8). It is his
ability to clothe Geoffrey's often schematic narrative in detail evocative of
contemporary life — the geography of south-west England in which he had
apparently travelled, knowledge of ships and the sea natural in a Channel Islander, his
lively dialogue inserted among the formal speeches of the *Historia*, his gift for
aphoristic summation, which give the *Roman de Brut* its courtly gloss. The solidity
and conviction of Arthur's realm stem from Geoffrey, but Wace gives the first
fleeting glimpses of England as a land of romance:

> De buens homes e de richesce
> E de plenté e de noblesce
> E de curteisie e d'enur
> Portout Engleterre la flur
> Sur tuz les regnes d'envirun
> E sur tuz cels que nus savum.
> Plus erent curteis e vaillant
> Neis li povre paisant
> Que chevalier en altres regnes,
> E altresi erent les femes.   (10493-502)

*(For fine men and great wealth, for abundance and noble deeds,
for courtesy and for honour, in Arthur's day England bore the
flower over every realm of which we know. Even the poor peasant
was more courteous and valiant than was a knight in other realms,
and the women were equally so.)*

Laʒamon's relationship to his sources

What has been said of Wace's *Brut*, might, with variation of terms, be said of
Laʒamon's poem: the narrative sequence, the thematic sweep, the sense of historical
conviction derive from Geoffrey; but Laʒamon has coloured the whole with the spirit,
the atmosphere, some of the expressive means of Old English epic. No one seriously
doubts that Wace's version was the intermediary: but Laʒamon's text, at 16,095 long
lines, each roughly equivalent to an octosyllabic couplet, is more than twice as long.
The disparity is such, passage after passage having no counterpart in Wace, that it
has been suggested Laʒamon's source must have been some version of the *Historia*
other than Wace's *Roman*: an extended text of Wace incorporating material which
might account for the additions in Laʒamon, or the lost version of Gaimar, or some

other lost redaction of Geoffrey. The supposition is a somewhat backhanded compliment to Laȝamon, valuing the additional material as too significant to have originated with a provincial English poet. But if Gaimar's version contained such interesting additions and showed anything of Laȝamon's dramatic sense — and his *Estorie des Engleis* makes the latter unlikely — it is difficult to see why it should have been displaced by Wace's less detailed text. The manuscripts of Wace so far analysed show comparatively trifling variations, verbal rather than narrative or thematic; and, whatever other lost redactions may have contained, it is difficult to believe that the archaic, traditional character of Laȝamon's *Brut*, to which much of the additional matter notably contributes, can have been inherited from a French source. In the future, fuller knowledge of the vernacular versions of the *Historia* may clarify the source of individual episodes; it is unlikely to account for the extent and nature of the additions in Laȝamon.

Laȝamon source studies have, to some extent, been distorted by concentration upon a number of passages which seem to offer support for various theories of the cultural influences upon the poet and, in particular, about the origin and transmission of the Arthurian legend. A characteristic instance is the presence at Arthur's birth of *aluen* who bestow on him gifts of valour, dominion and long life (9609-15). Supernatural intervention in the life of mortals suggests Celtic influence, traced by some scholars to Breton sources preserved only in late folklore form, by others to Irish legends of fairy gifts bestowed upon heroes, supporting a theory, not generally accepted, that Laȝamon was of Scandinavian-Irish origin and shows personal knowledge of Irish matters. But in Norse legends also, the Norns preside over birth and foretell the destiny of princes and, though there is nothing conclusive in the Germanic origin of the term *aluen* (often used to translate names of classical nature-spirits — dryads, naiads, nymphs), Laȝamon may equally well have drawn upon Germanic tradition. The concept of gift-giving fays is probably too widespread to be traced to a particular tradition without more precise detail than Laȝamon gives.

Other apparent additions also suggest that Laȝamon was embroidering upon established tradition rather than conflating differing versions or freely inventing. But for the few lines in Wace on the making of the Round Table (9747-60), he would no doubt have been credited with drawing directly on the Celtic traditions concerning it to which Wace alludes. Yet Wace's text supplies the essential framework for Laȝamon's much longer passage (11345-464); the implication that Arthur had the table made in response to the rivalry for pre-eminence among his followers apparently suggested to Laȝamon the contention for places in a hierarchical seating order, the blows which might follow, the throwing of loaves and wine-bowls, and the extreme punishments merited by the ringleaders. His excited imagination reflects not so much the regressive barbarism of which he has been accused as contemporary reality. The punishments are those for treason, an act of violence in the sovereign's presence threatening the stability of the state — a danger still reflected in the regulations of the Palace of Westminster, red tape in the cloakrooms for the hanging of swords, the two sword-lengths separating Government and Opposition benches in the chamber — and are extended to kinsmen and womenfolk on the accepted basis that treason is an inheritable taint in the blood. The initiative taken by one of Arthur's hostages to suppress the riot with the only weapons available, the carving knives laid before the king, is reminiscent of those occasions in Anglo-Saxon literature when hostages make common cause with their captors under assault. That the suggestion for the building of the table comes from a Cornish carpenter may imply a localised version of a common Celtic legend, but the precision of detail which gives sixteen hundred as the number of those who could be seated round it is as characteristic of Laȝamon's love of the concrete as the making of a sequence of scenes full of dialogue from Wace's outline narrative is typical of his dramatic instinct.

Other passages which have attracted interest because they provide additional details of key episodes of the Arthurian legend have a similar air of extrapolation within a widely diffused tradition. To Wace's bare mention of Arthur's departure to Avalon (13277-8), Laȝamon adds that there his wounds will be healed by the fay Argante (14277-80), identified with his sister Morgan in French romance where the same details are given. Their occurrence there might suggest that she was associated with Avalon in Breton legend, but does not rule out the possibility that the association was also part of the Celtic tradition more immediately available to Laȝamon. Another instance of imaginative extrapolation which owes little or nothing to Celtic tradition is Arthur's dream of the treachery of Modred and Guenevere (13981-14021), inserted by Laȝamon after news of it has been brought but not yet revealed to the king. The passage reduplicates the earlier dream in which Arthur, during the crossing to France, sees a dragon defeat a bear in combat, a dream which his attendants fear to interpret as ill-omened. The tension created by the uncertain significance of the dream is repeated here by the reluctance of the messenger to admit that it relates to the news he has so far concealed, though the imagery makes its meaning clear: Arthur dreams that he bestrides a great wooden hall with Gawain seated before him as champion, royal sword in hand; Modred hews through the supporting pillars while Guenevere pulls down the roof, and, as the hall collapses, king and nephew fall, Arthur breaking his right arm and Gawain both of his; but, taking his sword in his left hand, Arthur cuts down the traitors. Structurally and thematically the episode echoes Geoffrey; its imagery, reminiscent of the Anglo-Saxon hall as the seat of royal power and the associated concept of the *comitatus* as royal bodyguard and defender of the nation, seems unlikely to have come from Gaimar's Anglo-Norman version or from an extended text of Wace. The later part of the vision is blurred by reuse of the animal imagery of the earlier dream, obscure in significance; but the combination of the general tradition of prophetic dreams, Geoffrey's imagery and thematic application, and the inventive employment of English images is characteristic of Laȝamon.

His presentation of Arthur's armour (10542-62) represents a similar amalgam: to the general concept of the hero's arms as emblems of his valour exploited by Geoffrey in a passage (§147) where names drawn from Celtic tradition are given to Arthur's shield, sword and spear, a passage barely changed in Wace, Laȝamon adds further details of Celtic origin (that the sword Caliburn was made by magic skill in Avalon) and of Germanic colouring (that Uther's helmet was called Goswhit and his corslet Wygar made by Witege (Widia), son of the magical weapon-smith Weland). And when he returns to Arthur's equipment on a later occasion (11856-70), without warrant from Wace, he attributes the spear Ron, inherited from Uther, to the Carmarthen smith Griffin. Appreciating the significance of the hero's arms being made by specially skilled, even supernatural smiths, inherited from valorous ancestors, given individual names, Laȝamon clearly felt free to embellish the arming convention from the variety of racial traditions available to him in the melting-pot of post-Conquest England.

It is natural that, living where he did, he should be assumed to have drawn on Welsh sources for additional details of the Celtic Arthur. There are some details which suggest such an origin: the comment that Caerleon was accursed (12114); the statement that the battle between Arthur and Lucius was the third greatest ever fought (13717), as if referring to one of the triads in which Welsh tradition listed significant events or persons in threes as an *aide-mémoire* in recalling their stories; the Saxons' curious threat to make a bridge of Arthur's backbone, to lay his bones in the doorway of the hall where all men must pass (10473-9), reminiscent of the story in the *Mabinogi* of Bran the Blessed who used his body as a bridge on which his army might cross to Ireland. None offers conclusive proof, only the possibility that elements of Celtic tradition, widely dispersed in western Europe, were most readily available to Laȝamon in Wales, of whose geography he shows some knowledge.

Equally the few trifling details in which his version seems closer to that of Geoffrey than of Wace prove no direct knowledge of the *Historia*, the disparity often disappearing when the Wace variants are consulted. But there are undeniable echoes of Merlin's Prophecies which Wace omitted: to Merlin's bare announcement in the *Roman de Brut* that Uther shall have his way with Ygerne, wife of Earl Gorlois, Laȝamon adds his pronouncement that the child to be born of their union should have immortal fame, should rule in Rome, and should never die:

> 'Of him scullen gleomen   godliche singen;
> of his breosten scullen æten   aðele scopes;
> scullen of his blode   beornes beon drunke.
> Of his eȝene scullen fleon   furene gleden;
> ælc finger an his hond   scarp stelene brond.
> Scullen stan walles   biuoren him tofallen;

beornes scullen rusien, reosen heore mærken.' (9410-16)

('Of him shall minstrels splendidly sing; of his breast noble bards shall
eat; heroes shall be drunk upon his blood. From his eyes shall fly
sparks of fire; each finger on his hand shall be a sharp steel blade.
Stone walls shall fall down before him; men shall tremble, their banners
fall.')

In the *Historia* (§112.2), it is said of the Boar of Cornwall, champion of the oppressed British against the invading Saxons — manifestly Arthur: *'In ore populorum celebrabitur et actus eius cibus erit narrantibus'* ('It shall be extolled in the mouths of its peoples, and its deeds will be as meat and drink to those who tell tales'); and at §115.26 it is said of the Boar of Commerce, feasibly associated with Arthur: *'Pectus eius cibus erit egentibus et lingua eius sedabit sitientes'* ('Its breast will be as food to the hungry and its tongue will assuage the thirst of those who are dry'). These two sentences seem to have been conflated in Laȝamon's passage, but the extrapolation from the concept of a hero's reputation serving as meat and drink to the bards who sing of him to the Eucharistic imagery of a Saviour on whose body and blood his people are spiritually nourished is typical of the verbal exaltation which overcomes Laȝamon in moments of heightened thematic interest. The image of Arthur's fingers as blades of steel seems a similar imaginative invention, but the picture of him as a ruler of Rome before whom stone walls shall fall may echo another sentence in the Prophecies (§112.2): *'Tremebit Romulea domus seuitiam ipsius et exitus eius dubius erit'* ('The House of Romulus shall dread the Boar's savagery and the end of that House will be shrouded in mystery').

The combination of invention and extrapolation is characteristic; so also is the repetition of this passage at a later moment of exaltation, the founding of the Round Table (11489-517), with variation of terms which queries further the form in which Laȝamon can have known the Prophecies. It is combined there with Merlin's prognosis that the British would refuse to credit Arthur's death when he should later depart to Avalon, while his prophecy that the walls of Rome should fall down before the king is echoed at the moment when he is about to launch his final attack upon the empire (13964-70).

These echoes of the Prophecies, though sufficiently close to Geoffrey's text to imply a literary rather than an oral origin, are yet so vague as to suggest something recollected from memory rather than immediately based upon a text consulted. The same might equally be true of the only incident in Laȝamon's *Brut* which appears to derive from Bede, Pope Gregory's famous encounter with Anglo-Saxon slaves in the Roman forum which inspired the Augustinian mission for the conversion of their island. An episode so vital to the Christian history of the country might, however, have been widely enough diffused in popular tradition to account for its appearance in the *Brut* (14695-728). But there is some indication in the forms of Anglo-Saxon names given by Laȝamon, much more consistent and authentic than the variable, often almost unrecognisable, forms given in the Wace manuscripts, that Laȝamon had direct access to a text of the *Historia Ecclesiastica*, the original Latin or the Anglo-Saxon translation, either of which could have supplied more correct models. Two other apparent borrowings from Anglo-Saxon sources suggest where he might have had access to either text or both. There is a possibility that Laȝamon may have drawn upon the homilies of Ælfric, Abbot of Eynsham, in condemning idolatry when Brutus visits the Temple of Diana after the fall of Troy (569-637), and in his account of Vortigern's resort to sacrificing a child without a father to ensure the completion of his tower of refuge in the Welsh mountains (7721-880) where there may be echoes of matter associated with Ælfric's condemnation of the killing of illegitimate children. The echoes in both cases are scattered and inexact, like vague memories of earlier reading. Laȝamon may have read the homilies at Worcester where a large library of Old English manuscripts, including many Ælfric texts, was still preserved in the thirteenth century.[12]

The source evidence, imprecise though it still is, suggests that Laȝamon felt free to embellish his version of a masterwork, Geoffrey's *Historia*, with whatever his imagination found relevant among the materials, literary, oral and personal, stored in his mind. His treatment of Wace is characteristically medieval, unrestrained by any inhibiting respect for the integrity of the work or the authorial property of those who had preceded him, assuming the right, the duty to bring to it anything which would make it more meaningful, more persuasive for the particular audience for which he intended it. The liberty which Wace himself had assumed Laȝamon carried much further, yet without significant narrative additions, alterations or rearrangements in sequence. The great difference between their versions is not in matter but in the manner of narration, most characteristically in reduplication of incidents, imaginative extrapolation of given material, dramatisation of narrative in action, dialogue, formal speeches, extended similes, repeated formulae of imagery and expression. Repeatedly and constantly, the English *Brut* loses touch with the French text, sometimes for hundreds of lines, yet without introducing anything markedly alien or inappropriate to the context of the original. The effect is of effortless extrapolation from the known to the unknown, from familiar outline to intimate and novel detail.

The opening episode of the Arthurian section, the fathering of the hero, contains a characteristic example of narrative reduplication. In Wace, when Uther, frustrated in his passion for Ygerne, is advised to send for Merlin, the seer appears within a few lines (8676-82), having been with the royal army. The English adds a sequence of highly dramatised scenes, some seventy lines in all (9361-430): Uther confides in his thane Ulfin who tells him that there is a hermit with the army who knows Merlin, '"where he lies each night under the heavens; and Merlin often spoke with him and told him wondrous things"', and if they could win him over the king might gain his desires. At Uther's request, the hermit 'journeyed into the land to the west, to a vast forest, a wilderness where he had lived full many a year, and in which he had often encountered Merlin'. There he finds Merlin eagerly expecting him since, as he reveals in a long speech, he knows everything that has passed since the hermit left for the royal camp, including why he is so urgently needed: '"Uther is filled with longing for the lovely Ygerne, greatly besotted with the wife of Gorlois. But it will never happen, as long as time shall last, that he shall win her save by my magic skill; for there is no truer woman in this mortal world."'

Though not found in Wace, this is not truly invention on Laȝamon's part; in outline it reduplicates an earlier episode when Merlin is missing in a moment of need. Aurelius, Uther's brother and predecessor, seeks advice on a suitable monument to commemorate the British chieftains treacherously massacred by Hengest near Salisbury, and sends messengers far and wide who ultimately find Merlin by a fountain deep in Wales (8473-526). To this episode in Wace (8003-16), Laȝamon adds the king's promise of land and treasure, Merlin's rejection of all gifts, his foreknowledge of the mission to find him and of the coming death of Aurelius. These features recur in the reduplicated episode, as if Laȝamon were echoing his own version rather than Wace's, culminating in Merlin's foretelling of the winning of Ygerne and the future greatness of her son Arthur. The reduplication serves to reintroduce Merlin after an absence prolonged by the increased scale of the English version and renew his association with the mysterious west, to demonstrate his powers as a seer, and create narrative tension by allowing him to prophesy the seemingly impossible, Uther's winning of the virtuous Ygerne. The characteristic reuse of materials adds little that is new, narrative or thematic; but the patterned repetition places the vital prophecy, original with Laȝamon, at the climax of a long, highly dramatised sequence of preparatory material.

The episode which follows, leading to Uther's death and the succession of Arthur, shows the same sense of climax achieved by vivifying Wace's outline narrative with dramatic action cumulative in its emotional effect upon the reader. Wace describes how the Saxons, unable to overcome Uther in war, send spies disguised in ragged dress who, failing to get within striking distance of the king, poison the well from which he drinks and so kill him (8951-9000). Laȝamon, taking his imaginative clue from the ragged dress, sends the assassins to court disguised as beggars who, at the royal alms-giving, claim charity as men of worth brought to ruin by Saxon exactions: '"Neither fish nor flesh ever comes into our bowl, nor any kind of drink save a draught of water, nothing but water alone — that is why we are so lean."' In a sequence of dramatised scenes, full of dialogue, they are fed, clothed and lodged by Uther, overhear his doctor order a chamberlain to protect the well from falling rain, poison it and, when its water is brought to Uther in golden bowls, he drinks and dies (9797-882). The dramatisation underscores the irony, Laȝamon's invention, that Uther died by the hands of those who had enjoyed his charity, treachery characteristic of the Saxons in his presentation. Its principal effect is to highlight the climax which immediately follows Uther's burial at Stonehenge: in Wace, Arthur is crowned within four lines (9009-12), while Laȝamon makes an emotive scene of the boy's reaction to the news of his father's death:

> þus heo gunnen tellen   and Arður sæt ful stille;
> ænne stunde he wes blac   and on heuwe swiðe wak,
> ane while he wes reod   and reousede on heorte.
> þa hit alles up brac   hit wes god þat he spac;
> þus him sæide þerriht   Arður, þe aðele cniht:
> 'Lauerd Crist, Goddes sune,   beon us nu a fultume,
> þat ich mote on life   Goddes laȝen halden.'   (9923-9)

(Thus they spoke and Arthur sat quite still; one moment he was pale and quite lacking in colour, next instant he was red, with heartfelt grief. When it all burst out, what he said was fitting; Arthur, the noble knight, at once spoke thus: 'Lord Christ, son of God, be a help to us now, that I may uphold God's laws throughout my life.')

Such additions contribute to theme by emphasis, others by accumulation at much greater length. Arthur's early campaigns of foreign conquest occupy some seventy lines in Wace (9659-730) where, following his defeat of Gillomar, King of Ireland, the rulers of the Orkneys, Jutland, and Winetland come to him in his next conquest, Iceland, offering submission. Over some two hundred and thirty lines (11103-336), Laȝamon elaborates the pattern of the Irish campaign: brief conflict followed by a long speech of submission by the king, offering tribute, hostages, his sons to serve the conqueror, confirmed upon the relics of Irish saints; and Arthur's benign response accepting the hostages as guarantors of fidelity, remitting half the tribute and promising his protection. The same pattern is then repeated for each of the rulers in turn, omitting the initial fighting and diminishing slightly in length, varying the terms of submission but cumulatively reinforcing the picture of Arthur as ruthless in conquest and gracious in victory, characteristic of Laȝamon's presentation of the king. To the modern mind the repetitions may be tedious; to the medieval they may well have seemed ceremonious and fitting celebrations of the first foreign triumphs of a national hero.

In terms of Laȝamon's use of sources they confirm the general impression of a combination of narrative dependence and creative independence in the elaboration and dramatisation of Wace's outline by reduplication, extrapolation and the importation of congruent detail from other traditions. No doubt the more closely the imported detail conformed to the experience, personal and cultural, of the audience, the more effectively it served Laȝamon's purpose; but it is scarcely surprising that, in a multi-cultural society, so little of it can be traced to a specific source. This combination of narrative dependence and piecemeal originality has suggested a particular method of composition:

> . . . we infer that he took in good-sized masses of Wace's poem and
> let them settle down in his imagination and stimulate its own creation;
> hence his great expansion, especially after the early part . . . ; hence
> also his frequent small changes of order, his occasional contradictions of
> Wace, and forgetful dropping of very good passages, his constant insertion

of precise numbers, fresh proper names, and other concrete detail often
highly lifelike, perceptive, emotional — dialogue, speeches and the like,
often epic in breadth, good cheer, ideality, adapted to the recitative manner.[13]

Such a method of composition might well explain the varying estimates of Laȝamon's
dependency upon Wace, extensive in terms of matter, much less so in literary
expression.

Structure and proportions

A literary method which develops the narrative very variously in relation to what
Laȝamon judged the inherent interest or dramatic potential of individual episodes
seems unlikely to show much concern for structure. The underlying structure,
originating with Geoffrey, is that of chronicle, seemingly dictated by the mere
sequence of events. But Geoffrey's chronicle, being a literary artefact, demonstrates
an inherent sense of structure in the emphasis which is given to certain periods and
personalities by the amount of space devoted to them. Structure and proportion in
turn serve theme, highlighting the reigns of those who, before Arthur, had established
or exercised the right to rule Rome on which his claim to imperial power is later
based. Wace preserves this inherent structure without major changes of proportion or
thematic emphasis. Laȝamon's elaboration and dramatisation inevitably distort the
proportions of the *Roman de Brut*, but not without some signs that he appreciated the
interrelation of structure and theme. His occasional personal interventions in the
third-person narrative not only maintain the fiction of history recorded but track its
progress by marking the close of one episode or the opening of another. He marks a
transition with 'Nu ich þe wulle tellen a þissen boc-spællen' (9691) or 'Lete we nu
ane while þeos ferde bilæue / and speke we of Arðure' (12680-81). He may use such
interjections to remind his audience of the literary authority for his narrative:
'Seoððen hit seið in þere tale þe king ferde to Cornwale' (11422); 'Her mon mai arede
of Arðure þan king' (11337). Or he may use seasonal references to record the
passage of time: 'Þa þe winter wes agan and sumer com þer anan' (11103); 'Seouen
niht uppen Æstre, þa men hafden iuast' (11133). On other occasions, he uses the
moment of transition to excite interest in what is to follow: 'Ich mai sugge hu hit
iwarð, wunder þæh hit þunche' (11345); 'Þa þe Arður wes king — hærne nu seollic
þing' (9945). Or he may comment ironically on the unforeseen outcome of an
incident just narrated: '— ah he nuste whæt com seoððe sone þeræfter!' (9283);
'— þet him ofþuhte sære sone þerafter!' (10430); 'Wale þat Modræd wes ibore —
muchel hærm com þerfore!' (11084). Such interjections rarely coincide with the end
of an episode, but they help to create the impression of a historical record conducted
by a narrator with knowledge of events to come.

The marking of periodic divisions in the unbroken flow of British history
suggests that Laȝamon was conscious of the practical problems involved in putting
such a massive work before an audience. Within the Arthurian section at least, it

appears to be divided into episodes of roughly four hundred lines each, appropriate to an evening's recital to a listening audience or the attention-span of a private reader. And their sequence suggests some attempt to achieve variety in a work so largely concerned with warfare, both in the alternation of war and peace, action and ceremonial, and in the juxtaposing of contrasting episodes within the same section. So at the climax of Uther's struggle against the Saxons, comes an episode of internal conflict among the Britons, the perennial weakness of the Celtic cause, out of which is born Arthur who is to triumph over it and ultimately perish from its renewal (9222-619). After which the struggle against the Saxons is resumed at the covert level, resulting in the assassination of Uther (9620-981). Arthur's accession is marked by the open renewal of the conflict and his triumphant expulsion of the Saxons (9982-10430), an episode reduplicated in their treacherous return and final annihilation (10431-799). Arthur's restoration of peace at home is then celebrated in an episode which twins his victorious campaign against the Scots with his re-establishment of law and order and his marriage to Guenevere (10800-11102), followed by a similar twinning of the opening of his foreign conquests with his enforcement of national unity symbolised by the making of the Round Table (11103-517). The resumption of his foreign conquests in Europe (11518-12026) is followed by the demonstration of national harmony in the plenary court held at Caerleon (12027-341). Then, at the peak of national prosperity, come the challenge from the Emperor Lucius and Arthur's preparations for war (12342-734). Next, Arthur's troubled dream of conflict is followed by his combat with the Giant of Mont St Michel (12735-13049). His envoys, having defied Lucius, precipitate the beginning of hostilities (13050-538) leading to general carnage, the victory of Arthur and his honourable burial of the dead of both sides (13539-970). In the moment of triumph, an ominous dream heralds the treachery of Modred and the destruction of the Round Table company (13971-14297). The narrative pattern, as much as the events themselves, marks a major climax in the action.

Something of the same effect of formal proportions related to theme is apparent in the larger structures of the poem, despite Laȝamon's constant expansion and occasional compression of episodes and the periodic quickening and slackening of the narrative tempo The greatly expanded treatment of Arthur's reign has altered the proportional balance from one-fifth of the whole in Geoffrey's *Historia* to almost one-third in Laȝamon's version, nearly a half if the reign of Uther is included. The function of the Arthurian section as the thematic climax of the work is emphasised by its placing within the overall structure, being preceded by some three-quarters and followed by one quarter of the remaining material. The long, slow prelude, with its recurrent theme of national greatness assailed from abroad and undermined by treachery at home, leads up to the most triumphant statement of that theme in the prolonged sequence of Arthur's victories and to its inevitable outcome in the dissolution of the Round Table, followed by Britain's rapid slide towards national extinction. And within the Arthurian section there are similar variations of pace and proportion for thematic effect. Those early episodes in which Arthur establishes his authority at home are treated in considerable detail in some seventeen hundred lines. The campaigns of foreign conquest which follow, repetitive in pattern and accelerated in treatment — Ireland is subdued in some two hundred lines, a third of the space previously given to Scotland, and in a further two hundred Iceland, Orkney, Jutland and Winetland capitulate with mounting rapidity — suggest Laȝamon's structural control of material largely of his own contrivance. The extended treatment of the riot which led to the making of the Round Table, another of his inventions, allows the episode to be seen as paralleling, at the domestic level, Arthur's establishment of national order, and as prefiguring the national collapse which will ultimately result from treason within his own household. When his foreign conquests are renewed, the earlier structural pattern is reversed: rapid campaigns in Norway and Denmark are followed by the longer sequence of the taking of France, largely focussed on the personal prowess of the king, building to a climax in the still longer Roman campaign, involving massive forces and resulting in wholesale slaughter minutely detailed. After which the downfall of the Round Table appears an anticlimax, brief, bitter and devoid of military glory, a pre-echo of the ultimate dissolution of the British nation.

The poetic medium

The artistic control apparent in the structure of Laȝamon's *Brut* does not radically differentiate it from the versions of Geoffrey and Wace, though it moderates the diffusive effect of greatly increased scale. The poetic medium, on the other hand, is unique, setting the *Brut* apart from both Latin and French traditions, clearly rooted in native tradition yet in a manner which defies precise definition. Anglo-Saxon verse, being addressed to the ear rather than the eye, is based on the stress patterns of speech organised into rhythmic units consisting of two stressed and at least two unstressed syllables arranged in five or six recognised patterns. These units are interlinked in pairs by alliteration borne always by the first stress of the second half-line and by either or both the stresses of the first half-line. The brief pause or caesura between the two half-lines, often emphasised by a syntactical break dividing grammatical or sense units, creates a tension within the alliterative unit of the line, while enjambment holds the long line in tension against the verse-paragraph composed of a variable number of half-lines. The semantic effect is cumulative, compiling details of action, description, emotion in loose syntactic association; the rhythmic effect reinforced by alliteration is emphatic, incantatory, ideally suited to recitation.

There are occasional lines in Laȝamon's *Brut* which echo this classical medium so closely as to suggest that he had knowledge of the Anglo-Saxon tradition:

       Saxes gunnen sinken   —sorʒe heom wes ʒiueðe!   (10058)

There are even passages, especially those concerned with conventional topics of the classical tradition — battle, violent action or emotion, rhetorical tirades, where it is momentarily sustained:

       Seoððen speren chrakeden,   sceldes brastleden,
       helmes tohelden,   heʒe men uellen,
       burnen tobreken,   blod ut ʒeoten;
       ueldes falewe wurðen,   feollen here-mærken.
       Wondrede ʒeond þat wald   iwundede cnihtes oueral;
       sixti hundred þar weoren   totredene mid horsen;
       beornes þer swelten,   blodes aturnen;
       stræhten after stretes   blodie stremes.   (13707-714)

But the lack of alliteration in the first line, its irregular placing on the final stress in the last line, the numerous weak stresses of lines five and six, and the imperfect rhyme between the two halves of line two exemplify the constant variation which characterises Laʒamon's verse. For him alliteration seems no longer an essential organisational principle; in nearly one line in three it is entirely absent. Yet it is too frequent to be merely ornamental and, in some passages, so regularly associated with stress as to echo its classical usage. Similarly, though the majority of half-lines are of two stresses only, some have three or even four; other half-lines are rhythmically so uncertain as to leave the determination of the stress pattern to the individual reader. Though the classic pattern can be imposed on such a line as:

       and sófte hine adun leíden,   and fórð gunnen líðen   (14287)

the variety of stresses avoids the insistence of the classic line which, at least to the modern ear, can seem monotonous. Equally, the modern ear, accustomed to identify syllabic rather than stress patterns, identifies in such lines as:

       Arður lai alle longe niht   and spac wið þene ʒeonge cniht   (13975)

a metrical regularity reminiscent of the octosyllabic couplet which was the dominant medium of contemporary French literature. The effect is reinforced, in slightly less than half the lines, by rhyme (*lond/hond*; *bistriden/riden*) or near-rhyme (*sune/inume*; *live/driʒe*; *fallen/unnen*). There are rare moments of appropriate subject-matter when such couplets seem to echo the contemporary French lyric soon to be imitated in English:

       þa Æstre wes aʒonge
       and Aueril eode of tune,
       and þat gras was riue
       and þat water wes liðe . . .   (12074-5)

The contrast in manner and medium with the battle passage quoted above could hardly be greater.

    The origins of this idiosyncratic medium have been the subject of prolonged debate, which inevitably, in view of the period of cultural fusion in which the *Brut* was written, has been somewhat inconclusive. The classic line of Anglo-Saxon verse was used by conservative poets to the end of the eleventh century and beyond. But even before the Conquest, it had sometimes been interspersed with expanded half-line units of three stresses and a variable number of unstressed syllables; there had also been sporadic employment of rhyme and at least one experiment in its thoroughgoing use. The sparse fragments of verse preserved from the next century and a half show a much looser alliterative line, sometimes with medial rhyme at the caesura, intermixed with rhyming couplets having occasional alliteration, the combinations very variously handled in the different poems. Behind this scanty literary record lies the phantom of a popular oral tradition unbroken by the Conquest in which the formal characteristics of the literary medium may have been much more freely handled. Another potential model which also spanned the period of the Conquest was homiletic prose incorporating rhythmic alliterative phrases, blurring the distinction between prose and verse, examples of which, in Ælfric's much-copied works, would have been available to Laȝamon from the Worcester scriptoria.

Attempts to place Laȝamon's medium in a tradition linking Anglo-Saxon poetry to the alliterative verse produced up to the end of the Middle Ages have tended to present him as a passive participant in a historical process, an impression refuted by his very positive redaction of Wace. If the selection, invention and adaptation to national tradition shown in his treatment of matter was matched in the creation of his poetic medium, that too must have been a process of choice, of trial and contrivance, however unconscious. We cannot know the full range of metrical models available to him, nor whether they were predominantly literary or oral; but it is manifest that he was doing more than trying at one moment to recall the half-forgotten movement of the Old English alliterative line and at the next to imitate Wace's octosyllabic couplet. The former, however well suited to battle passages, has an air of pastiche or self-conscious echo; the latter, though fluid in narration, seems to trivialise the epic subject-matter. The hybrid long line with its sporadic rhyme and alliteration, often seems mere doggerel, though a skilled reciter may have been able to impose effective discipline on its metrical irregularity. The overall effect, however patchy, does not suggest passive reaction to an age of cultural confusion; and when, for a moment, the right tone is struck, a new medium with something of the rhythmic variety of blank verse seems to be emerging:

> Æfne þan worden   þer com of se wenden
> þat wes an sceort bat liðen,   sceouen mid vðen,
> and twa wimmen þerinne   wunderliche idihte;
> and heo nomen Arður anan,   and aneouste hine uereden
> and softe hine adun leiden,   and forð gunnen liðen.   (14283-7)

Diction and imagery confirm the impression of the medium as rooted in tradition, native and foreign, but individually and experimentally extrapolated. Unlike the other early Middle English poems metrically related to Laȝamon's, whose vocabulary is largely that of contemporary prose, his diction contains a specifically poetic element. Alliteration requires a stock of variants particularly for terms of frequent occurrence; for 'man' and 'warrior', virtually synonymous concepts in the period, Laȝamon uses *beorn, guma, hæleð, rinc, secg, wer,* all common in Old English poetry but rarely found in contemporary writing. Such variants, together with rare occurrences of the Anglo-Saxon poetic practice of phrasal variation, repeating key ideas in differing terms, and the exceptionally limited vocabulary of French origin contribute to the archaic character of Laȝamon's idiom. So also does his fondness for compound nouns and adjectives, many familiar from Old and early Middle English texts: *here* 'army' is used as a prefix in *hereburne* 'corslet', *heretoȝe* 'commander', and *hereȝeonge* 'military expedition'. But, significantly, Laȝamon appears to extend the range of recorded compounds, adding in this instance *heredring* and *herekempe* both meaning 'warrior', *herrefeng* 'plunder' *heremarken* 'standards' and *hærescrud* 'armour'.

Most effective in creating the impression of an archaic diction is his use of formulaic phrases, expressions repeated in similar narrative contexts with only minor if any variation of terms. Though many are mere tags, there are more than seventy half-line formulas, such as 'breken brade speren' or 'feollen þa fæie', and over fifty full-line examples, such as 'ah longe is æuere, þat ne cumeð nauere', averaging one occurrence every ten lines throughout the poem.[14] Though variants on 'fæge feollen' occur in *Beowulf* and other Old English poems of epic character, very few of Laȝamon's formulas are found in earlier verse or that of his own age; the models for many are idiomatic or colloquial expressions, rhyming or alliterating phrases found in prose as well as verse. But the great majority appear to be original with Laȝamon and it is their use rather than any traditional association which gives them their formulaic character. By their repetition he characterises an individual (Arthur is 'aðelest alre kinge' and 'Bruttene deorling'), ensures continuity by echoing earlier incidents ('and dæd is þe oðer, Aurilien his broðer', 'al þat Arður isæh, al hit him to bæh'), or gives an air of ritual to repeated actions ('he lette blawen beomen and bonnien his ferden'). The effect is often somewhat mechanical, but the artistic intention behind the extension of a traditional form of expression is obvious.

The most striking instance of such artistic extrapolation is Laȝamon's use of extended similes which have no counterpart in Old English tradition and no apparent source in Wace. Virgil provides an obvious model but, Laȝamon's dubious Latinity apart, his examples are organically related to their context in a way which does not suggest self-conscious literary ornamentation. There is a more obvious inspiration in the rare, brief similes in Wace who says of Britons slaughtering Saxons:

> Si cum li liuns orguillus,
> Ki de lunges est fameillus,
> Ocist mutuns, ocist berbiz,
> Ocist ainnels granz e petiz . . .   (8517-20)

> (*Just as the fierce lion, long famished, kills sheep,*
> *kills ewes, kills beasts both great and small . . .*)

Though he omitted it in its original context, Laȝamon clearly had it in mind when, on a similar occasion, he wrote:

> Vp bræid Arður his sceld   foren to his breosten,

> and he gon to rusien   swa þe runie wulf
> þenne he cumeð of holte   bihonged mid snawe,
> and þencheð to biten   swulc deor swa him likeð.   (10040-3)

(Arthur raised his shield before his chest and went rushing like the savage wolf when he comes from the snow-hung wood, bent on devouring whatever prey he pleases.)

There are such brief similes, usually no more than a single line, throughout the *Brut*, but they increase markedly as the Arthurian section approaches; there are fifteen in lines 7000 to 9000 dealing with the period from the settlement of the Saxons at Vortigern's invitation to the beginning of Uther's reign. But with the coming of Arthur they begin to grow in length and vividness, though mostly on the conventional basis, familiar from Wace, of comparing the behaviour of men to that of animals. Then, at the climax of Arthur's revenge upon the Saxons for the killing of Uther, come, in an astonishing burst, eight similes within six hundred lines, growing in length and complexity as the climax approaches.

Immediately following the comparison of Arthur with a ravening wolf, Arthur himself describes his army falling upon the enemy like a fierce wind pressing upon a lofty wood (10047-8), while the poet pictures one enemy leader as a wild crane separated from the flock, pursued by hawks in the air and by hounds on land (10061-7), and another as a hunted wolf (10114). The tendency for Laʒamon's similes to develop into self-contained narratives, already apparent in the image of the crane, is carried further in the twenty lines in which Arthur pictures the defeated Childric as a sportive fox surprised by the hunt in the midst of his pleasure, driven to the hills and then dug out of his den just as the Saxon has been by Arthur (10398-417). Two further brief images of Arthur himself falling on the enemy like a wild boar upon the tame swine amongst the beech mast (10609-10) and as a pursuing lion (10613) lead to a sequence of three similes, continuous and interlinked, totalling twenty five lines, which mark the moment of final triumph. The sequence opens by returning to the image of Arthur as a preying wolf and pictures Colgrim as a goat standing at bay in the hills above Bath (10628-36); the third simile pictures the fleeing Childric as a hunter pursued by horns, in flight from those who were once his quarry (10646-52). Between the two comes a remarkable vision of the end of the whole Saxon enterprise as Baldolf looks down on his companions slaughtered in crossing the Avon — 'then the river Avon was all bridged with steel!' (10616):

> þa ʒet cleopede Arður,   aðelest kingen:
> 'ʒurstendæi wes Baldulf   cnihten alre baldest;
> nu he stant on hulle   and Auene bihaldeð,
> hu ligeð i þan stræme   stelene fisces;
> mid sweorde bigeorede   heore sund is awemmed;
> heore scalen wleoteð   swulc gold-faʒe sceldes;
> þer fleoteð heore spiten   swulc hit spæren weoren.
> þis beoð seolcuðe þing   isiʒen to þissen londe,
> swulche deor an hulle,   swulche fisces in wælle!'   (10638-45)

(Then Arthur, noblest of kings, continued: 'Yesterday Baldolf was the boldest of warriors; now he stands on the hill and looks upon the Avon,

sees how steel fish lie in the river trammelled with swords, their swimming impaired; their scales gleam as if they were gilded shields; their fins drift in the water like spears floating there. This is a marvellous thing come to pass in this land, such beasts on the hill, such fish in the water!')

As in his imaginative elaboration of the prophecies of Merlin, verbal exaltation has drawn Laȝamon into vivid elaboration of the basic image on which his simile rests. In both instances the source of his excitement is his vision of Arthur triumphant. There seems no reason to look for any extraneous source for this remarkable group of similes; while Wace supplied the traditional model of animal imagery, the imaginative extrapolation is characteristic of Laȝamon's methods elsewhere, his fascination with Arthur's reputation providing the stimulus.

Arthur as hero

The narrative expansion and imaginative intensity with which Arthur is treated in the *Brut* indicates his importance in Laȝamon's interpretation; but his place in the dynastic pattern and his personal characterisation were pre-determined by Geoffrey of Monmouth. In the line of British heroes founded by Brutus he comes after the high point of Brenne and Belin's conquest of Rome when, with Maximian's withdrawal of the best of the nation for his continental campaigns and the consequent Saxon invasion, the ultimate fate of Britain is already fixed. His personal role as the supreme national champion is heightened by the underlying threats, never wholly forgotten, of foreign invasion and domestic treason. For such a role Geoffrey had time-honoured models in Alexander and Caesar, world-conquerors struck down at the height of their power, and in Charlemagne, though as founder of that empire with which the Angevins were to contend the possession of France rather than the legendary Charlemagne of the *chansons de geste*, old and wise, figure-head rather than active warrior. The legend of Alexander's mysterious, divine parentage perhaps suggested the illicit siring of Arthur by the aid of magic; his youthful accession, his personal prowess and the scale of his conquests may also owe something to the classical model. Charlemagne provided precedent for a secular leader in a patriotic cause against pagan forces uniting his followers by generosity and good government. But these external literary influences need have done no more than strengthen the concept of Arthur inherited from Welsh tradition: valiant war-leader, good Christian devoted to the Virgin Mary, inspiring his followers by his personal prowess, his valour expressed in his arms with their ancient names and reputations. Unrestrained by historical record, Geoffrey has created the figure of an ideal king in whom, nonetheless, many aspects of contemporary monarchy are reflected.

The idealised portrait was clearly acceptable to Laȝamon, though he chose to emphasise certain features and to reflect different aspects of reality. Many of his additions and elaborations heighten the idealisation of Arthur. The echoes he introduces from Geoffrey's Prophecies of Merlin establish his undying fame even before he has been born:

> 'Longe beoð æuere, dæd ne bið he næuere;
> þe wile þe þis world stænt, ilæsten scal is worðmunt;
> and scal inne Rome walden þa þæines.' (9406-8)

('As long as time lasts, he shall never die; while this world last
his fame shall endure; and he shall rule the princes in Rome.')

Another of his creative initiatives, invoking the tradition of gift-giving deities at the
birth of a prince, defines the sources of Arthur's greatness as warrior, king and
long-living, generous patron:

> heo ȝeuen him mihte to beon bezst alre cnihten;
> heo ȝeuen him anoðer þing, þat he scolde beon riche king;
> heo ȝiuen him þat þridde, þat he scolde longe libben;
> heo ȝifen him, þat kinebern, custen swiðe gode
> þat he wes mete-custi of alle quike monnen; (9610-14)

(. . . they gave him strength to be the best of all knights; they gave him
another gift, that he should be a mighty king; they gave him a third,
that he should live long; they gave him, that royal child, such good
qualities that he was the most liberal of all living men;)

The armour which is the emblem of his knighthood is given more explicit magical
associations than in Wace or Geoffrey:

> þa dude he on his burne ibroide of stele
> þe makede on aluisc smið mid aðelen his crafte;
> he wes ihaten Wygar þe Witeȝe wurhte.
> His sconken he helede mid hosen of stele.
> Calibeorne his sweord he sweinde bi his side;
> hit wes iworht in Aualun mid wiȝelefulle craften. (10543-8)

(. . . then he put on his corslet of woven steel which an elvish smith
had made by his noble skill; he who made Wygar was called Witeȝe.
He protected his legs with hose of steel. At his side hung his sword
Caliburn; it was made in Avalon by magic arts.)

And the numinous element is increased by the invention of Arthur's second dream
(13981-14021); though modelled at least in part upon the first, uninterpreted omen
(12764-93), the king reveals his own understanding of it by his concern for the
absent Guenevere who, in a dream, he had cut to pieces for her complicity in
Modred's treason. Finally, at his departure to Avalon, he admits foreknowledge that
the *aluen* who blessed him at birth promise healing for his fifteen terrible wounds
and eventual return to his kingdom (14277-82). But though greatly increased by
Laȝamon, the element of the occult is not thematically engaged; Arthur is not
supernaturally guided in his mission as national messiah, as his predecessors were by
Merlin whom Arthur never meets. It merely adds a gloss of fairy prince to his more
realistic roles as war-leader, world conqueror, lawgiver and Christian king.

In the medieval manner, Arthur is characterised in relation to those roles rather
than in terms of individuality; others are characterised only in relation to him as
beautiful, passive consort, loyal or traitorous nephews, obedient followers, rebellious
underlings, imperious or humbled opponents. Nor is there any development in his
presentation; at his accession aged fifteen, he is already wholly himself — 'and the

years had all been well employed, for he was fully mature' (9931). Immediately afterwards, at his coronation, his regal personality is sketched in terms which are to remain constant throughout his reign:

> þa þe Arður wes king —hærne nu seollic þing—
> he wes mete-custi ælche quike monne,
> cniht mid þan bezste, wunder ane kene;
> he wes þan зungen for fader, þan alden for frouer,
> and wið þan vnwise wunder ane sturnne;
> woh him wes wunder lað and þat rihte a leof.
> Ælc of his birlen and of his bur-þæinen
> and his ber-cnihtes gold beren an honden,
> to ruggen and to bedde iscrud mid gode webbe.
> Nefde he neuere nænne coc þat he nes keppe swiðe god,
> neuær nanes cnihtes swein þat he næs bald þein.
> þe king heold al his hired mid hæзere blise;
> and mid swulche þinges he ouercom alle kinges,
> mid ræhзere strengðe and mid richedome;
> swulche weoren his custes þat al uolc hit wuste.
> Nu wes Arður god king; his hired hine lufede
> æc hit wes cuð wide of his kinedome. (9945-61)

(When Arthur was king — now listen to a marvellous matter — he was generous to every man alive, among the best of warriors, wonderfully bold; he was a father to the young, a comfort to the old, and with the rash extremely stern; wrong was most hateful to him and the right was always dear. Each of his cup-bearers and his chamberlains and his footmen bore gold in hand, wore fine cloth on back and bed. He never had any cook who was not a good warrior, never any knight's squire who was not a bold thane. The king kept all his followers in great contentment; and by such means he defeated all kings, by fierce strength and by generosity; such were his virtues that all nations knew of it. Now Arthur was a good king; his followers loved him and it was known far beyond his kingdom.)

The ambivalence, benevolence and sternness, ferocity and generosity, is Laзamon's addition to the blander portrait in Wace and Geoffrey, and he occasionally restates it aphoristically as the key to Arthur's personality:

> Arður wes wunsum þer he hafde his iwillen,
> and he wes wod sturne wið his wiðer-iwinnen. (11235-6)

(Arthur was gracious whenever he achieved his purpose, and he was terribly stern with those who opposed him.)

As such, it manifests itself in each aspect of his multiple role.

His function as lawgiver, foretold by Merlin before his birth, sworn to by the young king at the moment of his accession, is periodically renewed at national hustings, exercised in foreign territories whose conquest is confirmed by the establishment of British law, and finally forms the basis of his charge to his successor, Constantin:

> 'Ich þe bitache here mine kineriche;
> and wite mine Bruttes a to þines lifes,
> and hald heom alle þa laзen þa habbeoð istonden a mine daзen,
> and alle þa laзen gode þa bi Vðeres daзen stode.' (14273-6)

('I here entrust my realm to you; and you defend my Britons as long as you live, and maintain for them all the laws that have been in force in my day, and all the good laws which existed in Uther's time.')

But though the king is presented as the fountain of justice, justice is as often equated with punishment as with mercy. The punishments decreed by Arthur for those who started the riot which led to the making of the Round Table seem very rough justice indeed:

> 'Nimeð me þene ilke mon   þa þis feht ærst bigon,
> and doð wiððe an his sweore   and draȝeð hine to ane more,
> and doð hine in an ley uen   þer he scal liggen;
> and nimeð al his nexte cun   þa ȝe maȝen iuinden
> and swengeð of þa hafden   mid breoden eouwer sweorden.
> þa wifmen þa ȝe maȝen ifinden   of his nexten cunden,
> kerueð of hire neose   and heore wlite ga to lose;
> and swa ich wulle al fordon   þat cun þat he of com.' (11393-400)

('Seize that man who first began this fight, put a cord about his neck and drag him to a marsh, and thrust him into the bog where he shall lie; and seize all his close kin whom you can find and strike off their heads with your broad swords. The women of his immediate family whom you can find, cut off their noses and let their looks be ruined; and so I will utterly destroy the race from which he came.')

But violence within the court, threatening the king's peace and the stability of the nation, is treason — for which Arthur imposes the traditional penalty: '"mid horsen todraȝen þat is elches swiken laȝen"' (11406). The infectious nature of treason, which justifies the killing of the traitor's kin, is demonstrated in the closing days of Arthur's reign when Modred, having seduced the citizens of Winchester from their loyalty to the king, betrays them in turn, slipping away with his forces and leaving the city to Arthur's punishment:

> And Arður Winchestre   þa burh bilai wel faste
> and al þat moncun ofsloh   —þer wes sorȝen inoh!
> þa ȝeonge and þa alde,   alle he aqualde.
> þa þat folc wes al ded,   þa burh al forswelde,
> þa lette he mid alle   tobreken þa walles alle.
> þa wes hit itimed þere   þat Merlin seide while:
> 'Ærm wurðest þu, Winchæstre;   þæ eorðe þe scal forswalȝe!'
> Swa Merlin sæide   —þe witeȝe wes mære.   (14195-202)

(And Arthur besieged the town of Winchester very closely and slew all the inhabitants — great was the sorrow there! He killed them all, both young and old. When the people were all dead, the city completely destroyed by fire, then he caused all the walls to be destroyed utterly. Then was it come to pass there as Merlin once prophesied: 'Wretched shall you be, Winchester; the earth shall swallow you up!' Thus spoke Merlin, who was a true prophet.)

Such passages have been cited as evidence of Laȝamon's sadistic temperament and the unsophisticated nature of his English audience. But an audience, many of whose members may have been born in an age of civil war, remembering the anarchy under Stephen when in the strongholds of baronial freebooters such tortures were inflicted that, according to the Anglo-Saxon Chronicle, 'men said openly that Christ and all his saints were asleep', might well have found Laȝamon's picture of a strong and ruthless ruler both realistic and attractive. Though the antique native roots of his idiom may have darkened that picture with epic colouring suggesting a return to more primitive values, the spectacle of Arthur wooing and coercing his followers to rally to the defense of the nation ('And whoever stayed away should suffer mutilation; and whoever came willingly, he should become rich'), restraining them when they assault the Roman ambassadors in his court (a detail not in Wace), and calming violent disputes between his closest kinsmen in council no doubt seemed admirable exercise of authority in the interests of the nation. Laȝamon wrote in an age when fear and favour were equally instruments of government and admits their parity in Arthur's methods of control:

> Alle Brut-leoden   luueden Arðuren.
> Alle heom stod him æie to   þat wuneden a þan ærde;   (13526-7)
>
> (*All the people of Britain loved Arthur. All who dwelt in the land stood in awe of him;*)

If he acknowledges the darker side of feudal polity to a greater degree than Wace, it is perhaps because the vividness with which his imagination pictures the reign of Arthur instinctively clothes it in the circumstances of his own age. Ultimately he undermines the heroic image he has been at such pains to create by distancing the king from those who should advise and support him. When the king has his first portentous dream, no one dares to offer an interpretation which might disturb his feudal lord 'lest he should lose limbs which he valued' (12792-3); and the messenger who brings news of Modred's treachery critically delays its delivery and even denies the significance of Arthur's second prophetic dream:

> þa andswarede þe cniht: 'Lauerd, þu hauest unriht;
> ne sculde me nauere sweuen   mid sorȝen arecchen.
> þu ært þe riccheste mon   þa rixleoð on londen
> and þe alre wiseste   þe wuneð under weolcne.
> Ȝif hit weore ilumpe,   swa nulle hit ure Drihte,
> þat Modred, þire suster sune,   hafde þine quene inume
> and al þi kineliche lond   isæt an his aȝere hond,
> þe þu him bitahtest   þa þu to Rome þohtest,
> and he hafde al þus ido   mid his swikedome,
> þe ȝet þu mihtest þe awreken   wurðliche mid wepnen,
> and æft þi lond halden   and walden þine leoden,
> and þine feond fallen   þe þe ufel unnen,
> and slæn heom alle clane   þet þer no bilauen nane.'   (14022-34)

> (*Then the knight answered: 'Lord, you are mistaken; one should never interpret dreams ominously. You who rule in this land are the most powerful and the wisest of all who dwell upon earth. If it should have happened, as our Lord forbid, that Modred your sister's son had seized your queen and taken into his own possession your entire kingdom, which you entrusted to him when you planned to go to Rome, and he had done all this by his treachery, still you might fittingly avenge yourself by force of arms, and possess your land again and rule your people, and destroy your enemies who wish you ill, kill them one and all that none of them survive.'*)

Such adulation rings hollow on the eve of Arthur's last campaign — against fellow Britons.

The dangers of internal dissension are never entirely forgotten: a sudden passion for a loyal subject's wife may precipitate civil war, rivalry for pre-eminence at court lead to riot, quarrels erupt between trusted lieutenants in council. Arthur imposes his authority by using the political means of a feudal age: personal example, public ceremonial, royal largess, state religion. His military prowess is demonstrated both as tactician marshalling forces from all over his empire against the might of Rome, and as national champion fighting the Roman tribune in single combat. Both roles originate with Geoffrey, but Laȝamon has developed them with vigour and imaginative realism. The single combat, four times longer than in Wace, results from a challenge issued by the enemy leader in the confidence that Arthur will refuse, 'for if Frolle, King of France, had known that Arthur would grant him what he had requested, he would not have done so for a ship full of gold'. Their meeting on an island in the Seine is treated with all the formality of a trial by combat, and victory over an opponent of equal valour is won by Arthur's personal prowess:

Þær Bruttes wolden ouer water buȝen
ȝif Arður up ne sturte stercliche sone
and igræp his sceld godne, ileired mid golde,
and toȝaines Frolle mid feondliche lechen;
breid biforen breosten godne sceld brade.
And Frolle him to fusden mid his feond-ræse
and his sweord up ahof and adunriht sloh,
and smat an Arðures sceld þat he wond a þene feld.
Þe helm an his hæuede and his hereburne
gon to falsie foren an his hafde,
and he wunde afeng feouwer unchene long—
heo ne þuhte him noht sær for heo næs na mare—
þat blod orn adun ouer al his breoste.
Arður wes abolȝe swiðe an his heorte
and his sweord Caliburne swipte mid maine,
and smat Frolle uppen þæne hælm þat he atwa helden
þurhut þere burne hod þat hit at his breoste atstod.
Þa feol Frolle, folde to grunde;
uppen þan gras-bedde his gost he bilæfde. (11951-69)

(The Britons would have crossed the river then had Arthur not instantly leapt up, grasped his fine shield with its golden rim and, raising his good broad shield before his chest, advanced upon Frolle with hostile intent. And Frolle rushed at him in fierce assault and, raising his sword and striking downwards, smote upon Arthur's shield so that it fell to the ground. The helmet on his head and the chain-mail on his forehead beneath gave way, and he received a wound four inches long — since it was no greater it did not seem painful to him — so that the blood ran down all over his chest. Arthur was greatly enraged at heart, and swinging his sword Caliburn with force, struck Frolle upon the helmet so that it split apart right through the coif of mail and the sword lodged in his chest. Then Frolle fell, stricken to the earth; upon the grassy ground he yielded up his life.)

As in the other battle passages, Laȝamon relishes the violence, the bodies cut in half, the sword lodging in the teeth of a cloven skull, the showers of arrows 'thick as falling snow', the streams of blood flowing along the forest paths, the wounded soldiers wandering over the wooded countryside. The contrast with Wace's comparatively bland and generalised battle pieces owes more, perhaps, to Laȝamon's preference for concrete detail and the vividness of his vocabulary than to the sadistic interests with which he is sometimes credited.

On another occasion when the king defends his people against an evil force, he evokes the beastliness of the Giant of Mont St Michel vividly (12960-13040), but not more grotesquely or at greater length than Wace (11450-598) whose comparison with Arthur's combat with the giant Riun, collector of royal beards, Laȝamon reduces to a bare allusion. But there is a significant contrast: in Wace's account, Arthur hopes to take the giant unawares; Laȝamon says 'Arthur would never attack him while asleep lest he should later suffer reproach'. Laȝamon has been said to lack appreciation of chivalry, yet he elaborates descriptively the few lines in the *Roman de Brut* telling how the body of the emperor Lucius was returned to Rome, recognising the honour due to a worthy opponent who 'had been a very brave man while he lived' and underscoring the irony of Arthur's message that the golden coffin was the only tribute he would send the Romans.

Laȝamon's appreciation of the place of ceremonial in medieval governance seems no less acute than Wace's: Arthur's arming is as splendid, his councils as formal if often more impassioned, his crown-wearing at Caerleon no less detailed, ceremonious or courtly, even if his followers show more interest in field sports and ball games than in the gambling and board games of Wace. The English poet is no less aware of the refinements of court life than the French, except in the matter of courtly wooing where he does no more than lip-service to Wace's rare passages of *amour courtois*.[15] Where he omits such references, as when Gawain praises peace as conducive to amorous dalliance (see the lines from Wace quoted on p.xxvii), it is in favour of a different idealism based on social good rather than personal happiness:

> 'for god is gri and god is fri e freoliche er halde wi—
> and Godd sulf hit makede urh his Goddcunde—
> for gri make godne mon gode workes wurchen
> for alle monnen bi a bet at lond bi a murgre.' (12455-8)

(' . . . *for peace and quiet are good if one maintains them willingly
— and God himself in his divinity created them — for peace allows
a good man to do good deeds whereby all men are the better and the
land the happier.*')

Ceremonial occasions display the unity and magnificence of the Round Table and the royal munificence which underpin both. Arthur rewards loyal service with kingdoms and castles, dismisses aged knights with rich gifts, restores forfeited lands to pardoned rebels (though not to traitors or perjurers), and feasts his followers to the sound of trumpets. Much of the detail is merely echoed or elaborated from Wace, but Laȝamon's understanding of the role of generosity in Arthur's regality is apparent from his initial characterisation: 'The king kept all his followers in great contentment; and by such means he defeated all kings, by fierce strength and by generosity'.

Religious observance plays an important part in Arthur's public life: clerics bless his enterprises, keep vigil before he fights Frolle, celebrate his victories; he, in turn, nominates archbishops, rebuilds ruined churches, takes oaths upon the relics of saints. Repeatedly, earnestly and with every appearance of sincerity he invokes divine aid: at the moment of his accession when he prays for help in upholding God's laws all his life, addressing, before every battle, the Virgin whose image he bears on his shield and, on waking in terror from an ominous dream, calling on Christ by formulaic titles as old as the oldest English verse:

> 'Lauerd Drihten, Crist,   domes waldende,
> midelarde mund,   monnen froure,
> þurh þine aðmode wil,   walden ænglen,
> let þu mi sweuen   to selþen iturnen!'   (12760-3)

> ('*Christ, our Lord and Master, Lord of destinies, Guardian of the world, Comforter of men, Ruler of angels, let my dream, through your gracious will, lead to a good end!*')

But here too prayer is a public act in the hearing of his men, just as elsewhere God is invoked in a political act as Arthur is about to execute youthful German hostages in a moment of anger against their leaders:

> 'Ah, swa me hælpen Drihten   þæ scop þæs dæies lihten,
> þerfore he scal ibiden   bitterest alre baluwen,
> harde gomenes   —his bone ich wulle iwurðen!
> Colgrim and Baldulf   beiene ich wulle aquellen,
> and al heore duȝeðe   dæð scal iðolien.
> Ȝif hit wule ivnnen   Waldende hæfnen,
> ich wulle wurðliche wreken   alle his wiðer-deden.
> Ȝif me mot ilasten   þat lif a mire breosten,
> and hit wulle me iunne   þat iscop mone and sunne,
> ne scal nauere Childric   æft me bicharren!'   (10515-24)

> ('*But, so help me God who created the light of day, he shall suffer for it the most bitter affliction, harsh treatment — I will be his slayer! I will kill both Colgrim and Baldolf, and all their followers shall suffer death. If the Ruler of Heaven grants it, I will fittingly avenge all his wicked deeds. If life endures within me, and He who created sun and moon grants it, never again shall Childric deceive me!*')

Since Arthur, the public figure, has no inner life, there is no indication of his personal faith, even in moments of greatest anguish: when he learns of the treachery of Modred and Guenevere — it is Gawain who invokes God's law in vowing their destruction; when he laments Gawain's own death; or in the slaughter at Camelford. Christian and magical elements having coexisted in his public life as easily as the roles of feudal sovereign and fairy prince in his persona, it comes as no surprise that he invokes the fairy Argante for his bodily healing and that it is Merlin who, like some Old Testament prophet, predicts his messianic return:

> Nis nauer þe mon iboren   of nauer nane burde icoren
> þe cunne of þan soðe   of Arðure sugen mare.
> Bute while wes an witeȝe   Mærlin ihate;
> he bodede mid worde   —his quiðes weoren soðe—
> þat an Arður sculde ȝete   cum Anglen to fulste.   (14293-7)

> (*No man ever born of noble lady can tell more of the truth about Arthur. But there was once a seer called Merlin who prophesied — his sayings were true — that an Arthur should come again to aid the people of England.*)[16]

The *Brut* as national epic

It seems ironic that Arthur's messianic return, the hope of the British, should here be promised to the English whose ancestors were their bitterest foes. The unexpected twist raises the issue of Laȝamon's central theme and the literary category to which the *Brut* belongs. The difficulty of definition arises partly from the unfamiliarity of modern critics with the concept of a verse chronicle neither factually historical nor yet an obvious literary construct with traditional criteria of form and content. The problem originates with Geoffrey whose *Historia*, definable today as a pastiche chronicle, fascinated its original audience precisely because it illuminated the dark past of their society with a certainty warranted by all the apparatus of academic historiography. Where modern readers of such a pastiche would expect to be given some perspective to encourage appreciation of the ironic disparity between the fictive material and its factual presentation, the completeness of the illusion seems to have been a large part of its appeal for medieval readers, even for those contemporary chroniclers who yielded reluctantly to its fascination. Certainly neither Wace nor Laȝamon betrays any hint of ironic detachment towards the *Historia*; their concern is to make its matter yet more relevant and convincing to their particular audiences. Categorisation is complicated, in Laȝamon's case, by his use of elements of poetic idiom associated in Old English tradition with works of epic character. But the surviving fragments of that tradition include nothing of the scale and historical scope of the *Brut*, whose idiom suggests compilation and extrapolation from a variety of models rather than inheritance of an established epic medium. If Laȝamon's poem is to be judged as a national epic, it must be on other grounds than continuity of national tradition, either of idiom or theme. The very fact that the elements in his idiom which lend it epic colouring stemmed from that society cast as the racial foe in the *Brut* suggests the improbability of thematic inheritance, just as the variety of its components reflects the period of cultural fusion in which the work was written.

The *Brut* also lacks the formal criteria of the wider epic tradition from which it was cut off by Geoffrey's imitation of Latin chronicle only faintly coloured with Virgilian overtones; without the learning and the literary self-consciousness of a Joseph of Exeter, Laȝamon probably lacked access to and possibly interest in the classical models. So his work shows nothing of the structural complexity, the variety of perspective, the thematic concentration of Virgilian or Homeric epic. Equally it lacks the episodic organisation of *Beowulf* and the *Chanson de Roland*. In contrast, the narrative is swift, spare, uncomplicated in motivation, the narrator occasionally weakening concentration by his interventions. But the formal characteristics of epic vary greatly from age to age, culture to culture. Essential characteristics common to acknowledged examples of the genre include great length, seriousness of treatment, concentration upon themes and values vital to a particular society, especially to its military survival, demonstrated in the careers of charismatic heroes of exceptional gifts and prowess. There can be no question that the *Brut* is of epic scale and scope, covering in over sixteen thousand lines some two thousand years of history. Nor can there be any doubt of its seriousness of purpose or thematic power; despite its narrative linearity and a certain thinness of texture, the underlying theme persists of a noble society, born out of disaster, striving at times for mere survival, at others for total dominance, only to fall again into disaster. The stature of its heroes, Brutus, Brenne, Belin, Aurelius, Uther, Arthur, and the extent to which each embodies the national cause, is manifest. That it celebrates multiple aspects of charismatic leadership and personal prowess in a variety of heroes, rather than a Beowulf, a Roland or a Cid, associates it with the *Iliad*. That it ends in heroic failure, leaving a shadow hanging over the future of the national cause need not invalidate it as epic; so do *Beowulf*, and the *Roland*. Nor need the fact that it transmutes repeated failure into national glory and perverts historical fact in the process, since the *Roland* also shows the power of the patriotic imagination to transform disaster into triumph just as the *Iliad* demonstrates how the accretion of legend can transform a grain of fact into an epic myth. Nor should it be devalued as epic by its origin in the *Historia* whose myth-making is a conscious process, since the *Aeneid* also is a literary artefact with specific models in mind and conscious designs upon the patriotism of its audience. That the *Brut* has not been seriously considered as an epic may suggest that its literary quality cannot bear comparison with these classic examples of the genre. But that in turn may reflect the extent to which its appreciation has been limited by the nature of the texts available, and its impact upon national tradition through English chronicles and the alliterative poetry of the later Middle Ages been underestimated because of lack of research.

But there is, perhaps, a more fundamental reason why its epic character has remained undefined. Each of the admitted masterpieces of the genre has come to be identified with a specific culture, composed at the moment when that culture achieved national identity, establishing or inventing its glorious origins, celebrating past triumphs, used as a rallying cry in crisis, a paen in victory (like the *Roland* at Hastings), transmuted by time into a cultural symbol. For Laȝamon's *Brut* no such national status seems possible, dealing as it does with a defeated and slighted culture in the language of its conquerors. Unless, that is, its fundamental theme is not culture but country, not race but land. It may not be merely a verbal slip which promises Arthur's return to aid the English, since Laȝamon initially declares his intention to 'relate the noble origins of the English, what they were called and whence they came who first possessed the land of England' (7-9), announcing his subject as the land and his starting point as the coming of its first inhabitants. The history of the island is then outlined as that of its successive conquerors who, each in turn, changed its name and gave it their own:

> þis lond was ihaten Albion   þa Brutus cum heron;
> þa nolde Brutus namare   þat hit swa ihaten weore,

ah scupte him nome   æfter himseluan.
He wes ihaten Brutus;   þis londe he clepede Brutaine,
and þa Troinisce men,   þa temden hine to hærre,
æfter Brutone   Brutuns heom cleopede;
and ȝed þe nome læsteð   and a summe stude cleouieð faste . . .
Heora aȝene speke Troinisce   and seoððen heo hit cleopeden Brutunisc;
ah Englisce men hit habbeð awend   seoððen Gurmund com in þis lond.
Gurmund draf out þe Brutuns   and his folc wes ihaten Sexuns,
of ane ende of Alemaine   Angles wes ihaten;
of Angles comen Englisce men   and Englelond heo hit clepeden.
þa Englisce ouercomen þe Brutuns   and brouhten heom þer neoðere
þat neofer seoððen heo ne arisen   ne her ræden funden. (975-81, 987-93)

(This land was called Albion when Brutus arrived here; Brutus did not wish
that it should any longer be so called, but he made a name for it in keeping
with his own. He was called Brutus; this land he called Britain, and the
Trojans who had made him their leader called themselves Britons after
Brutus; and the name yet endures and remains still in some places . . .
They afterwards called their own Trojan language British; but the English
have changed it since Gormund came into this country. Gormund drove out
the Britons and his people were called Saxons, from a region of Germany
called Anglia; from Anglia came the English and they called the land
England. The English overcame the Britons and brought them into subjection
so that they never rose again nor prospered here.)

The country's multi-cultural past is exemplified in the changing names of its capital,
called 'Troye þe Newe' by Brutus, later Trinovant, then Kaerlud in honour of King
Lud, changed to Lundene by the English and by the French to Lundres:

þus is þas burh iuaren   seððen heo ærest wes areræd,
þus is þis eitlond   igon from honde to hond
þet alle þa burhȝes   þe Brutus iwrohte
and heora noma gode   þa on Brutus dæi stode
beoð swiðe afelled   þurh warf of þon folke.   (1032-6)

(Thus has this city fared since it was first built; thus has this
island passed from hand to hand so that all the cities which Brutus
created have been brought low and their proper names which they
bore in the days of Brutus obliterated through change of peoples.)

The detailed location of the narrative in the British Isles originates with Geoffrey
who uses scores of place-names to relate the wide-ranging action to regions, rivers,
towns and ports familiar to his comparatively mobile, ruling-class audience, and to
add to the illusion of historical perspective by borrowing, occasionally perhaps
inventing, traditions associating place-names with persons or events in his story or by
evoking their association with Roman history. The technique obviously appealed to
Laȝamon's antiquarian temperament and he extended it, adding further place-names
and giving additional details about others. He betrays understandable ignorance of
continental locations but special, no doubt personal, knowledge of south and west
England and south Wales. The effect, as the wide-ranging action shifts from Loch
Lomond to Stonehenge, from the Humber to the Severn, Dumbarton to Teignwic,
York to Exeter, is of a legend rooted in known places, a familiar landscape. For
Laȝamon's provincial audience many of the British names may have seemed as exotic
as Mont St Michel, Bayeux, Poitiers, Autun and the Great St Bernard, some of which
places lay in territories ruled or claimed by their Angevin masters. Citizens of a

would-be imperial power, their patriotism may have been roused by evocative names and distant conquests just as later English audiences were by Kipling's tales from the Raj, with scarcely more knowledge of geographical setting and historical reality. Just as the Normans, to judge from the success of Wace's *Brut*, took pleasure in a legend which made them heirs to imperial claims rivalling those their French contemporaries had inherited from Charlemagne, so the English could take pride in the same shadowy claims to the Roman inheritance.

In an age when most men were land-bound and feudal states were often transient groupings of military or marital acquisitions, patriotism was rooted in place of origin and feudal alllegiance rather than in nationality, race or language. As territories changed hands, men's enduring allegiance was to the land which gave them their feudal status and their living, and to any ruler whose firm possession of it promised stability and protection. The ruler, however unwelcome initially, inherited with the land the feudal hierarchy of land-holders, the mutual rights and privileges which bound each to each, the immemorial usages which constituted its identity, the myths and legends which provided its historical roots. The Normans, who called themselves English even before they spoke the language and resented royal recruitment of their continental cousins for the suppression of unrest at home, rapidly identified themselves with the traditions of the land they had conquered. For the defeated English there was every temptation to sublimate their humiliation by associating their circumstances with those of the British whom they had similarly overwhelmed and displaced. To what extent that was a conscious process with Laȝamon, for whom the terms 'British' and 'English' seem interchangeable, cannot be determined. His constant demonstration and vilification of the viciousness of the Saxons and comparatively rare and benign references to the Angles suggests that he intended a distinction between the former as the Germanic invaders and the latter as the ancestors of the English — though he acknowledges their Germanic origin also. But his occasional references to Arthur as 'King of England' and the apparent modelling of his cognomen 'Bruttene deorling' on the medieval title for Alfred the Great, 'England's darling' may show a conscious intention to encourage his English-speaking compatriots to identify themselves with the British both as victors and victims. His lively and inventive version of Geoffrey's unified history of the island made it a more vivid and effective focus for patriotism in which all races could associate themselves with the victorious British and identify the foreign invader, whatever his nationality, as the perennial enemy. The tragedy in which it ends is the tragedy of a particular race, but as a national epic its underlying message is that all conquerors are themselves eventually conquered. So, just as the occasional disaffection of Arthur's followers and the treachery of Modred imply moral reasons for the Norman Conquest, the defeat of the Saxons may prefigure the eventual overthrow of the most recent invaders. Though Laȝamon could not have foreseen it, their overthrow was already implict in the sources, language and poetic medium of his *Brut*, exemplifying that cultural fusion which was to be the future of Britain. If Laȝamon's work is a national epic, its subject is Britain — with all the ambivalence the name has acquired across the centuries.

Arthur has become the symbol of that ambivalent national identity, embodying the land, its racial fusions, its traditions of law and justice, its Christian faith and its resistance to foreign invasion. Geoffrey's *Historia* which gave academic respectability and wide-spread currency to that symbol has nothing to say of the hope of the British that Arthur will return to lead them. But by stating within the same sentence that the king was mortally wounded at Camlann and that he was carried off to Avalon so that his wounds might be tended, Geoffrey acknowledges, with politic ambiguity, the myth of Arthur's return already current when he wrote (§178). Wace, in his account (13275-98), openly admits its currency, but hints at personal doubts by citing Merlin as prophesying merely that Arthur's end would remain uncertain. In Laȝamon's version (14288-97), the hope of the British is reasserted, supported by a positive prophecy of Merlin for whose truthfulness the poet vouches. Writing for an English audience, he had less to fear from official disapproval than those whose patrons belonged to the ruling class. The power of the messianic myth to cause unrest in a multiracial society had already been demonstrated before Geoffrey wrote: the chronicler Herman of Laon tells how, when canons of that city visited Bodmin in 1113, doubts cast by one of their servants on a Cornishman's assertion that Arthur still lived led to a near riot. Shortly afterwards, a commentator on the Prophecies of Merlin remarked that in Brittany anyone who doubted Arthur's survival would be lucky to escape stoning. The historian, William of Malmesbury, noted how the absence of a known grave for Arthur encouraged what he regarded as trifling fables about his survival. Meanwhile the restless Welsh, in frequent rebellion against Angevin authority, looked to Arthur as their expected leader in the reconquest of the island said, by Geoffrey, to have been prophesied by Merlin (§115.20).

The political solution was to find the grave; in 1191, the monks of Glastonbury, prompted by Henry II, discovered in the abbey cemetery, an oak coffin said to contain giant bones worthy of an epic hero and a lead cross inscribed: *Hic iacet sepultus inclitus Rex Arturius in insula Avalonia* (Here lies buried the renowned king Arthur in the isle of Avalon). But the power of a myth which embodies the dreams of a society was demonstrated across the centuries to come as the funerary inscription changed form to reflect what each age wished to believe. In the most influential of Arthurian texts, *Le Morte Darthur* (*c.*1470), which was to carry the legend triumphantly into the modern world, Sir Thomas Malory wrote:

> Yet som men say in many partys of Inglonde that kynge Arthure ys nat dede,
> but had by the wyll of oure Lorde Jesu into another place; and men say
> that he shall com agayne, and he shall wynne the Holy Crosse. Yet I woll
> nat say that hit shall be so, but rather I wolde sey: here in thys worlde
> he chaunged hys lyff. And many men say that there ys wrytten uppon the

tumbe thys: *Hic iacet Arthurus, Rex quondam Rexque futurus* (Here lies Arthur, once king, who shall be king hereafter).[17]

The dream lived on and was to go round the world. Already in the twelfth century the commentator on the Prophecies of Merlin saw the process well advanced:

> What place is there within the bounds of the empire of Christendom to which the winged praise of Arthur the Briton has not extended? Who is there, I ask, who does not speak of Arthur the Briton, since he is scarcely less known to the peoples of Asia than to the Cornish and Welsh, as our pilgrims returning from the east inform us? The peoples of the east speak of him as do the peoples of the west, though separated by the breadth of the whole earth. Egypt speaks of him, and the Bosphorus is not silent. Rome, queen of cities, sings his deeds, and his wars are not unknown to her former rival Carthage. Antioch, Armenia and Palestine celebrate his feats.[18]

In that process Laȝamon, parish priest of Areley Kings, played an honourable if, as yet, not fully appreciated part.

NOTES

1. On the implications of the palaeographical evidence for the dating of the composition and the surviving texts see E. G. Stanley, 'The date of Laȝamon's Brut', *Notes and Queries*, 213 (1968), 85-8.

2. See E. G. Stanley, 'Laȝamon's antiquarian sentiments', *Medium Aevum*, 38 (1969), 23-37.

3. Of the various attempts to date the *Brut* more precisely on the basis of supposed allusions to historical events or persons, none has proved conclusive (see Stanley, *Notes and Queries*, 213 (1968), 85-8).

4. References are to the chapter numbers of the edition of the *Historia* by Neil Wright (Cambridge, 1984).

5. Throughout the Introduction, in referring to persons and places mentioned by Geoffrey of Monmouth, Wace and Laȝamon, we have used the forms of proper names adopted by Laȝamon within the Arthurian section of the *Brut*. Otherwise we have used the forms conventionally adopted in Arthurian scholarship. Where relevant, forms used by Geoffrey and Wace are given in the Commentary.

6. See Neil Wright, 'Geoffrey of Monmouth and Gildas', *Arthurian Literature*, 2 (1982), 1-40, and 'Geoffrey of Monmouth and Gildas revisited', *Arthurian Literature*, 4 (1985), 155-63.

7. On Geoffrey's historiography see R. H. Hanning, *The Vision of History in Early Britain* (New York, 1966), pp.121-72.

8. On the contemporary relevance of the *Historia* see S. Knight, *Arthurian Literature and Society* (London, 1983), pp.38-67.

9. William of Malmesbury, *Historia Regum Anglorum* as cited in *Arthurian Literature in the Middle Ages*, ed. R. S. Loomis (Oxford, 1959), p.55.

10. Quotations from and references to the *Roman de Brut* are to the edition by Ivor Arnold, *Le Roman de Brut de Wace*, 2 vols (Paris, 1938-40).

11. Wace's relationship to Geoffrey can only be judged in general terms since the *Historia* texts represent two versions whose relationship has not been determined. Wace appears to have drawn on both, but until the redactive process has been studied in detail, the distinctive character of his version cannot be precisely judged.

12. See P. J. Frankis, 'Laȝamon's English sources' in *J. J. R. Tolkien, Scholar and Storyteller*, eds M. Salu and R. T. Farrell (Ithaca, N.Y., 1979), pp.64-75.

13. J. S. P. Tatlock, *The Legendary History of Britain* (Berkeley, Calif., 1950), p.489.

14. For a detailed analysis see J. S. P. Tatlock, 'Epic formulas, especially in Laȝamon', *PMLA*, 38 (1923), 494-529.

15. Laȝamon deals quite competently with love when it is necessary to his dynastic theme, witness the Ygerne episode; it is abstract theory which he appears to find irrelevant.

16. On the characterisation of Arthur see R. Morris, *The Character of King Arthur in Medieval Literature* (Cambridge, 1982), *passim* and P. Korrel, *An Arthurian Triangle: A Study of the Origin, Development and Characterisation of Arthur,*

Guinevere and Modred (Leiden, 1984), pp.146-72.

17. *The Works of Sir Thomas Malory*, ed. E. Vinaver, Oxford Standard Authors, second edition (London, 1971), p.717.

18. *Prophetia Anglicana*, formerly attributed to Alain de Lille (Frankfurt, 1603), partly reprinted in E. K. Chambers, *Arthur of Britain* (London, 1927), p.265.

THE NARRATIVE CONTEXT

Laȝamon's *Brut*, following the outline of British history given by Robert Wace and before him by Geoffrey of Monmouth, describes how the island of Albion was settled by refugees from fallen Troy, led by Brutus, great-grandson of Aeneas, who gave his name to the new nation and built its capital, New Troy, upon the river Thames.

Among his successors as kings of Britain are Bladud, founder of Bath, Leir, Cymbeline and Belin who, with his brother Brenne, is said to have invaded Gaul, besieged Rome and sacked the city. Myth merges into history with the coming of Julius Caesar and the Roman conquest, an epoc which ends when they eventually abandon the island, leaving it prey to the attacks of Picts, Scots, Danes and Saxons.

A tribal leader, Vortigern, seizes the throne, displacing the royal line of Constantine, and enlists the help of a Saxon force under Hengest and Horsa against the other foreign invaders. They treacherously murder many of the British nobles and begin the Germanic conquest of the island. Vortigern takes refuge in Wales, where he seeks the aid of the marvellous boy Merlin who prophesies his imminent death. He is killed when Aurelius and Uther, princes of the royal line he had displaced, return from exile among the British refugees in Brittany.

Aurelius, crowned king, defeats Hengest and has him executed. But the internal struggle among the British continues: Vortigern's son, Pascent, has Aurelius poisoned and is himself killed by Uther. The new king buries his brother at Stonehenge, within the Giants' Ring, transferred with Merlin's help from Ireland to Salisbury Plain as a monument to the British nobles murdered by Hengest.

Meanwhile Hengest's kinsmen, Octa, Ebissa and Ossa, renew the Saxon assault. They besiege York which Uther fails to relieve until his loyal lieutenant, Gorlois, Earl of Cornwall, advises a night assault upon the besiegers' camp. The surprise attach succeeds, Octa, Ebissa and Ossa are captured and taken prisoner to London, while Uther restores peace in Scotland and the north.

And seoððen, vmbe stunde,   he ferde to Lunden;

he wes þere an Æstre   mid aðele his uolke;   9230

bliðe wes þe Lundenes tun   for Vthere Pendragun.

He sende his sonde   ȝeond al his kinelonde;

he bæd þa eorles,   he bæd þa cheorles,

he bæd þa biscopes,   þa boc-ilærede men

þat heo comen to Lunden   to Vðer þan kingen,   9235

into Lundenes tun   to Vðer Pendragun.

Riche men sone   to Lundene comen;

heo brohten wif, heo brohten child,   swa hehte Vther þe king.

Mid muchele godnæsse   þe king iherde mæsse,

and Gorlois, þe eorl of Cornwale,   and mid him cnihtes uale.   9240

Muche blisse wes i þan tun   mid Vðer kinge Pendragun.

    þa þe mæsse wes isungen,   to halle heo þrungen;

bemen heo bleowen,   bordes heo brædden;

al þat folc æt and dronc   and blisse heom wes imong.

þer sæt Vðer þe king   an his hæh setle;   9245

forn aȝan him Gorlois,   hende cniht ful iwis,

þe eorl of Cornwale,   mid aðele his wife.

þa heo weoren alle iseten,   eorles to heore mete,

þe king sende his sonde   to Igærne þere hende,

Gorlois eorles wif,   wifmone alre hendest.   9250

Ofte he hire lokede on   and leitede mid eȝene,

ofte he his birles sende   fron to hire borde,

ofte he hire loh to   and makede hire letes;

and heo hine leofliche biheold   —ah inæt whær he hine luuede!

Næs þe king noht swa wis   ne swa ȝære-witele   9255

þat imong his duȝeþe   his þoht cuðe dernen.

    Swa longe þe king þis him droh   þat Gorlois iwærð him wrað

and him gromede swiðe   wið þene king for his wife.

þe eorl and his cnihtes   arisen forðrihtes

and forð mid þan wife,   cnihtes swiðe whraðe.   9260

Vther king þis isah   and herefore særi wes,

and nom him forðrihtes   twælf wise cnihtes

and sende after Gorlois,   gumenene ældere,

and beden hine an hiȝinge   cumen to þan

and don þan kinge god riht   and beon icnowen of his pliht,   9265

þat he hafde þene king iscend   and from his borde wes iwende,

And then, after a time, he went to London; he was there at Easter with his noble retinue; London town was glad that Uther Pendragon had come. He sent his messengers through all his kingdom; he commanded the nobles, he commanded the commons, he commanded the bishops, the learned men to come to London to Uther the king, to Uther Pendragon in London town. Men of high rank came at once to London, bringing wife and child as King Uther had commanded. With great devotion the king heard mass, and Gorlois, the earl of Cornwall, and many warriors with him. Great was the joy in the town at King Uther Pendragon's presence. #

When the mass had been sung, they thronged into the hall; trumpets were sounded, tables were spread; the whole company ate and drank and there was joy among them. There sat King Uther in his seat of honour; directly opposite him Gorlois, the earl of Cornwall, a truly valiant warrior, sat with his gracious wife. When the nobles were all seated at their meal, the king sent his respects to the fair Ygerne, the wife of Earl Gorlois, the fairest of all women. He looked at her often, flashing glances from his eyes, often sent his cup-bearers to her table, smiled at her and eyed her often; and she looked kindly upon him — but whether she loved him I do not know! The king was not so prudent nor so quick-witted that he could conceal his feelings from his followers. #

The king behaved in this fashion so long that Gorlois became angry and was greatly enraged with the king on account of his wife. The earl and his followers suddenly rose and went out with the woman, the warriors greatly infuriated. King Uther saw this and was grieved at it, and immediately summoned twelve prudent knights and sent them after Gorlois, that leader of men, and commanded him to come quickly to the king, and submit to the king and acknowledge his fault, that he had insulted the king and

he and his cnihtes,   mid muchele vnrihte,
for þe king him wæs glad wið   and for he hailede in his wif;
and 3if he nalde a3ein cumen   and his gult beon icnawen,
þe king him wold after   and don al his mahten,   9270
binimen him al his lond   and his seoluer and his gold.

   Þis iherde Gorlois,   gumenene lauerd,
and he andsware 3af,   eorlene wraðest:
"Næi, swa me helpe Drihte   þa iscop þas da3es lihte,
nulle ich nauere a3æn cumen   no his grið 3irnen;   9275
ne scal he neuere on liue   me scende of mine wife.
And suggeð Vðer kinge   at Tintaieol he mai me finden;
3if he þider wule ride,   þer ich him wulle abiden,
and þer he scal habbe hærd gome   and mucle weorldes scome."

   Forð wende þe eorl,   ire on his mode;   9280
he wes wærð wið þene king   wunder ane swiðe,
and þretede Vther þene king   and alle his þeines mid him—
ah he nuste whæt com seoððe   sone þeræfter!
Þe eorl anan wende   into Cornwaille.

He hafde þer tweie castles,   biclused swiðe uaste;   9285
þæ castles aðele weore,   of his eoldrene istreon.
To Tintaieol he sende   his leofmon þa wes hende,
Ygerne ihaten,   wifene aðelest,
and heo biclusde uæste   inne þan castle.
Ygerne wes særi   and sorhful an heorte   9290
þat swa moni mon for hire   sculden habbe þer lure.

   Þe eorl sende sonde   3eond al Brutlonde,
and bæd alcne ohte gome   þat he him sculde to cume
for gold and for seolure   and for oðere 3iuen gode,
þat heo ful sone   to Tintaieole comen;   9295
and his a3ene cnihtes   comen forðrihtes.
Þa heo togædere weoren,   sele þeines,
þa hafde he fulle   fiftene þusend,
and heo Tintaieol   faste bitunden.
Uppen þere sæ-stronde   Tintaieol stondeð;   9300
he is mid sæ-cliuen   faste biclused
þat ne bið he biwunne   þurh nanes cunnes monnen,
bute 3if hunger   cumen þer anvnder.
Þe eorl uerde þenne   mid seouen þusend monnen
and wende to ane oðere castle   and biclusde hine ful uæste;   9305
and bilefde his wif in Tintaieol   mid ten þusend monnen—

departed from his table, he and his knights, most improperly, since the king was pleased with him and had drunk a toast to his wife; and if he would not return and achnowledge his guilt, the king would pursue him and do all within his power, would deprive him of all his land and his silver and his gold.

Gorlois, prince of warriors, heard this and, a nobleman most grievously angered, he replied:
'No, so help me God who created the light of day, I will never return nor beg his pardon; never while he lives shall he dishonour me with my wife. And tell King Uther he can find me at Tintagel; if he will ride there, I will await him there, and there he shall have rough treatment and great public disgrace.'

Away went the earl with anger in his heart; he was very greatly inflamed against King Uther, and uttered threats against King Uther and all his thanes as well — but he little knew what was to occur shortly thereafter! The earl immediately made his way to Cornwall. He had two castles there, very strongly defended, famous castles inherited from his ancestors. To Tintagel he sent his beloved, gentle wife, called Ygerne, the fairest of women, and shut her up securely in the castle. Ygerne was sorrowful and sad at heart that so many men for her sake should lose their lives there.

The earl sent messengers throughout all Britain, and invited every brave man to join him in return for gold and silver and other rich rewards, so that they very quickly came to Tintagel; and his own knights came immediately. When they had assembled, the noble thanes, he had fully fifteen thousand, and they fortified Tintagel strongly. Tintagel stands upon the seashore; it is closely surrounded by cliffs so that it is not to be captured by anyone whatsoever, unless hunger should enter there. The earl then set out with seven thousand men and went to another castle and fortified it very securely; and he left his wife in Tintagel with

for ne þurue þa cnihtes,   dæies na nihtes,
buten biwiten þat castelȝat   and careles liggen slæpen—
and þe eorl wuste þene oðer,   and mid him his aȝen broðer.

þis iherde Vther   —þe king wes swiðe steorc—
þat Gorlois, his eorl,   his ferde hafde igadered
and wolde halde weorre   mid muchelere wraððe.

þe king bad his ferde   ȝeond al þissen ærde
and ȝeond al þan londe   þa stoden an his honde,
monies kinnes leoden,   liðen heom togæderes
and comen to Lundene,   to þan leod-kinge.

Ut of Lundene tun   ferde Vðer Pendragun;
he and his cnihtes   ferde uorðrihtes
swa longe þat heo comen   into Cornwæille,
and ouer þat water heo tueoȝen   þat hatten Tambre is *
riht to þan castle   þer heo Gorlois wusten.

Mid muchelere læðe   þene castel heo bilæien,
ofte heo toræsden   mid ræȝere strengðe,
tosomne heo leopen;   leoden þer feollen.

Fulle seouen nihte   þe king mid his cnihten
bilæi þene castel;   his men þer hafeden sorȝen;
ne miste he of þan eorle   naþing iwinnen;
and alle þa seouen nihte   ilaste þat selliche feoht.

þa iseh Vðer king   þat him ne spedde naðing.
Ofte he hine biþohte   whæt he don mahte,
for Ygærne him wes swa leof,   æfne alse his aȝen lif,
and Gorlois him wes on leoden   monnen alre læðest;
and ælches weies him wes wa   a þissere weorlde-riche,
for he ne mihte beon wurðe   naþing of his wille.

þa wes mid þan kinge   an ald mon swuðe hende;
he wes a swiðe riche þein   and ræh on ælche dome;
he wes ihaten Vlfin   —muche wisdom wes mid him.
þe king bræid up his chin   and bisah an Vlfin;
swiðe he murnede;   his mod wes iderued.

þa quað Vðer Pendragun   to Ulfin þan cnihte:
"Ulfin, ræd me sumne ræd   oðer ich beo ful raðe dæde;
swa swiðe me longeð   þat ne mai i noht libben
after þere faire Ygærne.   þis word halt me derne,
for, Ulfin þe leoue,   aðele þine lare,
lude and stille,   don ich heom wulle."

þa andswarede Ulfin   þan kinge þet spac wið him:

9310

9315

9320

9325

9330

9335

9340

9345

-6-

ten thousand men — for the soldiers there had no concern, by day
or night, save to guard the castle gate and lie sleeping at their
ease — and the earl held the other castle, and his own brother
with him.

Uther learnt this — the king was quite implacable — learnt
that Gorlois, his earl, had gathered his forces and intended to
wage war with great ferocity. The king commanded his forces
throughout all this kingdom and throughout all the lands which
were in his possession, people of many nations, to assemble
together and come to London, to the high king. Uther Pendragon
set out from London town; he and his warriors marched directly
onwards until they came to Cornwall, and they advanced across
the river called Tamar straight to the castle where they knew
Gorlois was. With great ferocity they besieged the castle,
repeatedly attacked with violent force, charged in a body; men
perished there. Fully a week the king and his followers besieged
the castle; his men suffered there, yet he could gain no advantage
over the earl; and that great battle went on all week long.

Then King Uther saw that he had no success. He often
considered what he could do, so dear to him was Ygerne, as dear
as his own life, and Gorlois of all men in the land the most
hateful to him; and everything in this mortal world was a misery
to him because he could achieve none of his desires.

There was then with the king a most noble old man; he was a
thane of the highest rank and bold in all matters of judgement; he
was called Ulfin — there was great wisdom in him. The king,
greatly dejected, troubled at heart, lifted his head and looked at
Ulfin. Then Uther Pendragon said to the knight Ulfin:

'Ulfin, give me some advice or I shall very shortly be dead; so
great is my longing for the fair Ygerne that I cannot live. Speak
in all confidence, dear Ulfin, for I will follow your wise counsel,
whatever it may be.'

Then Ulfin answered the king who had spoken to him:

"Nu ihere ich muche seollic   ænne king suggen!
þu luuest Ygærne   and halst hit swa deorne;
þe wifmon is þe to leof   and hire lauerd al to lað;
his lond þu forbernest   and hine blæð wurchest,   9350
and þrattest hine to slænne   and his cun to fordonne!
Wenest þu mid swulche hærme   to biʒeten Ygærne,
þenne heo sculde don   swa ne deð na wifman,
mid æie vnimete   halden luue swete.
Ah ʒif þu luuest Ygærne,   þu sculdest hit halden derne,   9355
and senden hire sone   of seoluere and of golde,
and luuien hire mid liste   and mid leofliche bihæste.
þa ʒet hit weore a wene   whar þu heo mihtes aʒe;
for Ygærne is wel idon,   a swiðe treowe wimmon;
swa wes hire moder   and ma of þan kunne.   9360
    To soðe ich þe suggen,   leofest alre kinge,
þat oðere weies þu most aginnen   ʒif þu hire wult awinnen.
For ʒurstendæi me com to   an æremite wel idon
and swor bi his chinne   þat he wuste Merlin,
whar he ælche nihte   resteð vnder lufte;   9365
and ofte he him spæc wið   and spelles him talde.
And ʒif we mihte Merlin   mid liste biwinnen,
þenne mihtest þu þine iwille   allunge biwinne."
þa wes Vðer Pendragun   þa softer an his mode
and ʒaf andsware red: "Vlfin, þu hauest wel isæd.   9370
Ich þe ʒiue an honde   þritti solh of londe
þat þu Merlin biwinne   and don mine iwille."
    Vlfin ʒeond þat folc wende   and sohte al þa uerde,
and he vmbe stunde   þene æremite funde
and an hiʒinge   brohte hine to þan kinge;   9375
and þe king him sette an hond   seouen sulʒene lond
ʒif he mihte bringen   Merlin to þan kinge.
þe æremite gon wende   in þene west ænde,
to ane wilderne,   to ane wude muchele
þer he iwuned hafde   wel feole wintre,   9380
and Merlin swiðe ofte   þerinne sohte.
Sone þe armite com in   þa ifunde he Mærlin
vnder ane treo stonden   and sære him gon longen.
þene æremite he isæh cume   alse while wes his iwune;
he orn him toʒænes,   beiene heo uæineden þas;   9385
heo clupten, heo custen   and cuðliche speken.

- 8 -

'Now I have heard a king say a very strange thing! You love Ygerne and yet keep it so secret; the woman is so dear to you and her husband so very hateful; you ravage his land and make him destitute, and threaten to slay him and destroy his kith and kin! If you think to win Ygerne by such violence, then she will behave as no woman ever does, feeling in extreme fear the sweetness of love. But if you love Ygerne, you should keep it secret, and quickly send her gold and silver, and woo her with cunning and with fair promises. Even so it would be doubtful whether you could possess her; for Ygerne is a good and very faithful woman, as her mother was and others of that family.

I tell you truly, best of kings, that you must try other means if you wish to win her. For yesterday a worthy hermit came to me and swore on his oath that he knew Merlin, knew where he lies each night under the heavens; and Merlin often spoke with him and told him wondrous things. And if by guile we could win over Merlin, then you might gain your object to the uttermost.'

Then Uther Pendragon was easier in his mind and made prompt reply:

'Ulfin, you have spoken well. I will give into your possession thirty ploughlands of land if you do my will and win over Merlin.' # #

Ulfin went through the army and searched the whole host, and after a time he found the hermit and quickly brought him to the king; and the king pledged to him seven ploughlands of land if he could bring Merlin to the king. The hermit journeyed into the land to the west, to a vast forest, a wilderness where he had lived full many a year, and in which he had often encountered Merlin. No sooner had the hermit come there than he found Merlin standing under a tree in eager expectation. When he saw the hermit coming as he had been wont to do, he ran towards him, both of them glad at that meeting; they embraced, they kissed and spoke like old friends.

þa sæide Merlin —muchel wisdom wes mid him:
"Sæie þu, mi leofe freond, wi naldest þu me suggen,
þurh nanes cunnes þinge, þat þu wældest to þan kinge?
Ah ful ȝare ich hit wuste, anan swa ich þe miste, 9390
þat þu icumen weore to Vðere kinge,
and what þe king þe wið spæc and of his londe þe bæd
þat þu me sculdest bringe to Vðer kinge.
And Vlfin þe sohte and to þan kinge brohte,
and Vðer Pendragun forðrihtes anan 9395
sette him an honde þritti solh of londe,
and he sætte þe an honde seoue sulhȝene lond.
Vther is oflonged æfter Ygærne þere hende,
wunder ane swiðe after Gorloises wiue.
Ah longe is æuere, þat ne cumeð nauere, 9400
þat he heo biwinne bute þurh mine ginne;
for nis na wimmon treowere in þissere worlde-riche.
    And neoðeles he scal aȝe þa hende Ygærne;
on hir he scal streonen þat scal wide sturien;
he scal streonien hire on ænne swiðe sellichne mon. 9405
Longe beoð æuere, dæd ne bið he næuere;
þe wile þe þis world stænt, ilæsten scal is worðmunt;
and scal inne Rome walden þa þæines.
Al him scal abuȝe þat wuneð inne Bruttene.
Of him scullen gleomen godliche singen; 9410
of his breosten scullen æten aðele scopes;
scullen of his blode beornes beon drunke.
Of his eȝene scullen fleon furene gleden;
ælc finger an his hond scarp stelene brond.
Scullen stan walles biuoren him tofallen; 9415
beornes scullen rusien, reosen heore mærken.
þus he scal wel longe liðen ȝeond londen,
leoden biwinnen and his laȝen sette.
    þis beoð þa tacnen of þan sune þe cumeð of Uðere Pendragune
and of Ygærne —þes speche is ful derne, 9420
for ȝet næt hit neoðer Ygærne no Uðer,
þat of Vðere Pendragune scal arisen swilc a sune,
for ȝet he beoð unstreoned þa sturieð al þa þeoden.
Ah, lauerd," quað Merlin, "nu hit is iwille þin
þat forð I scal fusen to uerde þas kinges, 9425
þi word ich wulle heren; and nu ich wulle wende

Then said Merlin — there was much wisdom in him:

'Tell me, my dear friend, why, for what reason, were you not willing to tell me that you were going to the king? Yet I knew it at once, as soon as I missed you, that you had gone to King Uther; and I knew what the king said to you and that he offered you land of his so that you should bring me to King Uther. And Ulfin sought for you and brought you to the king, and Uther Pendragon there and then immediately pledged to him thirty ploughlands of land, and he pledged to you seven ploughlands of land. Uther is filled with longing for the lovely Ygerne, greatly besotted with the wife of Gorlois. But it will never happen, as long as time shall last, that he shall win her save by my magic skill; for there is no truer woman in this mortal world.

And yet he shall have the fair Ygerne nonetheless; on her he shall beget one who shall rule far and wide; he shall beget on her a most wonderful man. As long as time lasts, he shall never die; while this world lasts, his fame shall endure; and he shall rule the princes in Rome. All who dwell in Britain shall obey him. Of him shall minstrels splendidly sing; of his breast noble bards shall eat; heroes shall be drunk upon his blood. From his eyes shall fly sparks of fire; each finger on his hand shall be a sharp steel blade. Stone walls shall fall down before him; men shall tremble, their banners fall. So for a long, long time he shall go about the world conquering nations and establishing his laws. #

These shall be the signs of the son who is to come from Uther Pendragon and from Ygerne — this prophecy is most secret, for as yet neither Ygerne nor Uther knows it, that such a son shall spring from Uther Pendragon, since he is not yet begotten who is to rule all the nations. But, my lord,' said Merlin, 'since it is your wish that I should hasten to the army of the king, I will do your bidding; and I will set out now and, for love of you, will go to Uther Pendragon; and you shall have the land which he pledged to you.'

and faren ich wulle for þire lufe   to Vthere Pendragune;
and habben þu scalt þat lond   þat he þe sette an hond."
Þus heo þa ispecken,   þæ æremite gon to weopen;
deorliche he hine custe,   þer heo gunnen dælen.   9430
    Merlin ferde riht suð   —þat lond him wæs ful cuð;
forðriht he fusde   to þes kinges ferde.
Sone swa Vðer hine isæh,   swa he him toȝeines bæh;
and þus quað Vðer Pendragune: "Mærlin, þu ært wilcume;
her ich sette þe an honde   al þene ræd of mine londe   9435
and þat þu me ræde   to muchere neode."
Vther him talde   al þat he walde,
and hu Ygærne him wes on leoden   wimmonnen leofest
and Gorlois hire lauerd   monnenen alre laðest;
"and buten ich habbe þinne ræd   ful raðe þu isihst me dæad."   9440
    Þa andswerede Merlin: "Let nu cume in Vlfin
and bitæc him an honde   þritti sulȝene lond,
and bitæc þan æremite   þat þu him bihete;
for nulle ich aȝæn na lond,   neouðer seoluer na gold,
for ich am on rade   rihchest alre monnen,   9445
and ȝif ich wilne æhte   þenne wursede ich on crafte.
Ah al þin iwille   wel scal iwurðen;
for ich con swulcne lechecraft   þe leof þe scal iwurðen,
þat al scullen þine cheres   iwurðen swulc þas eorles,
þi speche, þi dede   imong þere duȝeðe,   9450
þine hors and þine iwede,   and al swa þu scalt ride.
    Þenne Ygærne þe scal iseon,   a mode hire scal wel beon—
heo lið inne Tintaieol   uaste bituned;
nis nan cniht swa wel iboren,   of nane londe icoren,
þe mid strengðe of Tintaieol   þe ȝeten mihten untunen,   9455
buten he weoren ibirsted   mid hungere and mid þurste;
þat is þat soðe   þat ich þe sugge wulle.
Þurh alle þinge þu scalt beon   swulc þu eorl weore,
and ich wulle beon iwil del   swulc him is Brutael
þat is a cniht swiðe herd;   he is þeos eorles stiward.   9460
Iurdan is his bur-cniht;   he is swiðe wel idiht.
Ich wulle makien anan   Ulfin swulc is Iurdan;
þenne bist þu lauerd   and ich Brutael þi stiward,
and Ulfin, Iurdan þi bur-cniht,   and we scullen faren nu, toniht;
faren þu scalt bi ræde,   wuderswa ich þe læde.   9465
Scullen nu, tonihte,   half hundred cnihten,

When they had spoken thus, the hermit began to weep; as they parted, he kissed him lovingly.

Merlin journeyed due south; the region was well known to him and he hastened straight to the king's army. As soon as Uther saw him, he went to meet him; and thus spoke Uther Pendragon:

'Merlin, you are welcome; I here and now entrust to you the entire direction of my kingdom so that you shall advise me in my great necessity.'

Uther told him all that he desired, and that Ygerne was to him the dearest woman in the world and her husband Gorlois the most hateful of all men; 'and unless I have your counsel you will very shortly see me dead'.

Then Merlin replied:

'Now let Ulfin come in and deliver to him thirty ploughlands, and give the hermit what you promised him; for I will have no land, nor gold or silver, for I am the richest of all men in wisdom, and were I to covet possessions then I would diminish in skill. But all your desires shall be fully accomplished; for I know such magic arts as will be of value to you, such that your whole appearance shall become like the earl's, your speech, your bearing among the courtiers, your horse and your clothes, and you shall ride just like him.

When Ygerne shall see you, she will be happy at heart — she lies closely besieged in Tintagel; there is no man anywhere so noble, so excellent, who could open the gates of Tintagel by force, unless they were burst open by hunger and thirst; that is the truth which I wish to tell you. In all respects you shall be as if you were the earl, and I will be in every way just as is Bretel who is a very bold knight; he is the earl's steward. Jurdan is his chamberlain; he is very well trained. I will presently make Ulfin just like Jurdan is; then you will be the earl and I your steward Bretel, and Ulfin your chamberlain Jurdan, and we shall set out now, tonight; wheresoever I lead you, you shall proceed according to my advice. Now, tonight, half a hundred warriors, with spears

mid speren and mid scelden,   beon abuten þine telden,
þat nauere nan quik mon   ne cumen þer aneosten,
and ӡif þer aueræi mon cume   þat his hæued him beon binumen;
for þa cnihtes scullen suggen,   selen þine beornen,   9470
þat þu ært ilete blod   and restest þe on bædde."
      þas þinges forðrihte   þus weoren idihte.
Forð ferde þe king   —næs hit cuð naþing—
and ferden forð mid him   Vlfin and Merlin;
he tuӡen riht þen wæi   þa into Tintaieol læi.   9475
Heo comen to þas castles ӡæte   and cuðliche cleopeden:
"Vndo þis ӡæt-essel;   þe eorl is icumen here,
Gorlois þe læuerd,   and Britael his stiward,
and Iurdan þe bur-cniht;   we habbeoð ifaren al niht."
þe ӡæte-ward hit cudde oueral   and cnihtes urnen uppen wal,   9480
and speken wið Gorlois   and hine icneowen mid iwis.
þa cnihtes weoren swiðe whæte   and wefden up þa castles ӡæte
and letten hine binnen fare   —þa læsse wes þa heore care;
heo wenden mid iwisse   to habben muchel blisse.
þa hædden heo mid ginne   Merlin þer wiðinne,   9485
and Vðer þene king   wiðinne heore walding; *
and ledde þer mid him   his gode þein Ulfin.
      þis tidinde com biliue   in to þan wife
þæt hire læuerd wes icumen   and mid him his þreo gumen. *
Vt com Ygærne,   forð to þan eorle,   9490
and þas word seide   mid wunsume wurde:
"Wilcume, læuerd,   monne me leofest;
and wilcume Iurdan   and Britael is alswa.
Beo ӡe mid isunde   todæled from þan kinge?"
þa quæð Vðer ful iwis   swulc hit weore Gorlois: 9495
"Muchel þat monkun   þæt is mid Vther Pendragun;
and ich æm bi nihte   bistole from þan fihte
for æfter þe ic wes oflonged;   wifmonne þu ært me leofuest.
Buð into bure   and let mi bed makien,
and ich me wulle ræsten   to þissere nihte uirste   9500
and alle dai tomærwe   to blissien mire duӡeðe."
      Ygærne beh to bure   and lætte bed him makien;
wes þat kinewurðe bed   al mid palle ouerbræd.
þe king hit wel bihedde   and eode to his bedde;
and Ygærne læi adun   bi Uðere Pendragun.   9505
Nu wende Ygerne ful iwis   þat hit weoren Gorlois;

– 14 –

and shields, shall surround your tents, so that no man alive may approach the place, and if any man come there that he be deprived of his head; for the knights, your noble warriors, shall say that you have been let blood and are resting yourself in bed.'

These things were immediately arranged in this way. The king set out — nothing was known of it — and Ulfin and Merlin set out with him; they took the way which led directly to Tintagel. They came to the gate of the castle and called out in a familiar manner:

'Undo the bar of this gate; the earl is come here, the lord Gorlois, and his steward Bretel, and Jurdan the chamberlain; we have travelled all night.'

The gatekeeper spread the news widely and soldiers ran up onto the wall, and spoke with Gorlois and recognised him clearly. The soldiers were very quick and opened the castle gate and let him come in — they had little concern at that moment, confidently expecting great pleasure to come. Then, by a trick, they had Merlin there within, and Uther the king within their power; and he had brought there with him his good thane Ulfin.

The news quickly reached the woman that her husband had come and his three men with him. Ygerne came out, came towards the earl, and spoke these words of pleasant greeting:

'Welcome, my lord, my dearest one; and Jurdan and Bretel are welcome too. Did you escape from the king without harm?'

Then Uther said, exactly as if it were Gorlois speaking:

'There is a great host with Uther Pendragon; and I have stolen away from the battle by night because I was filled with longing for you, you who are to me the dearest of women. Go into the bedroom and have my bed made, and I will rest myself this whole night through and all day tomorrow for my soldiers' pleasure.'

Ygerne went to the bedroom and had his bed made; the bed, fit for a king, was all spread with rich coverings. The king looked at it with pleasure and went to his bed; and Ygerne lay down beside Uther Pendragon. Now Ygerne truly believed that it was

þurh neuere nænes cunnes þing   no icneou heo Vðer þene king.
þe king hire wende to   swa wapmon sculde to wimmon do,
and hæfde him to done   wið leofuest wimmonne,
and he streonede hire on   ænne selcuðne mon,   9510
kingen alre kenest   þæ æuere com to monnen;
and he wes on ærde   Ærður ihaten.
Nuste noht Ygerne   wha læie on hire ærme,
for æuere heo wende ful iwis   þat it weoren þe eorl Gorlois.

    Næs þer na mære uirst   buten þat hit wes dæiliht;   9515
þer forðrihtes   vnderзeten þa cnihtes
þat þe king wes iuaren   ut of þere uærde.
Þa sæiden þa cnihtes   —soð þæh hit neoren—
þat þe king wes ифloзen,   mid ærhþen afeolled;
ah al hit wes lessinge   þat heo seiden bi þan kinge;   9520
herof heo heolden muchel run   uppen Vðer Pendragun.

    Þa seiden þa eorles   and þa hæhste beornes:
"Nu þenne hit wat Gorlois,   hu hit iuaren is
þat ure king is ifaren   and his ferde bilæiued,
he wule forðrihtes   wepni his cnihtes   9525
and ut he wule to fihten   and feollen us to grunden,
mid woden his þeines   muchel wæl makien;
þenne weore us beteren   þat we iboren neoren.
Ah leten we blawen bemen   and bonnien ure uerde,
and Cador þe kene   scal beren þas kinges marke,   9530
hæbben haзe þene drake   biforen þissere duзeðe
and faren to þan castle   mid kene ure folke.
And þe eorl Aldolf   scal beon ure aldre,
and we him scullen here   swulc hit þe king weoren;
and swa we scullen mid rihte   wið Gorlois fihten.   9535
And зif he us wule speken wið   and зernen þis kinges grið,
setten sæhtnusse   mid æðen soðfæste,
þenne maзen we mid wurðscipen   heonene iwenden,
þenne nabbeoð ure æfterlinges   nane upbreidinges
þat we for ærhscipe   heonene atærnden."   9540
    Al þat leodliche folc   bilufde þesne ilke ræd;
bemen heo bleowen,   bonneden uærden,
up heo hafden þene drake,   ælches mærken vnimake.
Þer wes moni bald scalc   þe sceld weiden on sculdre,
moni þein kene,   and wenden to þan castle.   9545
Gorlois wes wiðinnen   mid kene his monnen;

– 16 –

Gorlois; in no way whatsoever did she recognise Uther the king. The king went unto her as a man should to a woman, and had his way with the woman most dear to him, and he begot on her a marvellous man, the boldest king who ever was born; and in this land he was called Arthur. Ygerne knew not who lay in her arms, for all the time she fully believed that it was the earl Gorlois.

All too soon it was daylight; then, all at once, the troops became aware that the king had gone from the army. Then the soldiers said — though it was not true — that the king had fled, stricken with cowardice; but what they said of the king, making much of it, muttering against Uther Pendragon, was all lies.

Then the earls and the men of highest rank said:
'Now when Gorlois knows this, knows how it has come to pass that our king has gone away and deserted his army, he will immediately arm his followers and come out to fight and will strike us down, make great slaughter with his furious thanes; then it would be better for us that we had never been born. But let us command trumpets to be blown and assemble our army, and the brave Cador shall bear the king's standard, raise high the dragon banner before this noble band and advance to the castle with our valiant army. And the earl Aldolf shall be our leader, and we shall obey him as if he were the king; and so in good order we shall fight against Gorlois. And if he will parley with us and beg for the king's peace, seal a truce with trustworthy oaths, then we can withdraw from here with honour, for then our followers will have no need to reproach us that we ran away from here out of cowardice.' # #

The whole army of the nation approved this plan; they sounded trumpets, assembled forces, they raised the dragon, best of banners. There was many a valiant man, many a brave thane who slung his shield on his shoulder and advanced upon the castle. Inside was Gorlois with his bold followers; he caused trumpets

he lette blawen beomen,   and bonnien his ferden;
leopen an steden,   cnihtes gunnen riden—
þæs cnihtes weoren swiðe wate—   and wenden ut at þan ȝate.
Tosomne heo comen sone;   fastliche heo onsloȝen;   9550
feolle fæie men,   uolden isohten.
Þer wes muche blod-gute,   balu wes on folke;
imong þan fihte ful iwis   mon sloh þene eorl Gorlois.
Þa gunnen his men fleon,   and þa oðere after teon;
heo comen to þan castle   and binnen heo þrasten.   9555
Sone hit comen binnen,   ba twa þa uerden,
þer ileste þat fiht   þurh þene dæiliht.
Ær þe dai weore al asceken,   wes þe castel biȝeten;
næs þer nan swa wracche swein   þat he nes a wel god þein.
    Comen þa tidinde   into Tintageol an hiȝende,   9560
forð into þan castle   þer Vðer wes inne,
þat islaȝen wes ful iwis   þe eorl heore læuerd Gorlois,
and alle his here-gumen,   and his castel inumen.
Þis iherde þe king   þer he læi an skenting, *
and leop ut of bure   swulc hit an liun weore.   9565
Þa quað þe king Vðer   —of þissen tiðende he wes wær:
"Beoð stille, beoð stille,   cnihtes inne halle!
Here ich æm ful iwis,   eore læuerd Gorlois,
and Iurdan mi bur-ward   and Brutael mi stiward.
Ich and þas tweie cnihtes   leopen ut of þan fihte   9570
and hider in we beoð idraȝen;   neore we noht þere islaȝen.
Ah nu ich wulle fusen   and sumnien mine ferde,
and ich and mine cnihtes   scullen al bi nihte
faren in ænne tun   and imeten Vðer Pendragun;
and buten he of sæhnesse speken,   ich wulle me wurðliche awrake.
And ȝe þesne castel   bicluseð swiðe uaste,   9576
and hateð me Ygerne   þat heo noht ne murne.
Nu ich fare forðriht;   habbeoð alle gode niht."
Biforen ferde Merlin   and þe þein Vlfin,
and seoððen Uðer Pendragun,   ut of Tintageolestun;   9580
æuere heo uerden alle niht   þat hit wes dæiliht.
    Þa com he to þan ærde   þer læi his ferde,
Merlin hafde a þene king   his wlite iset þurh alle þing;
þa icneowen cnihtes   heore kinelauerd;
þer wes moni oht Brut   mid blissen afeolled.   9585
Þa weoren inne Bruttene   blissen inoȝe:

to be blown, and his forces to assemble; warriors leapt upon horseback — those knights were very valiant — and went riding out at the gate. The two sides immediately engaged, battling fiercely; doomed men fell, sank to the ground. There was great bloodshed, misfortune came upon the army; for indeed in the thick of battle the earl Gorlois was slain. Then his men took to flight, and the others pursued them, came to the castle and forced their way in. When the two armies were both inside, the fighting continued there throughout the hours of daylight. Before the day had quite ended, the castle was taken; there was no camp-follower so menial that he was not a right good warrior.

The news quickly came to Tintagel, right to the castle where Uther was, that their lord, the earl Gorlois, was most certainly slain, and all his warriors, and his castle taken. The king learnt this where he lay at dalliance, and rushed out of the bedroom as if he were a lion. Then King Uther, alerted by these tidings, said:

'Be quiet, be quiet, knights in the hall! Here am I, your lord Gorlois in person, with Jurdan my chamberlain and Bretel my steward. I and these two knights slipped away from the army and have made our way here; we were not slain there. But now I will make haste to gather my forces, and I and my warriors shall journey through the night to the town and confront Uther Pendragon; and unless he speaks of reconciliation, I will avenge myself fittingly. And you defend this castle very closely and bid Ygerne from me that she have no concern. I am leaving now, at once; goodnight to you all.'

Merlin and the thane Ulfin went first, and after them went Uther Pendragon, out of the town of Tintagel; they travelled continually all night long till it was daylight.

Then the king came to the place where his army lay. Merlin had restored his appearance to him in all respects, and so the knights recognised their lord and king; many a valiant Briton there was filled with joy. In Britain then was much rejoicing: horns

hornes þer bleowen,   gleomen gunnen gleowen;
glad æuerælch cniht,   al mid pælle biþæht.
Þreo dæies wes þe king   wuniende þere,
and þan feorðe dæie   to Tintaieol he wende.   9590
He sende to þan castle   his selest þeines
and grætte Ygærne,   wifuene aðelest,
and sende hire taken   whæt heo i bedde speken,
hehte heo þat heo aȝeuen   þene castel biliue—
þer nes nan oðer ræd,   for hire lauerd wes dæd.   9595
Ȝet wende Ygærne   þat hit soð weoren
þat þe dæde eorl   isoht hafede his duȝeðe,
and al heo ilæfde   þat hit læs weore
þat þe king Vðer   æuere weoren icumen her.
Cnihtes eoden to ræde,   cnihtes eoden to rune,   9600
radden þat heo nalden   þene castel lengere halden;
heore brugge heo duden adun   and bitahte hine Vðer Pendragun.
þa stod al þis kinelond   æft an Vtheres hond.
    Þer Vðer þe king   nom Ygærne to quene;
Ygærne wes mid childe   bi Vðer kinge,   9605
al þurh Merlines wiȝel,   ær heo biwedded weore.
Þe time com þe wes icoren;   þa wes Arður iboren.
Sone swa he com an eorðe,   aluen hine iuengen;
heo bigolen þat child   mid galdere swiðe stronge:
heo ȝeuen him mihte   to beon bezst alre cnihten;   9610
heo ȝeuen him anoðer þing,   þat he scolde beon riche king;
heo ȝiuen him þat þridde,   þat he scolde longe libben;
heo ȝifen him, þat kinebern,   custen swiðe gode
þat he wes mete-custi   of alle quike monnen;
þis þe alue him ȝef,   and al swa þat child iþæh.   9615
Æfter Arður, wes iboren   þeo ædie burde;
heo wes ihaten Æne,   þat ædien maiden,
and seoððen heo nom Loð   þe Leones ahte;
heo wæs inne Loeneis   leodene læfdi.
    Longe liuede Vðer   mid muchelere blisse her,   9620
mid gode griðe, mid gode friðe,   freo on kinedome.
Þa þe he wes ald mon,   þa com him ufel on.
þat vfel hine læide adun,   seoc wes Vðer Pendragun;
swa he wes here   seoc seoue ȝere.
þa iwurðen Bruttes   swiðe ibalded; *   9625
heo duden ofte unwræste   al for æieleste.

were sounded there, minstrels made music; glad was each and every knight, clad all in fine clothes. Three days the king dwelt there, and on the fourth day he went to Tintagel. He sent his best thanes to the castle to greet Ygerne, the noblest of women, and sent her as a sign something she had said in bed, commanding her to yield up the castle instantly — there was no other recourse, for her lord was dead. Ygerne still believed the truth was that the dead earl had gone to join his troops, and she firmly believed it was not true that King Uther had ever come to her. Knights took counsel, knights held debate, decided that they would not defend the fortress any longer; they lowered their drawbridge and surrendered the castle to Uther Pendragon. Then this whole kingdom was once again in Uther's possession.

There and then Uther the king took Ygerne as queen; Ygerne was with child by King Uther before she was married, all through the magic of Merlin. The time predestined came; then Arthur was born. As soon as he came upon earth, fairies took charge of him; they enchanted the child with magic most potent: they gave him strength to be the best of all knights; they gave him another gift, that he should be a mighty king; they gave him a third, that he should live long; they gave him, that royal child, such good qualities that he was the most liberal of all living men; these gifts the fairies gave him, and the child thrived accordingly. After Arthur, the blessed lady was born; she was called Anna, that worthy maiden, and later she married Lot who ruled Lothian; she was queen of the people of Lothian.

Uther lived long here in great content, in good peace and quiet, at ease in his kingdom. When he was an old man, then misfortune came upon him. That misfortune laid him low; Uther Pendragon was ill, and here continued sick for seven years. Then the Britons were greatly emboldened; they often behaved wickedly merely out of contempt for his authority.

þe ȝet læi ibunden   in þe quarterne of Lunden
Octa, Hengestes sune,   þa at Eouerwic wes inume,
and his iueren Ebissa   and his oðer, Ossa.
Heom biuusten twælf cnihtes   dæies and nihtes,   9630
þa weoren weri oflæien   inne Lundenne.
Octa iherde suggen   of seocnesse þas kinges,
and spac wið þa wardes-men   þe hine witen scolden:
"Hærcneð me nu, cnihtes,   þat ich eou wulle cuðen.
We liggeð here i Lundene,   uaste ibunden,   9635
and ȝe monienne longne dæi   ouer us ilæien habbeoð.
Bettere us weoren to libben   inne Sexlonde
mid muchele richedome   þene þus reouliche here.
And ȝif ȝe wolden iwurðen   and don mine iwille,
ich eou wolden ȝiuen lond,   muchel seoluer and gold,   9640
þat a ȝe mihten riche   rixlien in þan londe,
and eoure lif libben   swa eou bið alre leofuest.
For no biden ȝe nauere ȝiuen gode   of Vðer kinge,
for nu ful raðe he bið dæd   and his duȝeðen al bilæueð;
þenne nabben ȝe nouðer   þat an no þat oðer.   9645
Ah biðenche eou, ohte men,   and doð us eoure mildze on,
and þencheð whæt eou weoren leof   ȝif ȝe þus ibunden leien,
and mihten in eouwer londe   libben inne winne."
Swiðe ofte Octa   wið þæs cnihtes spac swa.
Cnihtes gunnen runen,   cnihtes gunnen ræden;   9650
to Octa heo seiden ful stille: "We scullen don þine iwille."
Aðes heo sworen   swiken þat heo nalden.
Hit wæs in ane nihte   þat þe wind wende rihte;
forð iwenden cnihtes   to þere midnihte
and ledden uorð Octa,   and Ebissa, and Ossa;   9655
after þere Temese   tuhten forð into þere sæ;
forð heo iwenden   into Sæxlonden.
Heore cun heom com aȝeines   mid mucle flockes.
Heo liðen ȝeond þan leoden   swa heom wes alre leofuest;
me heom bitahte lond,   me ȝæf heom seoluer and gold.   9660
Octa hine biðohte   whæt he don mahte;
he þohten hider wenden   and wræken his fader wunden.
Ferden heo biȝæten   of folke vnimete;
to þere sa heo wenden   mid muchele þrætte;
to Scotlonde heo comen.   9665
Sone heo fusden alond   and mid fure hit igrætten.

There still lay imprisoned in the tower of London Octa, Hengest's son, who had been captured at York, and his two comrades, Ebissa and Ossa. Twelve soldiers guarded them night and day, who were weary with keeping watch in London. Octa heard tell of the king's illness, and spoke to the guards who had the keeping of him:

'Now listen to me, soldiers, listen to what I have to say to you. We lie here in London, closely imprisoned, and you have kept guard over us many a long day. It would be better for us to be living in Saxony with full royal power than so miserably here. And if you would agree to do as I wish, I would give you land and much gold and silver that you might ever after, as men of wealth, have power in the land, and live your lives as best pleases you. #

For you need not expect good gifts from King Uther, for very shortly now he will be dead and his followers utterly abandoned; then you will have neither the one reward nor the other. But take thought, brave men, and have compassion on us, and consider what you would long for if you lay bound like this, when you might be living in contentment in your own land.'

Many times Octa spoke with those soldiers in this way. The soldiers began to whisper, to consult together; very quietly they said to Octa:

'We will do what you wish.'

They swore oaths that they would not betray him.

It was on a night when the wind was favourable; towards midnight the soldiers set out and led forth Octa, and Ebissa, and Ossa; down the Thames they went, out onto the sea, and away they went to Saxony. Their kinsmen flocked to meet them in great numbers. They journeyed throughout the country as pleased them best; they were given land, they were given gold and silver.

Octa considered what he could do; he planned to return here and avenge his father's injuries. They assembled forces, countless men; they put to sea with a great power and came to Scotland. Immediately they rushed ashore and set the land ablaze. The

Sæxes weoren ræie;   Scottes heo sloʒen,
mid fure heo adun læiden   þritti hundred tunes,
Scottes heo sloʒen   moni and unifoʒen.

    Comen þa tidende   to Vðer kinge.   9670
Vðer wes swiðe wa   and wunderliche ihærmed,
and senden into Loæines   to leofen his freonden,
and grette Lot his aðum   and hehte hine beon an sund,
and hahte hine nimen an his hond   al his kinewurðe lond,
cnihtes and freomen,   and freoliche heom halden,   9675
and leden heom to ferde   swa laʒen beoð an ærde.
And he hæhte his cnihtes leoue   beon hærsume Loðe
mid leofliche læten   swulc he weoren leodene king.
For Lot wes swiðe god cniht   and hafde ihalden moni fiht,
and he wes mete-custi   æueralche monne,   9680
he bitahten him þa warde   of alle þissen ærde.

    Octa heold muche vnfrið   and Lot faht him ofte wið,
and ofte he ahte biʒæt   and ofte he heom losede.
Bruttes hafden muchel mode   and vnimete prute,
and weoren æielese   for þas kinges alde;   9685
and lætten swiðe hokerliche   of Lote þan eorle
and duden swiðe vnwraste   alle his haste,
and weoren alle twi-ræde   —heore teone wes þa mare!
þis wes isæid sone   seocken þan kinge
þat his hæʒe men   Lot al forhoʒeden.   9690

    Nu ich þe wulle tellen   a þissen boc-spællen
hv Vðer þe king   uundede hine seoluen.
He sæide þat he wolde   wende to his ferde
and mid his eʒene iseon   wæ þer wolde wel don.
He lette makien þere   gode horse-bere   9695
and letten beoden uerde   ʒeond al his kineærde,
þat ælc mon bi his liue   comen to him swiðe,
bi heore liue and bi heore leme,   to wræken þas kinges scome;
"and ʒif þær is æi gume   þæt nulle hiʒenliche cume,
ich wulle hine hiʒenliche fordon,   oðer slæn oðer anhon."   9700
Alle ful sone   to hirede heo comen;
no durste þær bilæuen,   na þæ uatte no þe læne.

    þe king forðrihtes   nom alle his cnihtes
and ferde him anan   to þan tune of Verolam.
Abuten Uerolames tun   com him Vðer Pendragun;   9705
Octa wes wiðinnen   mid alle his monnen.

Saxons were ruthless; they slew the Scots, they burned down three thousand towns, they slaughtered Scots beyond number.

News of this came to King Uther. Uther was much grieved and sorely afflicted, and sent to Lothian, to his good friends there, and greeted his son-in-law Lot, wishing him good health, and commanded him to take charge of his whole kingdom, knights and freemen, and rule them justly, and lead them in battle as is the custom of the country. And he ordered his good knights to show obedience to Lot with due respect as if he were king of the realm. Since Lot was a very good warrior and had taken part in many a battle, and was generous to each and every man, he entrusted to him the keeping of this whole land.

Octa kept up great hostility and Lot fought repeatedly against him, and often he gained territory and often lost it. The British had great spirit and excessive pride and, because of the king's old age, were not the least in awe of him; and they thought very meanly of the earl Lot and carried out all his commands very half-heartedly, and were all at variance — so much the worse for them! It was soon made known to the sick king that his nobles wholly despised Lot.

Now in this history I will tell you how Uther the king conducted himself. He said he would go to his army and see with his own eyes who was doing his duty there. There and then he had a good horse-litter made and had an army summoned from all over his kingdom, commanding that every man upon pain of death, of losing life and limb, come to him quickly to avenge the king's humiliation; 'and if there is any man who will not quickly come, I will swiftly put an end to him, either slay him or hang him'. Very soon they came to court; neither the fat nor the lean dared stay away.

The king immediately gathered all his followers and went at once to the town of Verolam. Uther Pendragon surrounded the town of Verolam; Octa was therein with all his men. Verolam

- 25 -

þa wes Verolam   a swiðe kinewurðe hom—
Seint Alban wes þer islæӡen   and idon of lif-dæӡen;
þe burh wes seoððe foruaren   and muchel folc þer wes islæӡen.
Vðer lai wiðuten   and Octa wiðinnen.   9710
Vðeres ferde   fusde to wale,
ræsden to feondliche   þeines riche;
ne mihte heo of þan walle   ænne stan falle,
no mid nare strengðe   þene wal amærre.

      Wælle bliðe wes þæ   Hangestes sune Octa   9715
þa he isæh Bruttes   buӡen from walle
and sorhful wenden   aӡæin to heore telden.
þa sæide Octa   to his iueren Ebissa:
"Her is icumen to Verolam   Vðer þe lome mon
and wulle wið us here   fihten in his bære;   9720
he wænde mid his crucche   us adun þrucche!
Ah tomærӡe, wæne hit dæi buð,   duӡeðe scal arisen
and oppenien ure castel-ӡæten;   þas riche we scullen al biӡeten;
ne scullen we nauære here liggen   for ane lome monne!
Ut we scullen riden   uppen ure steden goden,   9725
and to Uðere fusen   and his folc fællen,
for alle heo beoð fæie   þat hider beoð iridenen;
and nimen þene lome mon   and leggen in ure benden,
and halden þene wræcche   a þat he forwurðe.
And sa me scal lacnien   his leomes þat beoð sare   9730
and his ban rihten   mid bitele stelen!" *
þus him ispac Octa   wið his iuere Ebissa—
ah al hit iwrað oðer   þene heo iwenden!

      Amarӡe þa hit daӡede   duren heo untunden;
up aras Octa,   Ebissa, and Ossa,   9735
and hehten heore cnihtes   ӡarkien heom to fihte,
vndon her brade ӡæten,   burӡen untunen.
Octa him ut ræd   and muche folc him after glæd—
mid balden his beornen   þer he bælu funden!
Vðer him þis isæh   þat Octa heom to bæh,   9740
and þohten his ferde   feolen to grunde.
þa cleopede Uðer   mid quickere stefene þer:
"Wær beo ӡe, Bruttes,   balde mine þeines?
Nu is icumen þe ilke dæi   þe Drihten us helpen mai—
þat Octa scal ifinden,   þat he þrættede me to binden!   9745
Iþencheð on eoure aldren,   hu gode heo weoren to fehten;

– 26 –

was then a most royal city — St Alban was slain there and deprived of life; the city was later destroyed and many people slaughtered there. Uther lay outside the town and Octa within. Uther's army advanced to the walls, the noble thanes attacked most fiercely; they could not dislodge a single stone from the wall nor, for all their efforts, weaken the wall. #

Hengest's son Octa was very happy when he saw the British retreat from the walls and return in sorrow to their tents. Then Octa said to Ebissa, his companion in arms:

'Uther the cripple has come here to Verolam and wants to fight with us here in his litter, hoping to fell us with his crutch! But tomorrow, when it is daylight, our warriors shall arise and throw open our castle gates, and we shall capture all their leading men; we shall not stay cooped up here just because of a cripple! We shall ride out upon our good steeds, and charge at Uther and destroy his army, for all those who have ridden here are doomed; and we shall capture the cripple and put him in chains, and keep the miserable creature until he dies. And so his limbs that are infirm shall be healed and his bones straightened with biting steel!'

This is what Octa said to his comrade Ebissa — but it all turned out otherwise than they expected!

On the morrow when it dawned and doors were opened, up rose Octa, Ebissa and Ossa, and commanded their followers to prepare themselves for battle, unbar their broad gates and throw open the city. Octa himself rode out and a great host followed him — he and his bold warriors met with misfortune there! Uther himself saw this, saw that Octa was coming against him, intent upon felling his forces to the ground. Then Uther called out there in a rousing voice:

'Where are you, my Britons, my bold thanes? Now the day is come when the Lord may help us — as Octa shall discover, he who swore to fetter me! Remember your ancestors, how good

iþencheð þene wurðscipe   þat ich eou habbe wel biwiten;
ne læten ȝe næuere þas hæðene   bruken eoure hames,
þæs ilke awedde hundes   walden eouwere londes.
And ich wullen bidden Drihten   þat scop þæs dæies lihten,   9750
and alle þaie halȝen   þa an hæfene hæhȝe sitteð,
þat ich on þissen felde   mote beon ifroured.
Nu, fuseð heom to swiðe;   fulste eou Drihten,
þe alwaldinde God   biwiten mine þeines!"
    Cnihtes gunnen riden,   gæres gunnen gliden;   9755
breken bræde speren,   brusleden sceldes,
helmes þer scenden;   scalkes feollen.
þe Bruttes weoren balde   and bisie to fihten,
and þa hæðene hundes   hælden to grunde.
þer wes islaȝen Octa,   Ebissa, and Ossa;   9760
þer seouentene þusend   siȝen into helle.
Feole þer atwenden   touward þan norð enden;
al þene dæilihte   Vðeres cnihtes
sloȝen and nomen   al þat heo neh comen.
þa hit wes eauen,   þa wes hit al biwunnen.   9765
    þa sunggen hired-men   mid hæȝere strengðe,
and þæs word sæiden   inne murie heore songen:
"Her is Vðer Pendragun   icume to Verolames tun,
and he hæfueð idubbed swa   Octa, and Ebissa, and Ossa,
and itah heom a londen   laȝen swiðe stronge   9770
þat men maȝen tellen   heore cun to spelle,
and þerof wurchen songes   inne Sæxlonde."
þa wes Vðer bliðe   and igladed swuðe,
and spac wið his duȝeðe   þe deore him wes an heorte;
and þas word sæide   Vðer þe ald: 9775
"Sexisce men me habbeoð   for hene ihalden,
mine unhæle me atwiten   mid heore hoker-worden,
for ich wes here   ilad inne horse-bere,
and sæiden þat ich wes ded   and mi duȝeðe aswunden.
And nu is muchel sellic   isiȝen to þissere riche,   9780
þat nu haueð þeos dede king   þas quiken aqualden;
and summe he heom flæmde   uorð mid þan wedere!
Nu iwurðen herafter   Drihtenes wille!"
    Fluȝen Sæxisce men   feondliche swiðe
þe weoren bihalues   ihalden from þan fihte;   9785
forð heo gunnen scriðen   into Scotlonde,

they were in fighting; remember in what great splendour I have maintained you; never let the heathens possess your homes, these mad dogs here rule your lands. And I will pray God who created the light of day, and all the saints who sit in heaven on high, that I may be aided on this field of battle. Now, charge them quickly; may the Lord assist you, may almighty God protect my thanes!'

Warriors charged, weapons flew; broad spears broke, shields clashed, helmets shattered; men fell there. The Britons were bold and active in battle, and the heathen dogs fell to the ground. There Octa was slain, Ebissa, and Ossa; there seventeen thousand sank down to hell. Many there escaped towards the northern regions; all through the day Uther's warriors killed and took captive all whom they came upon. By the time it was evening the victory was complete.

Then the soldiers sang with mighty power, and in their mocking songs voiced these words:
'Uther Pendragon is come here to the town of Verolam, and he has drubbed Octa, and Ebissa, and Ossa so, and imposed very severe penalties on them in this land such that their kinsmen may hear of it, and songs be made of it in Saxony.'
Then Uther was happy and greatly pleased, and spoke to his nobles who were dear to his heart; the aged Uther uttered these words:
'The men of Saxony have treated me with contempt, taunting me with my infirmity in their scornful words because I was brought here in a horse-litter, and saying that I was dead and my followers helpless. And now a great marvel has come to pass in this kingdom, in that this dead king has now killed those living men; and some he drove before him like the wind! Now may God's will be done hereafter!'

The men of Saxony who had retreated from the battle fled with furious haste; away they flew into Scotland, and took

and nomen heom to kinge   Colgrim þene hende.
He wes Hængestes mæie   and monnen him leofuest,
and Octa hine lufede   þæ while þe he leouede.
Weoren þa Saxisce men   swiðe iswunten,   9790
and iscriðen heom tosomne   into Scotlonde;
and Colgrim þene hende   heo makeden to kinge,
and sumneden færde   wide ȝeond þan ærde,
and sæiden þat heo wolden   mid heore wiðer-craften
inne Winchastre tun   quellen Vðer Pendragun.   9795
Wa la wa   þat hit sculde iwurðen swa!
     Nu sæiden Saxisce men   in heore som-runen:
"Nime we six cnihtes,   wise men and wihte,
hæweres witere,   and senden we to hirede.
Læten heom uorð liðen   an almes-monnes wisen   9800
and wunien an hirede   mid heȝe þan kinge,
and æuerælche dæie   þurhgon al þa duȝeðe,
and gan to þas kinges dale   swulc heo weoren vnhale,
and imong þan wracchen   harcnien ȝeorne
ȝif mon mihte mid crafte,   a dæi oðer a nihte,   9805
inne Winchæstres tun   cumen to Vðer Pendragun,
and mid morð-spelle   þene king aquellen."
þenne weoren heore iwil   allunge iwurden!
þenne weoren heo carelæse   of Costantines cunne!
     Nu wenden forð þa cnihtes   al bi dæies lihten,   9810
on ælmes-monnes claðes   cnihtes forcuðest,
to þas kinges hirede;   þer heo hærm wrohten.
Heo eoden to þære dale   swulc heo weoren unhale,
and hærcneden ȝeornen   of þas kinges hærme,
hu me þæne king mihte   to dæðe idihte.   9815
þa imetten heo enne cniht,   from þan kinge he com riht;
he wes Vðeres mæi   and monnen him leofuest.
þas swiken, þer heo sæten   onlongen þere streten,
cleopeden to þan cnihte   mid cuðliche worden:
"Lauerd, we beoð wracche men   a þissere weorlde-riche;   9820
while we weoren on londe   for gode men iholden,
a þat Sæxisce men   setten us adune,
and al biræiueden us   and ure æhten binomen us.
Nu we beden singeð   for Vðer kinge.
Ælche dæie on a mæl   ure mete trukeð;   9825
ne cumeð nauere inne ure disc   neoðer flæs na no fisc, *

as their king the noble Colgrim. He was Hengest's kinsman and
the dearest of men to him, and Octa while he lived had loved him.
The Saxons were greatly dejected, and assembled together in
Scotland; and they made the noble Colgrim king, and gathered an
army from far and wide throughout the land, and said that by
their devious practices they would kill Uther Pendragon in
Winchester town. Alas that it should have happened so! #

Now in talking together the men of Saxony said:
'Let us choose six soldiers, wise men and valiant, skilful spies,
and send them to the court. Let them go there in the guise of
beggars and live at court with the high king, and mingle with all
the courtiers every day and go to the king's almsgiving as if they
were infirm, and among the needy people listen keenly whether
anyone could, by day or night, by any stratagem, get at Uther
Pendragon in Winchester, and kill the king by some murderous
plot.'
Then their hopes would be fully accomplished! Then they
would be freed from fear of the race of Constantin!

Now, the warriors, most wicked knights in beggars' clothes,
set out in the open light of day for the king's court; they did harm
there. They went to the almsgiving as if they were infirm, and
kept their ears open, eager to hear of anything that might be
harmful to the king, and learn how the king might be put to
death. Then they met with a knight who had come straight from
the king; he was Uther's kinsman and a man most dear to him.
Those treacherous men, where they sat by the side of the street,
called to the knight with friendly words:
'My lord, we are poor men in this realm; yet once we were
considered men of worth in the land, until the Saxons brought us
to ruin, and robbed us utterly and took our possessions from us.
Now we chant prayers for King Uther. Each day when we would
eat, we lack food; neither fish nor flesh ever comes into our bowl,

no nanes cunnes drænc   buten water scenc,
buten water clæne   —for þi we beoð þus læne."

    Þis iherde þe cniht;   aзæn he eode forðriht
and com to þan kinge   þer he lai on bure,   9830
and seide to þan kinge: "Lauerd, beo þu on sunde;
herute sitteð six men,   iliche on heouwen;
alle heo beoð iferen,   iscrudde mid heren.
While heo weoren   a þissere worlde-richen
godfulle þeines,   mid goden afeolled;   9835
nu habbeoð Sæxisce men   isæt hom to grunden,
þat heo beoð on weorlde   for wracchen ihalden;
no raccheoð heo to borde   buten bræd ane,
no to heore drenches   bute water scenches.
Þus heo leodeð heore lif   inne þire leode,   9840
and heore beoden biddeð   þat Godd þe lete longe libben."

    Þa quað Vðer þe king: "Let heom cumen hider in;
ich heom wulle scruden   and ich heom wulle ueden,
for mines Drihtenes lufe,   þa wille þa ich liuie."
Comen into bure   beornes þa swikele;   9845
þe king heom lette feden,   þæ king heom lette scruden,
and nihtes hom læiden   ælc on his bedde;
and ælc on his halue   heoзede зeorne
hu heo mihten þene king   mid morðe aquellen.
Ah ne mihten heo þurh naþing   aquellen Vðer þene king,   9850
ne þurh nane crafte   cumen to him ne mahten.

    Þa iwærd hit in ane time   þe ræin him gon rine.
Þa cleopede þer a læche   þer he læi on bure
to ane bur-cnihte   and hahte hine forðrihtes
irne to þere welle   þe wes onvæst þere halle   9855
and setten þere ænne ohte swain   to biwiten heo wið ræin;
"for þe king ne mai on duзeðe   bruken nanes drenches
buten cald welles stræm   þat him is iqueme,
þat is to his ufele   aðelest alre drenche."

    Þas speche uorðrihtes   iherden þas six cnihtes;   9860
to harme heo weoren wiþte   and ut wenden bi nihte,
forð to þere welle;   þer ho hærm wrohten.
Vt heo droзen sone   amppullen scone
ifulled mid attere,   weten alre bitterest;
six amppullen fulle   heo зeoten i þan welle;   9865
þa wes þa welle anan   al mid attre bigon.

nor any kind of drink save a draught of water, nothing but water alone — that is why we are so lean.'

The knight took note of this; he at once went back and came to the king where he lay in his chamber, and said to the king:

'Good health to you, my lord; outside sit six men, alike in appearance; they are all companions, all clothed in hair shirts. Once they were worthy thanes in this realm, possessed of wealth; now the Saxons have brought them low, so that they are held by all the world to be paupers; at meals they have nothing but bread alone, nothing to drink but draughts of water. And so they lead their lives among your people, and offer up their prayers that God may let you live long.'

Then said King Uther:

'Let them come in here; I will clothe them and I will feed them, for love of my Lord, as long as I shall live.'

The deceitful men came into the chamber; the king had them fed, the king had them clothed, and at night had each of them given a bed; and each on his part earnestly considered how they could murder the king. But they could not kill King Uther by any means, nor get at him by any stratagem.

Then one day it came to pass that rain fell. Then a doctor in the chamber where the king lay called to a chamberlain and ordered him to go at once to the spring which was hard by the hall and station there a trustworthy servant to protect it from the rain; 'for there is no drink in the court which the king can take that is palatable to him but cold spring water which is the best of all medicines for his sickness.'

The six soldiers heard these words at once; they were prompt in doing harm and went out by night, straight to the spring; they did evil there. At once they drew out fine phials filled with poison, bitterest of liquids; six full phials they poured into the well; then in an instant the well was all suffused with poison.

þa weoren ful bliðe   þæ swiken on heore liue,
and forð heo iwenden   —ne dursten heo þer bilæfen!
    þa comen þer forðrihtes   tweien bur-cnihtes;
heo beren on heore honde   twæie bollen of golde.   9870
Heo comen to þare welle   and heore bollen feolde;
aȝæin heo gunnen wende   to Vðer þan kinge,
forð into þan bure   þer he læi on bedde.
"Hail seo þu, Vðer;   nu we beoð icumen her
and we habbeoð þe ibroht   þat þu ær bedde,   9875
cæld welle water   —bruc hit on wunne."
Vp aras þe seocke king   and sat on his bedde;
of þan watere he dronc   and sone he gon sweten;
his heorte gon to wakien,   his neb bigon to blakien,
his wombe gon to swellen;   þe king gon to swelten.   9880
Næs þer nan oðer ræd;   þer wes Vðer king dæd;
alle heo iwurðen dede   þat drunken of þan watere.
    þa þat hired isah,   þat sorhȝen of þan kinge
and of þas kinges monnen   þe mid attre weoren fordone,
þa wenden to þere welle   cnihtes þe weoren snælle   9885
and þa welle forduden   mid derfulle swincche,
mid eorðe and mid stanen   stepne hul makeden.
þa nomen þa duȝeðe   þene king dede,
vnimete uolc,   and forð hine uereden,
stið-imodede men,   into Stanhengen,   9890
and hine þer bureden   bi leofen his broðer;
side bi side,   beiene heo þer liggeð.
    þa com hit al togadere,   þat hæhst wes on londe,
eorles and beornes   and boc-ilarede men;
heo comen to Lundene   to muchelere hustinge.   9895
Nomen heom to rade,   þeines riche,
þat heo wolden ouer sæ   senden sonde
into Bruttainne   after bezst alre ȝeoȝeðe
þa a þissere weorlden-riche   a þan dæȝen weore,
Ærður ihaten,   bezst alre cnihten,   9900
and suggen þat he cumen sone   to his kinedome;
for dæd him wes Vðer   alswa Aurilien wes ær,
and Vðer Pendragune   nefde nenne oðerne sune
þat mihte, after his daȝen,   halden Bruttes to laȝe,
mid wurðscipe halden   and þisne kinedom walden.   9905
For ȝæt weoren in þissen londe   Sæxes atstonden,

Then the traitors were the happiest men alive, and away they went
— they did not dare remain there!

Then shortly there came two chamberlains bearing in their
hands two golden bowls. They came to the spring and filled their
bowls; they returned again to King Uther, straight to the chamber
where he lay abed.

'Good health to you, Uther; we have come here now to bring
you what you earlier asked for, cold spring water — drink it with
pleasure.'

The sick king rose up and sat on his bed; he drank the water
and at once he began to sweat; his heart began to weaken, his face
to grow pale, his belly began to swell; the king was dying. There
was no other recourse; there and then King Uther died; all who
drank of the water died.

When the courtiers, who sorrowed for the king and for the
king's men who were killed by the poison, saw that, then warriors
fleet of foot went to the fountain and with laborious toil blocked
the well up, made a high mound with earth and stones. Then the
royal retainers, a countless throng, brave-hearted men, took the
dead king and bore him away to Stonehenge, and buried him there
beside his beloved brother; there they both lie, side by side. #

Then all came together, those who were the highest in the
land, nobles and warriors and learned men; they came to London
to a great council. The noble thanes agreed upon a plan, that they
would send messengers overseas to Brittany to search out the
finest young man who was in this mortal world in those days, the
best of all warriors, Arthur by name, and to say that he should
come at once to his kingdom; for Uther was dead like Aurelius
before him, and Uther Pendragon had no other son who could,
after his days, subject the British to law, rule them with honour
and govern this kingdom. For the Saxons were still established in

Colgrim þe kene   and moni þusend of his iueren
þa ofte ure Bruttes   makeden hufele burstes.

    Bruttes ful sone   þreo biscopes nomen
and ridæres seouene   ræize on wisdome;   9910
forð heo gunnen buzen   into Bruttaine
and heo ful sone   to Ærður comen:
"Hail seo þu, Arður,   aðelest cnihten;
Vðer þe græten   þa he sculde iwiten,
and bæd þat þu sculdest   a Brutten þe seoluen   9915
halden lazen rihte,   and hælpen þine folke,
and witen þisne kinedom   swa god king sculden don,
þine feond flæmen   and driuen heom of londen.
And he bad þe to fultume   þene milde Godes sune
þat þu mostes wel don,   and þat lond of Godde afon;   9920
for dæd is Vðer Pendragun   and þu ært Ærður his sune,
and dæd is þe oðer,   Aurilien his broðer."

    þus heo gunnen tellen   and Arður sæt ful stille;
ænne stunde he wes blac   and on heuwe swiðe wak,
ane while he wes reod   and reousede on heorte.   9925
þa hit alles up brac   hit wes god þat he spac;
þus him sæide þerriht   Arður, þe aðele cniht:
"Lauerd Crist, Godes sune,   beon us nu a fultume,
þat ich mote on life   Goddes lazen halden."
Fiftene zere wes Arður ald   þa þis tiðende him wes itald;   9930
and alle heo weoren wel bitozen,   for he wes swiðe iðoze.

    Ærður forðrihtes   cleopede his cnihtes,
and hæhte æuerælcne mon   bonnien his weppnen,
and heore hors sadelie   hizendliche swiðe,
for he wolde buze   to þissere Brutene.   9935
To þere sæ wenden   sele þeines
at Mihæles Munte   mid muchelere uerede;
þa sæ heo sætten a þat strond;   at Suðhamtune heo comen alond.
Forð him gon ride   Arður þe riche,
riht to Selechæstre   þer him sel þuhte,   9940
þer wes Bruttene weored   baldeliche isomned.
Muchel wes þa blisse   þa Arður com to burhze;
þer wes bemene blæst   and swiðe glade beornes.
þer heo houen to kinge   Arður þene zunge.

    þa þe Arður wes king   —hærne nu seollic þing—   9945
he wes mete-custi   ælche quike monne,

this land, the bold Colgrim and many thousands of his countrymen who often did our Britons grievous injury.

The Britons immediately chose three bishops and seven knights excelling in wisdom; they set out for Brittany and very quickly they came to Arthur:

'Health to you, Arthur, noblest of knights; Uther sent you greetings when he was dying, and commanded that you yourself should maintain just laws in Britain, and help your people, and protect this kingdom as a good king should, put your enemies to flight and drive them from the land. And he prayed the gracious son of God to help you that you might do well, and receive the land from God; for Uther Pendragon is dead and the other brother, Aurelius, is dead too; and you, Arthur, are Uther's son.'

Thus they spoke and Arthur sat quite still; one moment he was pale and quite lacking in colour, next instant he was red, with heartfelt grief. When it all burst out, what he said was fitting; Arthur, the noble knight, at once spoke thus:

'Lord Christ, son of God, be a help to us now, that I may uphold God's laws throughout my life.'

When this news was told him, Arthur was fifteen years old; and the years had all been well employed, for he was fully mature.

Arthur immediately called his followers, and commanded each and every man to prepare his weapons, and ordered them to saddle their horses in great haste, for he wished to cross to the land of Britain. Noble thanes put to sea at Mont St Michel with a great army; the sea brought them to the shore and they landed at Southampton. Away he rode, the noble Arthur, straight to Silchester where he longed to be, where the British army was bravely assembled. Great was the joy when Arthur came to the town; there was blowing of trumpets and great rejoicing among the men. There they raised the youthful Arthur to the kingship.

When Arthur was king — now listen to a marvellous matter — he was generous to every man alive, among the best of

cniht mid þan bezste,   wunder ane kene;
he wes þan ȝungen for fader,   þan alden for frouer,
and wið þan vnwise   wunder ane sturnne;
woh him wes wunder lað   and þat rihte a leof.   9950
Ælc of his birlen   and of his bur-þæinen
and his ber-cnihtes   gold beren an honden,
to ruggen and to bedde   iscrud mid gode webbe.
Nefde he neuere nænne coc   þat he nes keppe swiðe god,
neuær nanes cnihtes swein   þat he næs bald þein.   9955
Þe king heold al his hired   mid hæȝere blise;
and mid swulche þinges   he ouercom alle kinges,
mid ræhȝere strengðe   and mid richedome; *
swulche weoren his custes   þat al uolc hit wuste.
Nu wes Arður god king;   his hired hine lufede   9960
æc hit wes cuð wide   of his kinedome.
      Þe king huld i Lundene   ane muchele hustinge;
þerto weoren ilaðede   his leond-cnihtes alle,
riche men and hæne   to hæȝen þan king.
Þa þe hit wes al icume,   uolc vnimete,   9965
vp aræs Arður,   aðelest kingen,
and lette bringen him biforen   halidomes wel icoren;
þerto gon cneoli   þe king sume þrie;
nuste noht his duȝeðe   what he deme wolde.
Arður heold up his riht hond;   ænne að he þer swor   9970
þat næuere bi his liue,   for nanes monnes lære,
ne sculden inne Brutene   Sæxes wurðen bliðe,
londes beon wurðen   no wurðscipe bruke.
Ah he heom wolde flemen,   for heo weoren iuæid wið him,
sloȝen Vðer Pendragune   þe wes Costances sune,   9975
swa heo duden þene oðer,   Aurilien his broðer,
for þi heo weoren on londe   laðest alre uolke.
Arður forðrihtes   nom his wise cnihtes;
weore heom lef, weore heom lað,   alle heo sworen þene að
trouliche þat heo wolden   mid Arðure halden,   9980
and wreken þene king Vðer   þat Sæxes aqualden her.
      Arður his writen sende   wide ȝeond his londe
after alle þan cnihten   þe he biȝiten mihte,
þat heo ful sone   to þan kinge comen
and he heom wolde on londe   leofliche athalden,   9985
scipien heom mid londe   mid seoluere and mid golde.

warriors, wonderfully bold; he was a father to the young, a comfort to the old, and with the rash extremely stern; wrong was most hateful to him and the right was always dear. Each of his cup-bearers and his chamberlains and his footmen bore gold in hand, wore fine cloth on back and bed. He never had any cook who was not a good warrior, never any knight's squire who was not a bold thane. The king kept all his followers in great contentment; and by such means he defeated all kings, by fierce strength and by generosity; such were his virtues that all nations knew of it. Now Arthur was a good king; his followers loved him and it was known far beyond his kingdom.

The king held a great assembly in London; to it were invited all his dependants, rich men and poor, to honour the king. When they had all come, a numberless throng, up rose Arthur, noblest of kings, and caused to be brought before him most precious holy relics; some three times the king knelt before them; his followers knew not what he intended to decree. Arthur held up his right hand; he swore an oath then that never while he lived, through no man's urging, should the Saxons be at ease in Britain, possess land or enjoy honour. But he would put them all to flight, for they were at enmity with him, and had slain Uther Pendragon who was Constantin's son, as they had the other son, his brother Aurelius, and so they were the most hateful of all men in the kingdom. Arthur then summoned his wise warriors; willingly or unwillingly, they all loyally swore on oath that they would remain faithful to Arthur, and avenge King Uther whom the Saxons had killed here. #

Arthur sent his writs far and wide throughout his land in search of all the soldiers he could find, saying that they should come at once to the king and he would lovingly maintain them in the kingdom, provide them with land, with silver and with gold.

Forð þe king ferde   mid vnimete uerde;
folc he ledde sællic   and ferde riht to Eouerwic.
þer he læi ane niht,   amærwe he ferde forðriht
þer he wuste Colgrim   and his iueren mid him.   9990
      Seoððen Octa wes ofslaȝen   and idon of lif-dæȝen—
þe wes Hengestes sune   vt of Sæxlonde icumen—
Colgrim wes þe hæhst mon   þat ut of Saxlonde com
after Hengeste   and Horse his broðer,
and Octa, and Ossa,   and heore iuere Ebissa.   9995
Heold a þan ilke dæȝen   Colgrim Sæxes to laȝen,
ladde and radde   mid ræȝere strengðe;
muchel wes þat moncun   þat ferde mid Colgrim.
      Colgrim iherde tidende   of Arðure þan kinge,
þat he touward him com   and wolde him vfel don.   10000
Colgrim hine biþohte   whæt he don mahte,
and bonnede his uerde   ȝeond al þan norð ærde.
þer liðen tosomne   alle Scotleode,
Peohtes and Sæxes   siȝen heom togæderes,
and moniennes cunnes men   uuleden Colgrimen.   10005
Forð he gon fusen   mid vnimete verde
toȝaines Arðure,   aðelest kingen;
he þohte to quellen   þe king on his þeoden
and his folc uallen,   uolden to grunden,
and setten al þis kinelond   an his aȝere hond,   10010
and fallen to þan grunde   Arður þene ȝunge.
      Forð wende Colgrim   and his ferde mid him,
and wende mid his ferde   þat he com to ane watere;
þat water is ihaten Duglas   —duȝeðen hit aquelde!
þer com Arður him aȝein,   ȝaru mid his fehte;   10015
in ane brade forde   þa ferden heom imetten;
fastliche onsloȝen   snelle heore kempen,
feollen þa uæie,   uolden to grunde.
þer wes muchel blod-gute,   balu þer wes riue;
brustlede scæftes,   beornes þer ueollen.   10020
þat isæh Arður;   on mode him wes unneðe.
      Arður hine biðohte   whæt he don mahte,
and teh hine abacward   in enne uald brade.
þa wenden his feond   þat he flæn walde;
þa wes glad Colgrim   and al his ferde mid him;   10025
heo wenden þat Arður   mid arhðe weore afallæd þere

The king set forth with a vast host; leading a splendid force, he journeyed straight to York. Wherever he halted at night, in the morning he advanced straight towards where he knew Colgrim was and his companions with him.

Since Octa had been slain and deprived of life — he was the son of Hengest who came from Saxony — Colgrim was the greatest of those who had come from Saxony after Hengest and his brother Horsa, and Octa, and Ossa, and their comrade Ebissa. In those days Colgrim subjected the Saxons to law, led them and ruled them with stern authority; great was the multitude which followed Colgrim.

Colgrim heard news of King Arthur, heard that he was coming against him and intended to do him evil. Colgrim considered what he could do, and summoned his army throughout the whole northland. All the men of Scotland assembled, Picts and Saxons united together, and men of many clans followed Colgrim. With a huge army he hastened out to meet Arthur, the noblest of kings; he thought to kill the king in his own country and destroy his army, fell them to the ground, take all this kingdom into his own possession, and fell to the ground the youthful Arthur.

Forth went Colgrim and his army with him, and advanced with his forces until he came to a river; that river is called Douglas — it was the death of warriors! Arthur came to meet him there with his forces in battle order; at a broad ford the armies confronted each other; their brave warriors attacked vigorously, the doomed fell, thrust down to the ground. There was great bloodshed, death was rife there; spears bristled, warriors fell there. Arthur saw that and was troubled in his heart. #

Arthur considered what he could do, and withdrew into a broad plain. Then his enemies thought that he was intending to flee; Colgrim was glad then and all his army with him; they thought that Arthur had been overcome with cowardice there and

and tuȝen ouer þat water alse heo wode weoren.

Þa Arður þat isah, þat Colgrim him wes swa neh,
and heo weoren beien bihalues þan wateren,
þus seide Arður, aðelest kingen: 10030
"Iseo ȝe, mine Bruttes, here us bihalfues,
ure iuan uulle —Crist heom aualle!—
Colgrim þene stronge ut of Sæxlonde.
His cun i þisse londe ure ælderne aqualden;
ah nu is þe dæi icumen þe Drihten haueð idemed 10035
þat he scal þat lif leosen and leosien his freonden,
oðer we sculle dæde beon —ne muȝe we hine quic iseon.
Scullen Sæxisce men sorȝen ibiden,
and we wreken wurhliche ure wine-maies!"

Vp bræid Arður his sceld foren to his breosten, 10040
and he gon to rusien swa þe runie wulf
þenne he cumeð of holte bihonged mid snawe,
and þencheð to biten swulc deor swa him likeð.
Arður þa cleopede to leofe his cnihten:
"Forð we biliue, þeines ohte, 10045
alle somed heom to; alle we sculleð wel don,
and heo uorð hælden swa þe hæȝe wude
þenne wind wode weieð hine mid mæine."

Fluȝen ouer þe woldes þritti þusend sceldes
and smiten a Colgrimes cnihtes þat þa eorðe aȝæn quehte. 10050
Breken braden speren, brustleden sceldes;
feollen Sæxisce men, folden to grunden.
Þat isah Colgrim —þeruore wa wes him!—
þe alre hendeste mon þe ut of Sexlonde com.
Colgrim gon to flænne feondliche swiðe, 10055
and his hors hine bar mid hæhȝere strengðe
ouer þat water deope and scelde hine wið dæðe.
Saxes gunnen sinken —sorȝe heom wes ȝiueðe!
Arður wende his speres ord and forstod heom þene uord;
þer adruncke Sexes fulle seoue þusend. 10060
Summe heo gunnen wondrien swa doð þe wilde cron
i þan moruenne þenne his floc is awemmed *
and him haldeð after haurkes swifte,
hundes in þan reode mid reouðe hine imeteð.
þenne nis him neouðer god, no þat lond no þat flod: 10065
hauekes hine smiteð, hundes hine biteð.

– 42 –

they charged across the river as if they were mad.

When Arthur saw that Colgrim was so near him, and they were both on the same side of the stream, Arthur, noblest of kings, spoke thus:

'See, my Britons, close to us here, our bitter enemies — Christ strike them down! — the fierce Colgrim out of Saxony. His kinsmen slew our ancestors in this land; but now the day is come which the Lord has appointed when he shall be deprived of life and lose his friends, or we shall die — we cannot look upon him while he lives. The Saxon men shall endure sorrow, and we shall fittingly avenge our kinsmen!'

Arthur raised his shield before his chest and went rushing like the savage wolf when he comes from the snow-hung wood, bent on devouring whatever prey he pleases. Then Arthur called to his beloved warriors:

'Brave thanes, let us rush upon them all together! We shall all do well, and they shall fall before us like the lofty wood when the wild wind strikes it with force.'

Thirty thousand shields flew over the downs and fell upon Colgrim's warriors so that the earth shook in answer. Broad spears broke, shields clashed; Saxon men fell, flung to the ground. Colgrim, the most powerful of all those who came out of Saxony, saw that — he was grieved at it! Colgrim took to flight with furious haste, and his horse bore him with great strength over that deep river and saved him from death. The Saxons began to sink — sorrow was their lot! Arthur turned the point of his spear and denied them the ford; full seven thousand Saxons drowned there. Some went wandering as does the wild crane in the moorland fen when his flock is scattered and swift hawks pursue him, hounds ruthlessly attack him in the reeds. Neither the land nor the water is safe for him then: hawks strike him, hounds bite him. Then

þenne biðð þe kinewurðe foȝel   fæie on his siðe.
    Colgrim ouer feldes   flæh him biliues
þat he com to Eouerwic,   riden swiðe sellic.
He wenden into burȝe   and faste heo biclusde;   10070
hafuede he binnen   ten þusend monnen,
burh-men mid þa beztse   þe him bihalues weoren.
Arður halde after   mid þritti þusend cnihten,
and ferde riht to Eouerwic   mid folke swiðe sellic,
and bilæi Colgrim   þe weorrede aȝæin him.   10075
    Seouen niht þer biuoren,   wes suðward ifaren
Baldolf þe hende,   broðer Colgrimes,
and lai bi þare sæ-brimme   and abad Childrichen.
Childric wes i þan daȝen   cæiser of riche laȝen
inne Alemaine;   þat aðel wes his aȝene.   10080
Þa iherde Baldolf,   þer he bi sæ lai,
þat Arður hafde inne Eouerwic   Colgrim biclused;
Baldolf hæfde ibonned   seouen þusend monnen,
baldere beornnen,   þe bi sæ leien.
Heo nomen heom to ræden   þat aȝæin heo wolden riden   10085
and bilæuen Childric   and faren into Eouerwic,
and fehten wið Arðure   and aquellen al his duȝeðe.
Baldolf swor on his grome   þat he wolde beon Arðures bone,
and bruken al þas riche   mid Colgrime his broðere.
    Nolde Baldolf abide   þan keisere Childriche,   10090
ah þenne he ferde uorð   and droh him forðrihtes norð,
from dæie to dæie   mid baldre duȝeðe,
þat he com in ane wude   in ane wilderne
from Arðures ferde   fulle seoue milen.
He hafde iþohte bi nihten   mid seouen þusend cnihten   10095
to riden uppen Arður   ær þe king wore war,
and his folc afeollen   and hine seolf aquelle.
    Ah al hit oðer iwarð,   oðer he iwende;
for Baldolf hafede on hirede   ænne cniht Bruttiscne—
he wes Arðures mæi,   Maurin ihaten.   10100
Maurin bihalues   to þan wude halde,
þurh wude and þurh feldes,   þat he com to Arðures teldes,
and þus seide sone   to Arður kinge:
"Hail seo þu, Arður,   kingene aðelest;
ich æm hidere icume;   ich æm of þine cunne.   10105
Her is Baldulf icumen   mid swiðe hærde hære-gumen,

the royal bird is doomed in his tracks.

Colgrim fled in haste across the fields until he came to York, riding most skilfully. He went into the city and made it secure; inside he had ten thousand men, a garrison of the best warriors who were on his side. Arthur followed in pursuit with thirty thousand soldiers, and journeyed straight to York with a very great following, and besieged Colgrim who fought against him. #

A week earlier, the noble Baldolf, Colgrim's brother, had journeyed southwards and camped by the seashore, awaiting Childric. In those days Childric was a ruler of great authority in Germany, his own, his native land. Then Baldolf, where he lay encamped by the sea, heard that Arthur had besieged Colgrim in York; Baldolf had assembled seven thousand men, bold warriors, who were encamped by the sea. They decided that they would ride off without waiting for Childric and advance upon York, and fight with Arthur and slay all his followers. Baldolf, in his anger, swore that he would be Arthur's slayer, and take possession of this whole kingdom along with his brother Colgrim. #

Baldolf would not wait for the emperor Childric, but set out from there and, with his bold warriors, advanced due north, day after day, until he came to a wood in a wild region seven miles and more from Arthur's army. He had planned to ride down upon Arthur by night with seven thousand warriors before the king was aware of it, and slaughter his army and slay the king himself.

But it all turned out otherwise, quite otherwise than he expected; for Baldolf had in his following a British soldier called Maurin — he was a kinsman of Arthur's. Maurin slipped away to the woods, crept through forest and field till he came to Arthur's tents, and at once spoke to King Arthur thus:

'Health to you, Arthur, noblest of kings; I who have come here am a kinsman of yours. Baldolf has come here with hardy

and þencheð in þissere nihte   to slæn þe and þine cnihtes
to wracken his broðer   þe swiðe is vnbalded;
ah Godd him scal forwrænen   þurh his muchele mihten.
And send nu uorð Cador,   þene eorl of Cornwaile,   10110
and mid him ohte cnihtes,   gode and wihte,
fulle seoue hundred   selere þeines;
and ich heom wulle ræden   and ich hom wulle leden
hu heo muwen Baldulf   slæn alse enne wulf."

Forð ferde Cador   and alle þas cnihtes   10115
þat heo comen bihalues   þer Baldulf lai on comele.
Heo him to helden   on ælchere haluen;
heo sloȝen, heo nomen   al þat heo aneh comen;
þer weoren aqualde   niȝen hundred alle italde.
Baldulf wes bihalues   igan him aburhȝen   10120
and þurh þa wilderne flæh   feondliche swiðe,
and hafde his men leofe   mid reouðe bilæfued,
and fleh him swa feor norð   þat he com swa uorð
þer Arður lai in uolde   mid richen his ferde
al abuten Eouerwic   —king swiðe seollic!   10125
Colgrim wes wiðinnen   mid Sæxisce monnen.

Baldulf hine biþohte   what he don mihte,
mid wulches cunnes ginne   he mihte cumen binnen,
into þere burhȝe   to Colgrime his broðere
þe wes him on liue   leofest alre monne.   10130
Baldulf lette striken   to þan bare lichen
his bærd and his chinne   and makede hine to crosse.
He lette sceren half his hæfd   and nom him ane harpe an hond—
he cuðen harpien wel   an his childhaden—
and mid his harpe he ferde   to þas kinges hirede,   10135
and gon þær to gleowien   and muche gome to makien.

Ofte me hine smæt   mid smærte ȝerden,
ofte me hine culde   swa me deð crosce; *
ælc mon þe hine imette   mid bismare hine igratte.
Swa nauere na mon nuste   of Baldulfes custe   10140
buten hit weore crosse   icumen to þan hirede.
Swa he eode longe upward,   swa longe he eode adunward
þæt heo weoren warre   þe weoren þær wiðinnen
þat hit wes Baldulf,   Colgrimes broðer.
Heo wurpen ut enne rap,   and Baldulf hine faste igrap,   10145
and bruden up Baldolf   þat he binnen com.

warriors, and intends this night to slay you and your soldiers to avenge his brother who has been greatly humiliated; but God by his mighty power shall frustrate him. And now send out Cador, the earl of Cornwall, and valiant warriors with him, stout and strong, seven hundred brave thanes all told; and I will guide them and instruct them how they may hunt down Baldolf like a wolf.'

Cador and all the soldiers set forward until they came close to where Baldolf lay encamped. They rushed upon him from all sides; all that they came upon they killed or captured; nine hundred all told were done to death there. Baldolf slipped away to save himself and fled in furious haste through the forest fastness, abandoning his beloved followers with regret; and he fled so far north that he arrived just where Arthur lay in the field with his powerful force all about York — a most marvellous king! Inside was Colgrim with the men of Saxony.

Baldolf considered what he could do, by what sort of trick he could get inside, into the town to his brother Colgrim who was to him the dearest man alive. Baldolf had his beard and chin shaved to the bare skin and made himself seem a half-wit. He had half his head shaved and took a harp in his hand — in childhood he had been a skilful harper — and went with his harp to the king's encampment, and there proceeded to play, making great merriment. #

Often he was struck painful blows with a stick, often beaten as men do a lunatic; everyone who came upon him treated him with contempt. And so no one knew from Baldolf's manner that it was not a madman who had come to the camp. So for a long time he went up and down until those within the city became aware that it was Baldolf, Colgrim's brother. They threw out a rope, Baldolf grasped it firmly, and they drew him up until he

Mid swulches cunnes ginnes   Baldulf com wiðinnen.
        Þa wes bliðen Colgrim   and alle his cnihtes mid him,
and swiðe heo gunnen þratien   Arður þene king.
Arður bihalues wes   and þis gomen isæh,   10150
and wraðde hine sulfne   wunderliche swiðe,
and hæhte anan wepnien   al his wunliche uolc;
he þohte þe burhʒe   mid strengðe to biwinnen.
Alse Arður wolde   to þan walle ræse,
þa com þer riden   Patric þe riche mon   10155
þat wes a Scottisc þein,   scone an his londen,
and þus clupien agon   to þan kinge anan:
"Hail seo þu, Arður,   aðelest Brutten.
Ich þe wulle tellen   neouwe tidende
of þan kæisere Childriche,   þan wode and þan richen,   10160
þan strongen and þan balden.   He is inne Scottlonde
ihælde to are hafene,   and hames forberneð,
and waldeð al ure lond   after his ahʒere hond.
He haueð uerde wel idone,   al þa strengðe of Rome.
He sæið mid his ʒelpe,   þenne me him win scencheð,   10165
þat þu ne dærst in nare stude   his ræsses abiden,
no on uelde, no on wude,   no nauere nane stude;
and ʒif þu him abidest   he þe wule binden,
quellen þine leoden   and þi lond aʒen."
        Ofte wes Arðure wa,   nauere wurse þene þa,   10170
and he droh hine abac   bihalues þere burʒe,
clupede to ræde   cnihtes to neode,
beornes and eorles   and þa hali biscopes,
and bad þat heo him radden   hu he mihte on richen
mid his mon-weorede   his monscipe halden,   10175
and fehten wið Childriche,   þan stronge and þan richen,
þa hider wolde liðe   to helpen Colgrime.
Þa andswarede Bruttes,   þa þere weoren bihalues:
"Faren we riht to Lundene   and lete hine liðen after,
and ʒif he cumeð riden   sorʒe he scal ibiden;   10180
he seolf and his ferde   fæie scal iwurðen!"
Arður al bilufeden   þat radden his leoden;
forð he gon liðen   þat he to Lundene com.
        Colgrim wes in Eouerwic   and þær abad him Childric.
Chilric gon wende   ʒeon þan norð ende,   10185
and nom on honde   muchæl dal of londe.

was inside. By tricks of this kind Baldolf got into the city.

Then Colgrim rejoiced and all his warriors with him, and they began to threaten King Arthur fiercely. Arthur was close at hand and witnessed this behaviour, and grew exceedingly enraged; and he ordered all his splendid host to take arms immediately, intending to take the town by force. As Arthur was about to make an assault on the wall, there came riding up the nobleman Patrick who was a Scottish thane, a handsome man of that nation, and who at once began to address the king:

'Health to you, Arthur, noblest of Britons. I have fresh tidings to tell you of the fierce and mighty emperor Childric, a strong man and bold. He has come ashore at a harbour in Scotland, and is burning homesteads, and holds our whole land in his possession. He has a well-equipped army, the whole might of Rome. In his boasting, when wine is poured for him, he says that you dare not face his onslaughts anywhere, neither in field, nor in forest, not in any place whatsoever; and if you risk battle with him he will put you in chains, slaughter your people and seize your land.' #

Arthur had often been in difficulties, but never more so than then, and he drew back a short way from the town; he called his warriors to counsel in this time of need, commons and nobles and the holy bishops, and bade them advise him how he might uphold his honour in the kingdom with his army, fight against the strong and powerful Childric who was coming hither to help Colgrim. Then the Britons, those who were present there, answered:

'Let us go directly to London and let him follow after, and if he comes riding there he shall suffer misfortune; he and his army shall be doomed!'

Arthur approved all that his people advised, and marched onwards until he came to London.

Colgrim was in York awaiting Childric there. Childric advanced through the regions of the north, and took possession of a large stretch of territory. He gave the whole of Scotland to

Al Scotþeode   he ȝaf his ane þeine,
and al Norðhumberlond   he sette his broðer an hond;
Galeweoie and Orcaneie   he ȝaf his ane eorle;
himseolf he nom from Humbre   þat lond into Lundene.   10190
Ne þohte he naueremare   of Arður habben are
buten he wolden his mon bicume,   Arður, Vðeres sune!

     Arður wes in Lundene   mid alle Brutleoden;
he bed his ferde   ȝeond alle þissen ærde
þat æuerælc mon   þe him god vðen   10195
ræðe and ful sone   to Lundene comen.
þa wes Ænglene lond   mid ærmþe offulled;
her wes wop and her wes rop,   and reouðen vniuoȝe,
muchel hunger and hæte   at æuerælche monnes ȝete. *

     Arður sende ouer sæ   sele tweie cnihtes   10200
to Hoele his mæie,   þe wes him leofest monnen,
þe ahte Bruttaine,   cniht mid þan bezste,
and bad hine ful sone   þat he hider come,
liðen to londe   leoden to helpen;
for Chældrich hafde an honde   muchel of þissen londe,   10205
and Colgrim and Baldulf   him to iboȝen weoren,
and þohten Arður þene king   driuen ut of cuðen,
binimen him his icunde   and his kineriche.
þenne were his cun iscend   mid scomeliche witen,
heore wurðscipe iloren   a þissere worlde-richen.   10210
þenne weoren þan kingge betere   þat he iboren neore!

     þis iherde Howel,   þa hahste of Brutaine,
and he cleopien agon   his sele cnihtes anan,
and bæd heom to horse   hiȝenliche swiðe,
and faren into France   to þan freo cnihten,   10215
and seide heom þat heo comen   raðe and ful sone
to Mihæles Munte   mid muchere strenðe,
alle þa þe wolden   of seoluere and of golde
wurhscipe iwinne   a þissere weorlde-richen.
To Peito he sende   sele his þeines,   10220
and summe touward Flandres   feondliche swiðe;
and to Turuine   tweie þer wenden,
and into Gascuinne   cnihtes æc gode,
and hahten heom mid maine   touward Mihhæles Munte.
And ær heo eoden to ulode   heo sculden habbeon ȝiuen gode   10225
þat heo mihte þa bliðere   buȝen from heore ærde,

one of his thanes, and all Northumberland he committed to his brother's charge; Galloway and Orkney he gave to one of his earls; he himself took all the land from the Humber as far as London. He intended to have no mercy on Arthur unless he — Arthur, Uther's son! — would become his subject.

Arthur with all his Britons was in London; he ordered his forces throughout all this land, each and every man who wished him well, to come to London speedily and without delay. At that time there was misery throughout England; there was weeping and lamentation here, and widespread sorrow, much famine and want at every man's door.

Arthur sent two noble knights across the sea to his kinsman Howel, ruler of Brittany, a man most dear to him, the best of warriors, and besought him to come here without delay, sail to this land to aid the people; for Childric had much of this land in his possession, and Colgrim and Baldolf were in alliance with him, and they planned to drive King Arthur out of the country, deprive him of his kingdom and his rightful inheritance. Then his kinsmen would be brought to shame by ignominious torments, their honour lost in this mortal world. Then it would be better for the king that he had never been born!

Howel, ruler of Brittany, heard this, and he at once summoned his noble knights, and commanded them to mount with the greatest of speed, to travel to France to those warriors who were freemen there, and tell them to come speedily and without delay to Mont St Michel in great strength, all those who wished through silver and gold to win honour in this mortal world. He sent his noble thanes to Poitiers, and some in the greatest haste towards Flanders; and two travelled to Touraine, and good knights likewise into Gascony, and ordered all men to go in force to Mont St Michel. And before they set sail they should have generous gifts that they might depart the happier from their homeland,

and mid Howele þan hende   cumen to þissen londe
to helpen Arður,   aðelest kingen.

    Þreottene dæies igon weoren   seoððen þa beoden comen þære;
þa halden heo to sæ   swa hahȝel deh from wolcne.   10230
Twa hundred scipene   þer weoren wel biwitene;
me feolden heom mid folke   and heo forð wenden.
Wind stod and þat weder   after heore wille,
and heo at Hamtone   halden to londe.

    Up leoppen of scipe   wode scalkes,   10235
beren to londe   halmes and burnen;
mid spæres and mid sceldes   heo wriȝen al þa feldes.
Þer wes moni bald Brut;   þat beot wes aræred;
heo beoteden swiðe,   bi heore quiken liue,
þat heo wolden igræten   Cheldric þene richen,   10240
þene balde kæisere,   mid muchele harme þere.
And ȝif he nolde awæi fleon   and touward Alemaine teon,
and he wolde on londe   mid fehte atstonden,
mid balde his beornen   beorkes abiden, *
here heo sculde bilauen   þat heom weore alre leofest,   10245
hafden and heore honden   and heore white halmes,
and swa heo scullen on londen   losien heore freonden,
hælden into hælle   —hæðene hundes!

    Arður wes i Lundene,   aðelest kingen,
and iherde suggen   suðere spellen   10250
þat was icumen to londe   Howel þe stronge,
to Hamtune forðrihtes   mid þritti þusen cnihten;
and, mid vnimete uolke   þat wolleȝede þan kinge, *
Arður him toȝaines bah   mid hæhȝere blisse,
mid muchelere mon-weorede   toȝæines his mæie.   10255
Tosomne heo comen   —blisse wes on hirede—
custen and clupten   and cuðliche speken,
and anan, forðrihtes,   somneden heore cnihtes.
Þa weoren þer tosomne   sele twa ferden.
Howel sculde dihten   þritti þusend cnihten,   10260
and Arður hafde an londe   feouwerti þusend an honde.

    Forðrihtes he wenden   touward þan norð ænde,
toward Lincolne   þe Cheldric þe kaisere bilai;
ah he heo þa ȝæte   nefde noht biwunnen,
for þer weoren wiðinnen   seoue þusen monnen,   10265
ohte men and wihte   dæies and nihtes.

and come with the gracious Howel to this land to help Arthur, the noblest of kings. #

Thirteen days had passed since the messengers had arrived there; then men streamed down to the sea as hail does from the heavens. Two hundred ships, well equipped, were waiting there; they were then loaded with warriors and they set forth. Wind and weather were in their favour, and they came to land at Southampton.

Up leapt fierce warriors from the ships, bearing helmets and coats of mail ashore; they covered all the plains with spears and shields. Many a bold Briton was present there; boastful speeches were made; they boasted loudly, on their very lives, that there they would inflict great harm on the powerful Childric, the bold emperor. And if he would not withdraw and take himself off to Germany, but intended to remain in the land, to stand and fight, to face the hue and cry, he and his bold warriors, they should leave behind them here that which they most valued, their heads and their hands and their shining helmets, and thus they should lose their comrades in this land, and fall into hell — the heathen dogs!

Arthur, noblest of kings, was in London, and was informed by true report that the valiant Howel had just landed at Southampton with thirty thousand warriors; and, with a multitude of people following the king, Arthur went to meet him with great joy, went with a large army to meet his kinsman. They met each other, kissed and embraced and exchanged affectionate words — there was rejoicing in both armies — and at once, without delay, marshalled their warriors. Then two bold armies were united there. Howel could muster thirty thousand men, and Arthur had forty thousand at hand in the kingdom.

They set out immediately for the north, towards Lincoln which the emperor Childric was besieging; but he had not taken it as yet, for there were seven thousand warriors within, men brave

Arður mid his ferde   fusde touward burʒe;
and Arður forbæd his cnihtes   dæies and nihtes *
þat heo liðen stille   swulc heo stelen wolden,
liðen ouer leoden   and luden bilefden;   10270
hornes and bemen   alle weoren bilafde.
Arður nom enne cniht   þe wes oht mon and wiht,
and sende hine to Lincolne   to leuen his monnen;
and he heom to soðe   sæide mid muðe
þat cumen wolde Arður,   aðelest kingen,   10275
to þere middernihte,   and mid him moni god cniht;
"and ʒe wiðinne   þenne beoð eou iwarre
þat þenne ʒe ihereð þene dune   þat ʒe ʒæten untunen,
and fuseð ut of burʒe   and eoure feond felleð,
and smiteð a Cheldrichen,   þan strongen and þan richen—   10280
and we heom sculleð tellen   Bruttisse spelles!"
      Hit was to þere middelniht;   þe mone scæn suðriht.
Arður mid his ferde   fusde to burh—
þat folc wes swa stille   swa heo stelen wolden.
Forð heo comen liðen   þat heo iseiʒen Lincolne.   10285
Þus him cleopien agon   Arður, þe kene mon:
"Whar beo ʒe, mine cnihtes,   mine hære-kemppen?
Iseo ʒe þa teldes   þer Childrich lið i ueldes,
Colgrim and Baldulf,   mid baldere strengðe,
þat Alemainisce uolc   þat us hæfeð ihærmed   10290
and þat Sæxisce uolc   þat sorʒen us bihateð,
þat alle habbeoð aqualde   þa hæhste of mine cunne,
Constanz and Constantin   and Vðer þe wes fader min,
and Auriliæn Ambrosie,   mines fader broðer,
and moni þusend monnen   of aðele mine cunne?   10295
Uten we heom to liðe   and to grunde leggen,
and wreken wruðliche   ure cun and heore riche.
And alle somed, forðriht,   nu ride æueralc god cniht!"
      Arður gon to riden,   þa ferde gon gliden
swulc al þa eorðe   wolde forbærnen,   10300
and smiten i þa ueldes   imong Childriches teldes.
Þæt wes þæ æreste mon   þe þer cleopien agon,
Arður, þe heʒe gume,   þe wes Vðeres sune,
kenliche and lude,   swa bicumeð kinge:
"Nu fulste us Marie,   Goddes milde moder,   10305
and ich ibidde hire sune   þat he us beon a fultume."

and stout-hearted on all occasions. Arthur and his army hastened towards the town; night and day he restrained his warriors so that they moved stealthily as if bent on theft, travelling across country and avoiding noise; all horns and trumpets were left behind. Arthur chose a knight who was bold and valiant, and sent him to his beloved followers in Lincoln; and he told them truthfully, by word of mouth, that Arthur, noblest of kings, would come in the middle of the night, and with him many a good warrior; 'and you here within be heedful then, when you hear the din, that you open the gates, and rush out of the town and strike down your enemies, and smite the strong and powerful Childric — and we will tell them tales of the British!'

Midnight was near; due south shone the rays of the moon. Arthur with his army hastened towards the town — the army was quiet as if bent on theft. They advanced until they came within sight of Lincoln. The valiant Arthur addressed them thus:

'Where are you, my knights, my battle-warriors? Do you see those tents on the plain where lie Childric, Colgrim and Baldolf with a mighty power, that German army which has inflicted harm on us and that Saxon force which bodes us ill, which has killed all the noblest of my race, Constans and Constantin and Uther who was my father, and Aurelius Ambrosius, my father's brother, and many thousand men of my noble lineage? Let us charge them and strike them down, and worthily avenge our kinsmen and their realm. And now, at once, let all ride forward together, every brave warrior!'

Arthur rode forward, the army charged as if the whole earth were scorched with fire, and fell upon Childric's tents in the plain. Arthur, the great leader, Uther's son, was the first who called out there boldly and loudly, as befits a king:

'Now may Mary, merciful mother of God, help us, and I pray to her son that He be of aid to us.'

Æfne þan wordes turnden heo heore ordes,
stikeden and sloȝen al þat heo neh comen;
and cnihtes ut of burhȝe buȝen heom toȝæines.
ȝif heo fluȝen to burȝen, þer heo forwurden;   10310
ȝif heo floȝen to þa wude, þer hi heom forduden;
comen þer heo comen, æuere heo heom sloȝen.
Nis hit a nare boc idiht þat æuere weore æi fiht
inne þissere Bruttene þat balu weore swa riue;
for volken him wes ærmest þat æuere com to ærde.   10315
Þer wes muchel blod-gute, balu wes on folke;
dæð þer wes rife, þe eorðe þer dunede.

  Childrich þe kæisere hæfede ænne castel here,
a Lincolnes felde, þer he læi wiðinnen,
þe wes neouwen iworht and swiðe wel biwust;   10320
and þere weoren mid him Baldulf and Colgrim;
and iseȝen þat heore uolc fæie-sih worhten.
And heo forðriht anon on mid heore burnen,
and fluȝen ut of castle, kenscipe bidaled,
and fluȝen forðriht anan to þe wude of Calidon.   10325
Heo hafden to iferen seouen þusend rideren,
and ho bilafden ofslaȝen and idon of lif-daȝen
feowerti þusunde, ifeolled to þan grunde,
Alemainisce men mid ærmðe fordemed,
and þa Sexisce men ibroht to þan grunden.   10330
  Þa isæh Arður, aðelest kingen,
þat Childrich wes ifloȝen, into Calidonie itoȝen,
and Colgrim and Baldulf mid him iboȝen weoren
into þan haȝe wude, into þan hæȝe holme,
and Arður bæh after mid sixti þusend cnihten.   10335
Bruttene leoden þene wude al bileien,
and an are halfe hine feolden, fulle seoue milen,
treo uppen oðer treoliche faste.
An oðer halue he hine bilai mid his leod-ferde
þreo daȝes and þreo niht —þat wes heom muchel pliht!   10340
  Þa isæh Colgrim, alse he læi þerin,
þat þer wes buten mete scarp hunger and hete; *
ne heom no heore horsen hælp nefde nenne.
And þus cleopede Colgrim to þan kaisere:
"Sæie me, lauerd Childric, soðere worden,   10345
for whulches cunnes þinge ligge we þus here?

With these words they turned their sword points, stabbing and slaying all those they came upon; and warriors rushed out of the town to cut them off. If they fled towards the town, there they perished; if they fled to the wood, there they were slain; wheresoever they turned, still they were slaughtered. In no book is any such battle written of within this land of Britain where destruction was so widespread; for of all the armies that had ever come to this land, this was the most ill-fated. There was great bloodshed, slaughter among the army; death was widespread there, the earth was filled with noise.

Here, in the plain of Lincoln, the emperor Childric had a castle, newly built and very strongly fortified, in which he lay encamped; Baldolf and Colgrim were with him there and saw their army going to its doom. And immediately they donned their coats of mail and, stripped of courage, fled from the castle, fled directly to the wood of Calidon. They had in their company seven thousand horsemen, and they left behind them forty thousand dead, felled to the earth and deprived of life, German warriors wretchedly slaughtered, and the men of Saxony brought low. #

Then Arthur, noblest of kings, saw that Childric had fled, had retreated into Calidon, and that Colgrim and Baldolf had fled with him into the lofty wood, up to the high ground, and Arthur followed with sixty thousand warriors. The Britons surrounded the wood entirely, and on one side they felled, for fully seven miles, tree after tree in extreme haste. On the other side he surrounded it with his army three days and three nights — the enemy were in dire straits!

Then Colgrim became aware, as he lay in the wood, that there was keen hunger and thirst for lack of food; there was no help for either them or their horses. And so Colgrim said to the emperor: 'Tell me truthfully, my lord Childric, for what reason we

Whi nulle we ut faren   and bonnien ure ferden
and biginnen fehtes   wið Arður and wið his cnihtes?
For betere us is on londe   mid monscipe to liggen
þene we þus here   for hungere towurðen,   10350
iswencheð us sære   folke to scare.
Oðer we sendeð wið and wið   and ʒeornen Arðures grið,
and bidden þus his milce,   and ʒisles him bitechen,
and wurchen freondscipe   wið þan freo kinge."
þis iherde Childric,   þer he læi wiðinne dic,   10355
and he andswarede   wið ærmliche stefene:
"ʒif hit wulle Baldulf,   þe is þin aʒe broðer,
and ma of ure iferen   þe mid us sunden here,
þat we bidden Arðures grið   and sahtnesse him wurchen wið,
after æuwer wille   don ich hit wulle.   10360
For Arður is swiðe hæh mon   ihalden on leoden,
leof alle his monnen,   and of kinewurðe cunne
al of kingen icume   —he wes Vðeres sune.
And oft hit ilimpeð,   a ueole cunne þeoden,
þer gode cnihtes   cumeð to sturne fihte,   10365
þat heo ærest biʒiteð   after heo hit leoseð;
and al swa us toʒere   is ilumpen here,
and æft us bet ilimpeð   ʒif we moten liuien."
    Sone, forðrihtes,   andswareden þa cnihtes:
"Alle us biluuieð þisne ræd,   for þu hafest wel isæid."   10370
Heo nomen twælf cnihtes   and senden forðrihtes
þer he wes on telde   bi þas wudes ende;
þe an cleopeden anan   mid quickere stefne:
"Lauerd Arður, þi grið;   we wolden speken þe wið.
Hider þe kaisere us sent,   Childric ihaten,   10375
and Colgrim and Baldulf   beien tosomne.
Nu and æueremare   heo biddeð þine ære.
þine men heo wulleð bicumen   and þine monscipe hæʒen,
and heo wulleð ʒiuen þe   ʒisles inowe,
and halden þe for lauerd   swa þe beoð alre leofest   10380
ʒif heo moten liðe   heonene mid liue
into heore leoden   and lað-spæl bringen.
For her we habbeoð ifunden   feole cunne sorʒen,
at Lincolne bilæued   leofe ure mæies,
sixti þusend monnen   þa þer beoð ofslæʒene;   10385
and ʒif hit þe weore   wille an heorte

lie low here? Why do we not break out and assemble our armies
and do battle with Arthur and his warriors? For it is better that
we lie dead on the earth with honour than perish here with hunger
in this way, inflicting grievous harm upon ourselves to the scorn
of others. Or let us send at once and seek Arthur's clemency,
throw ourselves upon his mercy, give him hostages, and make
peace with the noble king.'

Childric, where he lay encamped, heard this, and he answered
in a voice full of sorrow:

'If Baldolf, who is your blood-brother, wishes it, and others of
our company who are here with us, that we seek peace with
Arthur and seal a truce with him, I will do so in accordance with
your wishes. For Arthur is widely held to be a very noble man,
dear to all his people, and of a royal race all descended from
kings — he was Uther's son. And it often happens, in many
different lands, where brave warriors engage in fierce battle, that
at first they gain victory and afterwards they lose it; just so it has
befallen us here on this occasion, and we may fare better
afterwards if we can survive.'

At once, without delay, the warriors answered:
'We all approve this plan, for you have spoken well.'
They chose twelve knights and immediately sent them to
where Arthur was in his tent at the edge of the wood; one of
them at once called out in a loud voice:

'Lord Arthur, be merciful; we wish to speak to you. The
emperor, Childric by name, has sent us here, as have both Colgrim
and Baldolf. They seek your mercy now and evermore. They are
willing to become your liegemen and render you homage, and they
will give you many hostages, and acknowledge you as overlord
since you are, of all men, the most highly esteemed, if they might
depart from here with their lives, return to their land, bringing
grim tidings. For we have suffered here many different
misfortunes, left behind at Lincoln our dear kinsmen, sixty
thousand men who lie slain there; and if it were truly your wish

þat we mosten ouer sæ   winden mid seile,
nulle we naueremare   æft cumen here,
for her we habbeoð forloren   leoue ure mæies.
Swa longe swa bið æuere   her ne cume we næuere!"   10390
     þa loh Arður   ludere stefene:
"Iþonked wurðe Drihtene   þe alle domes waldeð
þat Childric þe stronge   is sad of mine londe!
Mi lond he hafeð todæled   al his duzeðe cnihtes;
me seoluen he þohte   driuen ut of mire leoden,   10395
halden me for hæne   and habben mine riche,
and mi cun al foruaren   mi uolc al fordemen. * *
Ah of him bið iwurðen   swa bið of þan voxe
þenne he bið baldest   ufen an þan walde,
and hafeð his fulle ploзe   and fuзeles inoзe.   10400
For wildscipe climbið   and cluden isecheð,
i þan wilderne   holзes him wurcheð;
faren whaswa auere fare   naueð he næuere nænne kare.
He weneð to beon of duзeðe   baldest alre deoren.
     þenne siзeð him to   segges vnder beorзen   10405
mid hornen, mid hunden,   mid haзere stefenen.
Hunten þar talieð,   hundes þer galieð,
þene vox driueð   зeond dales and зeond dunes.
He ulih to þan holme   and his hol isecheð,
i þan uirste ænde   i þan holle wendeð.   10410
þenne is þe balde uox   blissen al bideled,
and mon him todelueð   on ælchere heluen;
þenne beoð þer forcuðest   deoren alre pruttest.
Swa wes Childriche,   þan strongen and þan riche;
he þohten al mi kinelond   setten an his aзere hond,   10415
ah nu ich habbe hine idriuen   to þan bare dæðe
whæðerswa ich wulle don,   oðer slæn oðer ahon.
     Nu ich wulle зifen him grið,   and leten hine me speken wið;
nulle ich hine slæ no ahon,   ah his bode ich wulle fon.
зisles ich wulle habben   of hæxten his monnen,   10420
hors and heore wepnen   ær heo heonne wenden.
And swa heo scullen wræcchen   to heoren scipen liðen,
sæilien ouer sæ   to sele heore londe,
and þer wirðliche   wunien on riche,
and tellen tidende   of Arðure kinge,   10425
hu ich heom habbe ifreoied   for mines fader saule,

that we might take ship across the sea, we will never again come back here, for here we have lost our dear kinsmen. As long as time lasts we shall never return!'

Then Arthur laughed with a loud voice:

'Thanks be to the Lord who controls all destinies that the mighty Childric is weary of my realm! He has divided all my land among his retainers; he planned to drive me myself out of my realm, treat me with contempt and seize my kingdom, kill all my kinsmen, destroy all my people. But it has befallen him as it does the fox when he is at his boldest up in the woods, and has his fill of sport and birds in plenty. From mere wantonness he climbs and seeks the hilltops, digs holes for himself in the waste places; wheresoever he may roam he has never a care. He considers himself to be the boldest of all animals in valour.

Then beneath the hills men come after him with horns, with hounds, with loud clamour. There hunters shout, hounds bay, driving the fox over hills and dales. He flees to the hilltop and makes for his earth, goes into the den at the nearest place. Then the bold fox is robbed of all his pleasure, and men dig him out from every side; then the proudest of all animals is there the most wretched. So it was with the great and mighty Childric; he planned to take my whole kingdom into his own possession, but now I have hounded him to the point of death whatever I choose to do, either slay him or hang him.

Yet I will show him mercy, and let him speak to me; I will not slay him or hang him, but will grant his request. I will have hostages from among the noblest of his followers, will take their horses and their weapons before they leave here. And so they shall return as outcasts to their ships, sail across the sea to their rightful land, live honourably there in that realm; and they shall tell tidings of King Arthur, tell how I set them free for the sake

and for mine freodome ifrouered þa wræcchen."

Her wes Arður þe king aðelen bidæled.

Nes þer nan swa rehʒ mon þe him durste ræden—

þet him ofþuhte sære sone þerafter!   10430

  Childric com of comela to Arðure þan kinge,

and he his mon þer bicom mid his cnihten alle.

Feouwer and twenti ʒisles Childric þer bitæhte;

alle heo weoren icorene and hæhʒe men iborenne.

Heo bitahten heore hors and heore burnen,   10435

scaftes and sceldes, and longe heore sweordes;

al heo bilæfden þat heo þer hæfden.

Forð heo gunnen siʒen þat heo to sæ comen;

þer heore scipen gode bi þere sæ stoden.

Wind stod on wille, weder swiðe murie;   10440

he scufen from þan stronde scipen grete and longe.

Þat lond heo al bilæfden and liðen after vðen

þat nænne siht of londe iseon heo ne mahten.

Þat water wes stille after heore iwille.

Heo letten tosomne sæiles gliden,   10445

bord wið borden; beornes þer spileden,

sæiden þat heo wolden eft to þissen londe

and wreken wurðliche heore wine-mæies,

and westen Arðures lond and leoden aquellen,

and castles biwinnen and wilgomen wurchen.   10450

  Swa heo liðen after sæ efne al swa longe

þat heo commen bitwiʒe Ænglelonde and Normandie.

Heo wenden heore lofes and liðen toward londe

þat heo comen ful iwis to Dertemuðe at Totteneis;

mid muchelere blisse heo buʒen to þan londe.   10455

Sone swa heo a lond comen þat folc heo asloʒen;

þa cheorles heo uloʒen þa tileden þa eorðen,

heo hengen þa cnihtes þa biwusten þa londes;

alle þa gode wiues heo stikeden mid cnifes,

alle þa maidene heo mid morðe aqualden,   10460

and þaie ilærede men heo læiden on gleden;

alle þa heorede-cnauen mid clibben heo aqualden.

Heo velleden þa castles, þat lond heo awæsten,

þa chirechen heo forbarnden —baluw wes on folke!

Þa sukende children heo adrenten inne wateren,   10465

þat orf þat heo nomen al heo sloʒen,

of my father's soul, and in my generosity have spared the wretches.'

In this King Arthur was lacking in good judgement. There was no man so bold that he dared contradict him — which very shortly afterwards he was bitterly to regret!

Childric came from his lair before King Arthur, and there became his liegeman together with all his followers. There Childric gave him four and twenty hostages; they were all men of worth and nobly born. The army surrendered their horses and their coats of mail, their spears and shields, and their long swords; they left behind everything they had there. They set forth and marched until they came to the sea; there, by the seashore, their good ships rode. The wind was favourable, the weather very pleasant; they thrust their ships, large and long, away from the shore. Leaving all land behind, they journeyed across the sea until they could see no sight of land. The water was calm, favouring their purpose. They let their ships glide close together, hull alongside hull; men spoke together there, saying that they would return to this land and fittingly avenge their kinsmen, lay waste Arthur's land and slay his people, seize castles and work their evil will.

So they journeyed thus across the sea for a long time until they were between England and Normandy. They changed course and sailed towards land so that they came directly to Totnes at the mouth of the Dart; with great joy they made for the shore. No sooner had they come ashore than they began to massacre the people; they drove off the peasants who were tilling the earth, and strung up the soldiers defending the land; they stabbed with knives all the married women, murderously slew all the young girls, and men of learning they laid upon burning coals; they clubbed to death all the servant boys. They razed the castles, laid waste the countryside, burned down the churches — there was devastation in the land! They drowned the suckling infants, they slaughtered all the livestock that they seized, bore it away to

to heore inne ladden   and suden and bradden;
al heo hit nomen   þat heo neh comen.

Alle dæi heo sungen   of Arður þan kinge,
and sæiden þat heo haueden   hames biwunnen   10470
þæ scolden heom ihalden   in heore onwalden,
and þer heo wolden wunien   wintres and sumeres.
And ʒif Arður weoren swa kene   þat he cumen wolde
to fihten wið Childrichen,   þan strongen and þan richen,
heo wolden of his rugge   makien ane brugge,   10475
and nimen þa ban alle   of aðele þan kinge
and teien heom togadere   mid guldene teʒen,
and leggen i þare halle dure   þer æch mon sculde uorð faren,
to wurðscipe Childriche,   þan strongen and þan riche.
þis wes al heore gome   for Arðures kinges sceome—   10480
ah al hit iwrað on oðer   sone þerafter;
heore ʒelp and heore gome   ilomp heomseoluen to scame.
And swa deð wel iwære,   þe mon þe swa ibereð!

Childric þe kaisere biwon   al þat he lokede on;
he nom Sumersete   and he nom Dorsete,   10485
and al Deuenescire,   þat volc al forferde;
and he Wiltunscire   mid wiðere igrætte;
he nom alle þa londes   into þære sæ-stronde.
þa, æt þan laste,   þa lette heo blawen
hornes and bemen   and bonnien his ferden,   10490
and forð he wolde buʒen   and Baðen al biliggen,
and æc Bristouwe   abuten birouwen—
þis was heore ibeot   ær heo to Baðe comen.

To Baðe com þe kæisere   and bilæi þene castel þere,
and þa men wiðinnen   ohtliche agunnen   10495
stepen uppen stanene wal,   wel iwepned oueral,
and wereden þa riche   wið þan stronge Childriche.
þer lai þe kaisere   and Colgrim his iuere,
and Baldulf his broðer,   and moni anoðer.
Arður wes bi norðe   and noht herof nuste;   10500
ferde ʒeond al Scotlond   and sette hit an his aʒere hond,
Orcaneie and Galeweie,   Man and Murene,
and alle þa londes   þe þerto læien.
Arður hit wende   to iwislichen þinge
þat Childric iliðen weore   to his aʒene londe   10505
and þat he naueremære   nolde cumen here.

their encampment and boiled or roasted it; all that they came upon they carried off.

All day long they sang songs about King Arthur, boasting how they had seized homesteads which they would keep in their possession and there they would dwell for evermore. And if Arthur were so bold that he would come to fight against the great and mighty Childric, they would make a bridge of his backbone, take all the bones of the noble king and bind them together with golden bands, and lay them in the doorway of the hall where all men must pass, to the greater glory of the mighty Childric. All this they cunningly devised to shame King Arthur — but it all turned out otherwise shortly thereafter; their boasting and their mockery brought shame upon themselves. And it is ever so with men who so behave!

The emperor Childric took possession of all he laid eyes on: he took Somerset and he took Dorset, and all Devonshire, slaughtering all the inhabitants, and he attacked Wiltshire with great ferocity; he seized all the counties as far as the coast. Then, after all this, he caused horns and trumpets to be blown and his army to assemble, intending to advance and encircle Bath completely, and also to blockade Bristol by ship — this they had vowed to do before they marched on Bath.

The emperor came to Bath and besieged the castle there, and the men within boldly mounted the ramparts, well armed from head to foot, and defended the city against the powerful Childric. The emperor encamped there with his ally Colgrim, and his brother Baldolf, and many others. Arthur was in the north and knew nothing of this; he marched through Scotland and took it all into his possession, Orkney and Galloway, Moray and the Isle of Man, and all the neighbouring regions. Arthur thought it a matter of certainty that Childric had sailed to his own land and that he would never come here again.

þa comen þa tidende   to Arthure kinge
þat Childric þa kæisere   icumen wes to londen,
and i þan suð ende   sorзen þer worhten.
þa Arður seide,   aðelest kingen: 10510
"Walawa, walawa,   þat ich sparede mine iua,
þat ich nauede on holte   mid hungere hine adefed, *
oðer mid sweorde   al hine toswungen!
Nu he me зilt mede   for mire god dede!
Ah, swa me hælpen Drihten   þæ scop þæs dæies lihten,   10515
þerfore he scal ibiden   bitterest alre baluwen,
harde gomenes   —his bone ich wulle iwurðen!
Colgrim and Baldulf   beiene ich wulle aquellen,
and al heore duзeðe   dæð scal iðolien.
Зif hit wule ivnnen   Waldende hæfnen,   10520
ich wulle wurðliche wreken   alle his wiðer-deden.
Зif me mot ilasten   þat lif a mire breosten,
and hit wulle me iunne   þat iscop mone and sunne,
ne scal nauere Childric   æft me bicharren!"
Nu cleopede Arður,   aðelest kingen: 10525
"Whar beo зe, mine cnihtes,   ohte men and wiðte?
To horse, to horse,   haleðes gode,
and we sculleð buзen   touward Baðe swiðe.
Leteð up fusen   heзe forken,
and bringeð her þa зæsles   biforen ure cnihtes,   10530
and heo scullen hongien   on hæзe treowen."
þer he lette fordon   feouwer and twenti childerren,
Alemainisce men   of swiðe heзe cunnen.
þa comen tidende   to Arðure þan kinge
þat seoc wes Howel his mæi   —þerfore he wes sari—   10535
i Clud ligginde. And þer he hine bilæfde,
hiзenliche swiðe   forð he gon liðe
þat he bihalues Baðe   beh to an uelde.
þer he alihte   and his cnihtes alle,
and on mid heore burnen   beornes sturne;   10540
and he a fif dæle   dælde his ferde.
þa he hafde al iset,   and al hit isemed,
þa dude he on his burne   ibroide of stele
þe makede on aluisc smið   mid aðelen his crafte;
he wes ihaten Wygar   þe Witeзe wurhte.   10545
His sconken he helede   mid hosen of stele.

Then the news reached King Arthur that the emperor Childric had landed and was wreaking havoc in the southern counties. Then said Arthur, noblest of kings:

'Alas, alas, that I spared my foe, that I did not starve him to death in the forest, or cut him to pieces with my sword! Now he rewards me for my good deed! But, so help me God who created the light of day, he shall suffer for it the most bitter affliction, harsh treatment — I will be his slayer! I will kill both Colgrim and Baldolf, and all their followers shall suffer death. If the Ruler of Heaven grants it, I will fittingly avenge all his wicked deeds. If life endures within me, and He who created sun and moon grants it, never again shall Childric deceive me!'

Then Arthur, noblest of kings, called out:

'Where are you, my knights, my brave and valiant men? To horse, to horse, good warriors, and we shall swiftly ride towards Bath. Let high gallows be set up, and fetch the hostages, and here before our warriors they shall hang on lofty beams.'

He had four and twenty German youths of the noblest rank put to death there.

Then news which saddened him came to King Arthur, that his kinsman Howel lay sick in Dumbarton. And there he left him, pressing onwards in great haste until he reached a plain close by Bath. There he and all his men dismounted, and the fearless warriors donned their coats of mail; and he divided his army into five companies. #

When he had ordered all things, and all was as it should be, then he put on his corslet of woven steel which an elvish smith had made by his noble skill; he who made Wygar was called Witeȝe. He protected his legs with hose of steel. At his side

Calibeorne his sweord   he sweinde bi his side;
hit wes iworht in Aualun   mid wiȝelefulle craften.
Halm he set on hafde   hæh of stele
þeron wes moni ȝimston,   al mid golde bigon;   10550
he wes Vðeres   þas aðelen kinges;
he wes ihaten Goswhit   —ælchen oðere vnilic!
He heng an his sweore   ænne sceld deore;
his nome wes on Bruttisc   Pridwen ihaten;
þer wes innen igrauen   mid rede golde stauen   10555
an onlicnes deore   of Drihtenes moder.
His spere he nom an honde   þa Ron wes ihaten.
þa he hafden al his iweden,   þa leop he on his steden.
þa he mihte bihalden,   þa bihalues stoden,
þene uæireste cniht   þe verde scolde leden.   10560
Ne isæh næuere na man   selere cniht nenne
þene him wes Arður,   aðelest cunnes!
    þa cleopede Arður   ludere stæfne:
"Lou war, her biforen us,   heðene hundes
þe sloȝen ure alderen   mid luðere heore craften,   10565
and heo us beoð on londe   læðest alre þinge!
Nu fusen we hom to   and stærcliche heom leggen on,
and wræken wunderliche   ure cun and ure riche,
and wreken þene muchele scome   þat heo us iscend habbeoð
þat heo ouer vðen   comen to Dertemuðen;   10570
and alle heo beoð forsworene   and alle heo beoð forlorene—
heo beoð fordemed alle   mid Drihtenes fulste.
Fuse we nu forðward   uaste tosomne,
æfne al swa softe   swa we nan ufel ne þohten.
And þenne we heom cumeð to,   miseolf ic wullen onfon   10575
an alre freomeste;   þat fiht ich wulle biginnen. *
Nu we scullen riden,   and ouer lond gliden;
and na man, bi his liue,   lude ne wurchen,
ah faren fæstliche   —Drihten us fulsten!"
    þa riden agon   Arður, þe riche mon,   10580
beh ouer wælde,   and Baðe wolde isechen.
þa tidende com to Childriche,   þan strongen and þan richen,
þat Arður mid ferde com,   al ȝaru to fihte.
Childric and his ohte men   leopen heom to horsen,
igripen heore wepnen   —heo wusten heom ifæied!   10585
þis isæh Arður,   aðelest kinge,

hung his sword Caliburn; it was made in Avalon by magic arts. Upon his head he placed a high helmet of steel on which were many jewels, all set in gold, and which had belonged to the noble King Uther; it was called Goswhit — there was no other like it! About his neck he slung a splendid shield whose name was Pridwen in the British tongue; on the inner side there was engraved in lines of red gold a noble likeness of the Mother of God. He took up his spear whose name was Ron. When he had all his war-gear on, then he leapt upon his horse. Then he who was present there might have seen the fairest knight who ever led an army. No man ever saw a better warrior than Arthur was, the noblest of his race! #

Then Arthur called out in ringing tones:

'Behold, here before us, the heathen dogs who slew our ancestors by their wicked stratagems, and who are to us the most hateful beings on earth! Now let us charge at them and attack them fiercely, and gloriously avenge our kinsmen and our realm, avenge the great shame with which they have dishonoured us by coming across the waves to Dartmouth; for they are all false to their pledge and are all doomed — with God's help they will all be destroyed. Let us advance now in close formation, yet very quietly as if intending no harm. And when we come within reach of them, I myself will engage first and foremost; I will begin the battle. Now we must ride, moving quietly forward; and let no man, upon his life, make a sound, but let us advance quickly — may the Lord help us!'

Then Arthur, the noble warrior, rode forward, advancing across the plain, and made towards Bath. The news came to the great and mighty Childric that Arthur was coming with his army, all ready for battle. Childric and his bold men leapt on their horses, seizing their weapons — they knew themselves to be the enemy! Arthur, noblest of kings, saw this; he saw a heathen earl

isæh he ænne hæðene eorl   hælden him toȝeines
mid seouen hundred cnihten,   al ȝærewe to fihten.
þe orl himseolf ferde   biforen al his genge,
and Arður himseolf arnde   biuoren al his ferde.   10590

    Arður þe ræie   Ron nom an honde,
he stræhte scaft stærcne,   stið-imoden king;
his hors he lette irnen   þat þa eorðe dunede;
sceld he braid on breosten   —þe king wes abolȝen!
He smat Borel þene eorl   þurhut þa breosten   10595
þat þæ heorte tochan,   and þe king cleopede anan:
"þe formeste is fæie   —nu fulsten us Drihte,
and þa hefenliche quene   þa Drihten akende."
þa cleopede Arður,   aðelest kinge:
"Nu heom to, nu heom to!   þat formest is wel idon!"   10600
    Bruttes hom leiden on   swa me scal a luðere don;
heo bittere swipen ȝefuen   mid axes and mid sweordes.
þer feolle Cheldriches men   fulle twa þusend,
swa neuere Arður ne les   næuere ænne of his!
þer weoren Sæxisce men   folken alre ærmest,   10605
and þa Alemainisce men   ȝeomerest alre leoden.
Arður mid his sweorde   fæiescipe wurhte;
al þat he smat to   hit wes sone fordon.
Al wæs þe king abolȝen   swa bið þe wilde bar
þenne he i þan mæste   monie swin imeteð.   10610
þis isæh Childric   and gon him to charren,
and beh him ouer Auene   to burȝen himseoluen.
And Arður him læc to   swa hit a liun weoren,
and fusde heom to flode   —monie þer weoren fæie!
þer sunken to þan grunde   fif and twenti hundred;   10615
þa al wes Auene stram   mid stele ibrugged!
Cheldric ouer þat water flæh   mid fiftene hundred cnihten;
þohte forð siðen   and ouer sæ liðen.
    Arður isæh Colgrim   climben to munten,
buȝen to þan hulle   þa ouer Baðen stondeð,   10620
and Baldulf beh him after   mid seoue þusend cnihtes;
heo þohten i þan hulle   hæhliche atstonden,
weorien heom mid wepnen   and Arður awæmmen.
þa isæh Arður,   aðelest kingen,
whar Colgrim atstod   and æc stal wrohte;   10625
þa clupede þe king   kenliche lude:

coming to oppose him with seven hundred warriors, all ready for battle. The earl in person led his whole company, and Arthur himself headed all his followers.

The bold Arthur took Ron in his hand, the valiant king advanced the stout shaft; he set his horse at a gallop so that the earth resounded; he raised his shield to his breast — the king was enraged! He pierced the earl Borel through the chest so that the heart was cleft, and at once the king called out:

'The leader is doomed — now may the Lord, and his mother the Queen of Heaven, assist us!'

Then Arthur, noblest of kings, called out:

'Now at them, at them now! The first blow is well struck!' #

The Britons fell upon them as one should on wicked men, giving bitter blows with swords and axes. Childric's men fell there, fully two thousand, yet Arthur lost not even one of his! Then the Saxons were the most wretched of all peoples, and the Germans the most miserable of all nations. Arthur wrought destruction with his sword; all those he struck at perished instantly. The king was consumed with rage as is the wild boar when he encounters herds of swine among the beechnuts. Childric saw this and turned to flee, retreating across the Avon to save himself. And Arthur pursued him like a lion, and drove them all into the river — many met their doom there! There five and twenty hundred sank to the bottom; then the river Avon was all bridged with steel! Childric fled across the river with fifteen hundred warriors, hoping to escape and sail across the sea.

Arthur saw Colgrim climbing the hillside, fleeing to the hill which stands above Bath, and Baldolf following him with seven thousand soldiers; they planned to resist stoutly on the hill, defend themselves with weapons and do Arthur injury. Then Arthur, noblest of kings, saw where Colgrim turned at bay and made a stand; and so the king called out very loudly:

"Balde mine þeines, buhȝeð to þan hulles!
For ȝerstendæi wes Colgrim monnen alre kenest;
nu him is al swa þere gat þer he þene hul wat,
hæh uppen hulle fehteð mid hornen 10630
þenne comeð þe wulf wilde touward hire winden.
Þeh þe wulf beon ane, buten ælc imane,
and þer weoren in ane loken fif hundred gaten,
þe wulf heom to iwiteð and alle heom abiteð.
Swa ich wulle nu, todæi, Colgrim al fordemen. 10635
Ich am wulf and he is gat —þe gume scal beon fæie!"
    Þa ȝet cleopede Arður, aðelest kingen:
"Ȝurstendæi wes Baldulf cnihten alre baldest;
nu he stant on hulle and Auene bihaldeð,
hu ligeð i þan stræme stelene fisces; 10640
mid sweorde bigeorede heore sund is awemmed;
heore scalen wleoteð swulc gold-faȝe sceldes; *
þer fleoteð heore spiten swulc hit spæren weoren.
Þis beoð seolcuðe þing isiȝen to þissen londe,
swulche deor an hulle, swulche fisces in wælle! 10645
    Ȝurstendæi wes þe kaisere kenest alre kingen,
nu he is bicumen hunte and hornes him fulieð;
flihð ouer bradne wæld, beorkeð his hundes.
He hafeð bihalues Baðen his huntinge bilæfued;
freom his deore he flicð and we hit scullen fallen, 10650
and his balde ibeot to nohte ibringen;
and swa we scullen bruken rihte biȝæten."
    Efne þan worde þa þe king seide,
he bræid hæȝe his sceld forn to his breosten,
he igrap his spere longe, his hors he gon spurie. 10655
Neh al swa swiðe swa þe fuȝel fliȝeð,
fuleden þan kinge fif and twenti þusend
whitere monnen, wode under wepnen,
hælden to hulle mid hæhȝere strengðe,
and uppen Colgrime smiten mid swiðe smærte biten. 10660
And Colgrim heom þer hente and feolde þa Bruttes to grunde,
i þan uormeste ræse fulle fif hundred.
Þat isæh Arður, aðelest kingen,
and wrað him iwræððed wunder ane swiðe;
and þus cleopien agon Arður, þe hæhȝe man: 10665
"War beo ȝe, Bruttes, balde mine beornes?

'Advance towards the hills, my bold warriors! For yesterday Colgrim was the bravest of men; now he is like the goat guarding the hilltop; high on the hillside it defends itself with its horns when the savage wolf comes slinking towards it. Though the wolf were alone, away from the pack, and there were five hundred goats in a single enclosure, the wolf will set upon them and savage them all. So now, this very day, will I destroy Colgrim utterly. I am the wolf and he is the goat — the man shall die!'

Then Arthur, noblest of kings, continued:

'Yesterday Baldolf was the boldest of warriors; now he stands on the hill and looks upon the Avon, sees how steel fish lie in the river trammelled with swords, their swimming impaired; their scales gleam as if they were gilded shields; their fins drift in the water like spears floating there. This is a marvellous thing come to pass in this land, such beasts on the hill, such fish in the water!

Yesterday the emperor was the boldest of all rulers; now he has become a hunter pursued by horns; he flees over the broad plain, his hounds barking. He has abandoned his hunting close by Bath; he is fleeing from his quarry and we shall put an end to his hunting, bring to naught his bold boasting; and so we shall regain our rightful possessions.'

As the king spoke these words, he raised his shield on high before his breast, grasped his long spear and spurred on his horse. Swiftly almost as the flight of a bird, five and twenty thousand brave men, armed and enraged, following the king, advanced upon the hill in great strength, and fell upon Colgrim with most bitter blows. And Colgrim engaged them there and felled the Britons to the ground, fully five hundred in the first onslaught. Arthur, noblest of kings, saw that, and grew furiously angry; and Arthur, the great leader, called out thus:

'Where are you, my Britons, my bold warriors? Here, before

Her stondeð us biuoren   vre ifan alle icoren;
gumen mine gode,   legge we heom to grunde."

Arður igrap his sweord riht   and he smat ænne Sexise cniht
þat þat sweord þat wes swa god   æt þan toþen atstod.   10670
And he smat enne oðer   þat wes þas cnihtes broðer,
þat his halm and his hæfd   halden to grunde.
þene þridde dunt he sone 3af   and enne cniht atwa clæf.
þa weoren Bruttes   swiðe ibalded, *
and leiden o þan Sæxen   læ3en swiðe stronge *   10675
mid heore speren longe   and mid sweoreden swiðe stronge.
Sexes þer uullen   and fæie-sih makeden,
bi hundred bi hundred   hælden to þan grunde;
bi þusund and bi þusend   þer feollen æuere in þene grund.
þa iseh Colgrim   wær Arður com touward him;   10680
ne mihte Colgrim for þan wæle   fleon a nare side.
þer fæht Baldulf   bisiden his broðer.
þa cleopede Arður   ludere stefne:
"Her ich cume, Colgrim;   to cuððen wit scullen ræchen.
Nu wit scullen þis lond dalen   swa þe bið alre laððest!"   10685
Æfne þan worde   þa þe king sæide,
his brode swærd he up ahof   and hærdliche adun sloh,
and smat Colgrimes hælm   þat he amidde toclæf,
and þere burne hod,   þat hit at þe breoste atstod.
And he sweinde touward Baldulfe   mid his swiðren honde   10690
and swipte þat hæfued of   forð mid þan helme.
þa loh Arður,   þe aðele king,
and þus 3eddien agon   mid gomenfulle worden:
"Lien nu þere Colgrim;   þu were iclumben ha3e;
and Baldulf þi broðer   lið bi þire side.   10695
Nu ich al þis kinelond   sette an eower ah3ere hond,
dales and dunes,   and al mi drihtliche uolc.
þu clumbe a þissen hulle   wunder ane hæ3e
swulc þu woldest to hæuene   —nu þu scalt to hælle!
þer þu miht kenne   muche of þine cunne.   10700
And gret þu þer Hengest,   þe cnihten wes fa3erest,
Ebissa and Ossa,   Octa, and of þine cunne ma,
and bide heom þer wunie   wintres and sumeres.
And we sculen on londe   libben in blisse,
bidden for eower saulen   þat sel ne wurðen heom nauære;   10705
and scullen her æuwer ban   biside Baðe ligen."

us, stand our enemies, most worthy opponents; let us strike them down, my good warriors.'

Arthur grasped his sword firmly and struck a Saxon warrior so that the sword, an excellent one, lodged in the teeth. And he struck another who was that warrior's brother, so that his helmet and his head fell to the ground. Instantly he delivered a third blow and cut a warrior in half. Then the Britons were greatly heartened, and inflicted very fierce strokes upon the Saxons with their long spears and their stout swords. Saxons fell there, met their doom, sank in their hundreds to the ground; thousands upon thousands without cease fell to earth there. Then Colgrim saw how Arthur was advancing upon him; and, because of the carnage, Colgrim could not flee in any direction. Baldolf fought at his brother's side there.

Then Arthur called out in a loud voice:
'I am coming now, Colgrim; we two shall contest the kingdom. We shall now divide this land between us in a way which will please you least!'
As the king spoke these words, he raised aloft his broad sword and brought it fiercely down, striking Colgrim's helmet so that he split it and the coif of mail beneath in half and the sword lodged in the chest. And he swung at Baldolf with his right hand and struck off his head along with the helmet.

Then the noble King Arthur laughed, and began to speak thus with mocking words:
'Now lie there Colgrim, you who had climbed so high, and your brother Baldolf shall lie by your side. I now entrust this whole kingdom to you in person, hills and dales, and all my worthy subjects. You climbed very high upon this hill as if you would climb up to heaven — now you shall sink down to hell! There you may meet many of your kinsmen. And greet Hengest there, who was the best of warriors, Ebissa, and Ossa, Octa, and others of your kin, and bid them remain there for evermore. And we shall live in this land well content, shall pray for your souls that no good ever come to them; and your bones shall lie here

Arður þe king cleopede   Cador þene kene—
of Cornwale he wes eorl;   þe cniht wes swiðe kene:
"Hercne me, Cador,   þu ært min aȝe cun.
Nu is Childric iuloȝen   and awæiward itohȝen;   10710
he þencheð mid isunde   aȝen cumen liðen. *
Ah nim of mire uerde   fif þusend monnen
and fareð forðrihtes   bi dæie and bi nihte
þat þu cume to þare sæ   biforen Childriche;
and al þat þu miht biwinnen,   bruc hit on wunnen.   10715
And ȝif þu miht þene kaisere   ufele aquellen þere, *
ich þe ȝifue to mede   al Doresete."
        Al swa þe aðele king   þas word hafede isæid,
Cador sprong to horse   swa spærc him doh of fure;
fulle seoue þusend   fuleden þan eorle.   10720
Cador þe kene   and muchel of his cunne
wenden ouer woldes   and ouer wildernes,
ouer dales and ouer dunes,   ouer deope wateres.
Cador cuðe þene wæi   þe toward his cunde læi;
an oueste he wende ful iwis   riht toward Toteneis   10725
dæies and nihtes;   he com þere forðrihtes
swa neuere Childric nuste   of his cume nane custe.
        Cador com to cuð̄ðe   biuoren Childriche,
and lette him fusen biforen   al þas londes folc,
cheorles ful ȝepe   mid clubben swiðe græte,   10730
mid spæren and mid græte waȝen   to þan ane icoren;
and duden heom alle clane   into þan scipen grunde,
and hæhte heom þere lutie wel   þat Childric of heom neore war;
and, þenne his folc come   and in wolden climben,
heore botten igripen   and ohtliche on smiten,   10735
mid heore waȝen and mid heore speren   murðren Childriches heren.
Al duden þa cheorles   swa Cador heom tæhte;
to þan scipen wenden   wiðerfulle cheorles,
in æuerælche scipe   oðer half hundred.
And Cador þe kene bæh   in toward ane wude hæh   10740
fif mile from þan stude   þær stoden þa scipen,
and hudde hine on wille   wunder ane stille.
        Childric com sone   ouer wald liðen;
walde to þan scipen fleon   and fusen of londen.
Sone swa Cador isæh,   þat wes þe kene eorl,   10745
þat Childric wes an eorðen   bitweonen him and þan cheorlen,

beside Bath.'

King Arthur called to the valiant Cador — he was the earl of Cornwall, a very brave knight:

'Listen to me, Cador, you who are my own kinsman. Childric has now fled and taken himself off, hoping to sail home in safety. But take five thousand men from my army and travel swiftly by night and day so that you reach the sea before Childric does; and all that you can seize, take it with pleasure. And if you can kill the evil emperor there, I will give you all Dorset as reward.'

No sooner had the noble king spoken these words than Cador sprang to horse as a spark does from the fire; seven thousand men all told followed the earl. The brave Cador and many of his kin travelled through woods and wildernesses, over hills and dales, across deep rivers. Cador knew the way which led to his own country; he travelled quickly and directly, both night and day, straight to Totnes, arriving there with such speed that Childric knew nothing whatsoever about his coming.

Cador reached the region before Childric, and had all the country people quickly brought before him, peasants of great shrewdness armed with very large clubs, with spears and large staves apt for his purpose; and he placed them, one and all, in the bottoms of the boats, ordering them to conceal themselves well there so that Childric would not be aware of them and, when his men arrived and wished to come aboard, to grasp their clubs and strike at them boldly, to butcher Childric's soldiers with their staves and their spears. The peasants did everything just as Cador had instructed them, went to the ships in defiant mood, a hundred and fifty peasants to each ship. And the bold Cador withdrew to a lofty wood five miles from the place where the ships rode, and stayed hidden for some time, keeping very quiet.

Soon Childric came, moving across the plain, meaning to flee to the ships and hasten from the land. As soon as Cador, who was a brave earl, saw that Childric was on the open ground

þa clupede Cador   ludere stefne:

"Wær beo ȝe, cnihtes,   ohte men and wihte?

Iþencheð what Arður   þe is ure aðele king

at Baðen us bisohte   ær we wenden from hirede.   10750

Leou war fuseð Childric,   and fleon wule of londe,

and þencheð to Alemaine   þer beoð his ældren,

and wule biȝiten ferde   and æft cumen hidere,

and wule faren hider in,   and þencheð awræken Colgrim

and Baldulf his broðer   þæ bi Baðen resteð.   10755

Ah no abide he næuere þære dæȝen   —ne scal he no ȝif we maȝen!"

Æfne þere spæche   þa spac þe eorl riche,

and onuest he gon riden   þe reh wes on moden.

Halden ut of wude-scaȝe   scalkes swiðe kene

and after Cheldriche,   þan strongen and þan richen.   10760

Cheldriches cnihtes   bisehȝen heom baften,

isehȝen ouer wolden   winden heore-mærken,

winnien ouer ueldes   fif þusend sceldes.

þa iwærð Childric   chærful an heorten;

and þas word sæide   þe riche kaisere: 10765

"þis is Arður þe king   þe alle us wule aquellen.

Fleo we nu biliue   and into scipen fusen,

and liðen forð mid watere,   ne recchen we nauere wudere."

þa Childric þe kaisere   þas word hæuede isæid,

þa gon he to fleonne   feondliche swiðe,   10770

and Cador þe kene   com him after sone.

Childric and his cnihtes   to scipe comen forðrihtes;

heo wenden þa scipen stronge   to scuuen from þan londe.

þæ cheorles mid heore botten   weoren þer wiðinnen;

þa botten heo up heouen   and adunriht sloȝen.   10775

þer wes sone islaȝen   moni cniht mid heore wahȝen;

wið heore picforcken   heo ualden heom to grunden.

Cador and his cnihtes   sloȝen heom baften.

þa isah Childric   þat heom ilomp liðerlic

þa al his folc mucle   feol to þan grunde!   10780

Nu isæh he þer bihalues   ænne swiðe mare hul;

þat water tið þerunder   þat Teine is ihaten;

þa hulle ihaten Teinnewic.   þiderward flæh Childric

swa swiðe swa he mihte   mid feouwer and twenti cnihten.

þa isæh Cador   hu hit þa uerde þer,   10785

þat þe kaisere flæh   and touwarde þæ hulle tæh;

between him and the peasants, then Cador called out in a loud voice:

'Where are you, knights, my bold and active men? Remember what Arthur, who is our noble king, asked of us at Bath before we separated from the army. See where Childric comes in haste, attempting to flee from the land, intending to go to Germany, the land of his forebears; he hopes to gather an army and return to this country, to re-enter it in order to avenge Colgrim and his brother Baldolf who lie buried near Bath. But he shall never live to see that day — not if we can help it!'

With these words which the noble earl spoke, he rode forward quickly, enraged at heart. Very bold warriors streamed from the thickets in pursuit of the great and mighty Childric. Childric's men looked behind them, saw battle-standards fluttering across the plain, five thousand shields coming across the fields. Then Childric's heart misgave him; and the mighty emperor spoke these words:

'There is King Arthur who will kill us all. Now let us flee with all haste and hurry aboard the ships, and sail away with the tide, not caring whither.'

When the emperor Childric had said these words, he took to flight in furious haste, and the brave Cador pursued him closely. Childric and his men made directly for the ships, intending to push out the sturdy vessels from the shore. The peasants, with their cudgels, were already on board; they raised their clubs aloft and brought them swinging down. Many a warrior was killed instantly by their clubs; with their pitchforks they thrust them to the ground. Cador and his knights fell on them from behind. When his vast army all lay slain, Childric knew they had met disaster there!

Then he saw there, close by, a very large hill, at whose foot flows the river called the Teign; the hill itself is called Teignwic. Childric, with twenty-four followers, fled towards it as fast as he could. Then Cador saw how things were going there, that the emperor had fled and was making for the hills; and Cador went

and Cador him after   swa swiðe swa he mahte,
and him to tuhte   and hine oftoc sone.
þa saide Cador,   þe eorl swiðe kene:
"Abid, abid, Childric!   ich wulle þe ȝefen Teinewic!"   10790
Cador his sweord anhof   and he Childric ofsloh.
Monie þe þer fluȝen   to þan watere heo tuhȝen;
inne Teine þan watere   þer heo forwurðen.
Al Cador acwælde   þat he quic funde;
and summe heo crupen into þan wude,   and alle he heom þer fordude.
þa Cador heom haueden alle ouercumen   and æc al þat lond inumen,
he sette grit swiðe god   þat þerafter longe stod;
þeh ælc mon beere an honde   behȝes of golde,
ne durste nauere gume nan   oðerne ufele igreten.
    Arður wes forð iwende   into Scotlonden   10800
for Howel lai inne Clud   faste biclused.
Hafden Scottes hine bilæien   mid luðere heore craften
and, ȝif Arður neore þe raðer icumen,   þenne weoren Houwel inumen,
and al his folc þer islaȝen   and idon of lif-daȝen.
Ah Arður com sone   mid selere strengðe,   10805
and Scottes to fleonne   feor of þan ærde,
into Muræine   mid mucle mon-weorede.
And Cador com to Scotlonde   þer he Arður ifunde.
Arður and Cador   into Clud ferden,
and funden þer Howel,   mid hahȝere blisse, an sel;   10810
of his seocnesse   isund wes iwurðen.
Muchel wes þa blisse   þæ þa wes in burȝe.
    Scottes weoren inne Mureine   and þer þeohten wunien;
and mid bolde heore worden   heore beot makeden,
and sæiden þat heo wolden   þa riche walden,   10815
and Arður þer abiden   mid baldere strenðe,
for ne durste nauere Arður   for his life come þer.
þa iherde Arður,   ærhðen bidæled,
whæt Scottes hafden isæid   mid heore hux-worden,
þa sæide Arður,   aðelest kingen: 10820
"Whær ært þu, Howel,   hæhst of mine cunne,
and Cador þe kene   ut of Cornwaile?
Leteð blæwen bemen   and bonnien ure ferden,
and to þere midnihte   we sculleð faren forðriht
toward Mureine   ure monscipe to bitellen.   10825
Ȝif hit wule Drihte   þe scop þæs daȝes lihten,

after him as quickly as he could, drew near to him and soon caught up with him. Then Cador, bravest of earls, said:

'Wait, Childric, wait! I will give you Teignwic!'

Cador raised his sword and slew Childric. Many who had retreated there fled to the river; there they perished in the river Teign. Cador killed all those he found alive; and some crept into the wood, and there he killed all those as well. When Cador had vanquished them all and seized all the land as well, he established a very secure peace which endured long thereafter; though men might wear bracelets of gold, no one dared treat another wrongfully. # #

Arthur had returned to Scotland, for Howel lay closely besieged in Dumbarton. The Scots, by means of their wicked stratagems, had surrounded him and, if Arthur had not come very quickly, Howel would have been captured and all his followers slain there, deprived of life. But Arthur came in time with a great power, and drove the Scots and their large army into Moray, far from their own country. And Cador came to Scotland and joined Arthur there. Arthur and Cador entered Dumbarton, and there, to their great joy, found Howel in good health; he had fully recovered from his illness. Great was the rejoicing in the town then.

The Scots were in Moray and intended to settle there; with bold words they made a vow, declaring that they would rule over the region, and await Arthur there with unflinching resolve, for Arthur would never dare come there for fear of his life. When Arthur, who was quite fearless, heard what the Scots had said in their derisive speeches, then Arthur, noblest of kings, said:

'Where are you, Howel, noblest of my kin, and bold Cador of Cornwall? Let trumpets be blown and our armies assembled, and at midnight we shall set out immediately for Moray to defend our honour. If the Lord, who created the light of day, grants it,

we heom sculle tellen   sorhfulle spelles,
heore ӡælp fellen   and heomseolue aquellen."
    To þere midnihte   Arður aras forðriht;
hornes me gon blawen   mid hahӡere stafnen,   10830
cnihtes gunnen arisen   and ræhӡe word speken.
Mid muche mon-weorede   into Mureine
forð gunnen þræsten,   þreottene þusend *
a feormeste flocke   feondliche kene men.
Seoðen com Cador,   þe eorl of Cornwæille,   10835
mid seouentene þusen   selere þeinen.
Seoððen com Heowel   mid his kempen swiðe wel,
mid an and twenti þusen,   mid aðelere kempen.
Seoððen com Arður,   aðelest kingen,
mid seouen and twenti þusend   siӡen heom afterward;   10840
sceldes þer cliseden,   lihten hit gon dæӡen.
    þat word com to Scotten   þær þar heo wuneden,
hu Arður þe king   com touward heore londe
feondliche swiðe   mid vnimete folke.
þa weoren ærhest   þat ær weoren baldest,   10845
and gunnen to fleonnen   feondliche swiðe
into þan watere   þer wunderes beoð inoӡe.
þat is a seolcuð mere   iset a middel-ærde
mid fenne and mid ræode,   mid watere swiðe bræde,
mid fiscen and mid feoӡelen,   mid uniuele þingen.   10850
þat water is unimete brade   —nikeres þer baðieð inne;
þer is æluene ploӡe   in atteliche pole.
    Sixti æitlondes   beoð i þan watere longe;
in ælc of þan æitlonde   is a clude hæh and strong;
þer næstieð arnes   and oðere græte uoӡeles.   10855
þe ærnes habbeoð ane laӡe,   bi æuerælches kinges dahӡen;
whænneswa æi ferde   fundeð to þan ærde,
þeonne fleoð þa fuӡeles   feor i þan lufte,
moni hundred þusen,   and muchel feoht makieð;
þenne is þat folc buten wene   þat reouðe heom is to cumene   10860
of summes cunnes leoden   þe þat lond wulleð isechen.
Tweien dæӡes oðer þreo   þus scal þis taken beo
ær unkuðe men   to þan londe liðen.
    Ӡet þer is sellic   to suggen of þan watere.
þer walleð in þan mæren   a moniare siden, *   10865
of dalen and of dunen   and of bæchen deopen,

we shall tell them stories full of sorrow, put an end to their boasting and destroy them all.'

At midnight the king promptly arose; loud notes were sounded upon horns, warriors sprang up, uttering fierce words. They pressed on into Moray with a great power, thirteen thousand most resolute men in the first company. Next came Cador, the earl of Cornwall, with seventeen thousand valiant soldiers. Then came Howel with his brave warriors, with twenty-one thousand excellent fighters. Last came Arthur, noblest of kings, marching behind them with twenty-seven thousand men, their shields glistening as day dawned.

News of this came to the Scots where they were, that King Arthur was marching in furious haste towards their land with a vast army. Then those who were formerly very bold were now the most cowardly, and began to flee in the greatest haste into that expanse of water where marvels abound. That loch, set in this mortal world, with marsh and reeds, with very broad waters, with fish and birds, with many other creatures, is a wondrous one. That lake is immensely wide — in it water-monsters bathe; there is sport of elves in that fearsome pool.

There are sixty islands in that stretch of water; on each island is a rocky peak, tall and massive, where eagles and other large birds make their nests. In the reign of each and every king, the eagles have a habit that whenever any army ventures into that land the birds fly high into the sky, hundreds of thousands of them, and set up a great squabbling; then the inhabitants are certain that calamity is to come upon them from some nation or other which intends to invade that land. This omen shall recur for two or three days before foreigners come to the land. #

There is yet another marvel to tell of that loch. There flow into that mere on many sides, from hills and dales, from deep

sixti wateres,   alle þer isomned;

swa neuere ut of þan mære   na man no uindeð

þat þer ut wenden,   buten an an ænde

an imetliche broc   þe of þan mere ualleð   10870

and swiðe isemeliche   into sæ wendeð.

    Þa Scottes weoren todeled   mid muclen vniselen

ȝeond þa monie munten   þa i þan watere weoren.

Arður biseohte scipen   and gon heom to wenden

and sloh þer vniuoȝe,   moni and inoȝe;   10875

and moni þusend þer wes dæd   for heom trukede ælc bræd.

Arður þe aðele   was an æst side,

Howel þe sele   wes a suð halue,

and Cador þe kene   bi norðen heom biwusten;

and his smale uolc   he setten alle bi weste siden.   10880

Þa weoren Scottes   ihalden for sottes

þer heo leien   ȝeond þa cliues, faste biclused;

þer weoren sixti þusend   mid sorreȝe forfarene.

    Þa wes Irlondes king   icume into hafene,

twalf milen from Arðure   þer he lai mid ferde,   10885

Scotten to hælpen   Howel to forfarene.

Þis iherden Arður,   aðelest kinge,

and nom his ane ferde   and þiderward fusden,

and funde þene king Gillomar   þe icumen wes to londe þar.

Arður him faht wið   and nolde him ȝiuen na grið,   10890

and feolde Irisce men   feondliche to grunden;

and Gillomar mid twalf scipen   teh from þan londe

and ferde to Irlonde   mid harme swiðe stronge.

And Arður a þan londe   sloh al þat he uunde;

and seoððen he wende to þan mere   þer he his mæi lette,   10895

Howel þene hende,   hahst of Brutlonde

wiðuten Arðure,   aðelest kingen.

    Arður Howel uunde   þer he wes bi hauene,

bi þan mere brade   þer he abiden hafde.

Þa fainede swiðe   folc an hirede   10900

of Arðures cume   and of aðele his dede.

Þer wes Arður forðriht   twei dæies and twa niht;

Scottes leie ȝeond clude,   moni þusend dede,

mid hungere foruarene,   folkene alre ærmest.

I þan þridde dæiȝe   faire hit gon daȝiȝen;   10905

þa tuȝen touward hirede   alle þat weoren ihadded;

valleys, sixty streams, all mingled there; yet no one knows of any there which flow out of the lake, save at one place a stream of moderate size which runs out of the lake and wends its way calmly to the sea.

The Scots, in dire straits, were scattered among the many mountains which were in the water. Arthur obtained ships and went after them and slew a great many there, a vast number; and many thousands perished there for lack of food. The noble Arthur was on the eastern side, the brave Howel on the southern side, and the valiant Cador hemmed them in on the north; and he had stationed his lesser thanes all along the western shores. Then they looked with contempt at the Scots where they lay, closely surrounded, among the rocky peaks; sixty thousand perished there in misery.

In the meantime the king of Ireland, hoping to help the Scots in destroying Howel, had landed at a harbour twelve miles from where Arthur lay with his army. Arthur, noblest of kings, heard of this and took one of his companies and hastened thither, and confronted King Gillomar who had come ashore there. Arthur fought with him and would show him no mercy, and in fury felled the Irishmen to the ground; and Gillomar withdrew from that land with twelve ships and returned to Ireland in sorry state. And Arthur slew all those he came upon on shore; and then he returned to the loch where he had left his kinsman, the gracious Howel, the greatest man in Britain save for Arthur, the noblest of kings. #

Arthur rejoined Howel near the harbour, beside the broad loch where he had remained. Then the soldiers of his army rejoiced greatly at Arthur's return and at his noble deeds. Two days and two nights Arthur remained there; the Scots lay scattered among the rocky peaks, many thousands of them dead, destroyed by hunger, the most wretched of mortals. On the third day it dawned fair; then all those who were in holy orders came to the army;

and þreo biscopes wise,   a boke wel ilæred,
preostes and muneckes   vnimete monie,
canones þer comen,   monie and wel idone,
mid alle þan halidomen   þa hahst an londe weoren,   10910
and ȝeornden Arðures grið   and his aðmeden.

  Þider þa wifes comen   þa i þan londen wuneden;
heo wæiden in hære ærmen   heore children ærmen.
Heo weopen on Arðure   wunder ane swiðe,
and heore uæx fæire   wælden to volde;   10915
curuen heore lockes   and þer niðer læiden
to þas kinges foten   biforen al his duȝeðen;
nailes to heore nebbe   þat æfter hit bledde;
neh þan alle clæne   nakede heo weoren.

  Sorhliche heo gunnen clupien   to Arðure þan kinge   10920
and summe þus iseiden,   þer heo on sið weoren: *
"King, we beoð on ærde   ærmest alre uolke.
We ȝeorneð þine milzce   þurh þæne milde Godd.
Þu hauest a þisse londe   ure leoden aslæȝen
mid hungere and mid hete,   mid feole cunne hærmen, *   10925
mid wapnen, mid wæteren,   mid feole wan-siðen,
vre children imaked faderlese   and frofre bidæled.

  Þu ært Cristine mon   and we alswa sunden;
Sæxisce men beoð   hæðene hundes.
Heo comen to þisse londe   and þis folc here aqualden.   10930
Ȝif we heom hereden,   þat was for ure hermen,
for we nefden nænne mon   þe us wið heom mihten griðien.
Heo us duden swiðe wa   and þu us dest al swa;
þa heðene us hatieð   and þe Cristine us sari makieð!
Wær scullen we bicumen?"   queðen þa wif to þan kinge.   10935
"Aȝef us ȝet þa quicke men   þa liggeð ȝeond þas cluden;
and ȝif þu ȝiuest milze   þisse moncunnen,
þi monscipe bið þa mare,   nu and æueremære.
Lauerd Arður, ure king,   leoðe vre benden.
Þu hafust al þis lond inomen   and al þis folc ouercumen;   10940
we beoð under uote   —a þe is al þa bote."

  Þis iherde Arður,   aðelest kingen,
þesne wop and þesne rop,   and reouðen vniuoȝe.
Þa toc he to ræde   and reosede on heorte;
he uunde on his ræde   to don þat heo hine beden.   10945
He ȝæf heom lif, he ȝef heom lumen,   and heore lond to halden.

three wise bishops, well versed in the scriptures, priests and monks in great numbers, canons, numerous and well educated, came there with all the sacred relics, the most precious in the land, and entreated Arthur's pardon and his mercy.

The women who dwelt in that country came there, carrying their poor children in their arms. In Arthur's presence they shed many a tear, cast their lovely hair upon the ground, tore their locks and threw them down there at the king's feet in the presence of all his nobles; they tore their faces with their nails and made them bleed; they were almost entirely naked.

In their grief they began to address King Arthur and some, in their distress, spoke as follows:

'O king, we are the most wretched of all people on earth. We entreat your forgiveness in the name of the merciful God. You have destroyed our people in this land by hunger and violence, by cruelties of many kinds, by force of arms and by drowning, by many other oppressions; you have made our children fatherless and left them comfortless.

You are a Christian and so, too, are we; the Saxons are heathen dogs. They came to this land and slaughtered the people here. If we submitted to them, that was due to our misfortune, that we had no one who could defend us against them. They caused us great distress and so, likewise, do you; the heathens hate us and the Christians cause us grief! What is to become of us?' said the women to the king. 'But restore to us the men still alive who lie among these crags; and if you show mercy to this nation, your honour shall be the greater, now and for evermore. Lord Arthur, our king, free us from bondage. You have seized this whole land and subdued all the people; we are at your mercy — our relief is wholly in your hands.'

Arthur, noblest of kings, heard this, this weeping and lamentation, and this violent grief. Then he took thought and pitied them in his heart; he found it in his heart to do what they begged him. He granted them life and limb, and possession of

He lette blæwen bemen   and þa Scottes bæcnien,
and heo ut of cluden   to þan scipen comen,
an auerælchen siden   siȝen touward londe;
heo weoren swiðe iharmede   mid scærpen þan hungre.   10950
Aðes heo sworen   swiken þat nalden,
and heo þa iȝefuen   ȝisles þan kingen;
and alle ful sone   þas kinges men bicomen.
And seoððen heo gunnen fusen;   þat folc þer todelden,
ælc mon to þan ende   þer he wes wuniende.   10955
And Arður þer grið sette,   god mid þan bezste.
     "Whær ært þu, Howel, mi mæi,   monne me leofest?
Isixst þu þisne muchelne mære   þer Scottes beoð amærred?
Isihst þu þas hæhȝe treon,   and sihst þu þas ærnes teon?
Inne þisse uenne   is fisc unimete.   10960
Isihst þu þas æitlondes   þe ȝeond þas watere stondeð?"
Seollic þuhte Howel   of swulchere isihðe,
and wondrede wide   bi þan watere flode;
and þus þer cleopede Howel   hæhes cunnes:
"Seoððen ich wes mon iboren   of mire moder bosme   10965
no isah ich a none londe   þus seolcuðe þinges
swa ich here biuoren me   mid æȝenen bihælde."
Wundreden Bruttes   wunder ane swiðe.
     Þa cleopede Arður,   aðelest kingen:
"Howel, min aȝe mæi,   monnen me leofest,   10970
lust mire worden   of mucle mære wunder
þat ic þe wulle tellen   of soðe mine spellen.
Bi þisse mære enden,   þer þis water wendeð,
is an lutel wiht mære,   monnen to wundre.
He is endlonge   feouwer and sixti munden;   10975
he is imeten a bræde   fif and twenti foten;
fif foten he is deop   —alfene hine dulfen!
Feower-noked he is,   and þerinne is feower kunnes fisc,
and ælc fisc an his ende   þer he his cun findeð;
ne mai þer nan to oðere   buten al swa tacheð his icunde.   10980
Nes næuer nan mon iboren,   ne of swa wise crafte icoren,
no libbe he swa longe,   þe maȝen hit vnderstonde,
what letteð þene fisc   to uleoten to þan oðere,
for nis þer noht bitwenen   buten water clæne!"
     Þa ȝet cleopede Arður,   aðelest kingen: 10985
"Howel, i þissen londes ænde,   neh þere sæ-stronde,

their own land. He caused trumpets to be blown, summoning the Scots, and they came from the crags towards the ships, approaching the shore from every direction; keen hunger had greatly weakened them. They swore oaths that they would not act treacherously, and they then gave hostages to the king; there and then they became the king's subjects. And then they hastened away; the people dispersed, each man to that region where he had his home. And Arthur established there a firm and lasting peace.

[Then Arthur said:] 'Where are you, Howel, my kinsman, dearest of men to me? Do you see this great loch where the Scots perished? Do you see these lofty trees, and these eagles flying? In this marshy lake are countless fish. Do you see these islands which lie throughout the lake?'

Such a sight seemed marvellous to Howel, and he was greatly amazed at the expanse of water; and then the high-born Howel exclaimed thus:

'Since I was born of my mother's womb I have not seen such wondrous things in any land as I now see with my own eyes here before me.'

The Britons marvelled very greatly indeed.

Then Arthur, noblest of kings, said:

'Howel, my own kinsman, dearest of men to me, listen to my tale of a much greater marvel, about which I will tell you truthfully in my own words. At the end of this loch, where the water flows out, is a certain small lake, a marvel to men. It is four and sixty spans in length; in breadth it measures five and twenty feet; it is five feet deep — elves dug it! It is four-cornered, and in it are four kinds of fish, each species in its own region where it finds its own kind; and one species may not mingle with another save as its nature dictates. No man has ever been born so excelling in wisdom, nor shall any live so long, as to be able to comprehend it, to understand what prevents one species swimming towards another, for there is nothing between them except clear water!'

Then Arthur, noblest of kings, continued:

is a mære swiðe muchel   —þat water is unfæle!
And whænne þa sæ vledeð   swulc heo wulle aweden
and falleð inne þene mære   vnimete swiðe,
no bið næuere þæ mere   on watere þa mare.   10990
Ah þenne þa sæ falleð in   and scen warð þa uolden,
and heo bið al inne   in alden hire denne,
þenne swelleð þe mære   and swærkeð þa vðen;
vðen þer leppeoð ut   vnimete grete,
fleoð ut a þat lond   þat leoden agriseð an hond.   10995
Ʒif þer cumeð æi mon   þat noht ne cunne þeron
þat seollic to iseonne   bi þere sæ-stronde,
ʒif he his neb wendeð   touwærd þan mære,
ne beo he noht swa loh iboren,   ful wel he beoð iborʒen;
þat water him glit bisiden   and þe mon þer wuneð softe,   11000
after his iwille;   he wuneð þer uul stille
þat no bið he for þan watere   naðing idracched."
Þa sæide Howel,   hæh mon of Brutten:
"Nu ic ihere tellen   seolcuðe spellen,
and seollic is þe lauerd   þat al hit isette!"   11005
    Þa cleopede Arður,   aðelest kingen:
"Blaweð mine hornes   mid hæhʒere stæfne
and suggeð mine cnihtes   þat ic fare forðrihte."
Bemen þer blewen,   hornes þer stureden,
blisse wes an hirede   mid bisie þan kinge;   11010
for ælc wes ifreoured,   and ferde toward his ærd.
And þe king forbæd heom,   bi heore bare liuen,
þat na mon on worlde   swa wod no iwurðe
no swa ærwitte gume   þat his grið bræke;
and ʒif hit dude æi mon   he sculden dom ðolien.   11015
Æfne þan worde   fusde þa uærde.
Þer sungen beornes   seolcuðe leoðes
of Arðure þan kinge   and of his here-þringen,
and sæiden on songe   to þisse worlde longe
neore neueremære swulc king   ase Arður þurh alle þing,   11020
king no kæisere   in næuere nare kuðæ!
    Arður forð to Eouuerwic   mid folke swiðe seollic,
and wunede þer wiken sixe   mid muchelere wunne.
Þa burh-walles weoren   tobroken and tofallen
þat Childric al forbarnden,   and þa hallen alle clæne.   11025
Þa cleopede þe king   Piram, ænne preost mæren;

'At the edge of this region, Howel, near the seashore, is a very large lake — its waters are evil! And when the sea rises as if in rage and pours into the lake with great force, there is, nonetheless, no more water in the lake than before. But when the sea recedes and the shore is left clear, and the waters are all back in their former bed, then the lake swells and the waves grow dark; enormous great waves spring up there, flood out over the land so that the people close by are terrified. If anyone comes there who knows nothing about it, comes to see that marvellous sight near the seashore, if he faces towards the lake he is fully protected, however low-born he may be; the water flows past him and the man remains at his ease there, just as he wishes; he stands there very calmly so that he is in no way harmed by the water.'

Then Howel, the ruler of Brittany, said:

'Wondrous tales I now hear tell, and wonderful is the Lord who created all this!' #

Then Arthur, noblest of kings, called out:

'Sound my horns with loud noise and tell my warriors that I set forth at once.'

There trumpets blew, horns were sounded, there was joy among the court with the king so active; for all were cheered, and set out for their homeland. And the king commanded them, on pain of death, that no one whatsoever should be so mad or so foolish a mortal as to break his peace; and if any man did so, he should suffer punishment. On this command the army set out. The soldiers sang wonderful songs of Arthur the king and his warrior host, proclaiming in song that to the end of the world there would never again be such a king in every respect as Arthur was, never such a king or emperor in any land!

Arthur journeyed to York with a splendid army, and remained there in great contentment for six weeks. The walls of the city, which Childric had completely burnt, had collapsed and fallen in, and the halls were utterly destroyed. Then the king summoned Priam, a famous priest; he was a very wise man and well read

he wes swiðe wis mon   and witful on bocken.
"Piram, þu ært min aȝe preost   —þe æð þe scal iwurðen!"
þe king nom ane rode,   hali and swiðe gode,
and bitok Piram an hond,   and þermid swiðe muchel lond;   11030
and þene ærchebiscopes staf   þer he Piram aȝaf.
"Ær wes Piram preost god;   nu he is ærchebiscop!"
      þa hæhte hine Arður,   aðelest kingen,
þat he rærde churechen   and þa songes rihten,
and Goddes folc biwusten   and fæire heom dihten.   11035
And he hæhte alle cnihtes   demen rihte domes,
and þa eorðe-tilien   teon to heore cræften,
and æuerælcne gume   oðerne igræten.
And wulc mon swa wurs dude   þene þe king hafde iboden
he wolde hine ifusen   to ane bare walme;   11040
and ȝif hit weore læð mon,   he sculde hongie for þon.
      þa ȝet cleopede Arður,   aðelest kingen,
hæhte þat alc mon   þe his lond hafde forgan,
mid wulches cunnes wite   swa he biwæiued weore,
þat he aȝain come   ful raðe and ful sone,   11045
þe riche and þe laȝe,   and hefde æft his aȝen—
bute he weore swa fule biwite   þat he weore lauerd-swike,
oðer touward his lauerd man-swore,   þene þe king demde forlore.
      þer come þreo ibroðeren   þe weore kiniborne,
Lot and Angel and Vrien,   welle hwulche þreo men.   11050
þeos here-þringes þreo   comen to þan kinge,
and setten an heore cneowen   biforen þan kæisere.
"Hal seo þu, Arður,   aðelest kingen,
and þi duȝeðe mid þe;   a mote heo wel beo.
We sundeð þreo broðeren,   iboren of kingen;   11055
is al ure icunde lond   igan ut of ure hond,
for habbeoð hæðene men   us hene imakede,
and iwæst us al Leonæis,   Scotlond and Muræf.
And we biddeð þe, for Godes luue,   þat þu us beo fultume
and, for þire mucle wurðscipe,   þat þu us wurðe milde;   11060
aȝif us ure icunde lond   and we þe sculleð luuien,
hælden þe for lauerd   an ælche leod-wisen."
      þis iherde Arður,   aðelest king,
hu þeos þreo cnihtes   fæire hine bisohten;
reousede on heorte   and he reordien gan,   11065
and þas word sæide   selest alre kinge:

in the scriptures.

'Priam, you are my own priest — the better shall it be for you!'

The king took a holy crucifix of great worth, and gave it into Priam's keeping, and much land along with it; and there he gave Priam the archbishop's staff.

'Until now Priam was a good priest; now he is archbishop!' #

Then Arthur, noblest of kings, exhorted him to build churches and to restore the singing there, and to care for God's people and instruct them properly. And he ordered all the knights to render true justice, and the farmers to follow their calling, and all men to respect each other. And whoever behaved less well than the king had commanded should be instantly condemned to death by burning; and if it were someone base, he should hang for it.

Then Arthur, noblest of kings, spoke further, proclaiming that every man who had forfeited his land, no matter what penalty had caused his expulsion, should instantly return without any delay, whether great or humble, and possess his own land again — unless he were so corrupt as to be a traitor to his lord, or a perjurer, whom the king judged beyond pardon.

There came three brothers who were royally born, Lot and Angel and Urien, three excellent men. These three warriors came before the king, and fell to their knees before the sovereign.

'Health to you, Arthur, noblest of kings, and to your followers also; may they prosper always. We are three brothers, descended from kings; we have been dispossessed of all our rightful lands, for heathen men have brought us low, and laid waste around us all Lothian, Scotland and Moray. And we entreat you, for the love of God, that you aid us and, for your greater glory, be merciful to us; restore to us our rightful lands and we shall honour you, obey you as our liegelord in all due respects.'

Arthur, noblest of kings, heard this, heard how these three knights appealed to him courteously; touched at heart, he began to speak; the best of all kings pronounced these words:

"Vrien, bicum mi mon;   þu scalt to Muræiue aȝæn;
þerof þu scalt beon icleoped   king of þan londe
and hæh an mine hirede   mid þine mon-weorede.
And Angele ich sette an hond   al togadere Scotland;   11070
habbe hit an honde   and beon king of þan londe;
from þan fader to þan sune   þerof þu scalt mi mon bicumen.
And þu, Lot, mi leofe freond,   Godd þe wurðe liðe;
þu hauest mine suster to wiue   —þæ bet þe scal iwurðe.
Ich þe ȝifue Loenæis   þat is a lond faier.   11075
And ich wulle leggen þerto   londes swiðe gode
biside þere Humbre   wurð an hundred punden.
For mi fader, Vðer,   þe while þe he wes king here,
lufede wel his dohter,   þe wes his bæd-iþohte. *
And heo is mi suster   and haueð sunen tweien;   11080
þeo me beoð on londe   children alre leofest."
þus spæc Arður þe king.   þa wes Wolwain lute child;
swa ves þe oðer,   Modræd his broðer.
Wale þat Modræd wes ibore   —muchel hærm com þerfore!
    Arður for to Lundene   and mid him his leoden.   11085
He heold inne londe   ane muchele hustinge
and sette alle þa laȝen   þat stoden bi his ælderne daȝen,
alle þa laȝen gode   þe her ær stoden.
He sette grið, he sette frið,   and alle freodomes.
    þenene he for to Cornwale,   to Cadores riche;   11090
he funde þer a mæide   vnimete fæier.
Wes þas mæidenes moder   of Romanisce mannen,
Cadores maȝe,   and þat maide him bitahte;
and he heo fæire afeng   and softe heo fedde.
Heo wes of heȝe cunne   of Romanisce monnen;   11095
næs in nane londe   maide nan swa hende
of speche and of dede,   and of tuhtle swiðe gode;
heo wes ihaten Wenhauer,   wifmonne hendest.
Arður heo nom to wife   and luuede heo wunder swiðe;
þis maiden he gon wedde   and nom heo to his bedde.   11100
Arður wes i Cornwale   al þene winter þere,
and al for Wenhæuere lufe,   wimmonne him leofuest.
    þa þe winter wes agan   and sumer com þer anan,
Arður hine biþohte   whæt he don mahte
þat his folc gode   aswunden ne læie þere.   11105
He ferde to Æxchæstræn   to þan mid-festen,

'Urien, you shall become my liegeman; you shall return to
Moray and be declared king of that land and hold high rank in my
army along with your followers.   And to Angel I entrust the
whole of Scotland; take it into your control and be king of that
land; you and your descendants shall be my liegemen there.   And
you, Lot, my dear friend, may God be gracious to you; you have
my sister as your wife — the better shall it be for you.   Upon you
I bestow Lothian which is a very beautiful region. And I will add
to it very good lands bordering the Humber, worth a hundred
pounds. For my father, Uther, while he was king here, loved well
his daughter, who was the object of his prayers.   And she is my
sister and has two sons who are to me the dearest children in the
world.'

Thus spoke Arthur the king.   At that time Gawain was a
small child; so was the other boy, his brother Modred.   Alas that
Modred was ever born — great harm came of it! #

Arthur went to London and his followers with him.   He held
a great assembly in the kingdom and confirmed all the laws which
had existed in the days of his ancestors, all the good laws which
once existed here.   He established law and order and confirmed all
rights and privileges.

From there he went to Cornwall, to the realm of Cador; there
he met with a maiden of exceeding beauty.   The mother of the
maiden was of Roman stock, a kinswoman of Cador; and she had
entrusted the girl to him, and he had received her courteously and
nurtured her tenderly.   She came of a noble Roman family; in no
land was there a maid so gracious in speech and behaviour, and so
refined in bearing; the most gracious of women, she was called
Guenevere. Arthur took her to wife and loved her very deeply; he
wedded this maiden and took her to his bed.   Arthur was there in
Cornwall all winter long, and all for love of Guenevere, to him the
dearest of women.

When the winter had passed and summer came again, Arthur
considered what he could do so that his splendid army should not
lie idle there.   At mid-Lent he marched to Exeter, and held

and heold þer his hustinge   of hehȝen his folke,
and seide þat he wolde   into Irlonde,
wenden al þat kinelond   to his æhȝere hond.
Buten þe king Gillomar   to him raþer come ær,   11110
and mid listen him speken wið,   and ȝirnde Arðures grið,
he wolde westen his lond   and luðere him gon an hond,
mid fure, mid stele   streit gomen wurchen,
and þat lond-folc aslæn   þe wolde stonden him aȝein.

      Æfne þan worde   þa þe king sæide,   11115
þa andswarede þat folc   fæire þan kinge:
"Lauerd king, hald þi word;   we beoð alle ȝarewe
to ganne and to ride   oueral to þire neode."

      Þer wes moni bald Brut   þe hafde beres leches,
heouen up heore bruwen,   iburst an heore þonke.   11120
Wenden touwarde innen   cnihtes mid heore monnen;
heo ruokeden burnen,   bonneden helmes; *
heo wipeden hors leoue   mid linene claðe,
heo sceren, heo scoiden   —scalkes balde weoren.
Sum scæft horn, sum scaft ban,   sum ȝarked stelene flan,   11125
sum makede þwonges,   gode and swiðe strong;
summe beoveden speren   and beonneden sceldes. * *
Arður letten beoden   ȝeond al his kineþeoden
þat æuerælc god cniht   to him come forðriht,
and euerælc oht mon   comen forðriht anan.   11130
And waswa bilæfden   his leomen he sculde leosen,
and whaswa come gladliche,   he sculden wurðe riche.

      Seouen niht uppen Æstre,   þa men hafden iuast,
þa comen alle þa cnihtes   to scipen forðrihtes;
wind heom stod an honde   þe scaf heom to Irlonde.   11135
Arður a þet lond ferde   and þa leoden amerden;
muchel uolc he asloȝ,   orf he nom vniuoh;
and æuere he hæhte ælcne mon   chireche-grið halden.

      Þet tidinde com to þan kinge   þe lauerd wes of þan londe
þat þer wes icumen Arður   and ærmþen iwrohte þer.   11140
He sumnede al his leoden   ȝeond his kinelonde,
and his Irisce uolc   fusden to fehte
toȝæines Arðure,   þan aðele kinge.
Arður and his cnihtes   heom wepnede forðrihtes
and foren heom toȝeines,   folc vnimete.   11145
Arðures men weoren   mid wepnen al biþehte;

there his assembly of his noble followers, and announced that he would go into Ireland and take that whole kingdom under his own control. Unless King Gillomar came to him first and in all haste, and spoke with him willingly, entreating Arthur's mercy, he would lay waste his land and deal mercilessly with him, playing rough games with fire and with steel, and slaying those inhabitants who sought to resist him. # #

To these words which the king spoke, the people responded readily, saying to the king:

'Lord king, do as you have declared; we all are ready to march and ride wherever you require.'

Many a bold Briton there had a bear-like look, wrinkling their brows, enraged at heart. Knights went to their quarters with their followers; they cleaned coats of mail, made ready their helmets; they rubbed down fine horses with linen cloths, they clipped them, they shod them — the men were skilled. Some shaved horn, some scraped bone, some prepared steel arrows, some made thongs, stout and very strong; some prepared spears and gathered shields together. Arthur had it proclaimed throughout all his kingdom that every good warrior should come to him directly, every brave man come at once without delay. And whoever stayed away should suffer mutilation; and whoever came willingly, he should become rich.

Seven days after Easter, when men had fasted, all the soldiers then immediately took ship; the wind favoured them and bore them to Ireland. Arthur marched into that country and attacked the inhabitants; he killed many people, seized innumerable cattle; but he always ordered everyone to respect the right of sanctuary.#

The news came to the king who was ruler of that land that Arthur had landed and was wreaking havoc there. He summoned all his people throughout his kingdom, and his Irish subjects hastened to do battle against the noble King Arthur. Arthur and his warriors, a vast host, immediately seized their weapons, and advanced to meet them. Arthur's men were fully clad in armour;

þa Irisce men weoren   nakede neh þan,
mid speren and mid axen   and mid swiðe scærpe sæxen.
Arður men letten fleon   vnimete flan,
and merden Irisc folc   and hit swiðe ualden;   11150
ne mæhten heo iþolien   þurh nanes cunnes þingen,
ah fluȝen awai on siðe   swiðe uæle þusend.
And Gillomar þe king flah   and awæwardes teh,
and Arður him after   and þene king ikahte;
he nom bi þan honde   þene king of þan londe.   11155
     Arður þe hæȝe   herbeorwe isohte;
an his mode him wes þa æðe   þat Gillomar him wes swa neh.
Nu dude Arður,   aðelest kingen,
swiðe muche freondscipe   atforen al his folke;
he lette þene king scrude   mid ælchere prude,   11160
and æc bi Arðure sat   and æc mid himseolue æt;
mid Arðure he win dronc   —þat him wes mucheles unðonc!
Naðeles, þa he isah   þat Arður wes swiðe glad,
þa cleopede Gillomar   —an his horte him wes sær:
"Lauerd Arður, þi grið;   ȝef me leomen and ȝif me lif.   11165
Ich wulle þi mon bicumen   and biteche þe mine þreo sunen,
mine sunen deore,   to don al þine iwille.
And ȝet ich wulle mare,   ȝif þu me wult ȝefen ære:
ich wulle þe bitache   ȝisles swiðe rich,
children sume sixti,   hæȝe and swiðe mæhti.   11170
Ȝet ich wulle mære,   ȝif þu me ȝifuest ære:
ælche ȝere of mine londe   seouen þusend punde
and senden heom to þine londe,   and sixti mark of golde.
And ȝet ich wulle mare,   ȝif þu wult me ȝifuen are:
alle þa steden   mid alle heore iweden,   11175
þa hæuekes and þa hundes,   and hehȝe mine mahmes
ich bitache þe to honde   of al mine londe.
And þenne þu hauest þis idon,   ich wulle nimen halidom
of seint Columkille   þe dude Godes iwille,
and seint Brændenes hæfed   þe Godd seolf haleȝede,   11180
and seinte Bride riht fot   þe hali is and swiðe god,
and halidomes inoȝe   þe comen ut of Rome,
and swerien þe to soðe   swiken þe þat ich nulle;
ah ich þe wulle luuien   and halden þe for lauerd,
halden þe for hahne king   and miseolf beon þin vnderling."   11185
     þis iherde Arður,   aðelest king,

there Irish men were almost naked, with only spears and axes and sharp knives. Arthur's men let fly arrows without number, and assailed the Irish force and slaughtered many; they could not hold out by any means, but many thousands fled speedily away. And Gillomar the king took flight and made off, and Arthur went after him and seized the king; he took the king of the country captive.

The mighty Arthur took up quarters there; in his heart he was the more pleased because Gillomar was so close to him. Now Arthur, noblest of kings, displayed very great friendship before all his people; he had the king dressed with all splendour, and moreover he was seated beside Arthur and also ate with him; he drank wine with Arthur — that was little pleasure to him! Nevertheless, when he saw that Arthur was very happy, then Gillomar called out with grief in his heart:

'Mercy, my lord Arthur; grant me life and limb. I will become your liegeman and entrust to you my three sons, my beloved sons, to do all that you wish. And I will do more also, if you will grant me grace: I will give you most noble hostages, some sixty youths of the very highest rank. I will give more still, if you will grant me grace: seven thousand pounds each year from my land and sixty marks of gold which I will send to your country. And more still I will give, if you will grant me grace: all the horses with all their trappings, the hawks and the hounds, and the greatest of my treasures from throughout my land I will surrender into your hands. And when you have granted it, I will take a holy relic of St Columba who did God's will, and the head of St Brendan whom God himself sanctified, and the right foot of St Bridget who is most good and holy, and many sacred relics which came from Rome, and swear to you truly that I will not deceive you; but I will honour you and acknowledge you as overlord, accept you as high king and myself be your subject.' #

Arthur, noblest of kings, heard this, and he began to laugh

and he gan lihȝen   luddere steftne,
and he gon andswerie   mid ædmode worden:
"Beo nu glad, Gillomar!   Ne beo þin heorte noht sær,
for þv ært a wis mon;   þa bet þe scal iwurðen,   11190
for æuere me æhte wisne mon   wurðliche igreten;
for þine wisdome   no scal þe noht þa wurse.
Muchel þu me beodest   —þe scal beon þa betere!
Her, forðrihtes,   bifore al mine cnihtes,
forȝiuen þe amare   al þæ haluen-dæle   11195
of golde and of gærsume;   ah þu scalt mi mon bicumen,
and half þat gauel sende   ælche ȝere to mine londe.
Halfe þa steden   and halfe þa iweden,
halue þa hauekes   and halue þa hundes
þæ þu me beodest,   ich wulle þe bilefen;   11200
ah ich wulle habben   þire hæhre monne children
þeo heom beoð alre leofuest   —ich heom mai þe bet ileouen!
And swa þu scalt wunien   in wurðscipe þire,
a þine kinedome,   i þine rihte icunden;
and ic þe wulle ȝeuen to   þat ne scal þe king woh don   11205
buten he hit abugge   mid his bare rugge!"
Þeo hit sæide Arður,   aðelest kingen;
þa hafden he an hond   al tosomne Irlond,
and þe king his mon bicumen   and bitæht him his þreo seonen.
    Þa spæc Ærður   to sele his cnihten: 11210
"Faren to Hislond   and nimen we hit to ure honde."
Ferde þer fusde   and com to Islonde.
Ælcus þe king wes ihaten,   hæh mon of þan ærd.
He iherde þa tidende   of Arðure þan kinge;
he dude al so wis mon,   and wende toȝeines him anan,   11215
anan forðrihtes,   mid sixtene cnihtes;
he bar on his honde   ænne mucle ȝeord of golde.
    Sone swa he Arður isæh   swa he on his cneowen bæh,
and þas word him iquað   —þe king wes afæred:
"Wulcume, Sire Arður,   wilcume lauerd.   11220
Her ich biteche þe an hond   al togadere Islond;
þu scal beon min hæhȝe king   and ich wul beon þin underling.
Ich þe wullen heren   swa mon scal don his hærren,
and ich wulle þi mon bicumen   and bitæche þe minne leofue sune,
Esscol is ihaten;   and þu hine scalt iæðelien,   11225
to cnihte hine dubben   alse þin aȝene mon;

with a loud voice, and with gracious words he replied:

'Be glad now, Gillomar! Let not your heart be sad, for you are a wise man; the better shall it be for you, for one ought always to treat a wise man honourably; because of your wisdom it shall not go ill with you. You offer me much — the better it shall be for you! Here, at once, before all my followers, I excuse you more than half of all the gold and treasure; but you shall become my liegeman, and each year send half that tribute to my land. I will leave you half the horses and half the trappings, half the hawks and half the hounds which you offer me; but I will have the children of your noblemen who are most dear to them — then I may the better trust them! And so you shall dwell with due honour in your kingdom, in your native land; and I warrant you that no sub-king shall do you wrong without atoning for it on his bare back!'

Thus spoke Arthur, noblest of kings; he had all Ireland wholly in his possession then, and the king had become his liegeman and surrendered to him his three sons.

Then Arthur addressed his trusty followers:

'Let us go to Iceland and take possession of it.'

The army hastened thither and came to Iceland. The king, ruler of that land, was called Ælcus. Hearing the news about King Arthur, he acted like a wise man, and at once went to meet him, without any delay, with sixteen attendants, bearing in his hand a long rod of gold.

As soon as he saw Arthur, he fell on his knees — the king was afraid — and spoke these words to him:

'Welcome, Sir Arthur, welcome lord. I here surrender Iceland wholly into your hands; you shall be my overlord and I will be your subject. I will obey you as a man should his liegelord, and I will become your liegeman and entrust to you my beloved son called Escol; and you shall ennoble him, dub him a knight as your

his moder ich habbe to wife,   þas kinges dohter of Rusie.
And æc ælche ȝere   ȝiuen þe wulle æhte,
seoue þusend punde   of seoluere and of golde,
and to æuerælche ræde   beon ȝæru to þire neode.   11230
þis ich wullen þe swerien   uppen mine sweorden;
þe halidom is a þere hilte   þe hexste of þisse londe.
Likien swa me liken   nulle ich þe nauere swiken."
      þis iherde Arður,   aðlest kingen;
Arður wes wunsum   þer he hafde his iwillen,   11235
and he wes wod sturne   wið his wiðer-iwinnen.
Arður þa liðe word iherde   of þan leod-kinge;
al þat he ȝirnde   al he him ȝette,
ȝisles and aðes,   and alle his ibodes.
      þa iherde suggen   soðere worden   11240
þe king of Orcaneie,   vnimete kene—
Gonwais wes ihate,   haeðene kempe—
þat Arður king wolde   cume to his londe,
mid muchele scip-ferde   fusen to leoden.
Gonwais him uerde toȝæines   mid wisen his þeines,   11245
and sette Arðure an hond   al Orcaneies lond
and twa and þritti æitlond   þe þider in liggeð,
and his mon-radene   mid muchelere mensce.
And he him hafde a uoreward   biforen al his duȝeðe
ælche ȝere to iwiten   fulle sixti scipen,   11250
mid his aȝere costninge   bringen heom to Londenne
ifulled to iwisse   mid gode sæ-fisce.
þis forward he iuaste   and ȝisles he funde,
and aðes he swor gode   swiken þat he nolde.
And seoððen he lefe nom   and forð he gon liðen: 11255
"Lauerd, haue wel godne dæi;   ich wulle cumen wenne ich mai,
for nu þu art mi lauerd,   leouest alre kingen."
      þa Arður hafde þis idon,   þa ȝet he wolde mare afon.
He nom his writen gode   and senden to Gutlonde,
and grætte þe king Doldanim   and hehte hine sone comen to him
and himseolf his mon bicume   and bringen him his tweien sunen;
"and ȝif þu þat nulle,   do þat þu wulle,
ich þe wulle sende   sixtene þusend
heȝe here-kempen   to mucle þine harmen;
scullen þi lond wasten   and þirre leoden aslan,   *   11265
and þat lond setten   swa heom bezst þincheð,

own liegeman; his mother, daughter of the king of Russia, is my wife. And, moreover, every year I will give you treasure, seven thousand pounds of silver and of gold, and be ready to meet your needs in everything you plan. This I will swear to you upon my sword; the relic in its hilt is the most sacred in this land. I will never play you false no matter how much I might wish to.' #

Arthur, noblest of kings, assented to this; Arthur was gracious whenever he achieved his purpose, and he was terribly stern with those who opposed him. Arthur listened to the humble words of the king of that land and agreed to accept from him all he had proffered, hostages and oaths, and all his other pledges.

Then the king of Orkney, an extremely fierce heathen warrior called Gonwais, was informed by truthful reports that King Arthur was coming to his country, hastening to the land with a great fleet. Gonwais went to meet him with his wise councillors, and surrendered to Arthur the whole land of Orkney and thirty-two islands which lie adjacent to it, and did him homage with great respect. And he made a pledge to him before all his followers to provide each year sixty ships all told, and convey them to London at his own expense filled full of good sea-fish. He confirmed this covenant and provided hostages, and he swore firm oaths that he would not prove false. And then he took his leave and away he went:

'A right good day, my lord; I will come to you whenever I can, for now you are my liegelord, dearest of all kings.' #

When Arthur had accomplished all this, he still wished to conquer more lands. He drew up and sent to Jutland his royal writs greeting Doldanim the king and ordering him to come to him immediately and bring with him his two sons and himself become his liegeman; 'and if you refuse this, do what you may, I will send you sixteen thousand noble warriors who, to your great harm, shall lay waste your country and slay your people, and dispose of the land as seems best to them, and you yourself

and þe seoluen binden   and to me bringen."
    Þis iherde þe king,   þræt þas kaiseres,
and he on uaste iueng   fæiere his iweden,
hundes and hafekes   and his gode horsses,   11270
muchel seoluer, muchel gold,   his tweien sunen an his hond,
and forð he gon wenden   to Arðure þan kingen.
And þas word sæide   Doldanim þe sele:
"Hail seo þu, Arður,   aðelest kingen.
Her ich bringe tweiene   mine sunen beiene;   11275
heore moder is kinges istreon   —quene heo is min aȝene;
ich heo biȝat mid ræflac   ut of Rusie. *
Ich tache þe mine leofen sunen;   miseolf ich wulle þi mon bicumen,
and ic wulle sende   gauel of mine londe;
æuerælche ȝere,   to ȝiueles þingen, *   11280
ich wulle senden þe into Lundene   seouen þusend punden.
Þat ic wulle swerien   þat nulle ich næuere swiken,
ah here ich wulle þi mon bicomen   —þi monscipe is þa mare;
swiken nulle ich nauere   swa longe swa beoð auere."
    Arður nom his sonde   and sende to Winentlonde,   11285
to Rumareð þan kinge,   and hehte him cuðen an hiȝinge
þat he hæfde in his hond   Brutlond and Scotland,
Gutlond and Irlond,   Orcaneie and Islond.
He hæhte Rumareð cumen   and bringen him his ældeste sune,
and ȝif he þat nolde   he wolde hine driuen of londe;   11290
and ȝif he mihte afon   he wolde hine slæn oðer anhon,
and his lond al fordon,   his leoden fordemen.
    Þis iherde Rumared,   þe riche king of Winete;
swiðe he wes afered   al swa þa oðere weoren arer;
laðe him weoren þa tidende   from Arðure þan kinge!   11295
Noðeles þe king Rumareð   hercnede rædes;
he nom his ældeste sune   and sele twælf eorles
and ferde to Arðure,   þan kinge aðele,
and set æt his foten   and feire hine gon greten:
"Hail seo þu, Arður,   aðelest Brutten;   11300
ich hatten Rumareð,   þe king of Winetlonde.
Inoh ich habbe iherd kenne   of kenscipe þine,
þat þu ært widen icuð   kingen alre kennest.
þu hauest moni kinelond   biȝiten al to þire hond;
nis na king an londe   þe þe maȝen stonde,   11305
king ne na kaisere,   in nauere nane compe;

— 104 —

they shall bind and bring to me.' #

The king heard this, heard the sovereign's threat, and he in haste took his fine armour, hounds and hawks and his good horses, much silver, much gold, and his two sons with him, and set out to meet King Arthur. And the noble Doldanim spoke these words:

'Health to you, Arthur, noblest of kings. I bring you here both my two sons; their mother, my own queen, is of royal stock — I took her as booty out of Russia. I entrust to you my beloved sons; I myself will become your liegeman, and will send you tribute from my land; each and every year, as a sign of tribute, I will send to you in London seven thousand pounds. I will swear that I will never prove false, but here and now will become your liegeman — the greater shall be your honour; I will never be disloyal so long as time shall last.'

Arthur chose his messengers and sent them to Winetland, to Rumareth the king, and ordered them instantly to inform him that he held sway over Britain and Scotland, Jutland and Ireland, Orkney and Iceland. He commanded Rumareth to come and bring him his eldest son, and if he would not do that he would drive him from his kingdom; and if he could capture him he would slay him or hang him, and destroy his country utterly, exterminate his people.

Rumareth, the noble king of Winetland, heard this; he was greatly afraid just as the others had been earlier; the tidings from King Arthur were hateful to him! Nevertheless King Rumareth heeded his counsel; he took his eldest son and twelve worthy earls and went to the noble King Arthur, and, kneeling at his feet, greeted him courteously:

'Health to you, Arthur, noblest of Britons; I am called Rumareth, the king of Winetland. Much I have heard tell of your courage, that you are known far and wide as the bravest of all kings. You have taken many kingdoms entirely into your possession; there is no ruler on earth, no king or emperor, who can withstand you in any form of warfare; in all that you undertake

of al þat þu biʒinnest   þu dest þine iwille.
Her ich æm to þe icume   and broht þe mine aldeste sune;
her ich sette þe an hond   me seoluen and mi kinelond,
and minne sune leofe   and mine leoden alle,   11310
wif and mine weden   and alle mine wunnen,
wið þat þu me griðie   wið þine grim ræsen.
And beo þu min hæhʒe king   and ich wulle beon þin underling,
and senden þe to honde   fif hundred pund of golde;
þas ʒeuen ich finde þe wulle   æueralche ʒere."   11315
       Al Arður him ʒette   þat þe king ʒirde.
And seoððen he heolde runen   wið sele his þeinen,
and seide þat he wolde   aʒæin to þisse londe
and iseon Wenhaiuer,   þe wuneliche quene.
Bemen he lette blawen   and bonnien his ferden,   11320
and to scipen wenden   wunder bliðe þeines.
Wind heom stod on willen,   weder alse heo wolden—
bliðe heo weoren alle for þi;   up heo comen at Grimesbi.
þat iherden sone   þa hæhste of þissen londe
and to þære quene com tidende   of Arðure þan kinge,   11325
þat he wes isund icumen   and his folc on selen.
       þa weoren inne Bruttene   blissen inoʒe:
her wes fiðelinge and song,   her wes harpinge imong,
pipen and bemen   murie þer sungen;
scopes þer sungen   of Arðure þan kingen   11330
and of þan muchele wurðscipe   þe he iwunnen hafeden.
Folc com to hirede   of feole cunne þeode;
widen and siden   folc wes on selen.
Al þat Arður isæh   al hit him to bæh,
riche men and pouere,   swa þe haʒel ualleð;   11335
nes þer nan swa wræcche Brut   þat he nes awælʒed.
       Her mon mai arede   of Arðure þan king,
hu he twelf ʒere   seoðen wuneden here
inne griðe and inne friðe,   in alle uæʒernesse.
Na man him ne faht wið,   no he ne makede nan unfrið;   11340
ne mihte nauere nan man   biþenchen of blissen
þat weoren in æi þeode   mare þan i þisse;
ne mihte nauere moncunne   nan swa muchel wunne
swa wes mid Arðure   and mid his folke here.
       Ich mai sugge hu hit iwarð,   wunder þæh hit þunche.   11345
Hit wes in ane Ʒeol-dæie   þat Arður in Lundene lai;

you achieve your purpose. I have come to you here and brought you my eldest son; I here surrender to you my person and my kingdom, and my beloved son and all my people, my wife and my robes and all my treasures, on condition that you withhold your fierce onslaught. If you will be my sovereign I will be your subject, and will deliver into your hands five hundred pounds of gold; each and every year I will render you this tribute.' #

Arthur agreed to accept from him all that the king proffered. And then he held counsel with his noble thanes, and said that he would return again to this country and see once more the fair Queen Guenevere. He caused trumpets to be blown and summoned his forces, and the thanes went on board in high spirits. The wind favoured them, the weather was as they wished — they all rejoiced at that; they came ashore at Grimsby. The greatest men in this land soon learnt of that and news of King Arthur was brought to the queen, that he had returned safe and sound and with his army in good heart.

Then there was in Britain great rejoicing: here sounds of viol and of voice, mingling with music of the harp, there pipes and trumpets ringing out merrily; there minstrels sang of Arthur the king and of the great honour which he had won. Men from many different nations came to court; far and wide the people were in great contentment. All who set eyes on Arthur, the great and the humble, all bowed down before him, as the hail falls; there was no Briton so abject that he was not enriched.

Here one may read of Arthur the king, how he afterwards dwelt here twelve years in peace and prosperity, in all splendour. No man fought against him, nor did he make war on anyone; no man could ever conceive of greater happiness in any country than there was in this; nor could any nation ever know such great joy as there was with Arthur and his people here.

Now I will tell what came to pass, wondrous though it may seem. It was on a day in the Christmas season when Arthur lay

þa weoren him to icumen   of alle his kinerichen,
of Brutlonde, of Scotlonde,   of Irlonde, of Islonde,
and of al þan londe   þe Arður hæfede an honde,
alle þa hæxte þeines,   mid horsen and mid sweines;   11350
þer weoren seouen kingene sunes   mid seouen hundred cnihten icumen
wiðuten þan hired   þe herede Arðure.
Ælc hafede an heorte   leches heȝe
and lette þat he weore   betere þan his iuere.
þat folc wes of feole londe;   þer wes muchel onde   11355
for þe an hine talde hæh,   þe oðer muche herre.

        þa bleou mon þa bemen   and þa bordes bradden;
water me brohte an uloren   mid guldene læflen,
seoððen claðes soften   al of white seolke.
þa sat Arður adun   and bi him Wenhauer þa quene;   11360
seoððen sete þa eorles   and þerafter þa beornes,
seoððen þa cnihtes,   al swa mon heom dihte.
þa heȝe iborne   þene mete beoren
æfne forðrihten   þa to þan cnihten,
þa touward þan þæinen,   þa touward þan sweinen,   11365
þa touward þan bermonnen   forð at þan borden.
þa duȝeðe wærð iwrað.ðed,   duntes þer weoren riue;
ærest þa laues heo weorpen,   þa while þa heo ilæsten,
and þa bollen seoluerne   mid wine iuulled,
and seoððen þa uustes   uusden to sweoren.   11370

        þa leop þer forð a ȝung mon   þe ut of Winetlonde com—
he wes iȝefen Arðure   to halden to ȝisle—
he wes Rumarettes sune,   þas kinges of Winette.
þus seide þe cniht þere   to Arðure kinge:
"Lauerd Arður, buh raðe   into þine bure   11375
and þi quene mid þe   and þine mæies cuðe,
and we þis comp scullen todelen   wið þas uncuðe kempen."
Æfne þan worde   he leop to þan borde
þer leien þa cniues   biforen þan leod-kinge;
þreo cnifes he igrap,   and mid þan anæ he smat   11380
i þere swere þe cniht   þe ærest bigon þat ilke fiht
þat his hefued i þene flor   hælde to grunde.
Sone he sloh ænne oðer,   þes ilke þeines broðer;
ær þa sweordes comen   seouene he afelde.
þer wes fæht swiðe græt,   ælc mon oðer smat;   11385
þer wes muchel blod-gute,   balu wes an hirede.

in London; there had come to him at that time from all his kingdoms, from Britain, from Scotland, from Ireland, from Iceland, and from all those lands which Arthur had in his possession, all the thanes of highest rank, with horses and with servants; seven kings' sons had come with seven hundred knights in addition to the household which served Arthur. Each had proud feelings in his heart and thought that he was better than his fellows. Those men were from many lands; there was fierce rivalry because the one accounted himself great, the other considered himself much greater.

Then trumpets were blown and the tables spread, water was brought into the hall in golden bowls, then soft cloths all of white silk. Then Arthur sat down and beside him Guenevere the queen; next the earls sat down and afterwards the other nobles, then the knights, in due order just as they were placed. Then noblemen immediately brought the food to the knights, then to the thanes, then to the retainers, then to the servers along the tables. The courtiers grew angry, blows were frequent there; first they threw the loaves, as long as they lasted, and the silver bowls filled with wine, and next fists flew at necks.

Then there leapt forward a young man who came from Winetland, the son of Rumareth the king of Winetland; he had been given to Arthur to hold as hostage. The knight then spoke to King Arthur thus:

'Lord Arthur, go quickly into your chamber and your queen with you and your closest kinsmen, and we shall put an end to the fighting between these foreign warriors.'

With these words he leapt to the table where the knives lay before the monarch; he seized three knives, and with one of them he struck in the neck the knight who first began that fight so that his head fell down upon the floor. Instantly he struck another, the brother of that thane; he had felled seven before the swords were brought. There was fierce fighting, every man striking another; there was much bloodshed, there was chaos in the court.

þa com þe king buȝen ut of his buren,
mid him an hundred beornen mid helmen and mid burnen;
ælc bar an his riht hond whit stelene brond.
þa cleopede Arður, aðelest kingen: 11390
"Sitteð! Sitteð swiðe, elc mon bi his liue!
And waswa þat nulle don he scal fordemed beon.
Nimeð me þene ilke mon þa þis feht ærst bigon,
and doð wiððe an his sweore and draȝeð hine to ane more,
and doð hine in an ley uen þer he scal liggen; 11395
and nimeð al his nexte cun þa ȝe maȝen iuinden
and swengeð of þa hafden mid breoden eouwer sweorden.
þa wifmen þa ȝe maȝen ifinden of his nexten cunden,
kerueð of hire neose and heore wlite ga to lose;
and swa ich wulle al fordon þat cun þat he of com. 11400
And ȝif ich aueremare seoððen ihere
þat æi of mine hirede, of heȝe na of loȝe,
of þissen ilke slehte æft sake arere,
ne sculde him neoðer gon fore gold ne na gærsume,
hæh hors no hære scrud þat he ne sculde beon ded 11405
oðer mid horsen todraȝen þat is elches swiken laȝen.
Bringeð þene halidom and ich wulle swerien þeron;
swa ȝe scullen cnihtes þe weoren at þissen fihte,
eorles and beornes, þat ȝe hit breken nulleð."
Ærst sweor Arður, aðelest kingen; 11410
seoððen sworen eorles, seoððen sweoren beornes,
seoððen sweoren þeines, seoððen sweoren sweines,
þat heo naueremare þe sake nulde arere.
Me nom alle þa dede and to leirstowe heom ladden.

Seoððen me bleou bemen mid swiðe murie dremen; 11415
weoren him leof weoren him læð, elc þer feng water and clæð
and seoððen adun seten sæhte to borden,
al for Arðure æiȝe, aðelest kingen.
Birles þer þurngen, gleomen þer sungen,
harpen gunnen dremen; duȝeðe wes on selen. 11420
þus fulle seoueniht wes þan hirede idiht.

Seoððen hit seið in þere tale þe king ferde to Cornwale.
þer him com to anan þat wæs a crafti weorcmon,
and þene king imette, and feiere hine grætte:
"Hail seo þu, Arður, aðelest kinge; 11425
ich æm þin aȝe mon. Moni lond ich habbe þurhgan,

Then the king came hastening out of his chamber, with him a hundred men with helmets and coats of mail, each bearing in his right hand a bright steel blade. Then Arthur, noblest of kings, called out:

'Sit down! Each man sit down at once, upon his life! And whoever will not do so shall be condemned to death. Seize that man who first began this fight, put a cord about his neck and drag him to a marsh, and thrust him into the bog where he shall lie; and seize all his close kin whom you can find and strike off their heads with your broad swords. The women of his immediate family whom you can find, cut off their noses and let their looks be ruined; and so I will utterly destroy the race from which he came. And if hereafter I ever again hear that any member of my household, of high rank or low, stirs up fresh strife because of this conflict, neither gold nor any treasure shall ransom him, neither tall steed nor battle armour save him from death or being drawn asunder by horses which is the penalty for all traitors. Bring the holy relics and I will swear an oath upon them; so shall you knights who were at this fight, you earls and nobles shall swear that you will not break it.'

First swore Arthur, noblest of kings; next swore the earls, then swore the nobles, then the thanes, then the retainers, that never again would they stir up strife. The dead were all taken up and carried to a place of burial.

Then trumpets were sounded with a cheerful noise; whether reconciled or not, everyone there made use of water and towel and afterwards sat down to table in amity, solely out of respect for Arthur, the noblest of kings. Cup-bearers thronged there, there minstrels sang, harps resounded; the company was in high spirits. For fully a week the court was maintained in this manner.

Next it says in the story that the king went to Cornwall. Presently there came to him one who was a skilled craftsman and, coming into the king's presence, greeted him with due respect:

'Health to you, Arthur, noblest of kings; I am a loyal subject of yours. I have journeyed through many lands, and know a great

ich con of treo-wrekes   wunder feole craftes.

Ich iherde suggen   biȝeonde sæ neowe tidende
þat þine cnihtes   at þine borde gunnen fihte
a Midewinteres dæi;   moni þer feollen,   11430
for heore mucchele mode   morð-gomen wrohten,
and for heore hehȝe cunne   ælc wolde beon wiðinne.
Ah ich þe wulle wurche   a bord swiðe hende
þat þer maȝen sitten to   sixtene hundred and ma
al turn abuten,   þat nan ne beon wiðuten,   11435
wiðuten and wiðinne   mon toȝæines monne.
Whenne þu wult riden   wið þe þu miht hit leden
and setten hit whar þu wulle,   after þine iwille;
and ne dert þu nauere adrede   to þere worlde longen
þat æuere ænie modi cniht   at þine borde makie fiht,   11440
for þer scal þe hehȝe   beon æfne þan loȝe."
Timber me lete biwinnen   and þat beord biginnen;
to feouwer wikene uirste   þat wrec wes iuorðed.

    To ane heȝe dæie   þat hired wes isomned,
and Arður himseolf beh   sone to þan borde,   11445
and hehte alle his cnihtes   to þan borde forðrihtes.
Þo alle weoren iseten   cnihtes to heore mete,
þa spæc ælc wið oðer   alse hit weore his broðer;
alle heo seten abuten,   nes þer nan wiðuten.
Æuere ælches cunnes cniht   þere wes swiðe wel idiht;   11450
alle heo weoren bi ane,   þa hehȝe and þa laȝe.
Ne mihten þer nan ȝelpen   for oðere kunnes scenchen
oðer his iueren   þe at þan beorde weoren.

    Þis wes þat ilke bord   þat Bruttes of ȝelpeð,
and sugeð feole cunne lesinge   bi Arðure þan kinge.   11455
Swa deð aueralc mon   þe oðer luuien con;
ȝif he is him to leof   þenne wule he liȝen
and suggen on him wurðscipe   mare þenne he beon wurðe;
ne beo he no swa luðer mon   þat his freond him wel ne on.
Æft ȝif on uolke   feondscipe arereð   11460
an æueræi time   bitweone twon monnen,
me con bi þan læðe   lasinge suggen;
þeh he weore þe bezste mon   þe æuere æt at borde,
þe mon þe him weore lað   him cuðe last finden.

    Ne al soh ne al les   þat leod-scopes singeð;   11465
ah þis is þat soð̄e   bi Arðure þan kinge.

many skills in carpentry. Beyond the sea I heard tell recent tidings that your knights began to fight at your table on Midwinter day; many fell on that occasion, having engaged in deadly play out of their excessive pride, each expecting by right of his noble lineage to be included there. But I will make you a very fine table round the full extent of which sixteen hundred and more may be seated, one man facing another round the outside and the inside, so that none shall be excluded. When you wish to travel you can take it with you and set it up wherever you want, as it suits you; and to the end of the world you need never fear that any proud knight shall ever stir up strife at your table, for there the great shall be on an equal footing with the humble.'

Timber was brought and the table begun; in the space of four weeks the work was accomplished.

On a feast day the court was assembled, and Arthur himself went first to the table, and summoned all his followers to table immediately. When the knights were all seated at their meal, then each spoke with the other as if they were brothers; they were all seated around it so that no one was excluded there. Each and every rank of noble was very well accommodated there; they were all equal, both the great and the humble. No one there could boast of having refreshment different from that of his companions who were at the table.

This was that table of which the Britons boast, telling fables of many kinds about King Arthur. Each and every man who feels love for another does the same; if he is dear to him then he will lie and say more in praise of him that he is worthy of; there is no man so base that his friend will not wish him well. If likewise, anywhere at any time, enmity arises between two men, lies can be told about the one who is hated; even though he were the best man who ever ate at table, the man who hated him would be able to find fault with him. #

What minstrels sing is not all truth nor all lies; but this is the truth about King Arthur. Never before was there such a king, so

Nes næuer ar swulc king,   swa duhti þurh alle þing;
for þat soðe stod a þan writen   hu hit is iwurðen,
ord from þan ænden,   of Arðure þan kinge,
no mare, no lasse,   buten alse his laȝen weoren.   11470
Ah Bruttes hine luueden swiðe   and ofte him on liȝeð,
and suggeð feole þinges   bi Arðure þan kinge
þat næuere nes iwurðen   a þissere weorlde-richen.
Inoh he mai suggen   þe soð wule uremmen
seolcuðe þinges   bi Arðure kinge.   11475
     Þa wes Arður swiðe heh,   his hired swiðe hende,
þat nas na cniht wel itald,   no of his tuhlen swiðe bald,
inne Wales no in Ænglelond,   inne Scotlond no in Irlond,
in Normandie no inne France,   inne Flandres no inne Denemarc,
no in nauere none londe   þe a þeos halfe Mungiu stondeð,   11480
þet weoren ihalde god cniht   no his deden itald oht
bute he cuðe of Arðure   and of aðelen his hirede,
his wepnen and his weden   and his hors-leden,
suggen and singen   of Arðure þan ginge
and of his hired-cnihten,   and of heȝe heore mihten   11485
and of heore richedome,   and hu wel hit heom bicomen.
Þenne weore he wilcume   a þissere weorlde-richen,
come þer he come,   and þeh he weore i Rome.
     Al þat iherde   of Arðure telle
heom þuhte muchel seollic   of selen þan kinge.   11490
And swa hit wes iuuren iboded,   ær he iboren weoren.
Swa him sæide Merlin,   þe witeȝe wes mære,
þat a king sculde cume   of Vðere Pendragune,
þat gleomen sculden wurchen burd   of þas kinges breosten,
and þerto sitten   scopes swiðe sele   11495
and eten heore wullen   ær heo þenne fusden,
and winscenches ut teon   of þeos kinges tungen,
and drinken and dreomen   daies and nihtes;
þis gomen heom sculde ilasten   to þere weorlde longe.
     And ȝet him seide Marlin   mare þat wes to comene: 11500
þat al þat he lokede on   to foten him sculde buȝen.
Þa ȝet him sæide Mærlin   a sellic þe wes mare:
þat sculde beon unimete care   of þas kinges forðfare;
and of þas kinges ende   nulle hit na Brut ileue
buten hit beon þe leste dæð   at þan muchele dome   11505
þenne ure Drihte   demeð alle uolke.

valiant through thick and thin; for the truth of what befell King Arthur from beginning to end has been recorded in the writings, his acts just as they were, no more, no less. But the Britons loved him greatly and often tell lies about him, and say many things of King Arthur which never happened in this mortal world. He who shall speak the truth can tell many marvellous things about King Arthur.

Arthur was then supreme, his court resplendent, so that there was no knight so well esteemed nor so bold in his deeds, in Wales or in England, in Scotland or in Ireland, in Normandy or in France, in Flanders or in Denmark, or in any land whatsoever lying on this side of the Great St Bernard Pass, who was reputed a good knight or his deeds accounted valiant unless he could discourse of Arthur and his noble followers, his weapons and his armour and his horsemen, could tell tales and sing songs of the youthful Arthur and of the knights of his court, and their great prowess and their power, and how well it became them. Then he would be welcome anywhere in this world wherever he might go, even though as far as Rome. # #

All who heard tell of Arthur marvelled greatly at the noble king. And so it had been foretold long ago, before he was born. Merlin himself, the famous prophet, said so, said that a king should descend from Uther Pendragon, that minstrels should make a table of that king's breast, and most excellent poets sit down thereat and eat all they wished before they went away, and draw draughts of wine from that king's tongue, and drink and make merry both day and night; this entertainment should suffice them to the end of the world. #

And Merlin further prophesied more that was to come: that all whom he looked upon should kneel at his feet. Then Merlin further prophesied a greater wonder still: that there should be boundless sorrow at this king's departure; and no Briton would believe it, believe in this king's death unless it should be the ultimate death at the great judgement when our Lord shall judge

Ælles ne cunne we demen   of Arðures deðen,
for he seolf sæide   to sele his Brutten,
suð inne Cornwale   þer Walwain wes forfaren
and himseolf wes forwunded   wunder ane swiðe,   11510
þat he uaren wolde   into Aualune,
into þan æitlonde,   to Argante þere hende,
for heo sculde mid haleweie   helen his wunden,
and þenne he weore al hal   he wolde sone come heom.
þis ilefde Bruttes,   þet he wule cumen þus,   11515
and lokieð a whenne   he cume to his londe
swa he heom bihahte   ar he heonne wende.
          Arður wes an weorlde   wis king and riche,
god mon and griðful;   his gumen hine luueden.
Cnihtes he hafede prute   and græte on heore mode,   11520
and speken to þan kinge   of seollichen þinge;
and þus þat hired cleopede   to heʒe þan kinge:
"Lauerd Arður, faren we   to Francene riche
and iwinnen al þat lond   to þire aʒere hond,
flemen alle þa Freinscen,   heore king feollen,   11525
alle þa castles bonien   and setten heom to mid Brutten,
and rixlien a þere riche   mid rehʒere strengðe."
          þa andswarede Arður,   aðelest kingen:
"Eouwer wille ich wulle don,   ah ær ich wulle to Norweien,
and ich wulle mid me leden   Lot minne oðem;   11530
he is Wælwaynes fader   þa ich wel luuie.
For beoð icumen of Norweiʒe   niwe tidende
þat Sichelin, king þer, is ded,   his duʒeðen bileued,
and hæ hafeð al his kineriche   biqueðe her Loððe.
For þe king is al bidæled   sune and eke dohteren,   11535
and Lot is his suster sune   —þe bet him scal iwurðe,
for ich hine wulle in Norwæʒe   neowe king makien
and hine wæl lere   to witeʒen wel þa leoden.
And þenne ich þus habbe idon,   ich wullen seoððen cumen ham
and ʒarkien mine ferde   and faren into France;   11540
and ʒif þe king me stont wið   and nulle ʒeornen mi grið,
ich hine wulle mid fehte   fallen to þan grunde."
          Arður lette blawen   hornes and bemen,
and lette beoden to sæ   Bruttes swiðe balde.
Scipen he hæfde gode   bi þere sæ-flode;   11545
fiftene hundred   fusden from londe

all mankind. In no other circumstances can we believe in Arthur's death, for he himself said to his noble Britons, south in Cornwall where Gawain was killed and he himself most grievously wounded, that he would journey to Avalon, to the island, to the fair Argante, for she should heal his wounds with healing balm, and when he was fully recovered he would soon come back to them. The Britons have always believed this, that he will come in this way, and ever await the hour when he shall return to his land as he promised them before he went hence. #

In this world Arthur was a wise and powerful king, a good man and peaceable, beloved of his subjects. He had proud warriors, men of great courage, and they spoke to the king of matters new and strange; his retinue addressed the high king thus:

'Lord Arthur, let us go into the realm of France and bring that whole land under your own control, drive out all the French, strike down their king, occupy all the castles and garrison them with Britons, and rule in the kingdom by force of arms.'

Then Arthur, noblest of kings, answered:

'I will do as you wish, but first I will go to Norway, and I will take with me my brother-in-law Lot; he is the father of Gawain whom I greatly love. For fresh tidings have come from Norway that Sichelin, the king there, is dead, his people abandoned, he having previously bequeathed his whole kingdom to Lot. For the king is without sons, or daughters either, and Lot is his sister's son — the better shall it be for him, for I will make him the new king in Norway and give him good advice how to govern the people rightly. And when I have done so, I will return home again and prepare my army and cross over into France; and if the king resists me and will not sue to me for peace, I will overthrow him in battle.'

Arthur caused horns and trumpets to be blown, and had the most valiant Britons summoned to the seashore. At the coast he had good ships; fifteen hundred pushed off from the shore and

and fluȝen after þere sæ   swulc heo fluht hafden,
and buhȝen into Norwæȝen   mid baldere strengðen.
Sone swa heo comen   hafne heo nomen,
mid muchelere strengðe   stepen a þa riche.   11550
Arður senden his sonde   wide ȝeond þan londe,
and hæhte heom cumen sone   and Lot habben to kinge;
and ȝif heo þat nolden   alle heom he wolde aslan.

    Þa nomen heore sonden   eorles Norenissce
and senden to þan kingen   and hahten hine aȝain wenden;   11555
"and ȝif þu nult aȝæin faren   sorhȝen þu scalt habben and kare;
for longe bið auere,   þat ne iwurð næuere,
þat we uncuðne mon   to kinge scullen hæbben.
For ȝif Sikelin is forðfaren,   her beoð oðere icoren
þe we maȝen, bi vre iwille,   hæbben to kinge;   11560
and þis is þat soðe   —nis þer nan oðer.
Oðer far þe awæiward   and wend þe riht hamward
oðer todæi a seoueniht   þu scalt habben græt fiht."

    Þa eorles Norenissce   nomen heom to ræde
þat king heo wolden habben   of seoluen heore cunden,   11565
for al Sikelines quiden   sotscipe heo heolden;
"and swa longe swa beoð æuere,   ne scal hit stonde næuere;
ah we scullen nimen Riculf,   þe is swiðe riche eorl,
and hebben hine to kinge   —þis is us iqueme—
and sumnen ure ferde   ȝeond al þissen ærde,   11570
and faren to Arðure   and flemen hine mid fehte;
and Lot we scullen fusen   and flemen of londen
oðer we mid fehten   sculleð hine fallen."
Heo nome Riculfe,   þene eorl of Norene,
and hefuen hine to kinge   þeh hit neore him noht icunde,   11575
and sumneden uerde   ȝeond Nornisce ærde.

    And Arður an his ende   ȝuond þat lond gon wende;
þat londe he þurharnde,   burhȝes he uorbarnde,
æhte he nom inoh,   muche moncun he þer ofsloh.
And Riculf him gon riden   toȝæines Arðure anan;   11580
togædere heo fusden   and veht heo bigunnen.
Bruttes buȝen heom to   —balu þer wes riue;
luken vt of scaþe   sweordes longe;
hefden fluȝen a þene uelde,   faluwede nebbes,
beorn aȝein beorne   scaft sette an breoste,   11585
burnen þer breken.   Bruttes bisie weoren;

flew over the sea as if they had wings, and made their way to Norway with powerful force. As soon as they arrived they entered harbour, disembarked in the kingdom with a great power. Arthur sent his messengers far and wide throughout the land, commanding the people to come quickly and accept Lot as king; and if they would not do that he would slay them all.

Then the Norwegian earls chose their messengers and sent to the king demanding that he depart again; 'and if you will not depart you shall have sorrow and care; for it shall never happen, as long as time lasts, that we shall elect a foreigner as king. For though Sichelin is dead, there are other excellent men here who we may, of our own free will, elect to be king; and this is the truth of the matter — there is no other. Either take yourself off and return directly to your home or a week from today you shall have a great battle.'

The Norwegian earls determined that they would have a king of their own race, for they considered everything Sichelin had said to be folly; 'and that shall never come to pass as long as time lasts; for we shall choose Riculf, who is a very powerful earl, and elect him as king — this is acceptable to us all — and assemble our forces throughout this whole land, march upon Arthur and put him to flight by force of arms; and we shall pursue Lot and expel him from the land or else strike him down in battle.'

They chose Riculf, the earl of Norway, and elected him to the kingship though it was not his by right, and assembled the army from all over the land of Norway. #

And Arthur in his region went through the land overrunning the countryside, burning down towns, taking much booty, slaying many men there. And Riculf at once rode out to meet Arthur; they charged against each other and joined battle. The Britons, drawing long swords from their sheaths, fell upon them — destruction was rife there! On the field of battle heads flew, faces grew pale, man fought man, aimed spear at breast, corslets shattered there. The Britons were active; shields bristled, men fell there.

brustleden sceldes,   scalkes þer ueolen.

And swa al þene dæiliht   ilaste þis muchele fiht;
ferden heo æst ferden heo west,   þer Noreine wes þa wurse;
ferden heo suð ferden heo norð,   þe Norrene þer feollen.   11590
Bruttes weoren balde;   þa Noreine heo aqualden;
Noreinisce men þer feollen,   fif and twenti þusend,
and Riculf king þer wes ofslaʒen   and idon of lif-dæʒen.
Lutel þer eode to læue   of þan leod-folke;
wulcswa hafuede þat wracche lif   ʒirde Arðures grið.   11595
Arður bisæh a Lot   þe leof him wes swiðe,
and þus him cleopien agon   Arður þe riche mon:
"Lot, wend hider to me,   þu art mi wine deore.
Her ich þe biteche   al þas kineriche;
of me þu scalt halden   and habben me to munde."   11600
   þa wes Walwain þider icumen,   Lottes ældeste sune,
of Rome, from þan Pape   þe Supplice wes ihate,
þa longe him wes dihte   and makede hine to cnihte.
Wælle wel wes hit bitoʒen   þat Walwain wes to monne iboren,
for Walwæin wes ful aðelmod,   an ælche þeouwe he wes god;   11605
he wes mete-custi   and cniht mid þan bezste.
Al Arðures hired   wes swiðe ifurðed
for Walwaine þan kene   þe icumen wes to hirede,
and for his fader Lote   þe iloten wes to kinge.
þa spac Arður him wið   and hehte hine halden god grið,   11610
and hehte hine luuien   his griðfulle leoden,
and þa grið nolden halden   fallen heom to grunde.
   þa ʒet cleopede Arður,   aðelest kingen:
"Whær beo ʒe, mine Bruttes?   Fareð nu forðrihtes,
ʒarkieð bi þan flode   mine scipen gode."   11615
Al duden þa cnihtes   swa Arður heom hæhte.
þa þa scipen weoren ʒaru,   Arður gon to sæ faren;
mid him he nom his cnihtes,   his Norenissce þeines
and balden his Bruttes,   and bah forð mid vðes;
and þe duhtie king   com to Denemarke.   11620
He lette slæn teldes   wide ʒeond þa feldes,
bemen he lette blawen   and his cume bodien.
   þa wes inne Denemarke   a king of mucle mæhte,
Æscil wes ihate,   hext ouer Denene.
He isah þat Arður biwon   al þat him wes on willen.   11625
Æscil king hine biþohte   whæt he don mahte;

And so this great battle lasted all through the daylight hours; whether they turned east or west, the Norwegians had the worst of it; whether they turned south or north, the Norwegians fell there. The Britons were bold; they slaughtered the Norwegians; five and twenty thousand Norwegians fell there, and there King Riculf was struck down and deprived of life. Few of the people of the country survived there; those who preserved their miserable lives begged for Arthur's mercy. Arthur looked upon Lot who was most dear to him, and the noble Arthur addressed him thus:

'Come here to me, Lot, you who are my dear friend. I here entrust to you this whole kingdom; you shall rule it under me and have me as your protector.'

Then arrived from Rome Gawain, Lot's eldest son; he had come from the pope who was called Supplice and who had long instructed him and had made him a knight. Most fortunately had it befallen that Gawain was born, for Gawain was very noble-minded, excelling in every virtue; he was a generous man and the best of warriors. All Arthur's followers were greatly heartened because the valiant Gawain had come to court, and because his father Lot had been appointed king. Then Arthur spoke with Lot and commanded him to keep the peace securely, and ordered him to treat his peaceable subjects well, and strike down those who would not keep the peace. #

Then Arthur, noblest of kings, said further:

'Where are you, my Britons? Go now at once, prepare my good ships on the seashore.'

The soldiers did all as Arthur commanded them. When the ships were ready, Arthur marched to the seashore, taking with him his warriors, his Norwegian thanes and his bold Britons, and set out upon the sea; and the valiant king came to Denmark. He caused tents to be pitched far and wide across the plains, he caused trumpets to be blown and his coming announced.

There was then in Denmark a king of great power called Æscil, ruler of the Danes. He saw that all Arthur wanted he acquired. King Æscil considered what he could do; he was loath

lað him wes to leosen   leouen his leoden.
He isah þat mid strengðe   stonden he ne mahte
aʒain Arður,   mid nauere nane compe.
He sende gretinge   to Arður kinge,   11630
hundes and hauekes   and swiðe gode horses,
seoluer and ræd gold,   mid ræhfulle worden.
And ʒet dude mare   Æscil þe mære:
he sende to þan hæxten   of Arðures hireden,
and bad heom arndien him   to hæhʒen þan kingen   11635
þat he moste his mon bicumen   and to ʒisle bitæchen his sune,
and ælche ʒere him senden   gauel of his londe,
ænne bæt mid isunde   from breorde to grunde
of golde and of gærsume   and of godliche pallen;
and seoððen he wolde swerien   swiken þat he nalden.   11640
      Þis iherden Arður,   aðelest kingen,
þat Æscil, Denene king,   wolde beon his vnderling
buten ælche fihte,   he and alle his cnihtes.
Þa iwrað iaðeled   Arður þe riche,
and þus andswærede   mid aðmode worden: 11645
"Wel wurðe þan monne   þe mid wisdome
biwineð him grið and frið   and freondscipe to halden.
Þenne he isiht þet he bið   mid strengðe ibunden,
iʒarked al to leosen   leofue his richen,
mid liste he mot leoðien   luðe his bendes."   11650
Arður hehte þene king cume,   and bringen his aldeste sune;
and he swa dude sone,   þe king of Denemarke;
Arðures iwille   sone he gon fulle.
Tosomne heo comen   and sæhten iwurðen.
      Þa ʒet cleopede Arður,   aðelest kingen: 11655
"Faren ich wulle to France   mid muchele mire ferde.
Ich wulle habben of Noreweie   niʒe þusend cnihtes,
and of Denemarke ich wulle leden   niʒe þusend of þan leoden,
and of Orkaneie   enleuen hundred,
and of Mureinen   þreo þuseond monnen,   11660
and of Galeweien   fif þusend of þan leoden,
and of Irlonde   elleuen þusend;
and of Brutaine   mine cnihtes balde
scullen þræsten biforen me,   þritti þusunde.
And of Gutlonde ich wulle leden   ten þuseond of þan leoden,   11665
and of Frislonde   fif þusend monnen,

to lose his beloved land. He saw that he could not withstand Arthur by force, by resistance of any kind. He sent greetings to King Arthur, sent him hounds and hawks and very fine horses, silver and red gold, and brave words with them. And the noble Æscil did more still: he sent to the chief officers of Arthur's army, entreating them to intercede for him with the mighty king that he might become his liegeman and entrust his son to him as a hostage, and send him annually tribute for his land, a ship laden from top to bottom with gold and treasure and precious fabrics; and, moreover, he would swear upon oath that he would not prove false.

Arthur, noblest of kings, heard this, heard that Æscil, King of Denmark, was willing to be his subject, he and all his followers, without any resistance. Then the mighty Arthur was glad at heart, and replied thus with gracious words:

'Well shall he fare who through wisdom gains peace and security and firm friendship for himself. When he sees that he is constrained by force, on the point of losing his beloved kingdom, he should ease his cruel bondage through prudence.'

Arthur bade the king come to him, bringing his eldest son; and he, the king of Denmark, did so immediately, promptly fulfilling Arthur's wish. They met together and concluded a treaty.

Then Arthur, noblest of kings, spoke once more:

'I will march into France with my vast army. From Norway I will take nine thousand warriors, and I will lead nine thousand men from Denmark, and eleven hundred from Orkney, and three thousand men from Moray, and five thousand from Galway, and eleven thousand from Ireland; and thirty thousand of my bold British warriors shall march on before me. And I will take ten thousand of the men of Jutland, and five thousand warriors from

and of Brutaine   Howel þene balde;
and mid swulche uolke   France ich wulle isechen.
And swa ich ibiden Godes ære,   ʒet ich wulle haten mare,
þat of alle þan londen   þat stondeð a mire honden   11670
ich haten ælcne ohtne mon   þe his wepnen beren con,
alse he wule liuien   and his lumen habben,
þat he faren wið me   to fehten wið Frolle
þat is Francene king   —fæie he scal iwurðe!
He wes iboren i Rome   of Romanisce cunne."   11675
    Forð ferde Arður   þat he com to Flandres;
þat lond he gon biwinnen   and sette hit mid his monnen.
And seoððe he beh þanene   into Buluine,
and al Buluines lond   nom hit to his aʒere hond;
and seoððen he nom þene wæi   þe in touward France læi.   11680
Þa bed he his bod   allen his beornen,
for þær heo uoren,   þat na wiht heo ne nomen
buten he mid rihte   hit biʒiten mihte
mid rihte chepinge   i þas kinges hirede.
    Þat iherde Frolle,   þer he wes inne France,   11685
of Arðures ispede   and of alle his deden,
and hu al biwonne   þat he lokede on,
and al hit him to beh   þat he mid eʒene isah.
Þa wes þe king Frolle   laðliche offered.
A þere ilke worlde   þa þis wes iwurðen,   11690
wes Francene lond   Gualle ihaten;
and Frolle wes from Rome   ifaren into France,
and ælche ʒere sende   gauel of þan londe,
ten hundred punde   of seoluer and of golde.
    Nu iherde Frolle,   þe ældere wes of France,   11695
of þere lond-sorʒe   þe Arður dude an londe.
Sonde he sende sone   an uest touward Rome
and hehte Romanisce folc   reden heom bitweonen
hu feole þusend cnihten   heo þider wolden senden
þat he þa æð mihte   wið Arðure uihte,   11700
and ulemen of londe   Arður þene stronge.
    Cnihtes gunnen riden   vt of Rom-leoden,
fif and twenti þusend   ferden touward France.
Þis iherde Frolle   mid muchele his ferde,
þat þe Romanisce uolc   riden touward londe.   11705
Frolle and his ferde   heom toʒeines ferde;

Friesland, and from Brittany the valiant Howel; and with this force I will invade France. And, moreover, as I hope for God's aid, I will further pledge that from all the lands in my possession I will command every brave man who is able to bear arms that, if he hopes to save life and limb, he should go with me to fight against Frolle who is king of the Franks — he is doomed to die! He was born in Rome of Roman stock.' #

Arthur advanced until he came to Flanders; he conquered that land and occupied it with his forces. And then he went from there into Boulogne, and took the whole region of Boulogne into his own possession; and afterwards he took the road which led towards France. Then he issued his edict to all his men that, wherever they went, they should take nothing except what they could rightfully obtain by honest trading within the king's army.

Frolle, in France, where he then was, heard this, heard of Arthur's success and of all his achievements, and how he conquered everything he saw, and every place he set eyes upon submitted to him. Then King Frolle was terribly afraid. In the world as it was at the time of these events, the land of the Franks was called Gaul; and Frolle had come from Rome into France, and every year he sent tribute from that land, ten hundred pounds of gold and silver.

Now Frolle, who was the ruler of France, heard of the widespread havoc which Arthur was wreaking in the land. He at once sent messengers post-haste to Rome and bade the Roman people decide among themselves how many thousand soldiers they would send him that he might the more readily resist Arthur, drive the mighty Arthur out of the land.

Warriors rode out from the Roman territories; twenty-five thousand men marched towards France. Frolle and his many followers heard this, that the Roman force was riding towards his land. Frolle and his army went to meet them; then from all over

þa heo comen tosomne,   kene men and wihte,
of alle þan ærde,   vnimete uerde.

     þæt iherde Arður,   aðelest kingen,
and sumnede his ferde   and heom toʒaines wende.   11710
Ah næs næuere king nan   þa quic wes an eorðen
þa eouere ær an uolde   swulc folc awalde,
for of alle þan kinelonde   þe Arður hafuede an honde
forð he ladde mid him   alle þa kenneste men,
þat nuste he neuere on weorlde   hu feole þusend þer weoren.   11715

     Sone swa heo comen tosomne,   Arður and Frolle,
harliche heo igrætten   al þat heo imette.
Cnihtes swiðe stronge   igripen speren longe
and ræsden heom togædere   mid ræhʒere strengðe.
Alle dæi þer weore   duntes swiðe riue;   11720
folc feol to uolden   and fæie-sið worhten;
græmende segges   gras-bæd isohten.
Gullen þa helmes,   ʒeoumereden eorles,
sceldes þær scenden,   scalkes gunnen reosen.

     Þa cleopede Arður,   aðelest kingen: 11725
"Whar beo ʒe, mine Bruttes,   balde mine þaines?
þe dæi him forð ʒeongeð;   þis folc us aʒein stondeð.
Lette we heom to gliden   scærpe gares inoʒe
and techen heom to riden   þene wæi touward Romen."
Æfne þan worde   þe Arður iseide,   11730
he sprong forð an stede   swa sparc deð of fure.
Him weore fuliende   fifti þusende,
hærde here-kempen   hælden to fihte,
smiten uppen Frolle   þær he wes on ulocke
and brohten hine of fleme   mid muclen his folke.   11735
Þer Arður ofsloh   muchel uolc and vniuoh.

     Þa fleh into Parise   Frolle þe riche
and þa ʒeten tunden   mid teonen inoʒe;
and þa word seide,   sorhful an heorte:
"Leouere me weore   þat ich iboren neore!"   11740
þa weoren inne Paris   plihtliche spelles, ful iwis,
sorhfulle iberen;   burhmen gunnen beouien.
Walles heo gunnen rihten,   þa ʒæten heo gunnen dihten;
mete heo nomen   al þat heo neh comen.
An ælchere halue   heo heolden to burʒe;   11745
heo uerden þider alle   þe heolden mid Frolle.

the region, brave and bold men came together, an immense host.

Arthur, noblest of kings, heard of that and, summoning his army, went to meet them. But never before had there been any king living upon earth who had commanded such an army in the field, for from all the kingdoms which Arthur had in his possession he led forth with him all the bravest men, so that he had no idea whatsoever how many thousands there were.

As soon as the forces of Arthur and Frolle engaged, they fiercely attacked all whom they encountered. Warriors of great strength grasped long spears and charged together with furious strength. All day long blows were rife; men fell to the ground and met their deaths; wounded warriors sought their deathbed on the grass. The helmets rang, warriors groaned; there shields shattered, soldiers fell.

Then Arthur, noblest of kings, called out:
'Where are you, my Britons, my bold thanes? The day is passing; this army is holding out against us. Let us hurl at them sharp spears in plenty and send them riding on the road to Rome!'
As Arthur spoke these words, he sprang forward on his horse as a spark springs from the fire. Fifty thousand brave warriors intent on battle followed him, rushed upon Frolle where he was in the press and put him and his vast force to flight. There Arthur slew many men, a countless number.

Then the mighty Frolle retreated into Paris and with great difficulty closed the gates; and, sad at heart, he spoke these words:
'Better were it for me that I had never been born!'
Then in Paris there were, to be sure, reports of disaster, outbursts of sorrow; citizens trembled with fear. They began to fortify the walls, to strengthen the gates; they collected all the food they could come by. From all sides they poured into the city; all those who were loyal to Frolle gathered there.

þat iherde Arður,   aðelest kingen,
þat inne Paris wunede Frolle   mid unimete uerde,
and seiden þat he wolde   wið Arðure stonden.
To Paris ferde Arður,   ærhðe bideled,   11750
and bilæi þa walles   and arerde his teldes.
A feower halue he heo bilai   fouwer wiken and enne dæi;
auared weoren þa leden   þa þere weoren wiðinnen.
þa burh wes wiðinnen   afulled mid monnen
and æten sone þene mete   þe þer wes isomned.   11755

    þa feouwer wiken weoren aзonged   þa Arður wes þær atstonden,
þæ wes inne burзe   vnimete sorзe
mid wræcche þan falke   þe leie þer an hungre.
þer wes wop, þer wes rop,   and reouðen vniuohзe.
Heo cleopeden to Frolle   and beden hine frið wurchen,   11760
Arðures mon bicumen   and his monscipe bruken,
and þene kinedom halden   of Arðure þan kenen,
and no lete noht þat wræcche uolk   uorfaren al mid hungre.
þa andswarede Frolle   —freo he wes an heorte:
"Nai, swa me helpe God   þæ alle domes awalt,   11765
ne scal ich nauere his mon bicume   no he mi kinelaued.
Miseolf ich wulle fihte   —a Gode is al þat rihte!"
    þa зet cleopede Frolle   —freo mon an heorte:
"Næi, swa me helpe Drihten   þe scop þas dæies lihten,
nulle ic naueremare   зirnen Arðures ære.   11770
Ah fehten ich wulle   buten ælche cnihte,
licame wið licame   biforen mine leoden,
hond aзain honde   wið Arðure kinge.
Whaðer unkere swa beoð þere wakere,   sone he bið þe laðere;
wahðer vnkere swa þer ma luuien,   his freonden he bið þe leouere;
and whaðer unkere þe mæi of oðere   þat betere biwinne   11776
habben al þis oðeres lond   and sette hit an his aзere hond.
    þis ic wulle зirne,   зif Arður hit wule зetten,
and þis ich wulle swerien   uppen mine sweorden;
and зisles ich wulle finden,   þreo kingene sunen,   11780
þat ich þis forward wulle   fastliche halden,
þat nulle ich hit liзen,   bi mine quike liuen.
For leouere me is to liggen   bifore mine leoden
þan ich iseo an uolde   forfaren heom mid hungre.
For we habbeoð mid fehte   ure cnihtes uorfarene—   11785
scalkes auælled   fifti þusende—

Frolle challenges Arthur to single combat

Arthur, noblest of kings, heard of that, heard that Frolle lay in Paris with a vast force, proclaiming that he would hold out against Arthur. Arthur, quite undaunted, marched upon Paris, encircled the walls and pitched his tents. Four weeks and a day he besieged it on all sides; those who were within were terrified. Inside, the city was crammed with people and soon they had eaten the food which had been collected there.

When four weeks had passed since Arthur had taken up his position there, then inside the city there was misery beyond measure among the wretched people who lay starving there. There was weeping, there was lamentation, and sorrow unbounded. They called out to Frolle, imploring him to make peace, to become Arthur's liegeman and, retaining his high estate, rule the kingdom under the valiant Arthur, and not allow the common people to perish utterly from hunger. Then Frolle answered — he was noble at heart:

'No, so help me God who controls the destinies of all, I shall never become his liegeman nor he my sovereign lord. I will fight in single combat — justice lies with God alone!'

Then Frolle — a noble man at heart — called out again:
'No, so help me God who created this light of day, never, at any time, will I entreat Arthur's mercy. But I will fight in single combat, man to man, hand to hand against Arthur, in the presence of my people. Whichever of us proves the weaker, he will at once be the more despised; whichever of us may survive there, he will be the dearer to his friends; and whichever of us can get the better of the other he shall have all the other's land and take it into his own possession.

This I would desire, if Arthur will agree to it, and this I will swear to upon my sword; and I will provide hostages, three kings' sons, as surety that I will adhere firmly to this agreement, that I will not break it, on my very life. For I had rather lie dead before my people than see them perish of hunger on all sides. For we two have decimated our forces in battle — fifty thousand men

and moni ænne gode wifmon   iwhorht to bleðere widewe,
moni child faderlæs   and frouere bidaled;
and nu þis folc mid hungre   wunderliche ihærmede.
Forþi hit is betere   bitwixen unke seoluen   11790
todælen and todihten   þis kinelond mid fihte;
and habbe hit þa betere   and bruken hit on wunne."
    Frolle nom twalf cnihtes,   mid þissen worden forðrihtes,
and sende heom an sonde   to Arðure kinge,
and iwuste ȝif he wolde   þis forewarde halde   11795
and mid his aȝere hond   bitelen þat kinelond,
oðer uoreliggen   his leoden to harmen;
and ȝif he hit bitalden   hafde hit on an onwalde.
    þat iherde Arður,   aðelest kingen;
næs he neuere swa bliðe   ær an his liue,   11800
for him likede tidende   from Frolle þan kinge.
And þas word seide   Arður þe sele:
"Wel saið Frolle   þe king is of France;
betere is þat wit tweie   bitelen þas riche
þene þer beon ofslaȝene   ure þeines snelle.   11805
þis foreward ich biluuie   bifore mine leoden,
to ane isette dæie   to don þat he beodeð.
þat scal beon tomarȝen,   biforen unker monnen,
þat fehten wit scullen unc seoluen   —and falle þe forcuðere!
And whaðer unker þe geð abake   and þis feoht wulle forsake,   11810
beon he in ælche londe   iqueðe for ane sconde.
þenne mæie me singe   of ane swulche kinge
þe his beot haueð imaked   and his cnihtscipe forsaken!"
    þæt iherde Frolle   þe king wes of France,
þat Arður fehten wolden   himseolf buten cnihte.   11815
Strong mon wes Frolle   and sterc mon on mode,
and his beot imaked hafde   biforen al his duȝeðe;
and he ne mihte for scome muchelen   scenden hine seoluen,
bilæuen his balde ibeot   þat he i burh hafde iseid.
Sæide þat he sæide   to soðe he hit wende   11820
þat Arður hit wolde forsaken,   and nawiht to þan fehte taken;
for ȝif hit wuste Frolle   þe king wes ane France,
þat Arður him ȝetten wolde   þat he iȝirnd hafde,
don he hit nolde   for a scip ful of golde!
Neoðeles, wes Frolle   to fihte swiðe kene,   11825
muche cniht and strong mon,   and modi on heorten,

cut down — and made many a good woman a desolate widow, many a child fatherless and bereft of comfort; and now all these people are grievously afflicted with hunger. It is better, therefore, to divide and dispose of this kingdom by combat between the two of us; and may the better man have it and enjoy it in contentment.'

With these words, Frolle at once chose twelve knights and sent them as envoys to King Arthur to learn if he would agree to this proposal and prove his claim to the kingdom with his own hands, or reject it to his people's loss; and if he won the kingdom he could rule it as his own.

Arthur, noblest of kings, heard this; never before in his life had he been so happy, for the message from King Frolle pleased him. And the noble Arthur spoke these words:

'Frolle, King of France, speaks true; it is better that we two should dispute this kingdom than that our brave warriors be slain. In the presence of my people I approve this agreement, to do as he proposes on a day to be appointed. Tomorrow shall be the day when, before our forces, we two shall fight each other — and may the less worthy lose! And whichever of us two takes flight, seeking to abandon this contest, he shall be spoken of with ignominy in every land. Then songs may be sung of such a king who had pledged his word and betrayed his knighthood!'

Frolle, King of France, heard this, heard that Arthur was willing to fight single-handed, without companions. Frolle was a powerful fighter and stout-hearted, and had pledged his word before all his retainers; and he could not, for very shame, disgrace himself, could not go back on his bold boast which he had uttered in public. In saying what he had said, he truly thought that Arthur would reject it, would by no means agree to the combat; for if Frolle, King of France, had known that Arthur would grant him what he had requested, he would not have done so for a ship full of gold! Nevertheless, Frolle was very brave in battle, a bold fighter, a strong man and stout-hearted, and said that he would

and sæide þat he wolde   þene dæi halde
in þan æitlonde   þe mid watere is bizeonge.
"þat æitlond stondeð, ful iwis,   inne þere burh of Paris;
þer ich wulle mid fehte   bitele mine irihte
mid scelden   and mid cnihtes iwede.
Nu, tomarzen bið þe dæi   —habben þe hit bizieten mæi!"
     Comen þa tiðende   to Arður þan kinge
þat Frolle wolde mid fæhte   France bitellen.
Næs he næuere swa bliðe   ær an his liue,
and he lehzen agon   ludere stæfnenen,
and þas word seide   Arður þe kene:
"Nu ich wat þat Frolle   wið me wulle fihte
tomarze, in þan dæie,   alse he seolf demde,
i þan aitlonde   þat mid watere is bistonde,
for hit bicumeð kinge   þat his word stonde.
Leteð blawen bemen   and bodien mine monnen,
þat æuerælc god mon   toniht wakien for þon
and bidden ure Drihten   þe alle domes awalt
þat he me iscilde   wið Frolle þene wilde,
and mid his riht honde   witeze me wið sconde.
And zif ich mæi þis kinelond   bizieten to mire azere hond,
auereælche ærmen mon   þe æð scal iwurðen,
and wurchen ic wulle   muchel Godes wille.
Nu me uulsten þerto   þe alle þing mai wel idon;
þe heze heueneliche king   stonde me an helping,
for ich hine luuien wulle   þa while þe ich liuie."
     þer wes al longe niht   songes and candelliht;
hæhliche sungen clarckes   hali Godes salmes.
þa hit dæi wes amarzen,   duzeðe gunne sturien.
His wæpnen he nom an honden   Arður þe stronge;
warp he an his rugge   a ræf swiðe deore,
ænne cheisil scurte   and ænne pallene curtel,
ænne burne swiðe deore,   ibroiden of stele.
Sette he an hefde   ænne helm godne;
to his side he swende   his sweorde Caliburne.
His sconken he helede   mid hosen of stele,
and duden on his uoten   spuren swiðe gode.
þe king mid his weden   leop on his stede.
Me him to rehte   anne scelde gode;
he wes al clane   of olifantes bane.

11830

11835

11840

11845

11850

11855

11860

11865

keep the appointed day, upon the island which is amidst the water.

'That island, as is well known, stands within the city of Paris; there, in combat, will I defend my rights with the shield and armour of a knight. Now, tomorrow is to be the appointed day — may he who triumphs carry the day!'

The news came to King Arthur that Frolle meant to defend his claim to France in combat. Never before in all his life had the valiant Arthur been so happy, and he began to laugh loudly, uttering these words:

'Now I know that Frolle will fight against me tomorrow, all day long, as he himself has agreed, on the island encompassed by water, for it behoves a king that he should keep his word. Let the trumpets be blown and my men summoned, so that all good men stay awake this night and pray to our Lord who controls all destinies that He protect me from the savage Frolle, and with his right hand shield me from humiliation. And if I may secure this kingdom for my own, every poor man shall fare the better, and I will fulfil the will of God Almighty. Now may He who can do all things well help me in this; may the high king of heaven be my aid, for I will worship him as long as I live.'

All night long there was singing by candlelight, clerics solemnly chanting God's holy psalms. At daybreak on the morrow, the host began to stir. The mighty Arthur donned his armour; he threw on his back a splendid panoply, a shirt of fine linen and a tunic of rich cloth, a magnificent coat of mail, woven of steel. Upon his head he set a splendid helmet; at his side he hung his sword Caliburn. He sheathed his legs with hose of steel, and put fine spurs upon his feet. The king in his armour leapt upon his horse. A good shield, made all of ivory, was given to

Me salde him an honde   enne scaft stronge;
þer wes a þan ænde   a spære swiðe hende;
hit wes imaked i Kairmeðin   bi a smið þe hehte Griffin;
hit ahte Vðer,   þe wes ær king her.   11870

    Þa þe iwepned wes þe rahȝe,   þa gon he to uarene;
he mihte þa bihalde   þe þer bihalfues weore
þene king richne   rehliche riden.
Seoððen þis weorlde wes astald   nes hit nowhar itald
þat æuere ai mon swa hende   wunden uppen horse   11875
swa him wes Arður,   sune Vðeres.
Riden after þan kinge   balde here-ðringes,
a þen feoremeste flocke   feouwerti hundred,
heȝe here-kempen   bihonged mid stelen,
baldere Brutten,   bisie mid wepnen.   11880
After þan fusden   fifti hundred;
þeo Wælwain ladde   þe wæs a wæl-kempe.
Seoððen þer gunnen ut siȝen   sixti þusende
Bruttes swiðe balde;   þat wes þa bacwarde.

    Þer wes þe king Angel;   þer wes Lot and Urien;   11885
þer wes Vrienes sune,   Ywæin ihaten;
þer wes Kæi and Beduer,   and biwusten þa uerde þer;
þer wes þe king Howel,   hah mon of Brutlond;
Cador þer wes æc,   þe kene wes on flocke.
þer wes of Irlonde   Gillomar þe strong;   11890
þer wes Gonwais þe king,   Orkaneies deorling;
þer wes Doldamin þe kene   ut of Gutlonde;
þer wes Escil þe king,   Denemarkes deorling.
Folc þer wes afoten,   swa feole þusend monnen,
þat nas nauere na swa witful mon   a þissere weorlde-richen   11895
a nauere nane spelle   þat mihte þa þusend telle
bute he hauede, mid rihte,   wisdom of Drihtene,
oðer he hafde mid him   þat him hafde Mærlin.

    Arður forð gon liðe   mid vnimete folke
þat he com ful iwis   into þere burh of Paris   11900
a west halue þan watere   mid mucle his genge.
An æst hælf wes Frolle   mid muchelere ferde,
ȝaru to þan fehte   biforen his cnihtes alle.
Arður nom ænne bat godne   and bæh þer an inne
mid scelde mid stede   and mid alle his iwede,   11905
and he þat scip stronge   scaf from þan londe

him. A stout lance was handed to him; at the tip was a finely made spearhead forged in Carmarthen by a smith called Griffin; it had belonged to Uther, who was king here once. **#**

When the bold man was armed, he went forth; then he who chanced to be present there would have seen the noble king ride boldly forth. Never since this world began has it anywhere been recorded that any man so magnificent as Arthur, the son of Uther, ever rode upon horseback. Behind the king rode bold warriors, four thousand in the foremost company, noble warriors clad in steel, bold Britons, their weapons at the ready. Behind them pressed five thousand; Gawain, who led them, was a deadly fighter. Then sixty thousand most valiant Britons sallied out there, forming the rearguard.

King Angel was there; so were Lot and Urien; Urien's son, named Ywain, was there; Kay and Bedevere, were there, holding command in the army; King Howel, ruler of Brittany, was there; Cador, a staunch warrior, was there as well. The mighty Gillomar from Ireland was there; King Gonwais, beloved of the men of Orkney, was there; the valiant Doldamin of Jutland was there; King Æscil, beloved ruler of the Danes, was there. So many thousand men were on the march there that there was no man in this mortal world so skilled in numbers that he could reckon the thousands unless he had, in truth, the wisdom of the Lord, or had in him that skill which Merlin possessed.

Arthur marched onward with a vast force until he came right to the city of Paris on the west bank of the river with his great host. Frolle was on the east bank with a large army, ready for the combat in the presence of all his warriors. Arthur took a sturdy boat and embarked in it with horse and shield and all his armour, pushed the stout boat away from the bank and landed upon the

and stop uppen þat æitlond,   and ladde his stede an his hond.
His men þe hine þer brohte,   alse þe king hehte,
leten þene bat buȝen   forð mid þan vðen.

Frolle into scipe ferde   —þe king wes unuele   11910
þat he auere þohte   wið Arðure to fehte.
Ferde to þan æite   mid aðele his wepnen;
uppen þan æit he stop   and his stede him after droh.
Þeo men þe hine þer brohten,   alse þe king hehte,
lette þene bat fusen   forð mid þan vðen,   11915
and þa kinges tweien   ane þer wuneden.
Þa me mihte bihalden   þe þer bihalues weoren
folc a þan uolde   feondliche adredde;
heo clumben uppen hallen,   heo clumben uppen wallen,
heo clumben uppen bures,   heo clumben uppe tures   11920
þat comp to bihalden   of þan tweom kingen.
Arðures men beden   mid muchele æðmoden
Godd þene gode   and þa hali his moder
þat heore lauerd þere   siȝe moste habben;
and þa oðere eke   bede for heore kinge.   11925

Arður stop a stel boȝe   and leop an his blancke,
and Frolle mid his iwede   leop on his steden,
þe an an his ænde   a þan æitlonde,
and þæ oðer an his ænde   i þan æitlonde.
Heo quehten heore scaftes,   kinewurðe cnihtes,   11930
heo græneden heore steden   —gode cnihtes heo weoren!
Næs he næuere ifunde,   a næuere nane londe,
nan swa wihtful mon   þat hit wuste ær þan
whæðer of þan kingen   ouercumen sculde liggen,
for beien heo weoren cnihtes kene,   ohte men and wihte,   11935
muchele men on mihte   and a maine swiðe stronge.

Heo muneȝeden heore steden   and tosomne gunnen riden,
fusden feondliche   þat fur him sprong after.
Arður smat Frolle   mid feond-stronge maine
uppen þene sceld hehȝe   11940
and þe stede þe wes god   leop ut i þe ulod.
Arður ut mid his sweorde   —balu wes a þan orde—
and puinden uppen Frolle   þer he wes an ulode
ær heore comp weore   icumen to þan ænde.
Ah Frolle mid honde   igræp his spere longe   11945
and kept Arður anan   alse he aneoust com, *

island, leading his horse by the bridle. His men who had brought him there, as the king commanded, let the boat drift away with the current.

Frolle embarked — the king was sick at heart that he had ever thought of fighting with Arthur. He went in his splendid armour to the island and landed upon it, leading his horse behind him. The men who had brought him there, as the king commanded, let the boat speed away with the current, and the two kings remained there alone. Then anyone who chanced to be present there would have seen people on the shore in dreadful fear; they climbed upon buildings, they clambered up walls, they clambered upon dwellings, they climbed up towers to see the combat between the two kings. Arthur's men prayed most humbly to the gracious Lord and his holy mother that their sovereign might have the victory there; and the others prayed for their king also.

Arthur put his foot in the stirrup and leapt upon his steed, and Frolle in his armour mounted his horse, the one at one end of the island, and the other at the other end. The royal warriors shook their lances, readied their horses for combat — they were skilled knights! There never was, in any land, a man so clever as to know beforehand which of the kings would fall in defeat, for they were both fierce warriors, brave men and valiant, men of great might and of powerful strength.

They spurred their horses and rode towards each other, charging fiercely so that sparks flew out behind them. Arthur struck Frolle with furious strength high upon the shield and the good steed leapt out into the water. Arthur drew his sword — death was in the point — and struck at Frolle where he was in the water lest their combat should come to nothing. But Frolle gripped his long spear in his hand and fended Arthur off as he

and þene stede balde   smat i þere breoste
þat þat spere þurh raf   and Arður adun draf.
þa aras þe mon-drem   þat þe uolde dunede aȝen;
aqueðen þa weolcne   for reme of þan uolke.   11950

    þær Bruttes wolden   ouer water buȝen
ȝif Arður up ne sturte   stercliche sone
and igræp his sceld godne,   ileired mid golde,
and toȝaines Frolle   mid feondliche lechen;
breid biforen breosten   godne sceld brade.   11955
And Frolle him to fusden   mid his feond-ræse
and his sweord up ahof   and adunriht sloh,
and smat an Arðures sceld   þat he wond a þene feld.
þe helm an his hæuede   and his hereburne
gon to falsie   foren an his hafde,   11960
and he wunde afeng   feouwer unchene long—
heo ne þuhte him noht sær   for heo næs na mare—
þat blod orn adun   ouer al his breoste.
Arður wes abolȝe   swiðe an his heorte
and his sweord Caliburne   swipte mid maine,   11965
and smat Frolle uppen þæne hælm   þat he atwa helden
þurhut þere burne hod   þat hit at his breoste atstod.
þa feol Frolle,   folde to grunde;
uppen þan gras-bedde   his gost he bilæfde.

    þa Bruttes lohȝen   ludere stefuene,   11970
and leoden to fleonen   feondliche swiðe.
Arður þe riche   wende to londe,
and þus cleopien agon   aðelest kingen:
"Whær ært þu, Walwain,   monne me leofest?
Heot þas Rom-wæren alle   mid griðen liðen heonne;   11975
ælc mon bruke his ham   swulc Godd hit him on.
Hat ælcne mon halde grið   uppen leome and uppen lif,
and ich hit wulle dihten   todæi a seouennihte.
Hat þis folc þenne   liðen al tosomne,
and cumen to me seoluen   —þæ bet heom scal iwurðen.   11980
Heo scullen me mon-radene   mid monscipe fremmen,
and ich heom wulle holden   a mine onwolden,
and setten i leode   laȝen swiðe gode.
For nu scullen Romanisce laȝen   to þan grunde reosen,
þa iuurn here   stoden mid Frolle   11985
þe lið on æite ofslaȝen   and idon of lif-daȝen.

came towards him, and struck the brave steed in the chest so that
the spear pierced it and Arthur fell to the ground. Then a roar
went up from the people so that the earth rang in echo; the
heavens resounded with the clamour of the crowd.

The Britons would have crossed the river then had Arthur not
instantly leapt up, grasped his fine shield with its golden rim and,
raising his good broad shield before his chest, advanced upon
Frolle with hostile intent. And Frolle rushed at him in fierce
assault and, raising his sword and striking downwards, smote upon
Arthur's shield so that it fell to the ground. The helmet on his
head and the chain-mail on his forehead beneath gave way, and he
received a wound four inches long — since it was no greater it
did not seem painful to him — so that the blood ran down all over
his chest. Arthur was greatly enraged at heart, and swinging his
sword Caliburn with force, struck Frolle upon the helmet so that it
split apart right through the coif of mail and the sword lodged in
his chest. Then Frolle fell, stricken to the earth; upon the grassy
ground he yielded up his life. #

The Britons laughed, shouted loudly, and the others fled in
furious haste. The mighty Arthur returned to land, and the
noblest of kings called out thus:
'Where are you, Gawain, dearest of men to me? Bid all these
Romans depart hence in peace; let each man possess his lands and
home as God grants him. Command each man upon pain of life
and limb to keep the truce, and I will ratify it in seven days' time.
Order this whole company to return then, and come into my
presence — the better shall it be for them. They shall pledge
homage to me with due honour, and I will govern them by my
authority, and establish just laws in the land. For now the Roman
laws shall be abolished, those which existed formerly under Frolle
who lies slain on the island, deprived of life. Very shortly now

Herafter ful sone   scal his cun of Rome
heren tidinge   of Arðure þan kinge,
for ich heom wulle wið speken   and Rome walles tobreken,
and munegie heom hu King Belin   Bruttes ladde þider in   11990
and iwon him þa londes alle   þat stondeð into Rome."

    Arður beh to þan ʒæte   forn at þere burʒe;
comen witfulle men   þe þa burh biwusten
and Arður letten binnen   mid alle his monnen,
bitahten him halles,   bitahten him castles,   11995
bitahten him ful iwis   al þa burh of Paris.
þer wes muchel blissce   mid Brutisce uolke.
þe dæi sæh to burhʒe   þe Arður iset hafde;
com al þa mon-weorede   and his men bicomen.

    Arður nom his duʒeðe   and atwa heom todalde,   12000
and þa haluendæle   Howele bitætte,
and hehte hine uaren sone   mid muchele þere uerde,
mid Brutisce monnen   londes iwinnen.
Howel dude al swa   alse Arður hine hehte;
he biwon Barri   and alle þa londes þerbi,   12005
Angou and Turuine,   Aluerne and Gascunne,
and þa hafuenes alle   þe herden to þan londes.

    Guitard þe duc hæhte,   þe Peytouwe ahte;
he nolde buʒen Howele   ah heold toʒæines him æuere.
Nolde he ʒirnen na grið,   ah Howel him faht wið;   12010
ofte he uolc ualde   and ofte he ulem makede.
Howel al þat lond weste   and ofsloh þa leode.
þa isæh Guitard,   þe i Peitou wes lauerd,
þat alle his leoden   him to lose eoden.
Wið Howele he grið makede   mid al his mon-weorede,   12015
and bicom Arðures mon,   þas aðele kingen.
Arður him warð liðe   and luuede hine swiðe,
and hehte hine his lond bruken   for he him bæh to foten.
þa hafde Howel   hæhliche agunnen.

    Arður hafde France   and freoliche heo sette.   12020
He nom þa his ferde   and wende ʒeond þan ærde;
to Burguine he wende   and sette hit an his honde,
and seoððen he gon liðen   into Loherne
and alle þa londes   sette himseolue an honde.
Al þat Arður isæh   al hit him to bæh;   12025
and seoððen he wende ful iwis   aʒain ham to Paris.

his kinsmen in Rome shall hear tidings of King Arthur, for I will have words with them and, breaking down the walls of Rome, will remind them how King Belin led the Britons into the city and won for himself all the lands which belong to Rome.' #

Arthur proceeded to the gate at the entrance to the city; the men of good sense who had charge of the city came and gave Arthur entry along with all his men, surrendered to him the halls, the castles, indeed the entire city of Paris. There was great rejoicing among the British army. The day which Arthur had appointed came; the people all assembled and became his subjects.

Arthur took his forces and divided them into two, and entrusted one half to Howel, ordering him to set out at once with that large army, to conquer the regions with British troops. Howel did just as Arthur had ordered him; he conquered Berry and all the land around it, Anjou and Touraine, Auvergne and Gascony, and all the harbours which belonged to those regions.

The duke called Guitard, who possessed Poitou, would not submit to Howel but continued to hold out against him. He would not sue for peace, so Howel fought on against him; often he repulsed the army and as often retreated. Howel laid waste that entire region and slaughtered the inhabitants. Then Guitard, who was ruler of Poitou, saw that all his people were losing their lives. He made peace with Howel, he and all his followers, and he became the noble King Arthur's liegeman. Arthur showed him kindness and favoured him greatly, and bade him keep his land since he had knelt in submission to him. So Howel had done well. #

Arthur held France and ruled it nobly. Then he took his army and marched through the land; he went to Burgundy and took it into his possession, and afterwards he proceeded into Lorraine and took all the lands there into his possession. Each region Arthur set eyes upon submitted to him; and then he returned directly to Paris.

þa hafde Arður France   mid gode griðe astalde,
iset and isemed   þat sel was an þeoden,
þa hehte he þa cnihtes alden,   þa he hafde ȝare athalden,
þat heo to þan kinge comen   and heore læn afængen,   12030
for heo feole ȝeren   hafden ibon his iueren.
Summen he ȝæf lond,   summen seoluer and gold,
summen he ȝæf castles,   summen he ȝaf claðes,
hehte heom uaren an wunne   and beten heore sunnen;
forbed heom to berne wapnen   for ælde heom eode ouenan,   12035
and hehte heom luuien swiðe   Godd in þissen liue
þat he an ende ful iwis   ȝefen heom his paradis,
þæt heo mosten bruken   blisse mid ænglen.
     Alle þa cnihtes alde   foren to heore londe,
and þa ȝunge bilæfden   mid leouen heore kingen.   12040
Alle þa niȝen ȝere   Arður wuneden þere,
niȝen ȝere he heold France   freoliche on honde,
and seoððen na lengere   þat lond he ne walde.
Ah þa while þe þat kinelond   stod an Arðures hond,
þinges seolcuðe   siȝen to þere þeode.   12045
Monienne modfulne mon   Arður makede milde,
and monienne hehne mon   he helde to his foten.
     Hit wes an ane Æstere   þat men hafden iuaste,
þat Arður an Æstere dæi hafde   his aðele men atsomne,
al þat hæhste moncun   þat herden into Francen   12050
and of alle þan londen   þe þider in læien,
þer he ȝette his cnihten   alle heore irihten;
elc ane he ȝef æhte   alse he iærned hafde.
þus him iquað Arður,   aðelest kingen:
"Kæi, bisih þe hiderward,   þu ært min haxte stiward: 12055
her ich Angou ȝiue þe,   for þire wel dede,
and alle þa irihte   þe þider in beoð idihte.
Cneole me to, Beduer,   þu art min hexte birle her;
þa while þa ich beo an liue   luuien ich þe wulle.
Her ich ȝiue þe Neustrie   aneuste mire riche."   12060
(þa hehte Neustrie   þat nu hatte Normandie.)
þe ilke tweien eorles weoren   Arðures deore men
at rede and at rune   an æuerælche tune.
     þa ȝet him seide Arður,   aðelest kingen:
"Wend þe hider, Howeldin,   þu ært mi mon and mi cun.   12065
Haue þu Bulune   and bruc his on wunne.

Arthur rewards his older knights for their loyal service

When Arthur had made a firm peace in France, established and imposed it so that the people were content, then he ordered that the older knights, those he had long retained in his service, should come to the king and receive their reward, for they had been his companions in arms for many years. To some he gave land, to some silver and gold, to some he gave castles, to some he gave robes, bidding them depart in contentment and atone for their sins; he forbade them to bear arms since old age had overtaken them, and exhorted them to worship God truly in this life so that He would assuredly grant them his paradise at the last, that they might have bliss among the angels.

All the old knights went back to their lands, and left the younger ones with their beloved king. Nine years all told Arthur remained there, nine years he held France without let or hindrance, and after that he ruled that land no longer. But while Arthur held that kingdom in his possession, wondrous things befell the people. Many a proud man did Arthur humble, and many a haughty subject he brought to heel.

It was one Eastertide when men had fasted, on Easter day when Arthur had all his nobles with him, all the men of highest rank who hailed from France and from all the regions round about, that he then granted his warriors all that was their due; he gave each one such rewards as he had deserved. Arthur, noblest of kings, spoke to them thus:
'Mark this, Kay, you who are my High Steward: in recognition of your loyal service, I give you here Anjou and all the rights and privileges attached thereto. Kneel to me, Bedevere, you who are my chief cup-bearer here; I will cherish you as long as I live. I give you here Neustrie, which adjoins my realm.'
(What is now called Normandy was then called Neustrie.) These two earls were men particularly valued by Arthur for counsel and advice on all occasions.

Then Arthur, noblest of kings, spoke further:
'Draw near, Howeldin, you who are both my liegeman and my kinsman. Take Boulogne as yours and possess it in contentment.

Cume ner, Borel, þu art cniht wis and war.
Her ich þene Mans þe   mid monscipe bitæche;
and bruc þu his on wunne   for þire wel dede."
Þus Arður þe king delde   his drihtliche londes   12070
after heore iwurhte   for he heom þuhte wurðe.
Þa weoren bliðe spelles   in Arðures hallen;
þer wes harepinge and song,   þer weoren blissen imong.

        Þa Æstre wes aȝonge   and Aueril eode of tune,
and þat gras was riue   and þat water wes liðe,   12075
and men gunnen spilien   þat wes Mæi at tune,
Arður nom his folc feire   and to þere sæ uerde,
and lette bonien his scipen,   wel mid þan bezsten,
and ferde to þissen londe   and up com at Londen.
Up he com at Lundene   leoden to blissen;   12080
al hit wes bliðe   þat hine isæh mid eȝen;
sone heo gunnen singe   of Arðure þan kinge
and of þere wurðscipe muchele   þe he iwunne hafde.
        Þer custe uader þene sune   and seide to him welcume,
dohter þa moder,   broðer þene oðer;   12085
suster custe suster   —þa softere heom wes an heorten.
A monie hundred studen   stoden bi þan weie,
folc fraininge   of feole cunne þingen;
and cnihtes heom talden   of heore onwalden,
and heore ȝeolp makeden   of muchele biȝeten.   12090
Ne mihte na mon suggen,   nære he na swa hende mon,
of halue þan blissen   þa weoren mid þan Brutten.
Ælc ferde, an his neode,   ȝeond þas kineþeode
from burhȝe to burhȝe   mid blissen uniuoȝe.
And þus hit ane stunde   stod a þan ilke;   12095
blisse wes on Brutene   mid balde þan kinge.

        Þa Æstre wes aȝeonge   and sumer com to londe,
þa nom Arður his red   wið riche his monnen
þat he wolde inne Karliun   bere his crune him on,
and a Whitesunedæi   his folc þer isomnie.   12100
A þen ilke daȝen   men gunnen demen
þat nes i nane londe   burh nan swa hende
na swa wide cuð   swa Karliun bi Uske,
buten hit weoren þa burh riche   þe Rome is ihaten.
Þa ȝet wes mid þan kinge   moni mon an londe   12105
þat quidde þa burh of Karlion   ricchere þene Rome,

Come near, Borel, you who are a wise and prudent knight. I here bestow Le Mans upon you with all honour; possess it in contentment in recognition of your loyal service.'

So King Arthur distributed his royal lands according to the merits of those men whom he thought worthy. Then there was joyful entertainment in Arthur's halls; there was harping and singing, and other pleasures as well. #

When Easter was over and April come to an end, and the grass was plentiful and the waters calm, and men began to say that May was here, Arthur took his splendid army and marched to the seashore, had his most excellent ships assembled, and sailed to this country, making landfall at London. He came ashore at London to the joy of the people; all who set eyes on him rejoiced, began at once to sing of King Arthur and the great renown which he had won.

There father kissed son and bade him welcome, daughter kissed mother, brothers each other; sister kissed sister — their hearts were the more at ease. In hundreds of places people lined the route, asking questions about all sorts of things; and the warriors told them of their conquests, loudly boasting of vast booty. No one, however skilled he were, could describe half the happiness there was among the Britons then. Each, as occasion required, travelled through this kingdom from city to city in great contentment. And so it continued thus for a time; there was joy in Britain with the presence there of the valiant king.

When Easter had passed and summer was come, then Arthur decided in counsel with his chief followers to wear his crown in Caerleon, and to assemble his people there upon Whit Sunday. In those days men judged that there was in no land a city so splendid nor famed so far and wide as Caerleon-upon-Usk, unless it were the splendid city which is called Rome. Indeed there was many a man with the king there who declared the city of Caerleon

and þat Uske weore   selest alre wateren.
Medewes þer weoren brade   bihalues þere burhȝe,
þer wes fisc, þer wes fuȝel,   and fæiernesse inoȝe;
þer wes wude and wilde deor,   wunder ane monie,   12110
þer wes al þa murhðe   þe æi mon mihte of þenche.
Ah nauer seoððen Arður þider bæh   þa burh seoððe no iþæh,
no nauere ne mæi   bitwene þis and Domesdæi.
Summe bokes suggeð to iwisse   þat þa burh wes biwucched,
and þæt is wel isene   soð þat hit sunde.   12115
    I þære burh weoren   twa munstres swiðe mære;
þat an munstre wes of Seint Aaron   —þerinne wes muchel halidom—
þat oðer of þan martir Seint Iuliæn   þe heh is mid Drihten.
þer weoren nunnen wel idon,   moni heh iboren wifmon.
þe biscop-stole wes at Seint Aaron   þer wes moni sel mon;   12120
canunes þer weoren   þe cuð weoren widen.
þer wes moni god clarc   þe wel cuðe a leore;
muchel heo ferden mid þan crafte   to lokien in þan leofte,
to lokien i þan steorren   nehȝe and feorren;
þe craft is ihate   Astronomie.   12125
Wel ofte heo þan kinge   seide of feole þinge;
heo cudden him on leoden   what him sculde ilimpen.
Swulc wes þe burh of Karliun;   þer wes muchel richedom,
þer wes muchel blisse   mid bisie þan kinge.
    þe king nom his sonde   and sende ȝeond his londe;   12130
hæhte cumen eorles,   hehte cumen beornes,
hehte cumen kinges   and æc here-ðringes,
hehte cumen biscopes,   hehte cumen cnihtes,
hahte alle þa freomen   þa euere weoren an londe,
bi heore life hehte heom beon   a Whitesunedæi at Kærleon.   12135
    Cnihtes gunnen riden   vnimete whiden,
riden touward Kairliun   of feole cunne londen.
To þan Whitesunedæie   þer com þe king Angel,
King of Scotlonde,   mid sceone his folke—
moni wes þe faire mon   þe folȝede þan kingen—   12140
of Mureiue King Vrien   and his fæire sune Ywæin,
Stater, King of Suð Wales,   and Cadwaðlan, King of Norð Wales,
Cador, Eorl of Cornwale,   þa þe king luuede,
Moruið of Glouchæstre,   Maurin of Winchastre,
Gurguint, Eorl of Herford,   and Beof, Eorl of Oxeuord.   12145
Gursal þe balde   from Baðe þer com ride,

more splendid than Rome, and that the Usk was the best of all rivers. About the city there were broad meadows, there were fish, there were birds, and many other delights; there were woods and wild animals in great abundance, all the pleasures any man could conceive. But never since the time when Arthur resorted there has the city flourished, nor ever shall from now to Doomsday. Some books state as a fact that the city was accursed, and that is clearly seen to have been true. #

In the city there were two very famous minsters, the one dedicated to St Aaron — in it there were many sacred relics — the other to St Julian the Martyr who is honoured by God. There were pious nuns, many women of noble birth. The seat of the bishop was at St Aaron where there were many holy men; there were canons famed far and wide. There were many good clerics who had much learning; they busied themselves much in the art of scanning the heavens, in gazing at the stars both near and distant; that art is called Astronomy. They very often spoke to the king about many matters; they revealed to him what should befall him here. Such was the city of Caerleon; there was much magnificence, there was much joy in the presence of the active king. #

The king chose his messengers and sent them throughout his kingdom; he commanded earls to come, nobles to come, kings and chieftains too to come, bishops and knights to come, and all noblemen whatsoever who were in the land, ordering them upon pain of death to be at Caerleon on Whit Sunday.

From far and wide, from many different lands, noblemen rode to Caerleon. On the Whit Sunday there came King Angel, King of Scotland, with his splendid company — many a handsome man followed the king; there came King Urien of Moray and his fair son Ywain, Stater, King of South Wales, and Cadwallan, King of North Wales, Cador, Earl of Cornwall, whom the king loved, Morvith of Gloucester, Maurin of Winchester, Gurguint, Earl of Hereford, and Beof, Earl of Oxford. The valiant Gursal came

Vrgent of Chastre,   Ionatus of Dorchestre,
Ærnald of Salesburi   and Kinmarc of Cantuareburi,
Balien of Silechæstre,   Wigein of Leirchæstre,
Argal, Eorl of Warwic,   mid folk swiðe sellic,   12150
Dunwale, Apries sune,   and Kegein, Elauðes sune.
Kineus þer wes, Coittes sune,   and Cradoc, Catelles sune,
Ædlein, Cledaukes sune,   Grimarc, Kinmarkes sune,
Run, Margoitt and Netan,   Clofard, Kincar and Aikan,
Kerin, Neton and Peredur,   Madoc, Traher and Elidur.   12155
        þis weoren Arðures   aðele eorles
and þa haxte þeines ohte   of alle þissere þeode,
wiðuten þan beornen   of Arðures borden;
þa na man ne mihte ikennen   ne al þat folc inemnen.
þa weoren ærchebiscopes þreo   inne þissere þeode,   12160
inne Lunden and in Eouerwic,   and inne Karliun Seint Dubric;
he wes swiðe hali mon,   þurh alle þinge wel idon.
To Lundene læi þe ærchebiscop-stol   þe to Cantwareburi wes
                                                          seoððe idon
seoððe Engliscemen   þis lond heom iwunnen.
        To tellen þat folc of Kairliun,   ne mihte hit na mon idon: 12165
þer wes Gillomar þe king,   Irisce monnen deorling,
Maluerus, King of Islonde,   Doldanet, King of Gutlonde,
King Kailin of Frislonde,   Æscil, King of Denelonde.
þer wes Loð þe kene,   þe king wes bi Norðe,
and Gonwæis, Orcaneie king,   utlaȝen deorling.   12170
þider com þe wilde,   þe eorl of Builuine,
Læȝer wes ihaten   and his leoden mid him;
of Flandres þe eorl Howeldin,   of Chærtres þe eorl Cherin.
þeos ferede mid him   al þat Frensce moncun:
twalf eorles swiðe ræihe   þe rixleden ouer France,   12175
Guitart, Eorl of Peiters,   Kæi, þe orl of Angers,
Beduwear, Eorl of Normandie   —þat lond hehte þa Neustrie;
of þe Mans com þe eorl Borel,   of Brutaine þe eorl Howel.
Howel eorl wes freo mon   and faire weoren his iwede,
and al þat folc Frensce   bihongen weoren feire,   12180
iwepned wel alle   and hors ho hafden uatte.
þer weoren, bisides,   fiftene biscopes.
Nes na cniht ne na swein,   ne oht mon þat weore þein,
from þa porz of Spaine   to þan tune of Alemaine,
þat þider icomen nere   ȝif he iboden weore,   12185
al for Arðures æie   aðeles cunnes.

riding there from Bath, Urgent of Chester, Jonathas of Dorchester, Ærnald of Salisbury and Kinmarc of Canterbury, Balien of Silchester, Wigein of Leicester, Argal, Earl of Warwick, with a splendid company, Dunwald, son of Apries, and Kegein, son of Elauth. Kineus, son of Coitt, was there and Cradoc, son of Catell, Ædlein, son of Cledauk, Grimarc, son of Kinnarc, Run, Margoitt and Netan, Clofard, Kincar and Aikan, Kerin, Neton and Peredur, Madoc, Traher and Elidur. #

These were Arthur's noble earls and the most valiant thanes in all this land, save for the members of Arthur's household; no man could identify or name all those present there. At that time there were three archbishops in this country, in London and in York, and St Dubric in Caerleon; he was a very holy man, excellent in all respects. In London was located the archbishopric which was later removed to Canterbury after the English had conquered this land for themselves.

That assembly at Caerleon could not be numbered: there was King Gillomar, beloved of the Irish, Malverus, King of Iceland, Doldanet, King of Jutland, King Kailin of Friesland, Æscil, King of Denmark. The bold Lot, who was king in the north, was there and Gonwais, King of Orkney, beloved of the renegades he ruled. That fierce man, the earl of Boulogne, called Læʒer, had come there and his followers with him; from Flanders had come the earl Howeldin, from Chartres the earl Cherin. They had brought with them all the men of France: twelve most valiant earls who ruled over France, Guitard, Earl of Poitiers, Kay, the earl of Angers, Bedevere, Earl of Normandy — that region was then called Neustrie; from Le Mans came the earl Borel, from Brittany the earl Howel. Earl Howel was a handsome man and his clothes were splendid, and that whole band of Frenchmen was finely arrayed, all well armed and strongly mounted. There were fifteen bishops also. There was no knight, no squire, no valiant soldier of any rank, from the ports of Spain to the towns of Germany, who would not have come there if he had been bidden, purely out of respect for the noble Arthur. #

þa al þis hired wes icumen,   ælc king mid his folke,
þer me mihte bihalde   þe þer bihalues weore
moni seolcuðne mon   þe isizen wes to burhzen,
and feole cunne tiðende   mid Arðure þan kinge;
þer wes moni sellic clað,   þer wes moni cniht wrað.
þer weoren herberze   hæhliche awurðe,
þer þa innes weoren   mid strengðe biwunnen.
Þer weoren on uelden   moni þusend telden;
þer com spic and water   and aten vnimete;
ne mai hit na mon suggen on his tale   of þan win and of þan ale;
þer com hey, þer com gras,   þer com al þat god was.
    Þa al þis folc isomned was   at sele þan kingge,
þa com þe Whitesunedæi   alse Drihten hine sende,
þa comen þa biscopes alle   biuoren heore kinge,
and þa ærchebiscopes þreo   biuoren Arðure,
and þene kinehelm nome   þa him wes icunde
and setten uppen his hafde   mid hezere blisse.
Swa heo hine gunnen lede,   al mid Godes rede:
Seint Dubris eoden biuoren,   he wes Criste icoren;
þe ærchebiscop of Lundene   eode an his riht honden
and bi his luft side   þe ilke of Eouerwike,
fiftene biscopes biuoren   of feole londen icoren;
heo weoren bihangen alle   mid palle swiðe balde
þe weoren alle ibrusted   mid barninge golde.
    Þer feouwer kinges eoden   biuoren þan kaiseren;
heo wezeden on heore honde   feouwer sweord of golde.
Þus hehte þa an,   þe wes a swiðe duhti mon,
þat wes Cador þe king,   Arðures deorling;
þe oðer of Scotlonde,   sweord he weide an honde,
and þe king of Norð Walles   and þe king of Suð Wales;
and þus heo gunnen leden   þe king to chirechen.
Þeo biscopes gunnen singe   biuoren þan leod-kinge;
bemen þer bleowen,   bellen þer ringeden,
cnihtes gunnen riden,   wifmen forð gliden.
To iwissen hit is isaid   and soð hit is ifunden
þat no isah no mon nauer ær,   mid eorðliche monne her,
half swa hahne richedom   a nauer nane hepen
swa mid Arðure was   aðeles cunnes.
    Into chirchen bicom   Arður þe riche mon;
Dubriz þe archebiscop   —Drihten him wes ful god;

12190
12195
12200
12205
12210
12215
12220
12225

When all this royal company had come, each king with his followers, whoever was present there would have seen many a man from foreign parts who had come to the city, and heard many a different tale in King Arthur's court; there was many a strange garment, many a fearsome warrior. The lodgings there were splendidly prepared, the guest quarters strongly built. In the plain were many thousand tents liberally provisioned with meat and oats and water; no one can recount the quantities of wine and ale; hay was brought, grass was brought, all things necessary were brought there.

When all this company had assembled at the good king's court and Whit Sunday had come as the Lord appointed, then all the bishops and the three archbishops came before Arthur their king, and took the crown which was his by right and set it upon his head amidst great rejoicing. So, with God's guidance, they led him in procession: St Dubric, who was God's elect, went before him, the archbishop of London walking on his right side and on his left the archbishop of York, preceded by fifteen consecrated bishops from many lands; they were all robed in most splendid vestments which were embroidered all over with shining gold. #

Four kings walked before the sovereign there, bearing in their hands four golden swords. The one was called King Cador, a very valiant man beloved by Arthur; the second, a Scottish king, also carried a sword, as did the King of North Wales and the King of South Wales; and so they conducted the king to church. The bishops, processing before the sovereign, began to chant; trumpets sounded there, bells rang out, knights rode past, women passed by. It is stated with certainty and is manifestly true that no man ever before saw here upon earth half so much royal pomp in any assembly whatever as there was with Arthur, that man of royal race.

Into church came the mighty King Arthur; the archbishop Dubric — God was most gracious to him; he was the Roman

of Rome he wes legat   and of þan hirede prelat—
he song þa hali masse   biuoren þan leod-kinge.
Comen mid þere quene   wifmen wel idone,
þere richchere monne wif alle   þe wunede on londe   12230
and þere hehere monnen dohtere   þa quene hafden isohte,
al swa þa quene hafde ihate   bi hire fulle wite. *
I þere chireche i þere suð halue   sat Arður þe king himseolf,
bi pere norð side   Wenhæiuer þa quene.
þer comen hire biforen   feouwer quenen icoren;   12235
ælc bar on luft honde   enne beh of rede gold
and þreo snauwhite culueren   setten an heore sculderen;
þæt weoren þa feouwer quenen,   þere cnihte wifen
þa beren an heore heonden   þe feouwer sweordes of golde
biuoren Arðure,   aðelest kingen.   12240
Moni mæide child wes þere   mid mære þere quene,
þær wes moni pal hende   on faire þan uolke.
    Of monies cunnes londe   þer wes muchel onde,
for ælc wende to beon   betere þene oðer.
Feole cnihtes anan   comen to þere chirechen,   12245
summe for guðinge,   summe for þan kinge,
summe to bihalden   þa wifmen þat weoren balde.
Songes þer weoren murie   þa ilaste swiðe longe;
ich weone ʒif hit weore   ilast seoue ʒere
þa ʒet heo weolden mare   þe þerat weoren.   12250
    Þa þe masse wes isungen,   of chircchen heo ðrunge;
þe king mid his folke   to his mete uerde;
mid mucle his duʒeðe   drem wes on hirede.
þa quene an oðer halue   hire hereberwe isohte;
heo hafde of wifmonne   wunder ane monien.   12255
Þa þe king wes isete   mid his monnen to his mete,
to þan kinge com þæ biscop   Seind Dubriz, þe wes swa god,
and nom of his hafde   his kinehælm hæhne—
for þan mucle golde   þe king hine beren nalde—
and dude enne lasse crune   on þas kinges hafde;   12260
and seoððen he gon do   a þere quene al swo.
Inne Troie þis wes laʒe   bi heore ælderne daʒe
þa Bruttes of come   þe weoren wel idone:
alle þa wepmen   at heore mete seten
sundi bi heomseoluen   —þat heom þuhte wel idon;   12265
and al swa þa wifmen   heore iwune hafden.

legate and chaplain of the court — sang the holy mass before the sovereign. There came with the queen, just as the queen had ordered upon pain of her extreme displeasure, women richly arrayed, all wives of the leading men who dwelt in the land and the daughters of noblemen whom the queen had chosen. In the church King Arthur himself sat on the south side, Queen Guenevere on the north side. There came before her four chosen queens, each wearing on the left hand a ring of red gold and with three snow-white doves sitting upon their shoulders; these four queens were the wives of the lords who bore in their hands the four golden swords before Arthur the noblest of kings. There was many a maiden with the noble queen, many a splendid robe in that fair company.

There was great rivalry between the people from many different lands, for each thought himself better than the other. Many knights came flocking to the church, some for the jousting, some for the king's sake, some for the women who were handsome to look upon. There was glorious singing which continued for a long time; I think even if it had lasted seven years those who were present would still have wished for more.

When the mass had been sung, they thronged out of the church; the king with his company went to his meal; there was rejoicing in the court among his numerous retinue. The queen went to her appointed place on the opposite side; with her she had a great company of women. When the king was seated with his followers at his meal, the archbishop St Dubric, who was most pious, came to the king and took from his head his splendid crown — the king could not wear it because of the great weight of gold — and placed a lighter crown on the king's head; and afterwards he did the same for the queen. This was the custom in Troy in the days of their ancestors, those from whom the noble Britons were descended: at their meals all the men sat apart by themselves as seemed to them most fitting, and the women likewise had their customary place. #

þa þe king wes isete   mid alle his duȝeðe to his mete,
eorles and beornes,   at borde þas kinges,
þe stiward com steppen   þe Kæy wes ihaten,
hæxt cniht on londe   vnder þan kinge   12270
of alle þan hæpe   of Arðures hirede.
Kay hehte him biuoren   moni hæh mon icoren:
þer weoren a þusend cnihtes bald   wunder wel italde
þat þeineden þan kingen   and his here-ðringen.
Ælc cniht hafde pal on   and mid golde bigon   12275
and alle heore uingeres   iriuen mid gold ringes; *
þas beorn þa sunde   from kuchene to þan kinge.

    An oðer half wes Beduer,   þas kinges hæȝe birle;
mid him weoren eorlene sunen   of aðele cunne iboren,
and þere hehȝe cnihtene sunen   þa þider weoren icumen,   12280
seouen kingene sunen   þat mid him quehten.
Bedeuer auormest eode   mid guldene bolle;
after him a þusend   þrasten to hirede
mid alle þas cunnes drenche   þe me cuðe on biðenche.
And þa quene, an hire ende,   wifmen swiðe hende,   12285
a þusend hire eode biuoren   riche men and wel icoren
to þæinen þere quene   and þan þat mid hire weoren. *

    Nes he næuere iboren   of nane cnihte icoren,
ilæred no læwed,   a nauere nare leode,
þe cuðe him itelle   an æies cunnes spelle   12290
of halue þan richedome   þe wes inne Kairliune,
of seoluere and of golde   and gode iweden,
of hehȝe iborene monnen   þa inne hirede wuneden,
of horsen and of hafueken,   of hunden to deoren,
and of riche iweden   þa a þan hirede weoren.   12295
And of alle þan folke   þe wuneden þer on folde,
wes þisses londes folk   leodene hendest itald,
and al swa þa wimmen   wunliche on heowen
and hahlukest iscrudde   and alre bezst itoȝene.
For heo hafden on iqueðen alle   bi heore quike liue   12300
þat heo wolden of ane heowen   heore claðes habben;
sum hafde whit, sum hafden ræd,   sum hafde god grene æc,
and alches cunnes fah clað   heom wes wunder ane lað.
And elche untuhtle   heo talden vnwurðe.

    þa hafde Ænglene ard   þat alre bezste here-word;   12305
and þis leodisce uolc æc   leofuest þan kinge.

When the king was seated at his meal with all his courtiers, earls and nobles, at the royal table, there came forward the steward who was called Kay; of all the company of Arthur's court, he was the greatest noble in the land under the king. In the king's presence, Kay commanded many a noble man of rank: there were a thousand bold knights of high repute who served the king and his warrior host. Every knight wore rich robes trimmed with gold and their fingers were all adorned with gold rings; they bore the dishes from the kitchen to the king.

On the other side was Bedevere, the king's chief cup-bearer; with him were the sons of earls born of noble stock and the sons of the principal knights who had come there, and seven kings' sons who bore him company. First Bedevere advanced with a golden bowl; after him a thousand others thronged towards the company with every kind of drink that one could imagine. And before the queen, most gracious of women, in her place, came a thousand noble and worthy men to serve the queen and those who were with her.

Never was there any man, learned or unlearned, born of any worthy man in any country whatsoever, who could recount in words of any kind half the magnificence there was in Caerleon, of silver and gold and fine trappings, of high-born men who frequented the court, of horses and hawks and hunting-dogs, and of rich robes which there were at the court. And of all the people who were in the world then, the men of this land were considered the most handsome, and the women also the fairest in beauty and most splendidly dressed and the most nobly bred. For they had all declared upon their very lives that they would have clothes of one colour only; some had white, some had red, some others had bright green, and variegated cloth of any kind was most displeasing to them. And they held in contempt ill-breeding of any kind.

At that time the land of England enjoyed the highest repute; and also the people of this country were most esteemed by the

þa wifmen hehȝe iborene   þa wuneden a þissen londe
hafden iqueðen alle   on heore quides soðe
þat nan lauerd taken nolde   inne þissere leode
næuer nænne cniht,   neore he noht swa wel idiht,   12310
bute he icostned weoren   þrie inne compe,
and his ohtscipen icudde   and ifonded hine seolue;
baldeliche he mitte þenne   ȝirnen him brude.
For þere ilke tuhtle   cnihtes weoren ohte,
þa wifmen wel idone   and þa betere biwitene.   12315
þa weoren i Brutene   blissen inoȝe.
    þa þe king iȝeten hafde   and al his mon-weorede,
þa buȝen of burhȝe   þeines swiðe balde:
alle þa kinges   and heore hereþringes,
alle þa biscopes   and alle þa clærckes,   12320
alle þa eorles   and alle þa beornes,
alle þa þeines,   alle þa sweines,
feire iscrudde,   helde ȝeond felde.
Summe heo gunnen ærnen,   summe heo gunnen urnen,
summe heo gunnen lepen,   summe heo gunnen sceoten,   12325
summe heo wræstleden   and wiðer-gome makeden,
summe heo on uelde   pleouweden vnder scelde,
summe heo driuen balles   wide ȝeond þa feldes.
Monianes kunnes gomen   þer heo gunnen driuen,
and whaswa mihte iwinne   wurðsciþe of his gomene   12330
hine me ladde mid songe   atforen þan leod-kinge
and þe king for his gomene   ȝæf him ȝeuen gode.
Alle þa quene   þe icumen weoren þere
and alle þa lafdies   leoneden ȝeond walles
to bihalden þa duȝeðen   and þat folc plæie.   12335
    þis ilæste þreo dæȝes,   swulc gomes and swulc plæȝes.
þa a þan ueorðe dæie   þe king gon to spekene
and aȝæf his gode cnihten   al heore rihten;
he ȝef seoluer, he ȝæf gold,   he ȝef hors, he ȝef lond,
castles and claðes eke   —his monnen he iquemde;   12340
þer wes moni bald Brut   biuoren Arðure.
    Nu comen to þan kinge   neouwe tidinde.
Arður þe balde king   sat at ane borde;
biuoren him seten kinges,   and feole here-ðringes,
biscopes and clærekes   and swiðe ohte cnihtes.   12345
þer comen into halle   spelles seolcuðe.

king. The women of high birth who lived in this country had all pledged upon their given word that none in the land would take as husband any man whatsoever, were he never so well fashioned, unless he had been tested three times in battle, his valour demonstrated and his worth proven; then he might boldly claim a bride for himself. Because of that special custom the knights were valiant, the women well bred and the more virtuous. There was great happiness in Britain then.

When the king and all his company had eaten, then the most valiant thanes proceeded out of the city: all the kings and their commanders, all the bishops and all the clerics, all the earls and all the nobles, all the thanes, all the retainers, finely clad, spread out over the plain. Some raced on horseback, some on foot, some engaged in leaping, some in shooting, some of them wrestled and contended together, some played a shield-game in the plain, some drove balls far over the fields. They played many kinds of sport there, and whoever achieved honour in his game was led with song before the sovereign and the king rewarded him well for his skill. All the queens and all the ladies who had come there leaned over the walls to watch the nobles and the people at play.

All this, these games and sports, lasted three days. Then on the fourth day the king addressed them and gave his faithful followers all their dues; he gave silver, he gave gold, he gave horses, he gave land, castles and robes as well — his men were well pleased; there was many a bold Briton in Arthur's following. #

Now fresh tidings came to the king. The valiant King Arthur was seated at table; kings sat with him, and a host of warriors, bishops and clerics and most valiant knights. Strange tidings were brought into the hall. There came twelve bold lords clothed

þer comen twalf þeines ohte   mid palle biþehte,
hæʒe here-kempen,   hehʒe men on wepne.
Ælc hafde on heonde   grætne ring of golde
and mid æne bende of golde   ælc hafde his hæfd biuonge.   12350
Æuer tweie and tweie   tuhte tosomne;
ælc mid his honde   heold his iuere,
and gliden ouer ulore   biuoren Arðure
swa longe þat heo comen   biuoren Arðure þan leod-kinge.
Heo grætten Arður anan   mid aðelen heore worden: 12355
"Hal seo þu, Arður king,   Bruttene deorling,
and hal seo þi duʒeðe   and al þi drihtliche uolc.
We sunden twælf cnihtes   icumen her forðrihtes;
riche and wel idone   we sundeð of Rome.
Hider we sunden icumene   from ure kaisere,   12360
Luces is ihaten,   þe waldoð Rome-leoden.
He hahte us hider wende   to Arðure þan kinge
and þe hat græten   mid his grim worden,
and sæið þat he awundred is   wunder ane swiðe
whar þu þat mod nime   a þisse midden-erde   12365
þat þu derst of Rome   wiðsuggen æi dome
oðer hebben up þin eʒen   aʒein ure ældren,
and wha hit þe durre ræden   þat þu swa reh ært iwurðen
þat þu þrattien darst   domes walden,
Luces þene kaisere,   hexst of quicke monnen.   12370
Þu haldest al þi kinelond   a þire aʒere hond
and nult noht þene kaisere   of londe ihere,
of þan ilke londe   þe Iulius hafde an honde,
þa inne iuurn daʒæn   biwon hit mid fehten,
and þu hit hauest atholde   a þire anwolde   12375
mid balden þine cnihten,   binimest us ure irihten.
      Ah sæi us Arður, sone,   and word send to Rome;
we sculleð bere þin ærde   to Luces ure kaisere.
Ʒif þu wult icnawen   þat he is king ouer þe
and þu his mon bicumen wulle   and hine for lauerd icnawen,   12380
and don riht þan kaisere   of Frolle þan kinge
þat þu mid woʒe   at Paris asloʒe
and nu haldest al his lond   mid unrihte a þire hond,
ʒif þu i þissen twælf wiken   temest to þan rihten
and þu wult of Rome   þolien æi dome,   12385
þenne miht þu libben   imong þine leoden.

in fine garments, warriors of high rank, noble men in arms. Each had on his hand a great ring of gold and each had his head encircled with a band of gold. They all came in together two by two, each holding his companion by the hand, and crossed the floor towards Arthur until they came into the presence of Arthur the high king. They immediately greeted Arthur in courtly speech:

'Health to you, King Arthur, beloved of the Britons, and health to your court and all your noble followers. We twelve knights have just now arrived here; men of power and worth, we have come from Rome. We have come here at the behest of our emperor, Lucius by name, who rules the people of Rome. He commanded us to journey here to Arthur the king and bade us greet you with stern words from him, saying that he is exceedingly astonished where in the world you got such courage that you dare gainsay any decree of Rome or raise your eyes to oppose our prince, and wonders greatly who dared advise you thus that you have become so bold as to dare challenge the lord of destiny, the emperor Lucius, greatest of living men. You hold your whole realm in your own possession and will not obey the sovereign lord of the land, that very land which Julius Caesar ruled, who in days of yore conquered it in battle, and which you with your bold warriors have kept in your control, so depriving us of our rights. #

Now answer us immediately, Arthur, and send a reply to Rome; we shall bear your answer to our emperor, Lucius. If you will acknowledge that he is sovereign over you and will become his liegeman and acknowledge him as overlord, and recompense the emperor for the death of Frolle the king whom you wrongfully slew at Paris and whose whole land you now unjustly hold in your possession, and if within these twelve weeks you submit to due authority and will accept any ruling Rome may impose, then you may be allowed to live among your people. And if you will not

And ʒif þu swa nult don,   þu scalt wursen vnderfon:
þe kaisere wule her cumen   swa king scal to his aʒen,
king swiðe kene,   and nimen þe mid strengðe,
ibunden þe lede   biuoren Rom-leoden;   12390
þenne most þu þolien   þat þu ærst forhoʒedest."
Æfne þisse worden   Bruttes buʒen from borden;
þer wes Arðures hird   hehliche awraðða̅ed
and muchene að sworen   uppen mære ure Drihten
þat alle heo dede weoren   þa þeos arunde beden;   12395
mid horsen al todraʒene   dæð heo sculden þolie.
þer heo buʒen to   Bruttes swiðe wraðe,
luken heom bi uaxe   and laiden heom to grunde.
þer weoren men Romanisce   reouliche atoʒene
ʒif Arður ne leope to   swulc hit a liun weore   12400
and þas word seide,   wisest alre Brutten:
"Bilæueð, bilaueð swiðe   þas cnihtes on liue!
Ne sceollen heo on mine hirede   nenne harm þolien;
heo beoð hider iriden   ut of Rom-leoden
swa heore lauerd heom hehte,   Luces is ihaten.   12405
Ælc mon mot liðen   þer his lauerd hine hateð gan;
nah na man demen   erendes-mon to dæðen
bute he weoren swa ufele biwiten   þet he weore lauerd-swike.
Ah sitteð adun stille,   cnihtes inne halle,
and ich me biræde wulle   of swulchere neode   12410
wulc word heo scullen aʒen beren   to Luces þan kaiseren."
    þa seten adun alle   þa duʒeðe on heore benche
and þa luding alæid   biuoren þan leod-kinge.
þa stod Arður him up,   aðelest kingen,
and he cleopede him to   seouen sune kinges,   12415
eorles and beornes   and þa þe weoren baldest,
and alle þa wiseste men   þa wuneden a þen folke.
Wenden into ane huse   þe wes biclused faste,
an ald stanene weorc   —stiðe men hit wurhten.
þer men gunnen rune   his red-ʒeuen wise   12420
wulc andswere he ʒiuen wolde   Luces þan kaisere.
þa iboʒen weoren alle   beornes to benche,
þa wes hit al stille   þat wuneden inne halle;
þer wes vnimete æie   mid mære þan kinge;
ne durste þer na man speken   leste þe king hit wolde awreken.   12425
    þa stod þer up Cador,   þe eorl swiðe riche ær,

do so, the worse shall it be for you: the emperor will come here as a king should come to his own land, will come like a bold ruler and take you by force, lead you in chains before the people of Rome; then must you endure what once you scorned to do.'

At these words the Britons leapt from the table; Arthur's followers were greatly enraged at that and swore solemn oaths in the name of our glorious Lord that all those who had delivered this message were doomed to die, that they should suffer death by being torn apart by horses. The Britons, furiously angry, then leapt upon them, seized them by the hair and threw them to the ground. The Romans would have been cruelly ill-treated there had not Arthur, wisest of all the Britons, leapt forward like a lion and uttered these words:

'Stop, stop at once! Let these knights live; they shall not suffer any injury in my court; they have ridden here from Rome as their lord, Lucius by name, ordered them. Every man must go where his lord orders him to go; no man has the right to condemn an ambassador to death unless he should be so disposed to evil as to betray his lord. But sit down quietly, knights in hall, and I will consider in this hour of need what message they shall take back to the emperor Lucius.'

Then all the nobles sat down on their benches and the clamour ceased in the royal presence. Then Arthur, noblest of kings, stood up and summoned before him seven kings' sons, earls and nobles and the boldest of warriors, and all the wisest men who dwelt in the land. They went into a building which was stoutly fortified, an old stone structure — strong men built it. There his wise counsellors discussed what answer he should give to the emperor Lucius. When all the nobles had taken their seats, then those who were in the hall were perfectly quiet; there was great awe in the presence of the famous king; no man there dared speak lest the king should punish him for it.

Then Cador, the most powerful noble there, stood up and

and þas word sæide   bifore þan riche kinge:
"Ich þonkie mine Drihte   þat scop þes dæies lihte
þisses dæies ibiden   þa to hirede is iboзen
and þissere tidinge   þe icumen is to ure kinge,   12430
þat we ne þuruen na mare   aswunden liggen here.
For idelnesse is luðer   on ælchere þeode
for idelnesse makeð mon   his monscipe leose,
ydelnesse makeð cnihte   forleosen his irihte,
idelnesse græiðeð   feole uuele craften,   12435
idelnesse makeð leosen   feole þusend monnen;
þurh eðeliche dede   lute men wel spedeð.
For зare we habbeoð stille ileien   —ure wurðscipe is þa lasse.
    Ah nu ic þonkie Drihtne   þæ scop þas daзes lihte
þat Romanisce leoden   sunden swa ræie   12440
and heore beot makieð   to cumen ure burhзes,
ure king binden   and to Rome hine bringen.
Ah зif hit is soð þat men saið,   alse segges hit telleð,
þat Romanisce leoden   sunden swa ræзe,
and sunden swa balde   and swa balufulle   12445
þat heo wulleð nu liðen   into ure londen,
we heom scullen зarekien   зeomere spelles;
heore ræhscipe scal heomseoluen   to reouþe iwurðen.
For nauere ne lufede ich longe   grið inne mine londe,
for þurh griðe we beoð ibunden   and wel neh al aswunden."   12450
    Þat iherde Walwain,   þe wes Arðures mæi,
and wraððede hine wið Cador swiðe   þa þas word kende;
and þus andswærede   Walwain þe sele:
"Cador, þu ært a riche mon!   Þine rædes ne beoð noht idon,
for god is grið and god is frið   þe freoliche þer haldeð wið—   12455
and Godd sulf hit makede   þurh his Goddcunde—
for grið makeð godne mon   gode workes wurchen
for alle monnen bið þa bet   þat lond bið þa murgre."
    Þa iherde Arður   þat flit of þissen eorlen
and þus spac þe riche   wið raзen his folke: 12460
"Sitte adun swiðe,   mine cnihte alle,
and ælc bi his lifen   luste mine worden."
Al hit wes stille   þat wunede inne halle.
Þa spak þe king balde   to riche his folke:
"Mine eorles, mine beornes,   balde mine þeines,   12465
mine duhti men,   mine freond deoren,

spoke these words before the mighty king:

'I thank my Lord who created the light of day that I have
lived to see this day dawn in the court and hear this news which
has come to our king, so that we need no longer lie idle here. For
idleness is hateful to all peoples since idleness causes a man to
lose his valour, idleness makes a soldier neglect his duty, idleness
leads to many evil deeds, idleness brings to ruin many thousands
of men; few men prosper through idle habits. For a long time we
have lain idle — our honour is the less.

But now I thank God who created the light of day that the
Romans are so angered that they are threatening to come to our
cities, to put our king in chains and take him to Rome. But if
what men say is true, as it is reported, that the Romans are so
fierce, are so bold and so hostile that they intend now to invade
our land, we shall prepare unpleasant greetings for them; their
ferocity shall lead to their own undoing. For I have never
favoured a prolonged peace in my land, for peace ties us down
and makes us all but impotent.'

Gawain, who was Arthur's kinsman, heard that and was
greatly enraged with Cador who had uttered these words; and the
noble Gawain replied thus:

'Cador, you are a mighty man! Your advice is not sound, for
peace and quiet are good if one maintains them willingly — and
God himself in his divinity created them — for peace allows a
good man to do good deeds whereby all men are the better and
the land the happier.'

Then Arthur heard that dispute between these noblemen and
the mighty king spoke thus to his angry followers:

'Sit down quickly, all my followers, and let each upon his life
listen to my words.'

All who were in the hall fell silent. Then the bold king spoke
to his noble company:

'My earls, my nobles, my bold thanes, my valiant men, my

þurh eou ich habbe biwunnen   vnder þere sunnen
þat ich æm swiðe riche mon,   reh wið mine feonden;
gold ich habbe and gærsume;   gumenen ich æm ælder.
No biwan ich hit noht ane,   ah dude we alle clæne.   12470
To moni feohte ich habbe eou ilad,   and æuere ȝe weoren wel irad *
swa þat feole kinelondes   stondeð a mine honde.
Ȝe beoð gode cnihtes,   ohte men and wihte;
þat ich habbe iuonded   i wel feole londen."

    Þa ȝet him spac Arður,   aðelest kingen: 12475
"Nu ȝe habbeoð iherd,   hæȝe mine þeines,
what Romanisce men   redeð heom bitwenen,
and wulc word heo sendeð us here   into ure londe
mid write and mid worde,   wið grætere wræððe.
Nu we mote biðenchen   hu we ure þeoden   12480
and ure muchele wurðscipe   mid rihte maȝen biwiteȝen
wið þis riche moncun,   wið þas Rome-leoden,
and andsware heom senden   mid aðelen ure worden,
mid mucle wisdome   vre writ senden to Rome
and iwiten at þan kæisere   for whan he us ofcunnen,   12485
for whan he us mid þrætte   and mid hokere igræteð.
Swiðe sære me gromeð   and vnimete me scomeð
þat he atwit us ure luren   þat we ifeorn habbeoð forloren;
heo suggeð þat Iulius Cesar hit biwon   mid compe i fehten.

    Mid strengðe and mid fehte   me deð feole vnrihte,   12490
for Cesar isohte Bruttene   mid baldere strengðe.
No mihte Bruttes wið him   heore lond werien,
ah mid strenðe heo eoden an hond   and bitahten him al heore lond, *
and þerafter sone   alle his men bicome.
Sum ure cun heo hadden islaȝen   and sum mid horsen todraȝen;   12495
summe heo ladde ibunden   ut of þissen londen,
and þis lond biwunne   mid unrihte and mid sunnen.
And nu axeð mid icunde   gauel of þissen londe!
Al swa we maȝen don   ȝef we hit don wulleð,
þurh rihte icunde   of Beline kinge   12500
and of Brennen his broðer,   þan duc of Burgunne.
Þeos weoren ure ældre   þa we beoð of icumene;
þeos bilæie Rome   and þa riche al biwunnen,
and biuoren Rome þere stronge   heore ȝisles anhenge;
and seoððen heo nomen al þat lond   and setten hit an heore aȝere hond.
And þus we mid rihte ahten   Rome us biriden.

dear friends, with you I have conquered all lands under the sun so that I am now a most mighty man and stern with my enemies; I have gold and treasure; I am a ruler of men. I did not triumph on my own, for we did it all together. I have led you in many a battle, and you were always most skilful so that many kingdoms are now in my possession. You are good warriors, brave men and valiant; I have put that to the proof in many a land.'

Then Arthur, noblest of kings, spoke further:
'Now, my noble thanes, you have heard what the Romans are plotting among themselves, and what kind of message they have sent us here in our land, expressed with great fury in letters and speeches. Now we must consider how we can fitly defend our subjects and our high majesty against this powerful nation, against these Romans, and give them answer in princely words from us, with all prudence send our reply to Rome and learn from the emperor for what reason he despises us, why he addresses us with threats and derision. It greatly shames and sorely angers me that he taunts us with our losses which we have suffered in the past, the loss of this land which, they say, Julius Caesar won by force of arms.

Men commit many wrongs in war by force of arms as Caesar did in attacking Britain with extreme violence. The Britons could not defend their land against him, but they yielded to force and surrendered all their land to him, and thereupon all immediately became his subjects. They caused some of our ancestors to be slain and some they had torn apart by horses; some they led from these lands in chains, and unjustly and wrongfully took possession of this realm. And now their descendants demand tribute from this land as of right! We can do the same if we choose to do so, through our rightful inheritance from King Belin and his brother Brenne, the duke of Burgundy. These were our ancestors from whom we are descended; they besieged Rome and subdued the whole region, and before mighty Rome itself hanged their hostages; and then they seized that whole land and took it into their own possession. And so we ourselves have the right to besiege Rome. #

Nu ich wulle leten Belin   and Brenne bilæuen,
and speken of þan kaisere,   Costantin þan stronge;
he wes Helene sune,   al of Brutten icume;
he biwon Rome   and þa riche awelde.   12510
Lete we nu of Costantin   þe Rome iwon al to him
and speken of Maximiæn   þat was a swiðe strong mon;
he wes king of Brutene;   he biwon France.
Maximien þe stronge   Rome he nom an honde,
and Alemaine he biwon eke   mid wunder muchele strengðe,   12515
and al from Romayne   into Normandie.
And þeos weoren mine ælderen,   mine aððele uoregenglen,
and ahten alle þa leoden   þa into Rome leien;
and þurh swuche dome   ich ahte to biȝeten Rome.
Heo ȝirneð me an honde   gauel of mine londe;   12520
al swa ic wille of Rome   ȝif ich ræd habbe.
    Ich wilnie a mine þonke   to walden al Rome,
and he wilneð me in Brutene   to binde swiðe uaste
and slæn mine Bruttes   mid his balu-reses.
Ah ȝif hit on mi Drihten   þe scop dæiȝes and nihten,   12525
he scal his balde ibeot   sære abuggen
and his Rom-leoden   þerfore scullen reosen;
and ic wulle ræh beon   þer he nu rixleð on.
Wunieð nu stille alle;   ic wulle suggen mine iwille;
ne scal hit na man oðer idon,   ah hit scal stonden þeron.   12530
He wilneð al and ich wilni al   þæt wit beiene aȝæð,
habben hit nu and aȝe,   þe hit æð mæȝen iwinne;
for nu we scullen cunne   wham hit Godd unne."
Þus spac þe balde   þe Brutene hafde an onwalde;
þat wes Arður þe king,   Bruttene deorling.   12535
    Setten his kempen   and his quides lusten;
summe heo sæten stille   mucle ane stunde,
summe heo muche runen   ræhten heom bitweonen.
Summe hit þuhte heom god;   summe hit mengden heore mod.
Þa heo hafden longe   ilustned þan kinge,   12540
þa spac Howel þe hende,   hah mon of Brutene,
and his quides ræhte   biuoren raien þan kinge:
"Lauerd king, hercne me   alse ich ær dude þe;
þu hafest isæid word soðe   —selehðe þe beoð ȝifðe!
Hit wes ȝare iqueðen   þat we nu sculleð cuðen,   12545
i þan iuurn ȝere   þat nu is ifunden here.

Arthur expounds his ancestral right to imperial power

Now I will let Belin be and say no more of Brenne, and speak of the mighty emperor Constantine; he was the son of Helena and was descended solely from Britons; he conquered Rome and ruled that realm. Now let us leave Constantine who conquered all Rome for himself and speak of Maximian who was a very powerful man; he was King of Britain and he conquered France. The mighty Maximian took possession of Rome, and Germany too he conquered with a mighty power, and every place from the Romagna as far as Normandy. And these were my ancestors, my noble predecessors, and they possessed all the lands which had belonged to Rome; and on that precedent I have the right to conquer Rome. Tribute from my land is now demanded of me; I will demand the same from Rome if I have my way. **#**

I long in my heart to rule all the Roman emperor's lands, and he wishes to enslave me here in Britain and slay my Britons by his hostile attacks. But if my Lord who created day and night grant it, he shall pay dearly for his bold boasting and his Romans shall perish for it; and I will be all-powerful where he now rules. Let all stay silent now; I will make my intention known; no one shall prevent it, but it shall be as I say. He and I both want everything that we each possess, to have and hold now and evermore, whoever can the more readily get it in his power; for now we shall learn to whom God will grant it.'

Thus spoke the valiant man who had rule over Britain; it was King Arthur, beloved of the Britons.

His warriors sat and listened to his words; some of them sat silent for a long time, some of them whispered much among themselves. To some of them it seemed good; it troubled the minds of others. When they had listened long to the king, then the gracious Howel, ruler of Brittany, spoke, uttering his thoughts before the fiery king:

'Lord king, listen to me as I did just now to you; you have spoken words of truth — good fortune be yours! That which we shall now find true, what is now revealed here, was prophesied

Sibeli hit sæide —hire quides weoren soðe—
and sette hit on bocke uolke to bisne
þat þreo kinges sculden buȝen ut of Brutlonde
þa biwinnen sculden Rome and al þa riche 12550
and alle þa londes þe þerto liggeð.
þe uorme wes Belin, þat wes a Brittisc king;
þe oðer wes Costantin, þe king wes on Brutene;
þu scalt beon þe þridde þe Rome scal habben.

And ȝif þu wult biginnen, þu hit scalt biwinnen; 12555
and ich wulle þerto helpe mid haȝere strenðe.
Ich wulle ouer sæ sende to selen mine þeinen,
to balden mine Brutten —þa bet we scullen fusen.
Ich wulle haten alle þa aðele of Bruttaine,
bi leomen and bi heore liue, ȝeond alle mine londe, 12560
þat heo beon ȝarewe sone mid þe uaren to Rome.
Mi lond ich wulle sette to wedde for seoluere,
and alle þe æhten of mine londe for seoluere and for golde.
And swa we scullen uaren to Rome and slan Luces þene kaisere
and bitellen þine irihten. I þe lede ten þusend cnihtes." 12565
þus Howel spilede, hext of Brutaine.

þa þe Howel iseid hafde þat him sel þuhte,
þa spæc Angel þe king, Scotlondes deorling,
and stod uppen ane boncke and beien his broðeren;
þat was Lot and Vrien, tweie swiðe aðele men. 12570
þus Angel þe king seide to Arðure þan kene:
"Læuerd Arður, ich sugge þe þurh soðe quides mine
þat ilke þat Howel hafeþ ispeken —ne scal hit na man awreken,
ah we hit scullen ilæsten, bi ure quicke liuen.
And, lauerd Arður þe hæhȝe, lust me ane stunde. 12575
Cleope þe to ræde þine eorles riche
and alle þa hæxte þa beoð in þine hirede,
and bide heom þe suggen mid soðen heore worden
whæt heo þe wulleð fulste þine iuan to fordonne.
Ich þe leden wulle cnihtes of mire leode: 12580
þreo þusend kempen, ohte alle icorene,
ten þusend men auote, to uehte swiðe gode;
and fare we to Rome and iwinnen þa riche.
Ful swiðe us mæi scomien and ful swiðe us mai gromien
þat heo sculle senden sonden after gauele to ure londe. 12585
Ah swa us helpe Drihte þæ scop þas daȝes lihte,

– 168 –

long ago in the days of old. The Sibyl said it — her sayings were true — and set it down in a book as a forewarning to men that three kings would come out of Britain who were to conquer Rome and all the wealth and all the lands belonging thereto. The first was Belin, who was a British king; the next was Constantine, who was king in Britain; you are to be the third who shall possess Rome. #

And if you will undertake it, you shall achieve it; and I will assist in that to the utmost of my power. I will send across the sea to my brave thanes, to my bold Bretons — the better shall we speed. I will command all the nobles of Brittany, throughout my whole land, that they be ready promptly upon pain of life and limb to march with you to Rome. I will put my land in pawn for silver, and pledge all the goods in my country for silver and gold. And so we shall march to Rome and slay the emperor Lucius and claim your rights. I will bring you ten thousand warriors.'

Thus spoke Howel, the ruler of Brittany.

When Howel had said what seemed to him fitting, then King Angel, beloved of the Scots, spoke, standing upon a bench with his two brothers Lot and Urien, two most noble men. King Angel addressed the valiant Arthur thus:

'Lord Arthur, I say to you truly in my own words the same as Howel has said — no one shall prevent it, but as we live and breathe, we shall accomplish it. And, Arthur, mighty lord, listen to me for a moment. Call to counsel your noble earls and all the greatest men who are in your court, and bid them tell you truly in their own words what help they will give you to destroy your enemies. I will bring you soldiers from my country: three thousand warriors, all picked men of valour, ten thousand foot soldiers, most brave in battle; and we will march on Rome and conquer the kingdom.

We may rightly feel humiliated and be justly enraged that they should send messengers to our country demanding tribute. But so help us God who created this light of day, they shall

heo hit scullen abugge   mid heore bare liue!
For þenne we habbeoð Rome   and alle þa riche,
we scullen nimen þa londes   þa þerto liggeð,
Peoile and Alemaine,   Lumbardie and Brutaine,   12590
France and Normandie"   —þa hit hæhte Neustrie—
"and swa we sculleð meðegie   heore mod vnimete."
Þa þe king isaid hafde,   þa andswarede alle:
"Iniðered wurðe þe ilke mon   þe þerto nule helpen
mid ahten and mid wepnen   and mid alle his imihten!"   12595
    Þa wes Arðures hired   sturneliche awrað– ð ed;
cnihtes anburste weoren   þat alle heo gunnen biuien.
Þa Arður iherd hafde   his hired iberen,
þa cleopien agon   —þe king wes abolȝen:
"Sitteð adun stille,   cnihtes inne halle,   12600
and ich eou wulle telle   what ich don wulle.
Mine writen ich wulle maken   þa wel beon idihte,
and sende þan kæisere   modes sorȝe and muchel kare;
and ich wulle ful sone   faren into Rome.
Nulle ich þider na gauel bringe,   ah þane kaiser ich wulle binden
and seoððen ich wullen hine anhon,   and al þat lond ich wulle uordon
and foruaren þa cnihtes alle   þe aȝein me stondeð i fehte."
    Arður his writ nom an honden   mid wiðerfulle worden
and þan beornen hit bitahte   þæ þa ærnde hafde ibrohte.
And seoððe he lette heom scruden   mid ælchere pruden   12610
mid þan hæxte scrude   þa he hafde on bure,
and hehte heom faren sone   to Luces of Rome;
and he cumen after wolde   swa raðe swa he mihte.
    Þas twælfe heore wai ferden   touward heore londen;
mid seolure and mid golde   12615
cnihtes swa iscrudde   no þurh al swa wel idihte;
þus Arður heom dihte   al for heore worde.
Þas twalf cnihtes foren   þat heo to Rome comen;
heo gretten heore kaisere,   heore kinelauerd:
"Hail seo þu Luces;   þu art hæxt ouer us.   12620
We woren at þan raȝe,   at Arðure þan kinge;
we habbeoð writen ibroht þe,   word swiðe grate.
Arður is þe kenneste mon   þat we æuere lokeden on,
and he is wunder riche,   and his þeines beoð balde.
Þer is æuerælc swein   swulc he cniht weore,   12625
þer is æuerælc swein   swulc he weore riche þein,

atone for it with their very lives! For when we have taken Rome and the rest of the kingdom, we shall seize the lands which belong thereto, Apulia and Germany, Lombardy and Brittany, France and Normandy' — it was then called Neustrie— 'and so we shall curb their excessive pride.'

When the king had spoken, then all responded:

'May ruin strike the man who will not help in this with his wealth and weapons and with all his might!' #

Then Arthur's followers were greatly enraged; his warriors were so incensed that they all shook with rage. When Arthur had listened to the clamouring of his followers, then he called out — the king was furious:

'Sit down quietly, knights in hall, and I will tell you what I intend to do. I will have my writs prepared and rightly drawn, and send to the emperor much care and sorrow of heart; and I will immediately march upon Rome. I will bring no tribute there, but I will bind the emperor and afterwards hang him, and I will ravage that whole land and slaughter all the warriors who oppose me in battle.'

Arthur took up his writ with its threatening words and handed it to the men who had brought the message. Then he had them clothed with all magnificence in the richest robes he had in store, and ordered them to go at once to Lucius of Rome; and he would follow after as quickly as he could.

Those twelve went on their way towards their homeland; no knights were so bedecked in silver and gold nor so well arrayed in every respect; Arthur treated them thus solely on account of their mission. These twelve knights journeyed until they came to Rome; they greeted their emperor, their sovereign lord:

'Health to you, Lucius, you who are our ruler. We have been with that fierce man, with Arthur the king; we have brought you letters, a message of great import. Arthur is the boldest man we ever set eyes upon, a man of great authority, and his thanes are valiant. There every squire is like a knight, there every servant

þer beoð þa cnihtes   swulc hit weoren kinges.
Mete þer is vnimete,   and men swiðe balde,
and þa ueiezereste wifmen   þa wunieð on liuen,
and himseolf Arður þe balde   uæizerest ouer alle   12630
Bi us he sende word þe   þat he wule to þisse londe;
na gauel he nule bringen   ah þe seoluen he wule binden,
and seoðð he wule þe anhon,   and þis lond al fordon
and Alemaine, Lunbardie,   Burguine, France and Normandie.
Frolle he sloh, is iua;   swa he wulle us alle do,   12635
and ahnien him ane   þa we azen alle clane.
Herto he wule leden kinges,   eorles and here-þringes;
and her we habbeoð an honden   writen þat he sende
þe þe quiddieð what he wule don   þenne he cumeð hider on."

    þa þæ ærnde wes iseid,   þæ kaisere wes ful særi mon,   12640
and astured weoren Rom-weren alle   mid sterclichere wræððe.
Ofte heo eoden to ræde,   ofte heo heolden rune
ær heom mihte iwurðen   waht heo don wolde.
Noðeles, a þan ende,   enne ræd heo ifunden;
þat was þurh þa senaturs   þa þet sinað heolden.   12645
þan kaisere heo radden   þat he write runen
and sende his sonde   zeond feole kinelonde,
and hehte heom cume sone   alle to Rome
of euerælche londe   þe heom oht lufeden,
and alle þa wulleð mid fehte   biziten lond oðer ahte.   12650
Folc þer com sone   to þere burh of Rome;
swa muchel swa þer neuere ærer   na mon no isumnede.
Heo seiden þat heo wolden   ouer Munt Giu iwenden
and wið Arðure fehten   wharswa heo hine ifunden,
and Arður slæn oðer anhon   and his hired al fordon,   12655
and ahnien þan kaisere   Arðures riche.
    þe æreste king þe þer com   —he wes swiðe kene mon,
Epistrod, King of Grece;   Ethion, Duc of Boece,
þer com mid mucle wize,   Irtac, King of Turckie,
Pandras, King of Egipte,   of Crete þe king Ipolitte,   12660
of Syrie þe king Euander,   of Frigie þe duc Teucer,
of Babilone Mæptisas,   of Spaine þe kaisere Meodras,
of Medie þe king Boccus,   of Libie þe king Sexstorius,
of Bittunie Pollidices,   of Iturie þe king Sexes,
Ofustesar, King of Aufrike   —nes þer na king his ilike;   12665
mid him com moni Aufrican;   of Ethiope he brohte þa bleomen.

is like a rich thane, there the knights are like kings. Food is plentiful there, and the men are most valiant, the women the fairest now living, and the noble Arthur himself the handsomest of men. He sends you word by us that he intends to come to this country; he will bring no tribute but instead he will fetter you, and then he will hang you, and utterly destroy this realm and Germany, Lombardy, Burgundy, France and Normandy. He slew his enemy, Frolle; so he will do all of us, and himself alone possess everything, all that we now own. He will come here leading kings, noblemen and warriors; and we have with us here letters he has sent which will inform you what he intends to do when he comes here.'

When the message had been delivered, the emperor was greatly cast down, and all the citizens of Rome roused to furious anger. Often they met in counsel, deliberated repeatedly before they could agree what they would do. At last, however, they came to a decision arrived at by the senators who formed the council. They advised the emperor that he should write confidential letters and send his envoys to many kingdoms, commanding all men to come at once to Rome from every realm which owed them fealty, and all who hoped to gain land or property through warfare. A multitude came at once to the city of Rome; never before had so many men assembled there. They declared that they would march across the Great St Bernard Pass and fight against Arthur wherever they should encounter him, slay or hang Arthur and utterly destroy his army, and seize Arthur's kingdom for the emperor.

The first king to arrive there was Epistrod, King of Greece — a very brave man; Ethion, Duke of Boece, came there with a large force; Irtac, King of Turkey, came, Pandras, King of Egypt, King Ipolitte of Crete, King Evander of Syria, Duke Teucer of Phrygia, Mæptisas of Babylon, Meodras, Emperor of Spain, King Boccus of Media, King Sextorius of Libya, Pollicides of Bithynia, King Sexes of Ituria, Ofustesar, King of Africa — there was no monarch to equal him; with him came many Africans; he brought the dark-skinned men from Ethiopia. The Romans also assembled there,

þa seolue Rom-leoden   liðen heom tosomne,
þat weoren at nexte   of Rome þa hexte:
Marces, Lucas and Catel,   Cocta, Gaius and Metel;
þis weoren þa sixe   þe þat senaht al biwusten.   12670
    þa þis folc isomned wes   of feole cunne londes,
þa sette þe kaisere   arimen al þæne here.
þa weoren þer riht italde   to fihte swiðe balde
feouwer hundred þusende   cnihtes a þan hæpe,
mid wepnen and mid horsen   swa bihoueð to cnihten.   12675
Nes he neuere iboren   i nauere nane burȝe
þat mihte þat folc tellen   þat þer eoden auoten.
Auormest heruestes dæie   uorð heo gunnen sturien
auer riht þene wæi   þet touward Munt Giu lai.
    Lete we nu ane while   þeos ferde bilæue   12680
and speke we of Arður,   aðelest kinge,
þa þe he bisoht hafde   his þeines sele,
and ælc wes ham iuare   þer he lond hafde
and raðe aȝæin comen   cnihtes to hireden,
mid wepnen wel idihten   þurh allen heore mihte,   12685
of Scotlond, of Irlond,   of Gutlond, of Islond,
of Noreine, of Denene,   of Orcaneie, of Maneie.
Of þan ilke londen   beoð an hundred þusende
iwepnede þeines ohte   on heore londes wise.
Neoren hit noht cnihtes,   no þes wæies idihte,   12690
ah hit weoren men þa kenlukeste   þa æi mon ikende
mid mucle wiaxen,   mid longe saxen.
    Of Normandie, of Angou,   of Brutaine, of Peitou,
of Flandres, of Bulunne,   of Loherne, of Luueine,
comen an hundred þusende   to þas kinges hirede,   12695
cnihtes mid þan bezsten,   þurhcostned mid wepnen.
þer comen þa Twalf Iueren   þa France sculden heren;
twelf þusend cnihtes   heo brohten forðrihtes;
and of þissen londe   Arður nom an honde
fifti þusend cnihtes kene   and ohte men to fihte.   12700
Howel of Brutaine,   cnihtes mid þan bezste,
ten þusend ladde   of his leod-folke.
Of ganninde monnen,   þa heo forð wenden,
þurh nane cunnes spelle   ne cuðe heom na mon telle.
    Arður þa hehte,   aðelest kinge,   12705
to ane isette time   þat folc isomnien,

those who were next in authority to the ruler of Rome: Marces, Lucas and Catel, Cocta, Gaius and Metel; these six men had total control of the Senate. #

When this host had assembled from many different lands, then the emperor had the whole army counted. Then there were duly numbered there four hundred thousand soldiers in all, very brave fighting men with weapons and horses as befits warriors. No man was ever born in any place whatever who could reckon the multitude on the move there. At the beginning of August they set out, following always the route which led directly to the Great St Bernard Pass. #

Let us now leave this army for a while and speak of Arthur, noblest of kings, at the time when he had convoked his good thanes, and each had gone back to where he held lands and all speedily returned as warriors to the host, they and their followers well equipped with weapons, from Scotland, from Ireland, from Jutland, from Iceland, from Norway, from Denmark, from Orkney and from the Isle of Man. From these many lands came a hundred thousand valiant warriors, well armed after the fashion of their own regions. They were not knights, nor armed in knightly fashion, but were equipped like the boldest men ever known, with great battleaxes and long swords.

From Normandy, from Anjou, from Brittany, from Poitiers, from Flanders, from Boulogne, from Lorraine and from Louvain a hundred thousand men came to the king's army, the best of warriors, well tried in arms. The Twelve Peers to whom France was subject came, bringing ten thousand warriors all told; and from this country Arthur mustered fifty thousand soldiers, men keen and brave in battle. Howel of Brittany, the best of knights, led ten thousand of his countrymen. When they set out, no man could, by any means whatsoever, reckon the number of men on the march there.

Then Arthur, noblest of kings, ordered the army, upon pain of death, to assemble at Barfleur at a time appointed, and there he

bi heore bare lifen,   at Barbefleote,
and þer he wolde gædere   sele his þede.
Þis lond he bitahte   ane selcuðe cnihte—
he wes Walwaines broðer;   næs þer nan oðer.   12710
Moddred wes ihaten   —forcuðest monnen;
treouðe nefde he nane   to nauer nane monne!
He wes Arðures mæi,   of aðelen his cunne,
ah cniht he wes wunder god   and he hafde swiðe muchel mod.
Arðures suster sune,   to þere quene wes his iwune.   12715
Þat wæs ufele idon   —his æme he dude swikedom!
Ah al hit wes stille   in hirede and in halle,
for na man hit ne wende   þat hit sculde iwurðe,
ah men to soðe iwenden   for Walwain wes his broðer,
þe alre treoweste gume   þe tuhte to þan hirede.   12720
Þurh Walwain wes Modræd   monnen þa leouere,
and Arður þe kene   ful wel him iquemde.
     He nom al his kinelond   and sette hit Moddræd an hond
and Wenhauer his quene,   wurðlukest wiuen
þa þe in þissere leode   wunede an londe.   12725
Arður bitahte   al þat he ahte
Moddrade and þere quene   —þat heom was iqueme!
Þat was ufele idon   þat heo iboren weoren!
þis lond heo forradden   mid ræuðen uniuoȝen;
and a þan ænden heomseoluen   þe Wurse gon iscenden   12730
þat heo þer forleoseden   lif and heore saulen,
and æuer seoððe laðen   in auerælche londe,
þat nauer na man nalde   sel bede beoden for heore saule
for þan swikedome   þat he dude Arðure his æme.
     Al þat Arður ahte   he Moddrede bitahte,   12735
lond and his leoden   and leofen his quene,
and seððen he nom his ferde   of folken swiðe hende
and ferde ful sone   touward Suðhamtune.
Þer comen seilien sone   ȝeond þa sæ wide
scipes uniuoȝe   to þas kinges folke.   12740
Þe king þat folc beide   ȝeond þa scipen longe;
bi þusend and bi þusend   to þan scipen þrasten.
Þe uader weop a þene sune,   suster a þene broðer,
moder a þa dohter   þa þa duȝeðe sturede.
Weder stod on wille,   wind wex an honde;   12745
ankeres heo up droȝen   —drem wes on uolken.

would assemble his splendid host. He entrusted this land to one who was no ordinary knight — he was Gawain's brother; he had no other. His name was Modred — the basest of men; he never kept faith with any man! He was Arthur's kinsman, of royal lineage, an extremely bold knight, and he had a very proud spirit. The son of Arthur's sister, he paid court to the queen. That was an evil deed — he committed treason against his uncle! But all was peace in court and hall, for no one imagined that it could be so, taking it upon trust because Gawain was his brother, the most loyal man who ever came to court. Because of Gawain, Modred was the more esteemed by men, and the valiant Arthur favoured him greatly.

He gave his whole kingdom into the keeping of Modred and of Guenevere his queen, the most excellent woman of all who lived here in this land. Arthur entrusted all that he possessed to Modred and to the queen — that was pleasing to them! It was a great misfortune that they were ever born! By countless wrongs they brought this land to ruin; and in the end the Devil brought destruction upon them whereby they lost their lives and damned their souls, and were hated ever after in every land, so that no one would offer prayers for the good of their souls because of the treason he had committed against his uncle.

Arthur entrusted to Modred all that he possessed, his land and people and his beloved queen, and then he took his army of most valiant men and straightway marched towards Southampton. Shortly there came across the open sea a large number of ships sailing towards the king's army. The king distributed the army among the long-keeled ships; they thronged in their thousands to the ships. Father wept for son, sister for brother, mother for daughter when the army embarked. The weather was favourable, the wind freshened; they hoisted anchor — there was rejoicing in

Wunden into widen sæ   þeines wunder bliðe.
Scipen þer forð þrungen,   gleomen þer sungen,
seiles þer tuhten,   rapes þer rehtten;
wederen alre selest   and þa sæ sweuede.   12750
   For þere softnesse   Arður gon to slæpen.
Alse þe king slepte   a sweuen him imette;
feorlic wes þat sweouen   þene king hit auerde.
Þa þe king him awoc   swiðe he wes idræcched,
and granen agon   ludere stefenen.   12755
Næs þer nan swa þriste   cniht under Criste
þat durste þene king fræine   of his fare-coste
ær þe king himseolf speke   and spilede wið his beornen þere.
And þus Arður him seide   þa he awoc of slæpe:
"Lauerd Drihten, Crist,   domes waldende,   12760
midelarde mund,   monnen froure,
þurh þine aðmode wil,   walden ænglen,
let þu mi sweuen   to selþen iturnen!"
   Þa spac Angel þe king,   Scottene deorling:
"Lauerd, sæi us þi sweuen;   seleȝehðe us beo ȝeueðe!"   12765
"Bluðeliche," quað þe king;   "to blisse hit iwurðe!
Þer ich lai a sweuete   agan ich forto slepe.
Me þuhte þat in þere weolcne   com an wunderlic deor,
æst in þan leofte   —ladlic an sehte!
Wið leite, mid storme,   sturnliche wende—   12770
nis in nare leode   nan swa ladlic beore!
Þa com þer westene,   winden mid þan weolcnen,
a berninge drake;   burhȝes he suelde;
mid his feure he liht   al þis lond-riche.
Me þuhte a mire sihȝeðe   þat þa sæ gon to berne   12775
of leite and of fure   þa þe drake ferede.
   Þes drake and beore,   beien tosomne,
radliche sone   togadere heo come;
heo smiten heom togaderen   mid feondliche ræsen;
floȝen of heore hæȝene   swulc furburondes.   12780
Ofte wes þe drake buuen,   and eft, seoððen, bineoþen.
Neoðeles, a þan ænde,   heȝen he gon wende
and he flah dunrihte   mid feondliche ræsen,
and þene beore he ismat   þat he to þere eorðe iwhat;
and he þer þene beore ofsloh   and hine lim-mele todroh.   12785
Þa þat feht wes ido,   þe drake aȝen wende.

the host. In high spirits the warriors set out upon the open sea. Then ships pressed onwards, minstrels sang, sails were hoisted, ropes adjusted; the weather was very calm and the sea lay quiet.

Because of the calm Arthur fell asleep. While the king was sleeping he had a dream; it was a hideous dream which terrified the king. When the king awoke he was sorely troubled, and began to groan aloud. There was no knight in Christendom so bold that he dared question the king about his behaviour until the king himself spoke in conversation with his companions there. When he awoke from sleep, Arthur spoke to them thus:

'Christ, our Lord and Master, Lord of destinies, Guardian of the world, Comforter of men, Ruler of angels, let my dream, through your gracious will, lead to a good end!'

Then King Angel, beloved of the Scots, spoke:
'Tell us your dream, my lord; may good come of it!'
'Gladly,' said the king; 'may it turn out well! As I lay at rest I fell asleep. It seemed to me that a wondrous beast appeared in the heavens, in the sky to the east — a hideous sight! It came on fiercely, among lightning and thunder — there is no bear on earth so terrible! Then there came from the west, whirling through the clouds, a fiery dragon, burning cities, setting the whole kingdom alight with his fire. It seemed in my vision that the sea burst into flames from the lightning and the fire which the dragon brought.

The dragon and the bear, both at the same time, came at each other with the utmost speed; they set upon each other in furious onslaught, sparks flying from their eyes like firebrands. Often the dragon was on top, and then, at other times, underneath. In the end, however, he rose up high and flew straight down with furious force, and struck the bear so that he plummeted to earth; and there he killed the bear and tore him limb from limb. When the fight was finished, the dragon departed. This is the dream I dreamed as I lay sleeping.'

þis sweuen me imette   þer ich lai and slapte."

　　Biscopes þis iherden   and boc-ilærede men,
þis iheorden eorles,   þis iherden beornes;
ælc, bi his witte,   wisdom sæiden,   12790
þis sweuen aræhten.

Ne durste þer na cniht   to ufele ræcchen na wiht
leoste he sculden leosen   his leomen þat weoren him deore.

　　Forð heo gunnen liðen   an eouste bilife;
wind heom stod on wille,   selest alre wedere;   12795
heo hæfden al þat heom wes neod;   to londen heo comen at Barbefleot.

To Barbefleot, at Costentin,   þer com muchel moncun in
of alle þan londe   þa Arður hafde an honde;
swa sone swa heo mihten   ut of scipe heom rehten.
þe king his folc hehte   herberwe isechen,   12800
an badien þe king wolde   þat his folc come.

　　Nes he þere buten ane niht,   þa com him to an hende cniht.
He talde tidinge   Arðure þan kinge,
he seide þat þer wes icumen   a scaðe liðe,
of westward Spaine,   wel dreori feond,*   12805
and inne Brutaine   bisi wes to harme;
bi þere sæside   þet lond he weste wide;
nu hit hatte Munt Seint Michel   þat lond ewelde iwidel.

"Lauerd king," queð þe cniht,   "to soðe ich þe cuðe herriht
he hafueð inome þine maȝe   mid hahliche strenðe,   12810
heȝe wimmon iboren,   Howeles dohter icoren,
Eleine wes ihaten,   aðelest maidenen.
To þan munte he heo uerede   aðelest maidene;
nu fulle feowertene niht   þe feond heo hafueð ihalden þerriht.
Nute we on liue   þeh he heo nabbe to wife.   12815
Alle he makeð him to mete   þa men þa he igripeð,
ruðeren, hors and þa scep,   gæt and þa swin eke;
al þis lond he wule forfare   buten þu afeollen ure kare,
lond and þas leode   —a þe is ure neode."

　　Ȝet þe cniht seide   to þan uolc-kinge: 12820
"Isihst þu, lauerd, þe munt   and þene wude muchele?
þer wuneð þe scaðe inne   þa scendeð þas leode.
We habbeð wið him iuohten   wel feole siðen
bi sæ and bi londe;   þes leoden he amærde,
ure scipen he aseingde,   þat folc he al adrente;   12825
þeo þat feuhten a þan londe   þeo he adun leide.

－ 180 －

The bishops and learned men heard this, the nobles and warriors heard it; each, according to his ability, spoke with wisdom in interpreting this dream. No one there dared interpret it as in any way ill-omened lest he should lose limbs which he valued. #

They sailed on swiftly eastwards; the wind was favourable, the weather very good, everything they needed they had; they reached land at Barfleur. At Barfleur, in the Cotentin, there landed a great host from all the realms which Arthur held; they disembarked as soon as they could. The king ordered his followers to search out quarters, and the king would remain there until his host assembled.

He had been there only one night, when a nobleman came to him. He brought tidings to King Arthur, said that a monster, a very wicked creature, had come westwards from Spain, and was busy doing mischief in Brittany, laying waste the land far and wide along the sea coast; he wholly controlled that region which is now called Mont St Michel.

'Lord king,' said the knight, 'I tell you truthfully here and now that he has seized with great violence your kinswoman, a lady nobly born, Howel's beloved daughter, the worthiest of women, called Helene. He has carried off that most noble maiden to the mountain; the fiend has now held her fully fourteen days in that place. We do not know at all whether or not he has taken her to wife. He makes his food of all the men he seizes, the cattle, horses and sheep, the goats and swine as well; unless you relieve our sufferings, he will destroy this whole region, destroy the land and its inhabitants — we are in need of you.'

The knight spoke further to the sovereign:
'Do you see, my lord, the mountain and the vast wood? Therein dwells the miscreant who is harming the people. We have fought with him many times by land and sea; he has ravaged this region, sunk our ships, drowning all our people, has slaughtered those who fought on land. We have suffered it so

We habbeoð idriuen þat swa longe   þat we hine læteð ane
faren heu swa he wule   after iwille him;
þis lond-cnihtes ne durren   wið him mare na fehten."

    Arður þis iherde,   aðelest alre kinge;   12830
he cleopede him to þene eorl Kæi   þe wes his stiward and his mæi;
Beduer eke to him he cleopede   —he wes þes kinges birle.
He hæhte heom forðriht   beon al war to midderniht
mid alle heore wepne   to wenden wið þan kinge
þat na mon under Criste   of heore uare nuste   12835
buten Arður þe king   and þa tweien cnihtes mid him,
and heore sweines sixe,   ohte men and wihte;
and þe cniht þe radde   hit þan king heom ladde.

    To þere midnihte,   þa men weoren aslepe,
Arður forð him wende,   aðelest alre kinge.   12840
Biforen rad heore lod-cniht   þat hit was dæiliht; *
heo lihten of heore steden   and rihten heore iweden.
þa iseȝen heo, nawiht feorren,   a muchel fur smokien
uppen ane hulle   mid sæ-ulode biuallen;
and anoðer hul þer wes swiðe heh   —þæ sæ hine bifledde ful neh;   12845
þeruuenon heo iseȝen a fur   þat wes muchel and swiðe stor.
þæ cnihtes þa tweoneden   to whaþere heo faren mihten
þet þe eotend war neore   of þeos kinges fore.

    þa nom him to rede   Arður þe ræȝe
þat heo sculden somed faren   aneosten þan ane furen;   12850
and ȝif hine þer funden   aquellen hine to deðen.
Forð þe king wende   þat he com aneuste;
noht he þer ne funde   bute a muchel fur þer berninde.
Arður eode abute   and his cnihtes bi his siden;
na whit heo ne funden   quikes uppen wolden   12855
buten þat fur muchele   and ban vnimete;
bi atlinge heom þuhte   þritti uoðere.

    Arður þa nuste   nenne red godne,
and bigon him to spekene   to Beduer his eorle:
"Beduer, far biliue   adun of þissen hulle   12860
and wend þe ouer þat water deope   mid allen þine iwede,
and mid wisdome   wend to þan fure,
and bihalues þe iga   and bihald ȝeorne
ȝif þu miht afinden   oht of þan feonden.
And ȝif þu hine miht ofȝiten   on aiȝes cunnes wisen,   12865
wend adun stille   þat cume to þan watere

long that we now leave him alone to do as he wishes, as it pleases him; the knights of that region dare no longer fight with him.' #

Arthur, noblest of all kings, paid heed to this; he called to him the earl Kay who was his kinsman and his steward, and Bedevere as well — he was the king's cup-bearer. He immediately ordered them to be fully prepared at midnight with all their accoutrements to go with the king so that no one whatsoever should know of their going save King Arthur and the two knights accompanying him, and six of their followers, stout-hearted men and valiant; and the knight who had made it known to the king should lead them.

At midnight, when all were asleep, Arthur, noblest of all kings, set out. Their guide rode ahead of them until it was daylight, when they dismounted from their horses and prepared their armour. Then they saw, not far off, the smoke of a great fire upon a mountain surrounded at high tide by the sea; and upon another lofty peak, round which the sea closely surged, they saw a fire which was large and burning fiercely. The knights were then uncertain in which direction they should go so that the giant might not be aware of the king's coming.

Then the bold Arthur himself decided that they should go together to one of the fires; and if they discovered him there they should put him to death. The king went forward until he was quite close; he found nothing there except a great fire burning. Arthur, with his knights at his side, circled it; they found no sign of life upon the high ground save that hugh fire and a large number of bones, thirty cartloads it seemed to them at a guess.

Arthur did not have any sure plan of action then, and addressed himself to his earl Bedevere:

'Bedevere, go down quickly from this mountain and cross the deep water in all your armour, and approach that other fire with caution; go near to it and look carefully if you can find any sign of the ogre. And if you manage by any means whatsoever to catch sight of him, come down quietly until you reach the water

and seien me þer sone   what þu iseȝen habbe.
And ȝif hit ilimpeð swa   þat þu liðen to þan fure,
and þe feond þe ofȝite   and þu to fuse,
hafe mine godne horn   þe al mid golde is ibon   12870
and blawe hine mid maine,   swa mon scal for neode,
and fus þe to þan feonde   and bigin to fihten;
and we þe scullen fusen to   swa we hit swiðest maȝen don.
And ȝif þu hine ifindest   aneouste þan fure
and þu al unaȝeten   aȝein miht iwende,   12875
þenne forbeode ich þe   bi þine bare life
þat þu nauere wið þene scucke   feht no biginne."
     Beduer iherde   what his lauerd him seide.
His wepnen he on him dude   and forð him iwende,
and up astæh þene munt   þe is unimete.   12880
He bar an his honde   ænne gære swiðe stronge,
ænne sceld an his rugge   irust al mid golde, *
hælm an his hafde   hehne of stele.
His bodi wes bifeong   mid fæire are burne;
he hafde bi his side   enne brond al of stele.   12885
And forð he gon steppen,   stið-imainede eorl,
þat he com fusen   an neouste þan furen,
and he under ane treo   gon him atstonden.
     Þa iherde he wepen   wunder ane swiðen,
wepen and weinen,   and wanliche iberen.   12890
Þa þe cniht wende   þat hit þe eotend weoren,
and he anbursten agon   swulc weore a wilde bar,
and forȝæt sone   þat his lauerd him sæide.
His sceld he bræid on breoste,   his spere he igrap faste,
and an neoste gon fuse   touward þan fure;   12895
he wende to finden   þene feond sturne
þat he fehten mihte   and fondien hine seolue.
Þa fond he þer ane quene   quecchen mid hafde,
heor-lockede wif   —weop for hire wei-sið,
wanede hire siðes,   þat heo wæs on liues—   12900
þat set bi þan fure   mid reolichen ibere,
and sæt and biheold æuere   ænne burinæsse,
and hire ȝeddes sæide   ȝeomere stefne:
"Wale, Eleine!   Wale, deore maide!
Wale þat ich þe uedde,   þat ich þe uostredde!   12905
Wale þat þæ wald-scaðe   here þe haueð þus foruare!

and there tell me at once what you have seen. And if it so happens that the ogre sees you approaching the fire and rushes at you, take this good horn of mine which is all adorned with gold and blow it with all your might, as a man should when in need, and rush towards the ogre and begin attacking him; and we will hasten to you as quickly as we can. And if you come upon him near the fire and you can slip away unnoticed, then I forbid you on your very life to start fighting with the demon at all.'

Bedevere paid heed to what his lord said to him. He put on his armour and set off, and climbed up the towering mountain. He bore in his hand a very stout spear, on his back a shield all encrusted with gold, on his head a tall steel helmet. His body was covered with a splendid coat of mail; at his side he had a sword all wrought of steel. The stout-hearted earl pressed on until, shortly, he came close to the fire and halted beneath a tree.

Then he heard very loud wailing, wailing and howling, and hideous shrieks. The knight thought then that it must be the giant and, growing as furious as a wild boar, immediately forgot what his lord had said to him. He slung his shield before his chest, grasped his spear firmly, and rushed towards the fire, expecting to encounter the fierce ogre so that he might do battle and prove himself worthy. Then he came upon a woman there, a grey-haired woman with trembling head, weeping in her wretchedness, lamenting her lot, that she was still alive; she sat by the fire crying bitterly, gazing fixedly at a grave, making her moan in a piteous voice:

'Alas, Helene! Alas, dear maid! Alas that I fed you, that I fostered you! Alas that the demon has brought you to such a

Wale þat ich wes iboren   —mine leomen he haueð tobroken!"

    Þa bisæh þat wif abuten   whar þe eotend come buȝen,
biseh a þene eorl Beduer   þa icumen wes þer.
Þa sæide þat wif hore,   þer heo sæt bi fure: *   12910
"Whæt ært þu, fære whit?   Eært þu angel, eært cniht?
Beoð þine feðer-heomen   ihaneked mid golden?
Ȝif þu ært of heuene   þu miht isund faren heonene;
and ȝif þu ært eorðlic cniht   ærm þu iwurðest forðriht,
for nu anan cumeð þe scaðe   þe alle þine leomen wule todraȝen;   12915
þeh þu weore stel al   he þe awalt iwildel.
He uerde to Brutaine,   to aðelest alre bolde,
to Howeles castle,   hæh mon inne Brutene.
Þa ȝaten alle he tobrac   and binnen he gon wende;
he nom þare halle wah   and helden hine to grunde;   12920
þæs bures dure he warp adun   þat heo tobarst a uiuen.
He funde i þan buren   fæirest alre bruden,
Eleinen wes ihaten,   aðelest kunnen,
Howeles dohter,   hæh mon of Brutene,
Arðures maȝe,   of swiðe heȝe cunne.   12925
Ich wes hire uoster-moder   and feire heo uostredde.
Þer þe eotend unc ifeng   forð mid himseoluen
fiftene mile
into þisse wilde wude,   hider, to þissen ilke stude;
þus he us diste   todæi a seouen nihte.   12930

    Sone swa he hider com,   swa he þat maide inom;
he wolde mon-radene   habben wið þan maidene.
Ælde næfde heo na mare   buten fihtene ȝere,
ne mihte þat maiden   his mone iþolien;
anan swa he lai hire mide,   hire lif heo losede sone,   12935
and her he heo biburede,   burden alre hendest,
Eleine, min aȝen uoster,   Howelles dohter.
Þa he hafde þis idon,   swa me seoluen inom,
a uolden he me laiden   and lai mid me seoluen.
Nu hafeð he mine ban alle   ladliche abrokene,   12940
mine leomen al toleðed;   mi lif me is alaðed!
Nu ich habbe þe itald   hu we beoð her ihæd;
flih nu swiðe   lest he þe ifinde,
for ȝif he cumeð abolȝen   mid his balu-ræsen,
nes he neuere iboren   þe maȝen stonden þe biuoren."   12945
    Efne þissen worden   þa þat wif seide,

cruel end in this place! Alas that I was ever born — he has broken my bones!'

When the woman looked in the direction from which the giant would approach, she caught sight of the earl Bedevere who had come there. Then the grey-haired woman, where she sat by the fire, said:

'What are you, fair creature? Are you an angel or a man? Are your wings threaded with gold? If you are from heaven you may leave here unharmed; and if you are a mortal man you will shortly be destroyed, for the demon is coming now and will tear you limb from limb; though you be clad all in steel he will utterly overpower you. He came to Brittany, to the most magnificent of all dwellings, to the castle of Howel, ruler of Brittany. He tore down all the gates and forced his way in; he grasped the wall of the hall and hurled it to the ground; he smashed down the chamber door so that it shattered into pieces. In the chamber he found the fairest of all women, a lady of royal blood, called Helene, the daughter of Howel, ruler of Brittany, a man of most noble lineage, Arthur's kinsman. I was her foster-mother and raised her fittingly. The giant carried both of us off with him fifteen miles from there into this wild wood, here, to this very place; this he did to us a week ago today.

As soon as he got here, he seized the maiden, meaning to have intercourse with the girl. The maiden was no older than fifteen and could not endure his violation; as soon as he lay with her, she died instantly, and he buried her here, the fairest of all women, my own foster-child Helene, Howel's daughter. When he had done this, he took me and threw me on the ground and lay with me. Now he has cruelly broken all my bones, disjointed all my limbs; my life is hateful to me! Now that I have told you how we have been used here, flee quickly now lest he discover you, for if he comes in a rage, in furious onslaught, there is no man alive who can protect you.'

At these words which the woman uttered, Bedevere began to

Beduer heo gon hirten   mid hendeliche worden:
"Leofe moder, ich æm mon,   and cniht æm wel idon;
and ich þe wule suggen   þurh soðe mine worden
næs nan kempen iboren   of nauer nare burden   12950
þat mon ne mæi mid strenðe   stupen hine to grunde,
and hire þe, ane alde wifmon   —swiðe lutle beoð þine mæhten. *
Ah hafuen nu swiðe godne dæi,   and ich wulle faren minne wæi."
    Adun him ferde Beduer   to his duзeðe-kinge
and talde him hu he hafde kare   and hu he hafde al ifare,   12955
and what þat wif alde   of þan maidene him talde,
and hu þe eotend ælche dæi   bi þan alde wiue lai.
Þer heo heom bitwenen   heolden heore runen
hu heo mihten taken on   þat þe scucke weore fordon.
    Þeo while com þe eotende faren   and fusden to his fure;   12960
he bar uppen his rugge   burðene grete,
þat weore twælf swine   iteied tosomne,
mid wiðen swiðe grete   ywriðen al togadere.
Adun he warp þa dede swin   and himseolf sæt þerbi.
His fur he beten agon   and muchele treowen læiden on;   12965
þa six swin he todroh,   and euere he to þan wiue loh;
and sone umbe while   he lai bi þan wife.
Ah he nuste noht þan tidende   þat comen to his wife-þinge.
He droh ut his gleden,   his flæsce he gon breden,
and þa six swin he gon æten alle   ær he arise of selde;   12970
al biwaled on axen   wanliche weoren þa sonden.
And seoððen he gon ræmien   and raxlede swiðe,
and adun lai bi þan fure   and his leomen strahte.
    Lete we nu þene eotend bilafuen   and atlien to þan kinge.
Arður, at þan watere,   his wapnen nom an honde,   12975
and þe eorl Beduer,   god cniht, wis and war;
and þe þridde wes Kæi,   þes kinges stiward and his mæi.
Ouer þan watere heo comen,   iwepned mid þan bezsten,
and stiзen up þan hulle   mid allen heore maine
þat heo comen fusen   aneuste þan furen   12980
þer þe eotende lai and slæp   and þa quene sæt and weop.
Arður hine teh   bisiden his iferen,
forbad heom bi heore leomen   and bi heore bare liuen
þat nan, neoren swa kene,   þat heom neh comen
buten he iseзen   þat hit ned weoren.   12985
Beduer atstod him þere   and Kæi his iuere.

comfort her with kind words:

'Dear mother, I am a mortal, and a well-trained knight; and I tell you truthfully that no warrior was ever born of woman whom someone could not by force bring low, and so aid you, an old woman who has very little strength. But now I bid you farewell, and I will go my way.'

Bedevere went down to his sovereign and told him what distress he had witnessed and how he had fared in all matters, and what the old woman had told him about the girl, and how each day the giant lay with the old woman. Then they discussed among themselves how they might contrive that the demon should be destroyed.

Meanwhile the giant came back, hastening to his fire; on his back he carried a great load, twelve swine bound together, tied all together with very stout thongs. He threw down the dead pigs and seated himself close by. He began to build up his fire, throwing much wood upon it; six of the swine he pulled to pieces, all the while eyeing the old woman; and almost immediately he lay with her. But he knew not what tidings had reached the woman he was abusing. He spread out his burning embers and began to roast his meat, and before he rose from where he sat he had eaten all six swine; the food was all smeared and blackened with ashes. And afterwards he yawned and stretched mightily, and lay down by the fire stretching out his limbs.

Let us now leave the giant and turn to the king. Arthur, at the waterside, took up his weapons, as did the earl Bedevere, a brave knight, alert and skilful; and the third man was Kay, the king's kinsman and his High Steward. Well armed, they advanced across the water and climbed up the hill with all their might until shortly they came close to the fire where the giant lay sleeping and the woman sat weeping. Arthur drew close to his companions, and forbade them upon pain of life and limb to advance any further, however eager they might be, unless they saw that it was necessary. Bedevere and his comrade Kay halted there.

Arður gon stepe vorð,   stið-imoded kempe,
þat he com to þan ulette   þer þe feond lai and slæpte.
Æuere wes Arður   ærhðe bideled;
þet wes sutel þeron,   sellic þah hit þunche,   12990
for Arður mihte þere   þene eotende al tohæuwe,
slan þene scucke   þer he lai and slapte.
Þa nolde Arður on slepen   na wiht hine areppen
leste he an uferre daзe   upbræid iherde.

Þa cleopede Arður anan,   aðelest kingen: 12995
"Aris, aris, feond-scaðe,   to þine fæie-siðe!
Nu wit scullen delen   þene dæd of mire maзen!"
Ær þe king hæfde   þæs ful isæide,
þe eotend up asturte   and igrap his mucle clubbe,
and wende mid þan dunten   Arður al todriuen.   13000
Ah Arður bræid heзe   his sceld buuen his hælme
and þe eotend smat þeranouenan   þat al he gon toscenen;
and Arður him swende to   an hiзende mid his sweorde
and þen chin him ofswipte   mid alle þan cheuele;
and sturte him biaften ane treo   þe þer stod aneouste,   13005
and þe eotend smat after biliue   and noht hine ne hutte,
ah he þat treo smat   þat al his clubbe todraf.
And Arður aneouste   þat treo bieorn abute;
and swa Arður and þe scucke   biurnen hit þreie abuten.
Þa wes þe eotend heui swiðe   and Arður wes swiftre   13010
and oftoc þene eotend,   and up ahof his gode brond
and þat þih him ofsmat,   and eotend adun wæt.
And Arður atstod and biheold   þa gon to spekene þe ueond:
"Lauerd, lauerd, зef me grið!   Wha is þat me fihteð wið?
Ne wende ich þat na man   a þissere weorlde-richen   13015
me mihte þus lehtliche   aleggen mid fehte
bute hit Arður weore,   aðelest alre Brutte;
and neoðeles næs ich nauere   of Arðure afæred sære."
Þa him sæide Arður,   aðelest kingen:
"Ich æm Arður þe king,   Bruttene deorling.   13020
Tel me of þine cunne   and whar beo heore beonste,
and wha þe weore on uolde   fader oðer moder ihalde,
and of wulche londe   þu art iliðen hidere,
and whi þu mine maзe   aualled hafuest mid morðe."
Þa andswarede þe feond   þer he læi and biheold: 13025
"Al þis ich wulle don,   and þine treoðe underfon

Arthur defeats the giant of Mont St Michel

Arthur, the stout-hearted warrior, went forward until he reached the place where the ogre lay sleeping. Arthur, as was plain to see, was quite undaunted — strange as it may seem — for Arthur could have cut the giant to pieces there and then, killed the demon where he lay sleeping. But Arthur would never attack him while asleep lest he should later suffer reproach.

Then Arthur, noblest of kings, immediately called out:
'Arise, fiendish devil, arise to meet your doom! Now we two shall settle accounts for the killing of my kinswoman!'
Before the king had quite finished speaking, the ogre leapt up and grasped his giant club, intending to destroy Arthur utterly at a blow. But Arthur raised his shield high above his helmet and the giant struck it so that it was completely shattered; and Arthur instantly swung at him with his sword and sliced off his chin and the whole jaw along with it; and then he leapt behind a tree which stood nearby, and the giant quickly struck again and did not touch him at all, but struck the tree so that his club was completely shattered. And Arthur immediately ran round the tree; and so Arthur and the demon circled it three times. The giant moved very slowly then and Arthur was the swifter and caught up with the giant and, raising his trusty sword, cut through his thigh so that the ogre fell to the ground. And Arthur stood and watched as the ogre began to speak:
'Lord, lord, have mercy on me! Who is it that is fighting against me? I thought no man in this mortal world might so easily defeat me in combat unless it were Arthur, noblest of all the Britons; and yet I was never greatly afraid even of Arthur.'

Then Arthur, noblest of kings, said to him:
'I am King Arthur, beloved of the Britons. Tell me of your race and where they have their dwelling-place, and who in this world might be accounted your mother or your father, and from which land you have come here, and why you have brutally killed my kinswoman.'
Then the ogre, where he lay gazing up, answered:
'All this I will do, and trust to your mercy if you allow

wið þat þu me lete liuien   and mine leomen hælen."

Arður hine iwræðöede   wunder ane swiðe
and he Beduer cleopede,   balde his kempe:
"Ga aneouste, Beduer,   and hefd him binim her,   13030
and fere hit forð mid þe   adun of þisse munte."
Beduer aneouste com   and his hæfued him binom;
and swa heo þeonene ferden   adun to heore iferen.
Þa sat þe king adun   and hine gon to resten,
and þas word seide   Arður þe sele: 13035
"No uæht ich nauere ueht non   uppen þissere uolden
buten þa ich sloh þene king Riun   uppen þan munte of Rauinite!"
Seoðöen heo uorð wenden   and to þere uerde comen.
Þa þe þat hafd iseʒe   sellic heom þuhte
whar weore under heuene   swulc hafed ikenned.   13040

Howel of Brutaine   beh to þan kinge
and þe king him seide   al of þan maidene.
Þa wes Howel sari   and sorhful an heorte forþi,
and nom al his feren   and ferde to þan munte
þer þat Brutisce maide   bibured læi on eorðe.   13045
He lette þer areren sone   ane chireche swiðe faire
a Seinte Marie nomen,   Drihtenes moder.
And seoðöen he ʒæf nome þan hulle   ær he þonne wende,
and hehte hine Æleine Tunbel;   nu hit hæhte Munt Seint Myhhel.

Þa wes Arðures hired   sellich isomned,   13050
of Irlonde and of Scotlonde   þider weoren iscriðene.
Þa lette þe king blauwen   bemen an hireden
and wenden of Brutaine   bisie men and kene
þurhut Normandie   þæ hehte þa Neustrie;
heo uerden þurhut France   and folc heom after ferde;   13055
heo buʒen ut of France   into Burguine.
His hauwæres þer comen   and heolden his iferen,
and cudde þan kinge,   þer i þare cuðöe,
þat Luces þe kaisere   and al his Romanisce here
þiderward heo comen   fromward heore þeoden,   13060
and swa heo wolden fusen   in touward France
and al þat biwinnen,   and seoðöen wenden hidere
and Bruttes alle aquellen   quicke þer heo heom funde,
and Arður þene kene   ibunde lede to Rome.
Þa wes abolʒen   baldest alre kingen   13065
and hehte a þan feldes   slen alle his teldes,

me to live and let my limbs be healed.'

Arthur was extremely angry and he called out to Bedevere, his bold warrior:

'Come quickly, Bedevere, and strike off his head upon the spot, and bring it down with you from this mountain.'

Bedevere at once came and struck off his head; and then they went down from that place to their companions. Then the king sat down to rest, and the valiant Arthur spoke these words:

'Never in this world have I fought such a fight save when I slew King Riun upon the mountain of Ravinite!'

Then they went on until they came to the army. Those who saw the head thought it wondrous that such a head might exist anywhere on earth. #

Howel of Brittany went to the king and the king told him all about the maiden. Then Howel was sad at that and sorrowful at heart, and took all his followers and went to that mountain where the Breton maiden lay buried in the earth. Then he had a magnificent church erected there, dedicated to St Mary, mother of the Lord. And then, before he went from there, he named the mountain, calling it Helene's Tomb; it is now called Mont St Michel. #

By then Arthur's forces had assembled in all their splendour, having made their way there from Ireland and from Scotland. Then the king caused trumpets to be blown throughout the host and active and eager men marched from Brittany across Normandy which was then called Neustrie; they marched through the whole of France and, the people of the region following them, passed from France into Burgundy. There his spies came and joined his company, and there, in that place, informed the king that the emperor Lucius and his whole Roman army were moving out of their own land in that direction, intending to press on so into France, conquer it all, and then come here and slaughter all Britons whatsoever, wherever they found them, and lead the valiant Arthur in chains to Rome. Then the boldest of all kings was enraged and ordered all his tents to be pitched in the field,

and þer he wikien wolde   þat he þat soðe wuste
whær he mihte þene kæisere   iwisliche kepen. *
þat water hehte Albe   þer lai þe king balde.

An wis cniht þer com ride   to þas kinges uerde   13070
þe wes al forwunded   and his folc afelled swiðe;
hafden Romanisce men   al his lond biræiued him.
He talde þan kinge   neouwe tiðende
whar lai þe kaisere   and al his Romanisce here,
and whær he hine mihte iwinde   ʒif he wolde wið him fihten *   13075
oðer grið makien   wið Romanisce monnen.
"Ah, lauerd Arður," quað þe cniht,   "ich þe wulle cuðen herriht
þat betere þe is freondscipe to habben   þene for to fihten,
for aʒan þine tweie   heo habbeoð twælue,
swa feole kinges   swa feole here-dringes.   13080
Nis he in nare kuððe   þe hit þe maʒe icuððe
for alle þan uolke   þe uulieð þan kinge,
wiðuten þan Rom-leoden   of his aʒere þeoden,
and wiðute þan uolke   þe ʒirneð þas kinges are."
    Þa þe talen weoren alle italde   and Arður heo hafden understonde,
þa cleopede þe king forðrihtes   his deoreste cnihtes
and radden heom bitwenen   enne castel to areren
onuast þan wateren   þe Albe wes ihaten.
On ane swiðe feiere stude   itimbred he wes ful sone.
Þer feng moni hond to;   an hiʒende he wes ido.   13090
For ʒif Arður misferde   þenne he come to fihte,
oðer his uolc ueolle   oðer setten to fleonne,
þenne þohte he to atstonden   at þan castle stronge.
    Þa cleopede he eorles tweie,   aðele men and wise,
heʒe men icunned,   þan kinge swiðe deore.   13095
Þæ an wes of Chartres and hehte Gerin   —muchel wisdom wunede mid_{him;}
þe oðer hehte Beof of Oxeneuord   —welle wide sprong þas eorles word.
Þe ʒet þe king cleopede Walwæin   þe wes his deoreste mæi,
for Walwain cuðe Romanisc,   Walwain cuðe Bruttisc—
he wes iued inne Rome   wel feole wintre.   13100
Þe king nom þas þreo cnihtes hende   and to þan kaisere heom sende,
and hehte hine mid his ferde   faren aʒæin to Rome,
and þat he næuere into France   his ferde no ladde;
"and ʒif þu þider wendest   and þine ferde ledest,
þu scalt beon underuonge   to þine uæie-siðe;   13105
for France is min aʒen   and ich heo mid fehte biwon.

intending to camp there until he knew clearly where he might be sure to encounter the emperor. That river beside which the valiant Arthur lay encamped is called the Aube. #

There came riding to the king's army a knight bearing news; he was gravely wounded and his following much depleted; Roman soldiers had deprived him of all his land. He gave the king fresh tidings where the emperor and all his Roman host lay encamped, and where he might find him if he wished to fight with him or if he wished to make peace with the Romans. 'But, lord Arthur,' said the knight, 'I must tell you here and now that it is better for you to make peace than to fight, for against every two of your men they have twelve, and as many kings as they have commanders. There is no man on earth who can tell you how many nations follow the king, besides the Roman people of his own country, and in addition to the nations who seek the king's protection.'

When the circumstances had been fully explained and Arthur had grasped them, then the king immediately summoned his most trusty knights and together they determined to build a castle beside the river which was called the Aube. Within a very short time it was built, in a most favourable position. Many set their hands to it; it was quickly finished. For if Arthur fared badly when he came to do battle, or his army was destroyed or took to flight, then he planned to make a stand in his well-fortified castle.

Then he summoned two earls, noble men and wise, men of high birth and very dear to the king. The one was the earl of Chartres called Gerin — he had much wisdom; the other, who was the earl of Oxford, was called Beof — his fame had spread far and wide. The king also summoned Gawain, his dearest kinsman, for Gawain knew both Latin and the British language — he had been brought up in Rome for many years. The king chose these three noble knights and sent them to the emperor, demanding that he return with his army to Rome, and that he should never lead his forces into France; 'and if you go there at the head of your army, you shall be brought to destruction; for France is mine

And ʒif þu nult bilauen   þat þider nult liðen,
fare wit to uihte,   and falle þe uorcuðere!
And lete we þat folc wræcche   wunien an ære.
While Rom-leoden   iwunnen þa þeoden   13110
and seoððen heo þa þeoden   mid fehte forloseden,
and ich heo mid feohte biwon   and mid fehte wule halden."

Forð þa cnihtes wenden,   godliche kempen,
þat weoren Gerin and Beof þe hende   and Walwain þe balde,
iburned and ihelmed   an hæʒen heore steden;   13115
and ælc weiede an sculdre   sceld swiðe godne;
heo beren on heore honde   gares swiðe stronge.
Forð heo gunnen ride,   riche men, from hirede.
Muchel of þere duʒeðe   þe mid Arðure wunede
mid Walwaine eoden   and æðmodliche hine beden   13120
þat he wið Rom-leode   summe sake arerde
"þat we maʒen mid fehte   fondien us seolue;
for hit is feole ʒere   þat heore þrættes comen here
and heore beot makieð   þat heo us wulle bihafdi.
Nu is hit muchel leod-scome   ʒif hit scal þus aligge,   13125
bute þer sum sake beo   ær we iwurðe sæhte,
scaftes tobrokene,   brunies totorne,
sceldes toscened,   scalkes toheouwen,
sweordes ibaðede   i blode þan rede!"

Forð þa eorles wenden   þurh æne wude muchelen   13130
and mærcoden enne wæi   þe ouer anne munte læi
þat heo bicomen sone   to þan uolke of Rome,
wurðliche iwepned,   wunden an horsen.
Þer me mihte bihalden,   þe mon þe bihalues weore,
moni þusenden   þrasten ut of telden   13135
al to bihalden   þeos þreo cnihtes balde,
and biheolden heore steden   and biheolden heore iweden,
and hercnede tidende   from Arðure þan kinge;
and aneouste forðrihtes   fræinede þa cnihtes
and ʒif þe king heom isend hæfde   to þan kaisere,   13140
to speken þan kæisere wið   and to ʒirnen his grið.

Ah for nauer nare speche   þas þreo eorles riche
nolden abiden   ær heo comen riden
forn to þas teldes deoren   þerinne wes þe kaisere.
Adun heo gunnen lihten   and bitahten hore steden,   13145
and swa heo, iwepned mid alle,   wenden into telde,

and I conquered it in battle. And if you will not desist and will not depart thence, let us two do combat — and may the worse man fall! And let us leave the unfortunate nation to live in peace. The Romans once conquered that land and afterwards they lost it in battle, and I conquered it in battle and will keep it by battle.' #

The knights, brave warriors, set out, Gerin and the noble Beof and the valiant Gawain, in helmet and armour on their tall steeds, each bearing a good shield on his shoulder; in their hands they grasped stout spears. Away they rode, those noblemen, leaving the army. Many of the warriors who were to stay with Arthur went some way with Gawain and earnestly urged him to stir up some cause for strife with the Roman people 'that we may prove ourselves in battle; for many years now their threats have been coming here, their boasts that they will cut off our heads. Now it will be a great disgrace to the nation if it so happens, unless there be some fighting before we come to terms, spears broken, armour hacked, shields shattered, warriors cut to pieces, swords bathed in red blood!'

The earls made their way through a large wood, following a track which ran across a mountain, until shortly they came, fittingly armed, riding on horseback, to the Roman host. Anyone who was present there would have seen many thousands thronging out of the tents just to look at those three bold knights; they gazed at their mounts, noted their garments, and listened for a message from Arthur the king. And then they asked the knights directly whether the king had sent them to the emperor, to speak with the emperor and to seek peace from him.

But those three noble earls would not pause for any speech whatsoever until they came riding right up to the entrance of the pavilion in which the emperor was. They dismounted and handed over their horses, and so went, fully armed, into the tent, into

forn to þan kaisere,   þe Luces wes ihate,
þer he sæt an his bedde.   Heore ærnde heo him cudde;
ælc his saȝe sæide   swa him sel þuhte,
and hehten hine wenden   aȝæin to his londen,   13150
þat he nauere mid unfriðe   France no isohte.

   Þa while þa þeos eorles þreo   seiden heore erende,
aset þe kaisere   swulc he akimed weore
and andsware nauer nan   no aȝæf þissen eorlen;
ah he lustnede ȝeorne   luðer on his þohte.   13155
Þa anbælh Walwain   swulc an iburst þein,
and þas word sæide   Walwain þe kene:
"Luces þe riche,   þu ært kæisere of Rome;
we beoð Arðures men,   aðelest Brutten.
He sent þe his sonde   wiðuten gretinge: 13160
he hat þe faren to Rome   þa riche is þin aȝen;
let hine halden France   þe he biwon mid fehte,
and hald þu richen   and þine Rom-leoden.
While þine aldren   France ieoden;
mid fehte heo þer biwunnen   unimete wunnen;   13165
swa ane while heo þer liueden,   and seoðen heo hit leoseden.
Mid fehte Arður hit biwon   and he hit wule walden.
He is ure lauerd,   we beoð his leod-kempen.
He us hæhte suggen   soð to þe seoluen;
ȝif þu nult aȝen buȝen   þi bone he wule iwurðen;   13170
and ȝif þu nult aȝen wenden   ah iwurðien þin iwillen,
and þu wult þat kinelond   bitellen to þire hond,
nu, tomorȝen is þe dæi;   haue ȝif þu biȝete mæi!"

   Þæ andswarede þe kaisere   mid grættere wræððe:
"Nulle ich noht aȝæin faren,   ah France ich wulle bitellen;   13175
mine ældren hit heolden   and ich hit wulle habben.
Ah ȝif he wolde bicumen mi mon   and for lauerd me icnawen,
and treouliche me heren   and me for hærre halden,
griðien ich him wulle   and his gumen alle
and lete halde Brutlond,   þæ Iulius hafde in his hond,   13180
and oðere londes monie   þe Iulius hafde an honde
þat he naueð nane rihte to   þæ riche þæh he walde;
þa he scal alle leose   buten he leoð makie."

   Þa andswarede Walwain,   þæ wes Arðures mæi:
"Belin and Brenne,   beiȝene þa ibroðere,   13185
Brutlond heo ahten   and France heo biwunnen,

the presence of the emperor, who was called Lucius, where he was sitting on his bed. They made known their mission to him, each saying his say as he thought right, and bade him return to his own country, never again to enter France with hostile intent.

All the while the three earls were delivering their message, the emperor sat as if he were struck dumb and made no answer whatsoever to these earls; but he listened intently with hatred in his heart. Then Gawain grew angry and, princely in his rage, the bold Gawain spoke these words:

'Mighty Lucius, you are Emperor of Rome; we are followers of Arthur, the noblest of Britons. He sends you this message of his without any greeting: he bids you return to Rome which is your own realm, and let him keep France which he conquered in battle; and you rule your realm and your Roman people. Your ancestors once before invaded France; there they won vast possessions in battle; so for a time they lived there, and afterwards they lost it. Arthur conquered it in battle and he intends to rule it. He is our lord, we are his warriors. He ordered us to speak to you in person, to tell you truly that if you will not withdraw he will be your slayer; and if you will not retreat, but intend to carry out your purpose, intend to take that kingdom into your possession, now, tomorrow is the day; take it if you can achieve it!'

The emperor answered then in great anger:

'I will not retreat, but will conquer France; my ancestors possessed it and I intend to have it. But if he would become my liegeman and acknowledge me as lord, serve me loyally and acknowledge me as his superior, I will grant peace to him and all his followers and let him hold Britain, which Julius Caesar had in his possession, and many other territories which Caesar held to which he has no right though he rules the realm; all this he shall lose unless he makes peace.'

Then Gawain, who was Arthur's kinsman, replied:

'The two brothers Belin and Brenne possessed Britain and they conquered France, and then immediately advanced and seized

and seoððen heo uerden sone   and biʒeten Rome,
and þer heo wuneden seoððe   wel feole ʒere.
þa þis wes al iuare,   þa wes Brennes kæisere
and walde Rom-leoden   and alle þa þeoden.   13190
And Rome is ure icunde,   þa þu haldest an honde,
and ʒif we mote libben   we hit wulleð habben,
beute ʒif þu wulle icnawen beo   þat Arður is king ouer þe
and ælche ʒere him senden   gæuel of þine londen;
and ʒif gæst him a leoð   þu miht libben þa eð."   13195
        þa sæt bi þan kaisere   a cniht of his cunne,
Quencelin ihaten,   hæh mon inne Rome.
þes cniht andswarede   biuoren þan kaisere,
and þus him seide   —þe cniht was unisele:
"Cnihtes, fareð eou aʒæin,   and cuðeð eower kinge   13200
Bruttes beoþ bolde   ac heo beoð unwræste italde;
for æuere heo ʒelp makieð   —heore monscipe is lutel."
Mare he þohte to suggen   þa Walwain bræid to sweorden
and smat hine ufenen þat hafde   þat he atweo hælde;
and he hiʒenliche anan   heolde to his horsen,   13205
and heo up leopen   mid grimliche lechen,
and þas word seide   Walwain þe sele:
"Swa me helpe þe ilke lauerd   þe scop þes daʒes lihte,
ʒif æueræie is swa kene   of eouwer moncunne
þat us after kenne,   ich hine wulle aquelle;   13210
he scal beo toswungen   mid brade mine sweorden."
        Efne þare ilke tale   þa cleopede þe kaisere:
"Haldeð heom, haldeð!   Alle heo sculleð heongien
heʒe uppen treouwe   oðer mid horsen beon todraʒene!"
Efne þissere sæʒe   þa þe kaisere seide,   13215
þe eorles gunnen riden   and spureden heore steden;
heo scæken on heore honden   speren swiðe stronge,
beren biforen breosten   brade heore sceldes.
Aneouste gunnen ride   eorles ræʒe,
and æuere þæ kaisere   lude gon cleopie: 13220
"Nimeð heom, slæh heom;   iscend heo us habbeoð!"
þer me mihte ihere   þe þer bihalues weore
clupien þusende   of þan þeod-folke:
"Hider, hider, wepnen!   Wende we heom æfter!
Hider ure sceldes   —þe scalkes atwendeð!"   13225
        Sone heom after wenden   iwepnede kempen,

Rome, and there they afterwards dwelt very many years. When this had all come to pass, then Brenne was emperor and ruled the Romans and all the subject peoples. And Rome, which you hold as yours, is ours by right, and if we live we intend to have it, unless you will acknowledge that Arthur is sovereign over you and send him each year tribute for your land; and if you approach him in a spirit of peace you may live the more pleasantly.' #

There was sitting by the emperor then a kinsman of his, a knight called Quencelin, a leading man in Rome. In the presence of the emperor this knight replied, expressing himself thus — he was a wicked man:

'Return again, knights, and tell your king that though the Britons are bold they are held in contempt; for they are always boasting yet their valour is slight.'

He was about to say more when Gawain grasped his sword and struck him upon the crown of the head so that it split in two; and at once he leapt speedily to his horse, and all three mounted with grim faces, and the noble Gawain spoke these words:

'So help me God himself who created this light of day, if any one of your men is so bold as to pursue us, I will kill him; he shall be cut to pieces by my broad sword.' #

At these words the emperor at once called out:

'Seize them, seize them! They shall all hang high upon the gallows-tree or be torn apart by horses!'

Even as the emperor spoke these words, the earls rode off, spurring on their steeds; they brandished in their hands stout spears and raised their broad shields before their breasts. The bold earls rode speedily away, and all the while the emperor called out loudly:

'Seize them, slay them; they have dishonoured us!'

Whoever was present there would have heard thousands of his people call out:

'Here, here, bring weapons here! Let us go after them! Bring here our shields — the scoundrels are escaping!'

Armed warriors at once went after them, here six, there

þer sixe, þer seouene;   þer æhte þer niȝene.
And æuere þa eorles   arnde biliues,
and æuere umbe stunde   biseȝen heom bihinde;
and euere þa cnihtes of Rome   after biliue come.   13230
And þer com aneouste   alre swiðest ærne,
and euere cleopede   kenlich swiðe:
"Wendeð aȝæin, cnihtes,   and werieð eo mid fihtes;
hit is eo muchel scome   þat ȝe wulleð atsceken."
Walwain icneo þene reme   of þan Romanisce men;   13235
he wende his stede   and to him gon ride,
and smat hine þurh mid þan spere   swa he ispited weore,
and bræid to him þat spere   —þe gume iwat sone;
and þæs word kende   Walwain þe kene:
"Cniht, þu ride to swiðe;   betere þe weore at Rome!"   13240
Marcel hehte þe cniht,   heȝere monnen.
Þa Walwain isæh   þat he to grunde bæh,
sone his sweord he ut abræid   and smat of Marcele þat hefd;
and þas word sæide   Walwain þe sele:
"Marcel, far to helle,   and tel heom þer spelles,   13245
and wune þer toȝere   mid Quencelien þin ifere,
and haldeð þer unker rune;   betere inc weoren inne Rome,
for þus we eou scullen techen   ure Bruttisce speche!"

Gerin isæh hu hit ferde,   hu þe Romanisce lai þer dune,
and his hors muneȝede   and ænne oðerne imette,   13250
and smat hine þurhut mid his spere   and þas word spilede:
"Rid nu swa, Romain,   and reos þe to hellen!
And þus we scullen grundien   ȝif Godd us wule fulsten.   *
Nis noht wurð þratte   buten þer beo dede æc."
Bos isæh, þe ohte mon,   hu his iueren hafden idon,   13255
and his hors wende   wunder ane swiðe,
and mid alle his mitte   teh to ane cnihte
and smat hine buuen þan scelde   þat tobarst his gode burne
and þurhut þene sweore   —þe swælt ful sone.

And þus þe eorl cleopien agon   kenliche on his feren: 13260
"Bruttes us wulleð scenden   ȝif we heonne wendeð
bute we bet aginnen   ær we heonene iwenden."
Efne þere speche   þe þe eorl kende
heo biwenden heom sone   wunder ane swiðe,
and ælc his sweord swiðe adroh   and ælc his Rumain ofsloh;   13265
and seoððen heore hors wenden   and heore wæi heolden.

seven; here eight, there nine. And the earls continued to ride speedily away, looking behind them every so often; and all the while the Roman warriors followed quickly behind. And he who rode swiftest of all came very close, continually calling out most boldly:

'Turn back, knights, and defend yourselves in fight; it is great dishonour to you that you seek to flee.'

Gawain, hearing the shouts of the Roman, turned his horse and rode towards him, and ran him through with his spear as if spitting him, and then withdrew the spear — the man died instantly; and the valiant Gawain uttered these words:

'Knight, you ride too fast; better for you had you stayed in Rome!'

The knight, a man of noble race, was called Marcel. Gawain, seeing him fall to the ground, immediately drew out his sword and struck off Marcel's head; and the noble Gawain spoke these words:

'Go, Marcel, to hell and tell them your story there, and dwell there hereafter with your comrade Quencelin, and there plot together; better for you both had you stayed in Rome, for this is how we shall teach you our British tongue!' #

Gerin saw how it had gone, how the Roman lay dead there and, spurring on his horse, charged at another, thrust him through with his spear, and spoke these words:

'Ride on now, Roman and sink down to hell! And so shall we triumph if God will help us. Threats are worth nothing unless there are deeds as well.'

Beof, the valiant man, saw how his comrades had fared and, wheeling his horse at great speed, charged with all his might upon a warrior and struck him above the shield so that his stout corslet split, and he was pierced right through the neck — he died instantly.

And the earl began to call defiantly to his comrades:

'The Britons will reproach us if we go from here without making a better showing before we withdraw.'

Even as the earl uttered these words they instantly wheeled about at great speed, and each quickly drew his sword and each

And þæ Romanisce men   riden eouere after heom;
ofte heo heom on smiten,   ofte heo heom atwiten,
ofte heo sæiden heom to   "abuggen ȝe scullen þa dede!"—
ah ne mihten heo þurh nane þinge   heore nenne adun bringe   13270
no nenne hærm þer don heom   i þan wiðer-happen.
Ah æuere umbe whilen   þe eorles aȝain wenden,
and ær heo totwemden   þe wurse wes Rom-leoden.

   þus heo iuerden   fiftene milen
þat heo comen to ane stude   vnder ane ueire wude,   13275
onuast þan castle   þer Arður lei uaste.
þreo milen þerfrom   to þan wuden þrungen
niȝe þusende   þe Arður þider senden,
baldere Brutten   þe bezst þat lond cneowen;
heo wolden wite þat soðe   of Walwain þan kene   13280
and of his iueren,   hu heo iuaren weoren,
whaðer heo liue weoren   þa heo bi wæie læien.

   þæs cnihtes siȝen þurh þene wude   wunder ane softe,
uppen ane hullen   and ȝeorne biheolden.
Heo letten alle þa horsmen   i þan wude alihten   13285
and rihten heore iwepnen   and alle heore iweden,
buten an hundred monnen   þe þer sculden bihalden
ȝif heo onȝiten mihten   þurh æies cunnes þingen.
þa iseȝen heo feorren   in ane uelde muchelen,
þreo cnihtes ærnen   mid allen heore mainen;   13290
after þan þreom cnihten   þritti þer comen;
after þan þrittie   heo iseȝen þreo þusende;
þerafter comen þrasten   þritti þusen anan
Romanisce leoden   mid ræue bihonged.
And þa eorles biuoren heom   aneuste atarnden,   13295
euere þene rihte wæi   þe touward þan wude lai
þer heore iueren   wel ihudde weoren.
þa eorles ærden to þan wuden,   þa Romanisce after riden;
þa Bruttes toræsden   on heore iræste steden
and smiten to auorenon,   and feollen an hundred anan.   13300
þa wenden Rom-leoden   þat Arður come riden
and weoren afered feondliche swiðe;   and Bruttes after heom
and sloȝen of þan folke   fiften hundred.

   þa com heom to fulste   of heore aȝe uolke,
þa Arður þider hafde isend,   sixtene þusund   13305
baldere Brutten   mid burnen bihonged.

slew his Roman; and then they turned their horses and continued on their way. And the Roman soldiers continued to pursue them, striking at them again and again, constantly taunting them, calling repeatedly to them 'you shall pay for your deeds!' — but they could not by any means bring any of them down nor do them any injury there in those clashes. But every so often the earls wheeled about, and before they broke off the Romans had the worse of it.

In this way they covered fifteen miles until they came to a place beneath a pleasant wood, close by the castle where Arthur lay secure. From there to the wood, three miles away, nine thousand men were thronging, bold Britons who knew that region best, whom Arthur had sent there to learn the truth about the valiant Gawain and about his companions, how they had fared, whether they were alive, since they were long upon their journey.

These soldiers moved with great caution through the wood, up onto a hill and looked eagerly around. All the horsemen were made to dismount in the wood and prepare their weapons and all their armour, except for a hundred men who were to be on the look-out there, whether by any means they could see anything. Then they saw, far off in a broad plain, three knights riding with all their might and main; behind the three knights there came thirty men; behind the thirty they saw three thousand; after them thirty thousand Roman warriors clad in armour came thronging all at once. And the earls rode speedily ahead of them, along the path which led straight towards the wood where their comrades lay well hidden. The earls rode into the wood, the Romans pursuing them; the Britons charged on their rested horses and fell upon the vanguard, striking down a hundred at once. Then the Romans thought that Arthur was attacking and were terrified; and the Britons pursued them and slew fifteen hundred of the force.

Then there came to their aid from their own army sixteen thousand bold Britons clad in armour whom Arthur had sent there.

þa com þer ride   þat wes an eorl riche,
Petreius ihate,   heh mon of Rome,
mid six þusend kempen   þan Romanisce to helpen;
and mid muchelere strengðe   leopen to þan Brutten,   13310
and lut þer ofnomen,   ah monie heo ofsloȝen. *
Bruttes to wude hælden,   þe oðere after wenden;
and þa Bruttes auoten   uaste aȝæin stoden.
And þa Romanisce men   fuhten ridende,
and Bruttes heom to heolden   and heore hors sloȝen,   13315
and moni þer nomen   and in þene wude droȝen.
þa iwarð Petreius wrað   þat his wes þa wurse þer,
and he mid his uerde   from þan wude wende;
and Bruttes heom to buȝen   and biæften heom sloȝen.
þa Bruttes weoren ut of wude   iȝein to þan felde,   13320
þa atstoden Rom-leoden   mid ræȝe strenȝe.
þa bigon þat muchele fiht;   þer ueollen eorles and moni god cniht,
þer ueollen a dæi   fiften þusend
aðelere monnen   ær hit weore æfen.
þer he finden mihte   þe his main wolde fondien   13325
hond aȝan honde,   strongne aȝein stronge,
sceld aȝein scelde;   scalkes þer ueollen.
Vrnen þa streten   mid blode-stræmen,
leien ȝeond þan ueldes   gold-faȝe sceldes;
al þene dæi longe   heo heolden þat feht stronge.   13330
Petreius, an his halue,   his folc heold tosomne;
þa iwræð sone   þat Bruttes hafden þat wurse.
þat isæh þe eorl heȝe   of Oxeneuorde,
Beof wæs ihæten,   hæh Bruttisc mon,
þat a nare wisen   ne mihte hit iwurðen   13335
þat Bruttes ne mosten reosen   buten heo ræd haueden.
þa eorl þa cleopede   cnihtes aðele,
of þan alre bezsten   of alle þan Brutten
and of þan kennesten   þe þer quike weoren,
and tuhte hine ut a þan felde   aneouste þere ferde   13340
and þus him iseide   —an heorte him wes unneðe:
"Cnihtes, hercnieð nu to me   —Drihten us helpe!
We beoð hidere icumen   and þis feht habbeoð undernumen
buten Arðures rede   þe is ure hexte.
Ȝif us oht ilimpeð   we him þa bet likieð;   13345
and ȝif us ilimpeð uuelen   he us wule hatien.

Then came riding up a noble earl, a Roman of high rank called Petreius, with six thousand soldiers to help the Romans; and they rushed upon the Britons with great force, capturing a few, but slaying many. The Britons made for the wood, the others in pursuit; and the Britons, dismounting, stood firm against them. The Roman soldiers fought on horseback, and the Britons, advancing on them, killed their horses, captured many men, and dragged them into the wood. Then Petreius was infuriated that he was getting the worse of it, and he and his force retreated from the wood; and the Britons pursued them and struck them down from behind. #

When the Britons emerged from the wood onto the plain once more, the Romans then made a stand, resisting fiercely. Then began that great battle; noblemen fell there and many a good knight, fifteen thousand brave men died there in one day before evening came. He who wished to prove his strength might test it hand to hand there, the strong against the strong, shield against shield; warriors fell there. The paths ran with streams of blood, gilded shields lay scattered over the fields; all day long they kept up that fierce conflict.

Petreius, on his side, kept his force together; then it quickly came about that the Britons had the worse of it. The noble earl of Oxford, a British nobleman called Beof, saw that, saw that nothing could prevent the Britons being defeated unless they had good guidance. The earl then called round him noble warriors, the very best of all the Britons and the bravest who still survived, and made his way out onto the plain close to those fighting and, uneasy at heart, spoke to them thus:

'Warriors, listen now to me — may the Lord help us! We have come here and have engaged in this battle without the guidance of Arthur who is our leader. If good fortune befall us we will the better please him; and if ill fortune befall us he will despise us. But if you want my advice, then let us ride forward

Ah ʒif ʒe wulleð minne ræd,   þenne ride we al glad;
we beoð þreo hundred cnihtes,   ihelmede þeines,
ohte men and kene,   aðele iborene.
Cuðeð eouwer cnihtscipe,   we beoð of are cuðð e;   13350
rideð þenne ich ride,   and fulieð mine rede:
alle haldeð him to,   to þan cnihte þa ich do;
ne nime ʒe nenne stede   no nanes cnihtes iwede,
ah æuerælc god cniht   slæn æuere adunriht."
    Æfne þan worde   þe þe cniht sæide of Oxeneuorde   13355
to his iueren bisiden,   þe gon he to riden
æfne al swa swiðe   swa hund þene heort driueð,
and his iueren after   mid allen heore mahten;
þurhut þene muchele uehte   al þa cniht-weorede
fluen an heore steden   —uolc heo þere aqualden!   13360
Wo wæs heom iboren   þa i þan weie heom weoren biuoren,
for alle heo hit totreden   mid horsen and mid steden,
and swa aneouste heo iwenden   and Petreium iuengen.
Beof him biarnde   and mid ærmen biclupte,
and bræid hine of his stede   and to eorðe hine istræhte;   13365
he wuste him bihalues   balde his cnihte.
Bruttes adun sloʒen,   Petreius heo droʒen,
and þa Rom-leoden   ræhliche fuhten,
and, a þan laste, ne mihte mon wite   wha oðerne smite;
þer wes muchel blod-gute,   balu wes on compe.   13370
    Þa isæh Walwain,   þer he wes bihaluen.
Mid seouen hundred cnihten   þider he gon hælden;
in his wæiʒe þat he funde   al he hit aqualde,
and ridende igrap Petreiun   on richen his steden,
and ladde uorð Petreiun,   læð þeh hit weore him,   13375
þat heo to þan wude comen   þer heo wel wusten
sikerliche to halden   þene riche mon of Rome;
and æft ut a þene ueld wenden   and bigonnen to fehten.
    Þer me iseon mihte   sorʒen inoʒe:
sceldes scenen,   scalkes fallen,   13380
halmes tohælden,   hæhʒe men toswelten,
blodie ueldes,   falewede nebbes.
Bruttes heom toræsden   þa fluʒen Rom-leoden.
Bruttes heom sloʒen   and monie heo quic nomen;
and þe dæi-ende þæ   wa wes Rom-leoden þa.   13385
    Þa bond men uaste   kempen Romanisce

in good heart; we are three hundred knights, helmeted warriors, brave men and bold, nobly born. Display your knightly prowess, show we are of the same breed; charge when I charge, and follow my example: all rush upon him, upon the same knight that I do; seize no horse nor take any knight's armour, but let every good warrior strike at all times with full force.'

With these words which the earl of Oxford addressed to his companions there, he rode off as quickly as a hound pursues a hart, and his companions followed with all their might and main; the whole company flew on their chargers through the great mêlée — they slaughtered many there! Disaster was visited upon those who stood in their way, for they trampled everything down with their horses and steeds, and so quickly came up with and seized Petreius. Beof, confident that his bold followers were by his side, rushed at him and, throwing his arms around him, pulled him from his horse and hurled him to the ground. As they dragged Petreius away, the Britons laid about them and the Romans resisted fiercely, and, in the end, no one could tell who was striking whom; there was much bloodshed, chaos in the battle.

Then Gawain, where he was nearby, saw that. He advanced in that direction with seven hundred soldiers, striking down all he found in his way, and as he rode snatched Petreius up onto his powerful horse and carried him away, reluctant though he was, until they came to the wood where they were sure that they could securely hold the Roman commander. And then they moved out into the plain and began to fight.

Much suffering was to be seen there: shields shattering, warriors falling, helmets splitting, noblemen dying, bloody fields, ashen faces. When the Britons charged them the Romans fled. The Britons slaughtered them and many they captured alive; and at the day's end the Romans were in distress.

Then the Roman warriors were bound fast and led to the

and lædden heom to þan wude   biuoren Walwaine.
Heom biwakeden a þere nihte   twenti hundred cnihten.
Þa hit dai wes amarȝen   duȝeðe gon sturie;
forð heo gunnen liðe   to heore kinelauerde,   13390
and swulc lac him brohte   þat leof him wes to habben.

    Þa spac Arður him þus: "Wulcume, Petreius;
nu ic þe wulle teche   Bruttisce spæche.
Þu ȝulpe biforen þan kaisere   þat þu me woldest aquellen,
nimen mine castles alle   and mine kineriche—   13395
and muchel þe sæl iwurðen   of þat þu wilnedest to habben!
Ich wulle bitachen þe ful iwis   minne castel inne Paris,
and þer þu scalt wunien   swa þe beoð alre leoþest;
ne scalt þu nauere mare   þi lif þenne lede!"

    Arður þa cnihtes nom   þe þer iuongen weoren.   13400
Þreo hundred rideres   he nom eke anan
þe alle weoren iueren,
cnihtes swiðe ohte   and kene men to uihte,
and hæhte heom amorȝen   monliche arisen,
binden Romanisce men   mid stronge rake-tehȝen,   13405
and lede Petreius   to þere borh of Paris.
Feouwer eorles he hæhte   forð heom ibringen,
Cador, Borel,   Beduer and Richer;
he hehte heom beon iueren   þat heo siker weoren
and cumen aȝain sone   to heore kinelauerde.   13410

    Þis wes al þus ispeken   —ah hit wes sone underȝeten;
hæwæres foren   ȝeond þas kinges ferden
and iherden suggen   soðere worden
wuder Arður wolde senden   þæ cnihtes þe he hafde i benden.
And þa hauweres forðrihte   wenden uorð bi nihte   13415
þat heo comen sone   to þan kaisere of Rome,
and talden al heore tale,   hu þas feouwer eorles sculden uare
and forð lede Petreius   to þære burh of Paris.
And al heo talden þene wæi   þe intowardes Parise læi,
and whar me heom kepen mihte   in ane slade deopen   13420
and biraiuien of heom   Petreiun þene riche mon,
and þa feouwer eorles ileggen   and fasten heom binden.

    Luces þis iherden,   þe kaiser of Rome,
and he leopt to wepne   swulc hit a liun weore,
and ten þusend hehte   kempen iþoȝene   13425
to horse and to wepnen   aneouste foren wenden.

wood, into Gawain's presence. Two thousand soldiers guarded them throughout the night. In the morning, when it was daylight, the troops began to stir; they marched back to their sovereign lord, bringing him a gift such as he was pleased to have.

Then Arthur addressed him thus:

'Welcome, Petreius; now I will teach you the British tongue. You boasted before the emperor that you would kill me, seize all my castles and my kingdom — and much good may it do you, all that you longed to possess! I will most certainly give you my castle in Paris, and there you shall so dwell that it will be most hateful to you; you shall never again dwell anywhere else!'

Arthur took charge of the knights who had been captured there. Then he immediately chose three hundred horsemen who were all comrades, very brave knights and dauntless fighters, and bade them on the morrow rise like men, bind the Romans with strong chains, and conduct Petreius to the city of Paris. He ordered four earls to escort them on the way, Cador, Borel, Bedevere and Richer; he bade them keep together that they might be secure and to return quickly to their sovereign lord. #

This was all agreed upon — but it was soon discovered; spies went through the king's army and heard tell truthful accounts where Arthur was going to send the knights he had in chains. And the spies immediately set out by night and quickly came to the emperor of Rome, and told their whole story, how the four earls were to proceed and were to conduct Petreius to the city of Paris. And they described the whole route which led all the way to Paris, and where men might ambush them in a deep valley and snatch from them the nobleman Petreius, and overpower the four earls and bind them fast.

Hearing this, Lucius, Emperor of Rome, leapt to arms like a lion, and ordered ten thousand seasoned warriors to arm and

He cleopede Sextorius   —of Libie he wes king, of Turkie dux—
he sende after Euander   þe of Babiloine wes icumen þer,
he cleopede to þan senaturs   Bal, Catel, Carrius—
þeos weoren alle kineborne   and þeos weoren alle icoren—   13430
aneouste to riden   and Petreium aredden.

 Anan swa hit was euen   forð heo iwenden;
heom ladden twelue   of þan leod-folke
þa swiðe ware weoren   and þa weizes cuðen.
þa riden Rom-leoden,   riseden burnen,   13435
quahten on hafden   helmes hezen,
seldes on rugge,   ræze Rom-leoden.
Heo ferden alle nihte   neodliche swiðe
þet heo comen in þe wai   þa into Parise lei;
þa weoren heo biuoren   and Bruttes biaften.   13440
Ah wale þat hit nuste   Cador þe kene,
þat þa Rom-leoden   heom forriden hafueden!
Heo comen in ænne wude   on ænne swiðe faire stude
in ane dale deope   dizelen bihælues;
sweoren heom bitwænen   þat þer heo wolden kepen.   13445

 Þer heo leien stille   ane lutle stunde;
and hit agon daizen   and deor gunnen wazezen.
þa comen Arðures men,   quecchen after streten,
riht þene ilke wæi   þer þe oðer uerde læi.
Heo riden singinge;   segges weoren bliðe.   13450
Neoþeles Cador wes þer   swiðe wis and swiðe war;
he and Borel þe eorl riche   buzen heom togæderes,
and nomen heom bitweonen   fif hundred cnihtes,
and biuoren wenden,   iwepnede kempen.
Richer and Beduer   wenden heom bafte þer,   13455
and þa cnihtes fereden   þa heo iuongen hafden,
Petreium and his iueren   þa iwunne weoren.

 Þa heo comen riden   uppen Rom-leoden,
and Rom-leoden ræsden to   mid ræzere strengðen
and smiten a þan Brutten   mid swiðe bitele duntes; *   13460
breken Bruttene trume   —balu wes on folke;
þe wude brastlien gon,   beornes þer feollen.
Bruttes heom wiðstoden   and stærcliche heom weoreden.
þat iherde Richer   and þe eorl Beduer,
hu heore iueren   heom biuoren fuhten.   13465
Petreiun heo nomen   and heore inume allen

mount and march out quickly. He summoned Sextorius who was King of Libya and Duke of Turkey, he sent for Evander who had come there from Babylon, he called upon the senators Bal, Catel and Carrius — they were all of royal birth and all excellent men — to ride in haste and rescue Petreius. #

As soon as it was evening they set out; they were guided by twelve of the local people who were well skilled and knew the paths. Then the Romans rode off, bold Romans, corslets clinking, tall helmets nodding on their heads, shields on their shoulders. They journeyed all night in furious haste until they came to the track leading to Paris; they were then in front and the Britons were behind them. But alas that the valiant Cador did not know of it, that the Romans had ridden ahead of them! They came into a wood, to a very pleasant place thereby in a deep and secluded valley; they agreed among themselves that they would lie in wait there.

They lay quiet there for a short time; and dawn began to break, the beasts to stir. Then came Arthur's men, advancing along the route, the very same path where the other force lay. They sang as they rode; the men were in high spirits. Cador, however, was very alert and vigilant there; he and the noble earl Borel joined forces and, taking with them five hundred soldiers, armed warriors, marched ahead. Richer and Bedevere marched behind them there, escorting the knights whom they had taken, Petreius and his compatriots who had been captured.

Then as they rode they came upon the Romans, and the Romans rushed out with great force and fell upon the Britons with most bitter blows, breaking the British ranks — there was chaos in the host; the woods resounded, men fell there. The Britons resisted them and defended themselves stoutly. Richer and the earl Bedevere heard that, heard how their comrades ahead of them were embattled. They took Petreius and all the prisoners and sent

and mid þreo hundred sweinen   into wude senden,
and heomseolue fusden   toward heore ifæren,
and smiten a Rom-leoden   mid raȝere strengðen;
þer wes moni dunt iȝeuen   and moni mon þer wes islaȝen.   13470
    Þa underȝæt Euander   —þe heðene king wes swiðe war—
þat heore uolc gon waxen   and Bruttes gunnen wonien,
and buȝen heom tosomne   his cnihtes seleste
and uuenon þan Brutten   swulc heo heom wolden abiten.
Bruttes wokeden þa   and heore wes þat wurse;   13475
heo sloȝen, heo nomen   al þat heo neh comen.
Wa wes Brutten þere   buten Arðure;
heore hele wes to lutel þere   at heȝere neode. *
Þer wes Borel ofslaȝen   and idon of lif-daȝen;
Euander king hine aqualde   mid luðere his crafte,   13480
and þreo Bruttes eke,   heȝe men iborene.
Þer islaȝen weoren   þreo hundred of heore iueren,
and monie quike nomen   and narwe heom ibunden.
Þa nusten heo godne ræd nanne,   for alle heo wenden beon dede;
neoþeles heo fuhten   swa ohtliche swa heo mahte.   13485
    Þa wes ut ifaren   from Arðures ferden
þæ king of Peytouwe,   har mon iblowen;
Guitard he hehte,   Gascunne he ahte.
He hæfde to iueren   fif hundred rideren,
þreo hundred scuhten,   kene men to uehten,   13490
and seouen hundred auoten   þa fuse weoren to harmen.
Heo weoren ifaren into þan londe   fodder to biwinnen,
æiþer uodder and mete   to læden to heore ferde.
Þa luden heo iherden   of þan Rom-leoden;
heore deden heo bilafden   and þiderward gunnen liðen,   13495
stið-imodede men and swifte,   slauþe bidæled,
þat heo comen sone   anneouste þan fehte.
    Guitard and his cnihtes   þerriht forðrihtes
igripen heore sceldes,   swiðe balde cnihtes,
and alle þa scuten   scuuen heom bisides   13500
and þa men auoten   to gunnen fusen,
and alle somed smiten on   mid smarten heore dunten.
At þan uorme smællen   Romaniscen veollen,
fiftene hundred,   folden to grunden.
þer wes islæȝen Euander,   þe king wes ful sturne ær;   13505
Catellus of Rome   forȝæt his domes þære!

them into the wood with three hundred young squires, and they themselves hastened towards their comrades, and fell upon the Romans with great force; many a blow was given there and there many a man was slain.

Then Evander — the heathen king was very wily — perceived that the British began to falter and his side to have the upper hand, and his best warriors banded themselves together and fell upon the Britons as if they would devour them. The Britons gave ground then and had the worse of the encounter; the Romans slew or captured all those they came upon. Disaster faced the Britons there in Arthur's absence; their strength was not sufficient in their hour of need. There Borel was struck down and deprived of life; King Evander slew him by his deadly skill, and three other Britons, men of noble birth. Three hundred of their comrades were slaughtered there, and many taken alive and closely bound. They had then no sure resource, for they all expected to die; nevertheless they fought on as bravely as they could.

There had earlier marched out from Arthur's army the king of Poitou, called Guitard, ruler of Gascony, famed as a doughty warrior. He had a company of five hundred horsemen, three hundred archers, keen fighters, and seven hundred foot soldiers who were deadly in action. They had marched into the countryside to get fodder, both fodder and provisions to take to their army. Hearing the clamour of the Romans, they abandoned their task and headed in that direction until, stout-hearted men, swift-moving and prompt in action, they shortly came close to the battle. #

Guitard and his soldiers, very bold warriors, thereupon immediately grasped their shields, and all the archers advanced with them and the foot soldiers hastened forward, and all charged together in fierce onslaught. At the first onset fifteen hundred Romans fell, stricken to the earth. There King Evander, who had fought fiercely, was slain; there Catellus of Rome forgot the

þæ astalden þer flem   þat ær staðel heolden;
þa rugges towenden   and fluʒen Rom-leoden.
Bruttes heom after buʒen   and mid baluwe heom igrætten;
and swa monie heo þer nomen   and swa monie heo þer sloʒen   13510
þat no mihte Bruttene uerde   biueolen namare.
And þa Romanisce men   þe þer atfaren mihten
atarnede ful sone   to þan kaisere
and talden him tidende   of Arður þan kinge,
for heo wenden to soðe   þat Arður þider comen.   13515
þer wes auared swiðe   þe kaisere and his ferde
þe Bruttes islaʒen hafden   —þat heom sel þuhten.

Aʒeinward heo buʒen þa   mid baldere biʒete
and to þan stude wenden aʒæin   þer þat feht hafde ibeon,
and bureden þa deden   and þa quike gunnen forð leden;   13520
and senden after Petreiun   þæ heo ær nomen
and after his iueren   þæ ær inumen weoren,
and senden heom alle ful iwis   into þære burʒe of Paris,
and þreo castles fulden   and faste heom biclusden,
after Arðures heste,   aðelest kingen.   13525

    Alle Brut-leoden   luueden Arðuren.
Alle heom stod him æie to   þat wuneden a þan ærde;
swa dude þan kaisere   —of Ærður e he hafde muchele kare;
and alle Rom-leoden   of Arður e weoren afærde.
þa wæs mid soðe ifunde   þat Mærlin sæide whilen: 13530
þat sculden for Arður e   Rome ifullen afure,
and þa wal of stanen   quakien and fallen.
þas ilke tacninge sculde beon   of Luces þan kæiseren
and of þan senature   þa mid him come of Rome,
and of þan seoluen wisen   þæ þer gunnen resen.   13535
þat Merlin i furn-daʒen seide   al heo hit funden þere,
swa heo duden ære   and seoðen wel iwhare—
ær Arður iboren weore   Merlin al hit bodede!

    þe kaisere iherde suggen   soðere worden
hu his men weoren inumen   and hu his folc æc ofslaʒen.   13540
þa weoren inne his ferde   feolevalde sorʒe;
summe mænden heore freond,   summe þrætteden heore ueond,
summe bonneden wepnen   —balu heom wes ʒeueðe.
þa iseh Luces   þat luðere him ilimped wæs,
for ælche dæi he losede   of his leod-folke,   13545
ah he herm iuredde,   his heʒe men he losede.

orders given him! Then those who had previously stood firm took to flight; and the Romans turned their backs and fled. The Britons pursued and violently assailed them; and they captured so many and slaughtered so many there that the British force could kill no more of them. And the Romans who managed to escape there fled in great haste to the emperor and brought him word of Arthur the king, for they truly believed that it was Arthur who had come there. Then the emperor, and his followers whom the Britons to their great satisfaction had stricken, were greatly alarmed. #

The Britons then withdrew with princely booty and returned to the place where the battle had been, and buried the dead and led the survivors away. And they sent for Petreius whom they had captured previously and for his comrades who had been taken earlier, and sent them all without fail to the city of Paris and, following the instructions of Arthur, noblest of kings, imprisoned them securely, filling three castles.

All the people of Britain loved Arthur. All who dwelt in the land stood in awe of him; so did the emperor — he had great dread of Arthur; and all the Roman people were afraid of Arthur. Then what Merlin had once said was found to be true: that, because of Arthur, Rome should be put to the torch, and the stone walls tremble and fall. These same prophecies were to prove true of the emperor Lucius and the senators who had come with him from Rome, and of the very manner in which they came to grief there. All that Merlin had spoken in former days they then found true, as men everywhere had done and were to do — Merlin foretold it all before Arthur was born! #

The emperor received truthful reports how his men had been captured and also how his followers had been slaughtered. Then there were in his army many signs of grief and anger, some lamenting their friends, some threatening their enemies, some preparing weapons — misfortune had come upon them. Then Lucius saw that things went badly for him, for each day he lost some of his people, and suffered also the misfortune of losing his

He iwærð afered þa wunder ane swiðe,
and nom him to ræde and to som-rune
þat he wolde to Æust mid alle his iuerde;
forð bi Lengres he wolde uare —of Arðure he hafde muchele kare!
Arður hafde his hauwares an hirede þas kaiseres
and sone duden him to witen whuder he wolde wenden.
Arður lette sone somnien his ferde
stilleliche bi nihte, his cnihtes seleste;
and forð þe king wende mid sele his folke. 13555
An his riht honde he lette Lengres stonde,
and i þæne wæi biforen ferde þe Luces faren wolde.
Þa he com in ane dale vnder ane dune,
þer he gon atstonden, kennest alre kingen.
(Þat dale is mid soðe Sosie ihaten.) 13560
Arður þer adun lihte and hæhte al his duʒeðe
græðien heom to fihte swa scolden cnihtes ohte,
þat whenne Rom-leoden þer comen riden
þat heo uengen heom on swa ohte cnihtes sculden don.
Alle þa sweines and þa unwræste þeines 13565
and of þan smale uolke feole þusunde
þe king heom sette in ane hulle mid feole here-marken—
þat he dude for ʒepscipe þerof he ʒelpen þohte,
al swa hit iwarð seoððe þerafter ful sone.
Arður ten þusend nom of aðelen his cnihten, 13570
sende a riht honde mid raue bihonge;
he lette oðere ten þusende an his lift honde,
ten þusend biuoren, ten þusend biæften;
mid heomseoluen heo heolden sixtene þusund.
Bihalues he sende into ane wude hende 13575
seouentene þusend selere cnihten,
wel iwepnede men, þene wude to biwiteʒen
þat heo mihte þider uare, ʒif him neod weore.
Þa wes inne Gloucestre an eorl mid þan bezste,
Moruið wes ihate, mon swiðe kene. 13580
Him he bitahte þene wude and þa ferde;
"and ʒif hit ilimpeð, swa wule þe liuiende Godd,
þat heo ouercumen beon and biginnen to fleon,
setteð heom after mid allen æouwer mahten
and al þat ʒe oftake maʒen doh hit of lif-daʒen, 13585
þa uatte and þa lene, þa riche and þa hene.

commanders. He was very greatly afraid then, and he took counsel and reached a decision that he would proceed to Autun with all his army, march out by way of Langres — he had great dread of Arthur!

Arthur had his spies in the emperor's train and they soon let him know where he intended to go. Arthur immediately caused his army, his best warriors, to be quietly assembled by night; and the king marched out with his splendid host. Leaving Langres on his right hand, he advanced along the route which Lucius would take. When he came into a valley beneath a hill, the boldest of kings halted there. (The rightful name of that valley is Sosie.) Arthur dismounted there and ordered all his followers to prepare themselves for battle as bold warriors should, so that when the Romans came riding that way they might fall upon them as valiant warriors should do. #

All the young squires and the serving-men unfitted for fighting and many thousands of the lesser folk were stationed by the king on a hill with many battle-standards —he did that as a stratagem, hoping to boast of it as, very shortly afterward, he had cause to do. Arthur took ten thousand of his noble warriors, clad in armour, and sent them to the right flank; he placed another ten thousand on his left flank, ten thousand in the van, ten thousand in the rear, keeping sixteen thousand in his own party. He sent apart into a nearby wood seventeen thousand excellent soldiers, men well armed, to guard the wood so that, if it were necessary, they might retreat there.

There was an earl of Gloucester, the best of earls, a most valiant man called Morvith. He entrusted to him the wood and the force guarding it; 'and if it so happens, as the living God wills, that they are defeated and take to flight, pursue them with all your might and kill all those you can overtake, the fat and the

For no beo in nauer nare leode,   no in none leode,
cnihtes al swa sele   swa beoð mid me seolue,
cnihtes al swa ræʒe,   cnihtes al swa riche,
cnihtes al swa stronge   in nauer ane londe.   13590
ʒe beoð under Criste   cnihten alre kennest;
and ich æm rihchest alre kinge   vnder Gode seolue.
Do we wel þas dede   —Godd us wel spede!"
Cnihtes þa andswarede   stilleliche under lufte:
"Alle we scullen wel don   and alle we scullen touon;   13595
niðing wurðe þe cniht   þe ne cuðe his mahten herriht!"
        þa sænde heo a ba siden   al þa men auoten;
þa lette he sette up þene drake,   here-mærken unimake,
bitæhte hine ane kinge   þe wel hine cuðe halde.
Angel, Kinge of Scotlonde,   þa uormeste uerde heold an honde; 13600
Cador, þe eorl of Cornwaille,   þa uerde heold baften;
Bof hafde ane,   þe eorl of Oxenuorde;
þe eorl of Chæstre, Gerin,   þa ueorðe uerde heold mid him.
þa uerden uppen þere dune   heold Escil king þe Denisce;
Lot heold þa ane,   þe leof was þan kinge;   13605
Howel of Brutaine   heold ane oðere.
Walwain þe kene   wes bi þan kinge.
Kai wuste ane,   stiward wæs þas kinges;
Beduer ane oðer,   þe wes þes kinges birle.
þe eorl of Flandres, Howeldin,   ane uerde hefde mid him;   13610
ane muchele uerde hefde Guitard,   þe king of Gascunnes ærd;
Wigein, Eorl of Leicestre,   and Ionatan, Eorl of Dorchestre,
heo wusten þa twa uerden   þe þer weoren auoten.
þe eorl of Chastre, Curselein,   and eorl of Baðe þe hehte Urgein,
ho biwusten ba þa uerden   þa weoren þær auoten;   13615
þeos sculden a twa haluen   halden to þan uehte.
To þissen twam eorlen   þa ohte cnihtes weoren
hafden Arður treouðe;   þe eorles weoren treowe.
        þa weoren alle þa uerden isette   alse Arður sel þuhte,
þa cleopede him to   þe king of Brutaine   13620
his redʒiuen alle   þa ræiʒest weoren to dome;
and þus seide Arður anan   to aðelen his monnen:
"Hercneð nu touwardes me,   mine wines deore.
Iræsed ʒe habbeoð tweien   to Romanis monnen,
and twien heo beoð ouercumen,   and islaʒen and inumen,   13625
for heo al mid wronge   wilneden of ure londe;

lean, the great and the humble. For in no country, nor among any nation, are there such excellent warriors as I have on my side, such bold and mighty warriors, such powerful fighters in any land whatsoever. You are the bravest of all warriors in Christendom; and I am the mightiest of all kings under God himself. Let us do all things well, and may God prosper us!' The knights there present then answered quietly:

'We shall do our best and endeavour all; may the knight who does not display his valour here and now be judged a coward!'

Then all the foot-soldiers were despatched on either hand; then he had the dragon banner, the matchless standard, raised, entrusting it to a king who could protect it well. Angel, King of Scotland, commanded the leading troop; Cador, the earl of Cornwall, led the next company; Beof, the earl of Oxford, had one; Gerin, the earl of Chester, had the fourth division under his command. Æscil, the Danish king, led the forces on the hillside; Lot, who was dear to the king, led one company; Howel of Brittany led another. The valiant Gawain was beside the king. Kay, who was the king's steward, commanded one division; Bedevere, who was the king's cup-bearer, another. Howeldin, the earl of Flanders, had a division under him; Guitard, the king of Gascony, had a large force; Wigein, Earl of Leicester, and Jonatan, Earl of Dorchester, commanded two divisions who were on foot there. Curselin, the earl of Chester, and the earl of Bath called Urgein, commanded two more divisions on foot there who were to advance to the battle on both flanks. Arthur trusted in these two earls who were valiant knights; and the earls were worthy of his trust. # #

When all the divisions had been marshalled as Arthur thought fit, then the king of Britain summoned to him all his counsellors who were most decisive in judgement; and thereupon Arthur spoke to his noble followers thus:

'Listen now to me, my dear friends. Twice you have attacked the Romans, and twice they have been overcome, slaughtered and taken captive, because they most wickedly coveted our land;

and min heorte seið me,   þurh ure Drihten hehne,
þat ȝet heo scullen beon ouercumen,   baðe islæȝen and inumen.
Ȝe habbeoð ouercumen Noreine,   ȝe habbeoð ouercume Denene,
Scotlond and Irlond   al iwunen to eouwer heond,   13630
Normandie and France   biwunnen mid fehte.
Þreo and þritti kinelond   ich halde a mire aȝere hond
þæ ȝe hit under sunnen   habbeoð me biwunnen.
And þis beoð þa forcuðeste men   of alle quike monnen,
hæðene leode   —Godd heo seondeð laðe!   13635
Ure Drihten heo bilæueð   and to Mahune heo tuhteð;
and Luces þe kæisere   of Godd seolf naueð nane care,
þat hafueð to iueren   haðene hundes,
Goddes wiðer-iwinnen!   We heom scullen awelden,
leggen heom to grunde,   and us seoluen beon isunde   13640
mid Drihtenes willen   þe waldeð alle deden."
Þa andswarede eorles þare: "Alle we beoð ȝarewe *
to libben and to liggen   mid leouen vre kingen!"
Þa þas ferde wes al idiht,   þa wes hit dailiht.

Luces at Lengeres boȝede   and al his Rom-leode.   13645
He hehte his men blawen   his guldene bemen,
bonnien his ferden;   forð he wolde riden
from Lengres to Auste   swa læi his weie rihte.
Forð gunnen riden   Romanisce leoden
þat heo ane mile comen   neh Arðure.   13650
Þa iherde Rom-leoden   ræȝe tiðenden:
iseȝen alle þa dales,   alle þa dunes,
alle þa hulles   mid helmes biþahte,
heȝe hare-marken,   hæleðes heom heolden,
sixti þusende   þrauwen mid winde,   13655
sceldes blikien,   burnen scinen,
palles gold-faȝe,   gumen swiðe sturne,
steden lepen   —sturede þa eorðe!
Þe keiser isah þæne king fare,   þer he was bi wude-scaȝe.
He, Luces, þa sæide,   þæ lauerd of Rome,   13660
and spac wið his monnen   ludere stefnen:
"What beoð þeos utlaȝen   þa þisne wei us habbeoð foruaren?
Nime we ure wepnen   and heom to wenden;
heo sculleð beon islaȝene,   and summe quic iulaȝene;
alle heo sculle beon dede,   mid wite fordemde!"   13665
Efne þan worden   heo iuengen heore wepnen;

and my heart tells me that, with the help of our Lord Almighty, they shall yet again be overcome, some slain and some taken captive. You have conquered Norway, you have conquered Denmark, you have taken all Scotland and Ireland into your possession, won Normandy and France in battle. I hold sovereignty over three and thirty earthly kingdoms which you have won for me. And these Romans are the most wicked race on earth, a heathen people — they are hateful to God! They deny our Lord and commit themselves to Mahoun; and the emperor Lucius takes no heed of the true God, Lucius who consorts with heathen dogs, enemies of God! We will vanquish them and, by the will of God who controls all actions, lay them low, and ourselves be safe and sound.'

Then the nobles present there answered:

'We are all ready to live and die with our beloved king!' By the time the army was fully prepared, it was daylight. #

Lucius and all the Romans were encamped at Langres. He ordered his men to sound his golden trumpets, to assemble his forces; he intended to ride out from Langres towards Auste as his line of advance required. The Roman host rode forward until they came within a mile of Arthur. Then the Romans learnt harsh tidings: they saw all the valleys, all the downs, all the hillsides covered with helmets, sixty thousand lofty standards borne by warriors fluttering in the wind, shields glittering, corslets gleaming, golden tunics, fearsome warriors, steeds leaping — the earth shook!

The emperor, where he was at the edge of the woods, observed the king's movements. Then he spoke; Lucius, the ruler of Rome, addressed his men in a loud voice:

'Who are these outlaws who have barred our right of way? Let us take our weapons and fall upon them; they shall be put to death, and some flayed alive; they shall all die, perish in torment!'

At these words they seized their weapons; as soon as they

þa heo igæred weoren   mid gode heore wepnen,
þa spac Luces sone,   þæ lauerd of Rome:
"Biliue we heom to   —alle we scullen wel do!"
     þer weoren icumen mid him   fif and twenti kingen,   13670
heðene uolc alle   þa heolden of Rome,
eorles and dukes eke   of æstene weorlde.
"Lauerdinges," quæd Luces þa,   "Mahun eou beo liðe;
ȝe beoð kinges riche,   and hereð into Rome.
Rome is mi rihte,   rihcchest alre burȝe,   13675
and ich ah hæxst to beon   of alle quike monnen.
ȝe iseoð her, on uolden,   þa ure ifan sunden;
heo þencheð to rixlien heȝe   ouer ure riche,
halden us for hænen,   heomseoluen riche iwurðen.
Ah we heom scullen forbeoden   mid baldere strengðen,   13680
for ure cun hæxst was   of alle quike monnen
and alle þa lond biwinnen   þa heo on lokeden;
and into Brutlonde   ferde Iulius þe stronge
and biwon him to hondes   feole kinelondes.
Nu wolden ure underlingges   beon ouer us kingges;   13685
ah heo hit scullen abuggen   mid heore bare ruggen;
no scullen heo nauere liðen   aȝæin to Brutaine!"
     Æfne þan worde   þa sturede þa uerde;
bi þusend and bi þusende   heo þrunggen tosomne;
ælc king of his folke   ȝarkede ferde.   13690
þa hit al was iset   and ferden isemed,
þa weoren þarriht italde   fulle fiftene ferden.
Twein kinges þere   æuere weoren ifere;
feouwer eorles and a duc   dihten heom togadere;
and þe kæisere himseolf   mid ten þusend kempen.   13695
þa gon þat folc sturien   —þa eorðen gon to dunien;
bemen þer bleowen,   bonneden ferden;
hornes þer aqueðen   mid hæhȝere stefnen,
sixti þusende   bleowen tosomne.
Ma þer aqueðen   of Arðures iueren   13700
þene sixti þusende   segges mid horne;
þa wolcne gon to dunien,   þa eorðe gon to biuien.
     Tosomne heo heolden   swulc heouene wolde uallen.
Ærst heo lette fleon to   feondliche swiðe
flan al swa þicke   swa þe snau adun ualleð.   13705
Stanes heo letten seoððen   sturnliche winden.

were armed with their stout weapons, then Lucius, the ruler of
Rome, said:

'Let us fall upon them — we shall all fight bravely!'

Five and twenty kings had come there with him, all heathens,
owing allegiance to Rome, as well as earls and dukes from eastern
lands. Then Lucius said:

'May Mahoun be merciful to you, sirs; you are mighty rulers,
and obedient to Rome. Rome, the greatest of all cities, is mine by
right, and I ought, by right, to be the greatest of all mortal men.
Here, in this place, you see those who are our foes; they plan to
rule supreme over our realm, to keep us in submission and
themselves become all-powerful. But we shall resist them with the
utmost force, for our ancestors were the greatest of all mortal men
and conquered all the lands they set eyes upon; and the mighty
Julius Caesar invaded Britain and took many other kingdoms into
his possession. Now our vassals wish to be sovereign over us; but
they shall atone for it upon their bare backs; never again shall
they return to Britain!'

At these words the forces began to move; they thronged
together in their thousands, each king forming a company from
among his own subjects. When all was prepared and the forces
marshalled, fully fifteen companies were duly numbered there.
There two kings kept close together at all times; four earls and a
duke joined forces; and the emperor himself led ten thousand
warriors. Then that host began to move — the earth resounded;
there trumpets sounded, troops wheeled; there horns rang out with
a splendid noise, sixty thousand sounding in unison. From
Arthur's army more than sixty thousand trumpeters answered; the
welkin rang, the earth shook.

They clashed together as if the heavens were falling. First
they let fly with furious speed arrows as thick as falling snow.
Next they sent stones fiercely whirling. Then spears clashed,

Seoððen speren chrakeden,   sceldes brastleden,
helmes tohelden,   heʒe men uellen,
burnen tobreken,   blod ut ʒeoten;
ueldes falewe wurðen,   feollen here-mærken.   13710
Wondrede ʒeond þat wald   iwundede cnihtes oueral;
sixti hundred þar weoren   totredene mid horsen;
beornes þer swelten,   blodes aturnen;
stræhten after stretes   blodie stremes.
Balu wes on uolke;   þe burst wes vnimete.   13715
Swa al swa suggeð writen   þæ witeʒen idihten,
þat wes þat þridde mæste uiht   þe auere wes here idiht,
þ[at] at þan laste   nuste nan kempe
whæm he sculde slæn on   and wham he sculde sparien,
for no icneou na man oðer þere   for vnimete blode.   13720
      Þa hæf þat fiht of þan studen   þer heo ær fuhten,
and bigunnen arumðe   ræsen tosomne,
and neouwe ueht bigunnen,   narewe iþrungen;
þer weoren Rom-leoden   reouliche iladde.
Þa comen þer kinges þreo   of hæðene londe;   13725
of Ethiope wes þe an,   þe oðer wes an Aufrican,
þe þridde wes of Libie,   of hæðene leode.
Heo comen to þere uerde   a þere æst ænde
and þene sceld-trume breken   þe Bruttes þer heolden,
and anan fælden   fiftene hundred   13730
baldere þeinen   of Arðures þeoden;
þa wenden Bruttes   sone to þa rugges.
      Þa comen þer riden   tweien eorles kene—
þat was Beduer and Kæi,   Arðures birle and his mæi.
Heore Bruttes heo isehʒen   mid bronden tohawen;   13735
þer iwurðen tobursten   eorles swiðe balden;
mid ten þusend cnihten   hælden to þan uihten,
amidden þan þrunge   þer heo þihkest weoren;
and sloʒen Rom-leoden   reouliche swiðen,
and ʒeond þan uehte wenden   after heore iwillen.   13740
Þa weoren heo to þriste   and to ufele heom biwusten—
wala wa, wala wa,   þat heo neoren war þa,
þat heo ne cuðen biwiten heom   wið heore wiðer-iwinnen,
for heo weoren to kene   and to ærwene,
and to swiðe fuhten   and to ueor wenden,   13745
and spradden to wide   ʒeond þat feht brade.

- 226 -

shields splintered, helmets split, noblemen fell, corslets shattered, blood gushed forth; the earth turned red, banners fell. Wounded soldiers wandered over the wooded countryside; there six thousand were trampled underfoot by horses; warriors perished there, blood flowed; streams of blood flowed along the forest paths. Disaster came upon the armies; the destruction was vast. Just as is stated in the accounts which wise men have compiled, that was the third greatest battle which was ever fought; such a battle that in the end no warrior knew whom he should strike down and whom he should spare, for no man recognised another because of the excess of blood.

Then the conflict shifted from the place where they had been fighting, and they began to attack each other over a wide area, beginning a new engagement, closely contested, in which the Romans were hard beset. Then there came three kings from heathen lands; one was from Ethiopia, the second was an African, the third was from Libya, from a pagan nation. They engaged the army on the eastern flank and broke through the shield-wall which the Britons had formed there, and struck down in an instant fifteen hundred bold warriors of Arthur's host; then the Britons quickly took to flight.

Then there came riding two bold earls — they were Bedevere and Kay, Arthur's cup-bearer and his kinsman. Seeing their fellow Britons cut down with swords, those most valiant earls grew enraged; with ten thousand soldiers they charged into the mêlée, into the midst where the press was thickest, striking down the Roman warriors with great ferocity, and cutting through the battle at will. Then they became too daring and too careless in defending themselves — alas, alas, that they were not more wary then, that they took no care to defend themselves against their enemies, for they were too eager and too reckless, and fought too rashly and advanced too far, and spread themselves too widely over the broad battlefield.

þa com þe king of Mede,   þe muchele and þe brade,
heðene here-þrihng,   þer he hærm wrohte;
he ladde to iueren   twenti þusend rideren.
He heold on his honde   ænne gare swiðe stronge;   13750
þene gare he uorð strahte   mid strongen his maine
and smat þene eorl Beduer   forn, a þan breoste,
þat þa burne tobarst sone   biuoren and bihinde;
anopened wes his breoste,   þa blod com forð luke.
þer feol Beduer anan   ded uppen uolden;   13755
þer wes sarinesse,   sorreʒen inoʒe!
    þer Kai funde Beduer   ded liggen him þer;
and Kai þat lich wolde   leden mid himseolue.
Mid twenti hundred cnihten   he hælde þer abuten,
and feondliche feuhten   and falden Rom-leoden,   13760
and of Medie þer sloʒen   moni hundred monnen.
þat ueht wes strong swiðe   and heo weoren þer to longe.
þa com þer liðen   a swiðe ladlic king an
mid sixti þusend monnen   sele of his londen,
Setor þe kene,   þe com him from Libie.   13765
þer þe king stronge   wið Kæi him gon fehte,
and forwundede Kai swiðe   inne strongen þan fehte,
to þan bare deðe   —reoulich wes þa dede!
His cnihtes þerrihte   hine ladden of þan uihte,
mid muchelere strengðe   þurh þat feht stræhten.   13770
Wa wes Arðure kinge   for þa tidinge!
    þæt iseh þe riche þein,   Ridwaðelan wes ihaten,
Bedueres suster sune,   of heʒe Bruttes he wes icume,
þat Boccus mid his spere stronge   Bedver hafde istunge.
Wa wæs him on liue   þa his æm wes an deðe,   13775
for he of alle monnen   mæst hine lufede.
He cleopede of his cunne   cnihtes swiðe gode,
and of þan alre leofeste   þe he on liue wuste;
fif hundred bi tale   fusden tosomne.
Riwaðlan þa sæide,   riche mon of Brutene: 13780
"Cnihtes, ʒe beoð of mine cunne;   cumeð hidere to me,
and wreke we Beduer min æm   þa bezst wes of ure cunne,
þa Buccus hafd ofstungen   mid his spere strongen.
Fuse we alle tosomne   and ure ifan feollen!"
    Æfne þan worde   forð he iwende,   13785
and alle mid him anan   aðele his iueren,

Then came the king of Media, a heathen warrior, tall and burly, leading a force of twenty thousand horsemen — he wrought havoc there! He had in his hand a very stout spear; with his full might he thrust forward the spear and struck the earl Bedevere in the front, through the chest, so that the corslet instantly shattered back and front; his chest was laid open, the warm blood gushed out. Bedevere instantly fell dead upon the ground there; great was the grief, the sorrow at that! #

Then Kay found Bedevere where he lay dead; and Kay wished to bear the body away with him. With two thousand warriors he surrounded the place and, fighting furiously, cut down the Romans, and slew there many hundreds of Median warriors. The fighting was very fierce and they were embroiled there too long. Then came up a most wicked king, the bold Seftor, who had come from Libya with sixty thousand valiant warriors from his land. The powerful king began to fight with Kay, and in the fierce encounter wounded Kay severely, to the point of death — a cruel deed! His knights immediately bore him from the battle, pressing through the mêlée with great force. Sad was King Arthur at news of that! #

The great nobleman Ridwathelan, Bedevere's sister's son, descendant of noble Britons, saw that Boccus had pierced Bedevere with his stout spear. To be alive now that his uncle was dead was misery for him, for he had loved him more than any other man. He called together from among his kinsmen the bravest knights, the worthiest of those whom he knew to be still alive; five hundred all told hastily assembled. Then Ridwathelan, the noble Briton, said:

'Knights, you who are my kinsmen, come here to me, and let us avenge my uncle Bedevere who was the noblest of our race, whom Boccus has fatally pierced with his stout spear. Let us all charge as one and strike down our enemies!' #

With these words he advanced, and with him on the instant

and Buccus þene king icneowen   þer he was i compen—
mid his spere and mid his scelde   monine king he aqualde!
Riwadðlan braid ut his sweord sone   and him to sweinde,
and smat þane king a þene helm   þat he a twa toueol,   13790
and æc þere burne-hod,   þat hit at þe toðen atstod;
and þe heðene king   hælde to grunde,
and his fule saule   sæh into helle.

Riwærdðlan þa seide,   ræh he was on mode:
"Boccus, nu þu hafst aboht   Beduer þu sloȝe   13795
and þi saule scal toȝere   beon þas wurse iuere!"
Æfne þan worde   swulc hit þe wind weore
he þraste to þan fihte;   swa þode doð on felde
þenne he þat dust heȝe   aȝiueð from þere eorðe,
al swa Riwadðlan   ræsde to his feonden.   13800
Al heo hit sloȝen   þat heo aneh comen,
þe while þe heo mihte walden   heoren kinewurðe wepnen.
Neouren in al þan fihte   cnihtes nane betere
þe while þat heom ilaste   þat lif on heore breoste.
Boccus þene king heo ofsloȝen   and a þusend of his cnihten;   13805
þa wes Beduer awræken,   wel mid þan bezsten!

Þer wes an oht eorl   aðeles cunnes,
Leir wes ihaten,   lauerd of Buluine.
He isæh i þan fihte   enne ueond fusen,
þat on admirail,   of Babiloine he wes ældere—   13810
muchel uolc he aualde,   uolde to grunde!
And þe eorl þat bihædde;   an heorte him was unneðe.
He bræid an his breoste   ænne sceld bradne
and he igrap an his hond   a sper þat wes swiðe strong,
and his hors muneȝeden   mid alle his imaine   13815
and þene admiral hitte   mid smærten ane dunte
vnder þere breoste   þat þa burne gon to berste,
þat him þer bæfte   þat sper þurhræhte
fulle ane ueðme;   þe ueond feol to grunde.

Þat isah sone   þeos admirale sone,   13820
Gecron is ihate,   and his spere grap anan
and smat Leir þene eorl sære   a þa lift side,
þurhut þa heorte;   þe eorl adun halde.
Walwain þat bihedde   þer he wes on uehte,
and he hine iwraðede   wunder ane swiðe.   13825
Þat isæh Howel,   hæh mon of Brutten,

all his noble companions, and they recognised King Boccus where he was in the mêlée — with his spear and shield he had killed many a king! Ridwathelan immediately drew his sword and swung at him, striking the king on the helmet so that it and the mail coif too split apart, and the sword lodged in the teeth; and the heathen king fell to the ground, and his evil soul sank down into hell.

Then Ridwathelan, enraged at heart, said:

'Boccus, you have now paid for slaying Bedevere, and henceforth your soul shall keep company with the Devil!'

With these words he rushed like the wind into the battle; as a whirlwind does in the plain when it drives the dust high from the ground, just so did Ridwathelan rush upon his foes. All they came upon they slew, as long as they could wield their princely weapons. In the whole battle there were no better knights while life remained in their bodies. They slew King Boccus and a thousand of his warriors; then Bedevere was fully avenged, to the uttermost!

There was a brave earl of royal lineage, called Leir, ruler of Boulogne. He saw an enemy making towards him in the battle, an emir who was the ruler of Babylon — he had felled many a warrior to the ground! And the earl, observing that, was troubled at heart. He flung a broad shield before his chest and grasped a very stout spear in his hand, and, spurring on his horse with all his might, struck the emir a fierce blow under the breast so that the coat of mail shattered, and the spear pierced through him a full fathom's length; the foe fell to the ground.

The son of this emir, called Gecron, saw this at once and, quickly grasping his spear, struck the earl Leir grievously on the left side right through the heart; the earl fell to the ground. Gawain, where he was in the press, saw that, and grew exceedingly angry. Howel, ruler of Brittany, saw it, and he rushed

and he þider halde   mid fiftene hundred monnen;
herde here-kempen   mid Howele fusden,
and Walwain heom uuenon,   swiðe stið-imoded mon.
He hefde to iferen   fif and twenti hundred   13830
baldere Brutten.   þa bigunnen heo to fehten.
    þer weoren Rom-leoden   reouliche iledde:
Howel heom kepte,   Walwain heom imette.
þer wes wunderlic grure: þa welcnen aqueðen,
þa eorðe gunnen to buuien,   stanes þer bursten,   13835
urnen stremes of blode   of ærmen þan folke,
þat wel wes unimete;   þa weoren Bruttes werie.
Kinard, þe eorle of Strugul,   bilefde þene king Howel
and inom mid him Labius,   Rimarc and Boclouius.
þis weoren þa keneste men   þat æi king ahte,   13840
þeos weoren on moncunne   eorles main stronge.
Heo nalden for heore mucle mode   fulien Howele þan gode,
ah bi heomseoluen heo sloȝen   alle þe heo neh come.
    þat isæh a riche mon   of þan Rom-leoden,
hu Kinard þe kene   heore uolc þer aqualde;   13845
and þe cniht gon him alihten   of leofuen his steden,
and nom him on his honde   a spere imaked of stele
and biwalede hine a blode,   and bihalues him eode
þat he com a þan ende   þer fæht Kinard þe stronge;
Kinardes burne he up ahof   and he þene eorl þer ofsloh.   13850
þa ȝeiden lude   alle Rom-leode
and buȝen to þan Brutten,   and heore trume breken;
feollen here-marken,   uolc adun helden. *
Sceldes þer scenden,   scalkes þer feollen,
þer ueollen to grunde   fiftene þusende   13855
baldere Brutten;   balu þer wes riue.
Swa ilaste longe   þat uiht swiðe stronge.
    Walwain gon ȝeonge   ȝeond þat wæl muchele
and somnede his cnihtes alle   þer he heom funde i fihte.
Aneouste þer com ride   Howel þe riche;   13860
heo somneden heore beire uolc anon   and forð heo gunnen fusen,
and riden to Rom-leoden   mid raȝere wraððen,
and fastliche heom to buȝen   and breken þere Freinsce trumen.
And Walwain forðrihte   þer he ifunde
Luces þene kaiser   leouien under scelde,   13865
and Walwain him to sweinde   mid þe stelene sweorde,

there with fifteen hundred men; fierce warriors hastened with Howel, and Gawain, the most resolute of men, along with them. He had as comrades in arms five and twenty hundred bold Britons. Then they joined battle there. #

The Romans were hard pressed there: Howel attacked them, Gawain assailed them. Awesome were the terrors there: the heavens resounded, the earth shook, stones shattered there, streams of blood ran from the wretched men, the slaughter was immense; the Britons were weary then. Kinard, Earl of Strugul, parted from King Howel, taking with him Labius, Rimarc and Boclovius. These were the bravest men that any king had in his service, leaders of might unmatched among mortal men. Because of their great pride they would not follow the good Howel, but of their own accord they slew all whom they came upon. #

A man of high authority among the Romans saw that, saw how the valiant Kinard was killing his countrymen there; and the knight dismounted from his trusty steed and, taking in his hand a spear of wrought steel, dipped it in blood, and strode forwards until he reached the spot where the mighty Kinard was fighting; thrusting under Kinard's coat of mail, he slew the earl there and then. Then all the Romans shouted aloud and, charging at the Britons, broke through their ranks; banners fell, the British force gave ground. There shields shattered, there warriors fell, fifteen thousand bold Britons sank to the ground; destruction was widespread there. That most violent of battles lasted long.

The youthful Gawain went through the carnage rallying all his followers wherever he found them on the battlefield. Shortly there came riding the valiant Howel; they quickly united their two forces and advanced swiftly, rode towards the Romans in furious anger and, rushing upon them speedily, broke through the Frankish ranks there. And there Gawain presently came upon the emperor Lucius actively defending himself, and Gawain struck at

and þe kaisere hine.   þat com wes swiðe sturne, *
sceld aȝein scelden   —sciuren þer wunden;
sweord aȝein sweorde   sweinde wel ilome,
fur fleh of þe stelen   —þa ueond weoren abolȝen.   13870
þer wes viht swiðe strong;   stureden al þa ferden.
þe kaisere wende   Walwain to scende
þat he miht an uuere daȝe   ȝelpen uor þere deden.
Ah Bruttes him þrungen to   þræfliche swiðe;
and þa Romanisce men   arudden heore kæiseren,   13875
and heo tosomne heolde   swulc heouene wolde ualle.
    Alle þene dailiht   heo heolden seoððen þat fiht.
Ane lutle stunde   ær þe sunne eode to grunde
Arður þa cleopede,   aðelest alre kinge:
"Nu we heom to alle,   mine cnihtes ohte;   13880
and Godd seolf us fulste   ure feond to afallene!"
Æfne þan worden   þa bleou men þa bemen;
fiftene þusend anan   þraste to blauwen
hornes and bemen;   þa eorðe gon beouien
for þan vnimete blase,   for þan mucle ibeote.   13885
Rom-leoden wenden   rug to þan feohten;
feollen here-marken,   heȝe men swulten,
fluȝen þa þe mihten;   þa ueie þær feollen.
Muchel mon-slæht wes þere;   ne mihte hit na man tellen
hu feole hundred monnen   toheouwen þer weoren   13890
i þan mucle þrunge,   i þan mon-slæhte.
    Wes þe kaisere ofslæȝen   a seolcuðe wisen,
þat nuste hit nauer seoðen   na mon to sugen
of nauer nare cuððe   wha þene kaisere qualde;
bute þa þet feht was al idon   and þat folc wes al iblissed,   13895
þa funde men þene kaisere   ofstungen mid ane spere.
    Word com to Arður   þer he wes on telde
þat þe kaisere wes ofslaȝen   and idon of lif-dæȝen.
Arður lette slæn an teld   amidden ænne bradne ueld
and þider iberen lette   Luces þene kaisere,   13900
and lette hine bitillen   mid gold-faȝe pallen,
and biwiten hine þer lette   þreo daȝes fulle
þe while he wurchen lette   an werc swiðe riche,
ane cheste longe,   and wreon heo al mid golde;
and lette leggen þerinne   Luces of Rome—   13905
þat wes a swiðe duhti mon   þa while his daȝes ilasten.

him with his blade of steel, and the emperor at him. That encounter was very fierce, shield against shield — splinters flew there, sword repeatedly struck against sword, sparks flew from the steel — the adversaries were enraged. The conflict there was very keen; the whole host was aroused. The emperor hoped to kill Gawain that he might boast of the deed in days to come. But the Britons in great anger rushed upon him; and the Roman soldiers rescued their emperor, and each side charged at the other as if the heavens were falling.

They continued fighting all through the daylight hours. Then, a little while before the sun sank to the earth, Arthur, the noblest of all kings, called out:

'Now let us all assail them, my brave knights; and may God himself help us to strike down our enemies!'

Then, with these words, trumpets were blown; fifteen thousand men immediately assembled to sound horns and trumpets; the earth shook at the mighty blast, at the great clamour. The Romans retreated from the battle; banners fell, noblemen perished, those who were able to, fled; the doomed fell there. There was great slaughter there; no one could reckon how many hundreds of men were cut to pieces there in the great mêlée, in the general carnage.

The emperor was slain in a strange manner, so that no man of any country whatsoever was ever afterwards able to say who killed the emperor; but when all the fighting had ended and the whole host was rejoicing, then the emperor was found pierced through by a spear.

Word came to Arthur where he was encamped that the emperor had been slain and deprived of life. Arthur had a tent pitched in the middle of a broad plain and caused the emperor Lucius to be brought there, and had him covered with a golden pall, and watched over there a full three days while he had a most splendid piece of work, a long coffer, made and covered all over with gold; and he caused Lucius of Rome to be laid therein — he had been a very brave man while he lived.

þa ȝet dude Arður mære,   aðelest alre Brutte:
Arður asechen lette   alle þa riche
kinges and eorles   and þa riccheste beornes
þa i þan fehte weoren islaȝen   and idon of lif-dæȝen;   13910
he lette heom burien   mid baldere pruten.
Buten þreo kinges he beren lette   Luces þan kaisere,
and lette makien beren   riche and swiðe maren,
and lette heom sone   senden to Rome.
And grette Rom-weren alle   mid græten ane huxe,   13915
and seide þat he heom sende   þat gauel of his londe,
and efte wold heom alswa   senden heom gretinge ma
ȝif heo ȝirnen wolden   of Arðures golden;
and þerafter wulle sone   riden into Rome
and tellen heom tiðinge   of Brutlondes kinge,   13920
and Rome walles rihten   þe ȝare weoren tofallen—
"and swa ich wulle awelden   þe wode Rom-leoden!"
Al þis ȝelp wes idel ido,   for eoðer weis hit eode,
al oðer hit itidde   —þe leoden he bilæfden,
al þurh Modred is mæin,   forcuðest alle monnen! *   13925
    A þan muchele fihte   Arður of his cnihtes losede
fif and twenti þusend   a uolden tohawen
of Brutten swiðe balde,   biræued at liue.
Kæi wes forwunded seore,   wunder a swiðe;
to Kinun he wes ilad   and sone þerafter he wes ded.   13930
Bibured he wes þere,   bihalue þan castle,
imong heremiten;   þat wæs þe riche mon!
Kæi hehte þe eorl,   Kinun þe castel.
Arður ȝæf him þene tun   and he þerto tumbede, *
and sette þer þene nome   after himseoluen;   13935
for Keises dæðe   Kain he hit hehte;
nu and auere mare   swa hit hehte þere.
    Seoððen Beðuer wes islæȝen   and idon of lif-dahȝen,
Arður hine beren lette   to Bæios, his castle,
and biburied he wes þere   inne þere burȝe;   13940
wiðuten þan suð ȝæte   in eorðe me hine sette.
Howeldin iulut wes   forð into Flandres,
and alle his bezste cnihtes   þer flutten uorðrihtes
into þan eorldomen   þenne heo þer comen.
And alle þa dede   in eorðe me heom leide;   13945
inne Teruane   heo liggeoð alle clane.

The dead are buried with great splendour

Then Arthur, the noblest of all Britons, did still more: Arthur caused all the mighty kings and earls and the greatest warriors who had been cut down and deprived of life in the battle to be sought out; he had them buried with great splendour. But he ordered three kings to take the emperor Lucius and, having had a costly and most magnificent bier made, dispatched them at once to Rome. And he greeted all the citizens of Rome with a gross insult, saying that he was sending them that tribute from his land, and, moreover, would send them more such greetings thereafter if they should still yearn for Arthur's treasure; and shortly thereafter he would ride into Rome and bring them tidings of the king of Britain, and secure the walls of Rome which once upon a time were overthrown — 'and so I will rule the unruly Romans!' All this vaunting was quite futile, for it turned out otherwise, turned out quite differently — he departed from his people, all through the might of Modred, the basest of all men!

In the great battle Arthur lost five and twenty thousand of his warriors, the bravest of Britons cut down and deprived of life. Kay was most grievously, mortally wounded; he was borne to Kinun and shortly afterwards he died. He was buried there, near the castle, among hermits, he who had been a mighty man! The earl was called Kay, the castle Kinun. Arthur had given him the town and he buried him there, and named it after him; because of Kay's death he called it Caen; now and for evermore that place is to be so called. #

After Bedevere had been cut down and deprived of life, Arthur caused him to be borne to his castle, Bayeux, and he was buried there within the fortress; he was interred outside the south gate. Howeldin was borne across the sea to Flanders, and all his best knights sailed directly there, to the earldoms from which they had come. And all the dead were laid in the earth; they lie all together in Therouanne.

Leir þene eorl me ladde   into Buluine;
and Arður þeræfter seoððe   wunede in ane londe
inne Burguine   þer him bezst þuhte.
Þat lond he al biwuste   and alle þe castles sette   13950
and seide þat he wolde   himseolue þat lond holde.
And seoððen he his beot makede,   a sumere þat he wolde
faren into Rome   and ahnien al þa riche,
and beon himseolf kaisere   þe Luces wuneden ære.
And monie of Rom-leoden   wolden þat hit swa eoden,   13955
for heo weoren adradde   to heore bare deðe
þat monie þer awæi fluȝen   and heore castles bibuȝen;
and monie sende sonde   to Arðure þan stronge,
and monie him speken wið   and ȝirnden Arðures grið.
And summe heo wolde   aȝein Arðure halden,   13960
and halden wið him Rome   and weren þa leode;
and neoðeles heo auered weoren   for heore uæie-siðen
þat nusten heo under Criste   nenne ræd godne.

     Þa wes hit itimed þere   þat Merlin saide while,
þat Rom-walles sculden   aȝein Arðure touallen.   13965
Þat was agan þære   bi þan kaisere
þa ueol þerinne fehte   mid fifti þusund monne;
ruren þer to grunde   riche Rom-leoden.
Þa Arður wende to soðe   to aȝen al Rome,
and wunede inne Burguine,   richest alre king.   13970

     Þa com þer in are tiden   an oht mon riden,
and brohte tidinge   Arðure þan kinge
from Moddrede, his suster sune   —Arðure he wes wilcume
for he wende þat he brohte   boden swiðe gode.
Arður lai alle longe niht   and spac wið þene ȝeonge cniht;   13975
swa nauer nulde he him sugge   soð hu hit ferde.

     Þa hit wes dæi a marȝen   and duȝeðe gon sturien,
Arður þa up aras   and strehte his ærmes;
he aras up, and adun sat   swulc he weore swiðe seoc.
Þa axede hine an uæir cniht: "Lauerd, hu hauest þu iuaren toniht?"
Arður þa andswarede   —a mode him wes uneðe:
"Toniht a mine slepe,   þer ich læi on bure,
me imætte a sweuen;   þeruore ich ful sari æm.
Me imette þat mon me hof   uppen are halle;
þa halle ich gon bistriden   swulc ich wolde riden;   13985
alle þa lond þa ich ah   alle ich þer ouer sah,

The earl Leir was borne to Boulogne; and then Arthur settled thereafter in a region of Burgundy where it best pleased him. He ruled that whole land and established all the castles, and declared that he himself would hold that land. And then he declared his intention, that in the summer he would march into Rome and take possession of the whole realm, and himself be emperor where previously Lucius had been. And many of the Romans wished it so to be, for they were so in fear for their very lives that many had fled, abandoning their castles; and many sent messengers to the mighty Arthur, and many appealed to him, entreating his protection. And some of them wished to resist Arthur, and defend Rome against him and protect the realm; and yet they were so in fear of their fate that they knew no sure resource in all the world.

Then there had come to pass there what Merlin had once said, that the walls of Rome should fall before Arthur. That had been fulfilled by the fall in battle there of the emperor and fifty thousand men; the might of Rome was there brought low. Arthur, mightiest of all kings, then lay waiting in Burgundy, fully expecting to possess all the lands of Rome. #

Then at a certain time there came riding a valiant man, bringing tidings to Arthur the king from Modred, his sister's son — Arthur welcomed him because he thought that he was bringing good tidings. All night long Arthur stayed talking with the young knight who yet could not bring himself to tell him the truth of what had befallen.

On the morrow when it was daylight and people began to stir, Arthur arose and stretched his arms; he stood up, and sat down again as if he were very unwell. A courteous knight then asked him:

'My lord, how have you fared this night?'

Then Arthur answered — he was uneasy at heart:

'In my sleep tonight, as I lay in my chamber, I dreamt a dream; I am ill at ease because of it. I dreamt that I had been seated high upon a hall, bestriding the hall as if I were riding it; there I looked over all the land that I possess, and Gawain sat

and Walwain sat biuoren me;   mi sweord he bar an honde.

þa com Moddred faren þere   mid unimete uolke;
he bar an his honde   ane wiax stronge.
He bigon to hewene   hardliche swiðe   13990
and þa postes forheou alle   þa heolden up þa halle.
þer ich iseh Wenheuer eke,   wimmonnen leofuest me;
al þere muche halle rof   mid hire honden heo todroh.
þa halle gon to hælden   and ich hæld to grunden
þat mi riht ærm tobrac.   þa seide Modred: 'Haue þat!';   13995
adun ueol þa halle,   and Walwain gon to ualle
and feol a þere eorðe;   his ærmes brekeen beine.
And ich igrap mi sweord leofe   mid mire leoft honde,
and smæt of Modred is hafd   þat hit wond a þene ueld.
And þa quene ich al tosnaðde   mid deore mine sweorede;   14000
and seoððen ich heo adun sette   in ane swarte putte.

And al mi uolc riche   sette to fleme
þat nuste ich under Criste   whar heo bicumen weoren;
buten miseolf ich gon atstonden   uppen ane wolden.
And ich þer wondrien agon   wide ȝeond þan moren;   14005
þer ich isah gripes   and grisliche fuȝeles.
þa com an guldene leo   liðen ouer dune,
deoren swiðe hende   þa ure Drihten makede.
þa leo me orn foren to   and iueng me bi þan midle,
and forð hire gun ȝeongen   and to þere sæ wende.   14010
And ich isæh þæ vðen   i þere sæ driuen;
and þe leo i þan ulode   iwende wið me seolue.
þa wit i sæ comen   þa vðen me hire binomen;
com þer an fisc liðe   and fereden me to londe.
þa wes ich al wet   and weri of sorȝen and seoc.   14015

þa gon ich iwakien;   swiðe ich gon to quakien;
þa gon ich to biuien   swulc ich al furburne. *
And swa ich habbe al niht   of mine sweuene swiðe iþoht,
for ich what to iwisse   agan is al mi blisse;
for a to mine liue   sorȝen ich mot driȝe.   14020
Wale þat ich nabbe here   Wenhauer mine quene!"

þa andswarede þe cniht: "Lauerd, þu hauest unriht;
ne sculde me nauere sweuen   mid sorȝen arecchen.
þu ært þe riccheste mon   þa rixleoð on londen
and þe alre wiseste   þe wuneð under weolcne.   14025
Ȝif hit weore ilumpe,   swa nulle hit ure Drihte,

before me bearing my sword in his hand.

Then Modred came marching up with a vast host, bearing in his hand a stout battleaxe. He began to hew with great vigour and cut through all the posts which supported the hall. There I also saw Guenevere, the dearest of women to me, pulling down the whole roof of the great hall with her hands. The hall began to sway and I fell to the ground, breaking my right arm. Then Modred said: "Take that!"; the hall collapsed, and Gawain tumbled down and fell upon the ground, breaking both his arms. And I, grasping my beloved sword in my left hand, struck off Modred's head so that it rolled to the ground. And I hacked the queen all to pieces with my trusty sword; and then I thrust her down into a black pit.

And all my noble subjects took to flight so that I knew not where in the wide world they were; but I myself was left standing upon a hill. And I then went wandering far and wide over the moors; there I saw griffins and hideous birds. Then there came roaming across the hills a golden lion, the most noble beast our Lord created. The lion came running towards me and seized me by the waist, and made off, moving towards the sea. And I saw the sea-waves surging; and the lion went with me into the water. Once we two were in the sea the waves parted us; then a fish came swimming by and bore me to the land. I was all wet and weary then, sick with sorrow.

Then I awoke; I began to tremble greatly, then to shiver as if I was all consumed with fever. And so all night long I have reflected much upon my dream, for I know with certainty that all my happiness is ended; for as long as I live I must endure sorrow. Alas that Guenevere my queen is not here with me!' #

Then the knight answered:

'Lord, you are mistaken; one should never interpret dreams ominously. You who rule in this land are the most powerful and the wisest of all who dwell upon earth. If it should have happened, as our Lord forbid, that Modred your sister's son

þat Modred, þire suster sune,   hafde þine quene inume
and al þi kineliche lond   isæt an his aȝere hond,
þe þu him bitahtest   þa þu to Rome þohtest,
and he hafde al þus ido   mid his swikedome,   14030
þe ȝet þu mihtest þe awreken   wurðliche mid wepnen,
and æft þi lond halden   and walden þine leoden,
and þine feond fallen   þe þe ufel unnen,
and slæn heom alle clane   þet þer no bilauen nane."
    Arður þa andswarede,   aðelest alre kinge: 14035
"Longe bið æuere   þat no wene ich nauere,
þat æuere Moddred mi mæi
wolde me biswiken   for alle mine richen,
no Wenhauer mi quene   wakien on þonke;
nulleð hit biginne,   for nane weorld-monne."   14040
    Æfne þan worde forðriht   þa andswarede þe cniht:
"Ich sugge þe soð, leofe king,   for ich æm þin vnderling,
þus hafeð Modred idon: þine quene he hafeð ifon,
and þi wunliche lond   isæt an his aȝere hond;
he is king and heo is quene   —of þine kume nis na wene,   14045
for no weneð heo nauere to soðe   þat þu cumen aȝain from Rome.
Ich æm þin aȝen mon   and iseh þisne swikedom,
and ich æm icumen to þe seoluen   soð þe to suggen.
Min hafued beo to wedde   þat isæid ich þe habbe
soð buten lese   of leofen þire quene,   14050
and of Modrede, þire suster sune,   hu he hafueð Brutlond þe binume."
    Þa sæt hit al stille   in Arðures halle.
Þa wes þer særinæsse   mid sele þan kinge;
þa weoren Bruttisce men   swiðe vnbalde uor þæn.
Þa umbe stunde   stefne þer sturede;   14055
wide me mihte iheren   Brutten iberen,
and gunne to tellen   a feole cunne spellen
hu heo wolden fordeme   Modred and þa quene,
and al þat moncun fordon   þe mid Modred heolden.
    Arður þa cleopede,   hendest alre Brutte: 14060
"Sitteð adun stille,   cnihtes inne halle,
and ich eou telle wulle   spelles vncuðe.
Nu, tomærȝe, þenne hit dæi bið   and Drihten hine sende,
forð ich wulle buȝe   in toward Bruttaine;
and Moddred ich wulle slan   and þa quen forberne,   14065
and alle ich wulle fordon   þa biluueden þen swikedom.

had seized your queen and taken into his own possession your entire kingdom, which you entrusted to him when you planned to go to Rome, and he had done all this by his treachery, still you might fittingly avenge yourself by force of arms, and possess your land again and rule your people, and destroy your enemies who wish you ill, kill them one and all that none of them survive.'

Then Arthur, noblest of all kings, replied:

'As long as time shall last, I will never believe that, that my kinsman Modred would ever betray me, not for all my kingdom, or that Guenevere my queen would weaken in resolve; never would she do so, not for any man on earth.'

At these words the knight immediately answered:

'Dear king, I tell you truthfully, because I am your subject, Modred has done so: he has seized your queen, and taken your fair land into his own possession; he is king and she is queen — there is no expectation of your return, for in truth they do not believe that you will ever come back from Rome. I am your own liegeman and witnessed this treachery, and I have come to you in person to tell you the truth. Let my head be forfeit if I have not told you the truth without deception about your beloved queen, and about Modred, your sister's son, how he has taken Britain from you.' #

Then all was silence in Arthur's hall. There was grief then in the presence of the noble king; then the Britons were much dispirited therefore. Then after a time voices were raised there; from all sides could be heard the clamour of the Britons, declaring in many and various words how they would put Modred and the queen to death, and kill all the people who supported Modred.

Then Arthur, noblest of all the Britons, called out:

'Sit down quietly, knights in the hall, and I will tell you matters strange to hear. Now, tomorrow, when it is day and the Lord has made it light, I will set out towards Britain; and I will slay Modred and burn the queen, and I will destroy all who approved that treachery. And I will leave behind here the

And her ich bileofuen wulle   me leofuest monne,
Howel, minne leofue mæi,   hexst of mine cunne;
and half mine uerde   ich bilæfuen a þissen ærde
to halden al þis kinelond   þa ich habbe a mire hond.   14070
And þenne þas þing beoð alle idone,   aȝan ich wulle to Rome,
and mi wunliche lond bitæche   Walwaine mine mæie,
and iuorþe mi beot seoððe   bi mine bare life;
scullen alle mine feond   wæi-sið makeȝe!"

þa stod him up Walwain,   þat wes Arðures mæi,   14075
and þas word saide   —þe eorl wes abolȝe:
"Ældrihten Godd,   domes waldend,
al middel-ærdes mund,   whi is hit iwurðen
þat mi broðer Modred   þis morð hafueð itimbred?
Ah, todæi, ich atsake hine, here,   biuoren þissere duȝeðe;   14080
and ich hine fordemen wulle   mid Drihtenes wille,
miseolf ich wulle hine anhon   haxst alre warien.
þa quene ich wulle mid Goddes laȝe   al mid horsen todraȝe.
For ne beo ich nauere bliðe   þa wile a beoð aliue *
and þat ich habbe minne æm   awræke mid þan bezste."   14085
Bruttes þa andswarede   mid baldere stefne:
"Al ure wepnen sunden ȝarewe;   nu, tomarȝen, we scullen uaren!"

A marȝen, þat hit dæi wes   and Drihten hine senden,
Arður uorð him wende   mid aðelen his folke;
half he hit bilæfde   and half hit forð ladde.   14090
Forð he wende þurh þat lond   þat he com to Whitsond;
scipen he hæfde sone,   monie and wel idone,
ah feowertene niht fulle   þere læi þa uerde,
þeos wederes abiden,   windes bidelde.

Nu was sum forcuð kempe   in Arðures ferde;   14095
anæn swa he demen iherde   of Modredes deðe,
he nom his swein aneouste   and sende to þissen londe,
and sende word Wenhaueren   heou hit was iwurðen,
and hu Arður wes on uore   mid muclere ferde,
and hu he wolde taken on   and al hu he wolde don.   14100

þa quene com to Modred,   þat wæs hire leofuest monnes,
and talde him tidende   of Arðure þan kinge,
hu he wolde taken an   and al hu he wolde don.
Modræd nom his sonde   and sende to Sexlond
after Childriche   —þe king wes swiðe riche—   14105
and bæd hine cume to Brutaine   þerof he bruke sculde.

dearest of men to me, my beloved kinsman Howel, noblest of my race; and I will leave half my army in this land to hold all of this kingdom which I have in my possession. And when these deeds are all accomplished, I will march upon Rome again, entrusting my fair land to my kinsman Gawain, and then fulfil my vow upon my very life; all my enemies shall meet a fearful end!'

Then up rose Gawain, who was Arthur's kinsman, and spoke these words — the earl was enraged:

'Almighty God, ruler of destinies, guardian of this mortal world, how has it come to pass that my brother Modred has stirred up this rebellion? But here and now, before this company, I disown him; and, God willing, I will destroy him, I myself will hang him higher than any criminal. I will have the queen torn apart by horses in accordance with God's law. For I shall never rest content while they are alive and until I have avenged my uncle in the most fitting manner.'

The Britons then answered with bold words:

'All our weapons are ready; now, tomorrow, we shall march!'#

On the morrow, when it was day and the Lord had made it light, Arthur set out with his princely following, leaving half the army behind and leading half away. Forth he went across the country until he came to Wissant; he quickly obtained ships, many and well equipped, but for a whole fortnight the army lay there lacking a wind, waiting upon the weather. #

Now there was a certain treacherous soldier in Arthur's army; as soon as he heard Modred's death decreed, he immediately chose one of his servants and sent him to this country, bringing word to Guenevere of what had happened, and how Arthur was on the march with a vast army, and how he was going to act and everything he intended to do.

The queen went to Modred, who was the dearest of men to her, and told him the news of King Arthur, how he was going to act and everything he intended to do. Modred chose his messengers and sent to Saxony for Childric, who was a very

Modræd bad Childriche,   þene stronge and þene riche,
wide senden sonde   a feouwer half Sexlonde,
and beoden þa cnihtes alle   þat heo biʒeten mihte
þat heo comen sone   to þissen kinedome,   14110
and he wolde Childriche   ʒeouen of his riche,
al biʒeonde þere Humbre,   for he him scolde helpe
to fihten wið his æme,   Arðuren kinge.
Childrich beh sone   into Brutlonde!

     Þa Modred hafde his ferde   isomned of monnen,   14115
þa weoren þere italde   sixti þusende
here-kempen harde   of heðene uolke
þa heo weoren icumen hidere   for Arðures hærme
Modred to helpen,   forcuðest monnen.
Þa þe uerde wes isome   of ælche moncunne,   14120
þa heo weoren þer on hepe   an hundred þusende,
heðene and cristene,   mid Modrede kinge.

     Arður lai at Whitsond   —feouwertene niht him þuhte to long;
and al Modred wuste   wat Arður þær wolde;
ælche dai him comen sonde   from þas kinges hirede.   14125
Þa ilomp hit an one time   muchel rein him gon rine,
and þæ wind him gon wende   and stod of þan æst ende;
and Arður to scipe fusde   mid alle his uerde;
and hehte þat his scipmen   brohten hine to Romerel
þer he þohte up wende   into þissen londe.   14130

     Þæ he to þere hauene com,   Moddred him wes auornon;
ase þe dæi gon lihte   heo bigunnen to fihten;
alle þene longe dæi   moni mon þer ded læi.
Summe hi fuhten a londe,   summe bi þan stronde;
summe heo letten ut of scipen   scerpe garen scriþen.   14135
Walwain biforen wende   and þene wæi rumde,
and sloh þer aneuste   þeines elleouene;
he sloh Childriches sune   þe was þer mid his fader icume.
To reste eode þa sunne.   Wæ wes þa monnen;
þer wes Walwain aslæʒe   and idon of lif-daʒe   14140
þurh an eorl Sexisne   —særi wurðe his saule!

     Þa wes Arður særi   and sorhful an heorte forþi,
and þas word bodede   ricchest alre Brutte:
"Nu ich ileosed habbe   mine sweines leofe.
Ich wuste bi mine sweuene   whæt sorʒen me weoren ʒeueðe: 14145
islaʒen is Angel þe king,   þe wes min aʒen deorling,

powerful king, inviting him to come to Britain and he should share possession of it. Modred bade the strong and powerful Childric to send messengers far and wide to the four quarters of Saxony, commanding all the warriors whom they could find that they should come at once to this kingdom, and he would give Childric part of his realm, everything beyond the Humber, so that he should help him to fight against his uncle, King Arthur. With all speed Childric came to Britain! #

When Modred had assembled his host of followers, then there were sixty thousand all told, fierce warriors of heathen race who had come here for Arthur's undoing and to help Modred, the most wicked of men. When from every nation the army had assembled, then there were present with King Modred there one hundred thousand men all told, both heathen and Christian.

Arthur lay at Wissant — a fortnight seemed to him too long; and Modred knew all that Arthur purposed there; each day news came to him from the king's camp. Then it happened that on a certain day much rain began to fall, and the wind veered and blew from the east. And Arthur hastened to take ship with his whole army, and commanded that his sailors bring him to Romney where he intended to land in this country. #

When he came to the port, Modred was there to oppose him; as day dawned they began to fight; all day long men died there in great numbers. Some fought on land, some on the beach; some sent sharp spears flying from the ships. Gawain went foremost and cleared the way, swiftly striking down eleven thanes; he slew Childric's son who had come there with his father. The sun sank to rest. There was grief among men; Gawain was cut down there and deprived of life by a Saxon earl — sorrow befall his soul!

Then Arthur was sad at that and sorrowful at heart, and the noblest of all Britons uttered these words:

'Now I have lost my beloved retainers. I knew from my dream what sorrows were in store for me: King Angel who was beloved by me is slain, and Gawain, my sister's son — woe is me

and Walwaine, mi suster sune   —wa is me þat ich was mon iboren!
Up nu of scipen biliue,   mine beornes ohte!"
Æfne þan worde   wenden to fihte
sixti þusend anon   selere kempen   14150
and breken Modredes trume;   and wel neh himseolue wes inome.

        Modred bigon to fleon   and his folc after teon,
fluȝen ueondliche   —feldes beoueden eke,
ȝurren þa stanes   mid þan blod-stremes.

þer weore al þat fiht idon,   ah þat niht to raðe com;   14155
ȝif þa niht neore   islaȝen hi weoren alle.

þe niht heom todelde   ȝeond slades and ȝeon dunen;
and Modred swa vorð com   þat he wes at Lundene.
Iherden þa burh-weren   hu hit was al ifaren, *
and warnden him inȝeong   and alle his folke.   14160

        Modred þeone wende   toward Winchastre,
and heo hine underuengen   mid alle his monnen.
And Arður after wende   mid alle his mahte
þat he com to Winchestre   mid muchelere uerde,
and þa burh al biræd;   and Modred þerinne abeod.   14165
Þa Modred isæh   þat Arður him wes swa neh,
ofte he hine biþohte   wæt he don mahte.
Þa a þere ilke niht   he hehte his cnihtes alle
mid alle heore iwepnen   ut of burhȝe wenden,
and sæide þat he weolde   mid fihte þer atstonden.   14170
He bihehte þere burȝe-were   auermare freo laȝe
wið þan þa heo him heolpen   at heȝere neoden.
þa hit wes dæiliht,   ȝaru þa wes heore fiht.

        Arður þat bihedde   —þe king wes abolȝe;
he lette bemen blawen   and beonnen men to fihten.   14175
He hehte alle his þeines   and aðele his cnihte
fon somed to fihten   and his ueond auallen,
and þe burh alle fordon   and þat burh-folc ahon.
Heo togadere stopen   and sturnliche fuhten.
Modred þa þohte   what he don mihte;   14180
and he dude þere,   alse he dude elleswhare,
swikedom mid þan mæste,   for auere he dude unwraste.
He biswac his iueren   biuoren Winchestren;
and lette him to cleopien   his leofeste cnihtes anan
and his leoueste freond alle   of allen his folke,   14185
and bistal from þan fihte   —þe Feond hine aȝe!—

that I was ever born! Now up, my brave thanes, up quickly from
the ships!'

At these words sixty thousand splendid warriors immediately
advanced to battle and broke through Modred's battle-line; and he
himself narrowly escaped capture.

Modred took to flight and, his troops following behind, they
fled in desperation — at that the plains shook, the stones jarred in
the gushing flow of blood. That whole conflict would have ended
there, but the night came too quickly; had it not been for the
darkness they would all have been slain. The night scattered them
throughout valleys and among hills; and Modred went on so far
that he arrived at London. The citizens learnt how it had all
turned out, and denied entry to him and all his followers.

Modred went from there towards Winchester, and they
received him with all his men. And Arthur gave chase with all his
might until he came to Winchester with a vast force, and
completely surrounded the town; and within it Modred stood at
bay. When Modred saw that Arthur was so close to him, again
and again he considered what he could do. Then, that very night,
he ordered all his soldiers to march out of the town with all their
weapons, saying that he intended to stand and fight there. He
promised the citizens free jurisdiction ever after on condition that
they would help him in his great need. By the time it was
daylight, their forces were marshalled.

Seeing that, King Arthur was enraged; he caused trumpets to
be blown and soldiers marshalled for battle. He ordered all his
thanes and his noble warriors to join battle and strike down his
enemies, and utterly destroy the town and hang the citizens. They
charged at each other and fought fiercely. Then Modred
considered what he could do; and there, as he had done elsewhere,
he committed treachery in the highest degree, for he always acted
evilly. He betrayed his comrades before Winchester; he caused
his most favoured knights from his whole army and all his closest
companions to be summoned to him at once, and stole away from
the battle — the Devil take him! — and left those brave soldiers

and þat folc gode lette   al þer forwurðe.
Fuhten alle dæi;   wenden þat heore lauerd þer læi
and weore heom aneouste   at muchelere neode.
     Þa heold he þene wai   þat touward Hamtone lai,   14190
and heolde touward hauene,   forcuðest hæleðe,
and nom alle þa scipen   þa þer oht weore
and þa steormen alle   to þan scipen neodde,
and ferden into Cornwalen,   forcuðest kingen a þan daȝen.
     And Arður Winchestre   þa burh bilai wel faste   14195
and al þat moncun ofsloh   —þer wes sorȝen inoh!
Þa ȝeonge and þa alde,   alle he aqualde.
Þa þat folc wes al ded,   þa burh al forswelde,
Þa lette he mid alle   tobreken þa walles alle.
Þa wes hit itimed þere   þat Merlin seide while: 14200
"Ærm wurðest þu, Winchæstre;   þæ eorðe þe scal forswalȝe!"
Swa Merlin sæide   —þe witeȝe wes mære.
     Þa quene læi inne Eouwerwic   —næs heo næuere swa sarlic;
þat wes Wenhauer þa quene,   særȝest wimmonne.
Heo iherde suggen   soððere worden   14205
hu ofte Modred flah   and hu Arður hine bibah;
wa wes hire þere while   þat heo wes on life!
Ut of Eouerwike   bi nihte heo iwende
and touward Karliun tuhte   swa swiðe swa heo mahte;
þider heo brohten bi nihte   of hire cnihten tweiȝe.   14210
And me hire hafd biwefde   mid ane hali rifte,
and heo wes þer munechene,   karefullest wife.
Þa nusten men of þere quene   war heo bicumen weore,
no feole ȝere seoððe   nuste hit mon to soðe
whaðer heo weore on deðe   . . .   14215
þa heo hireseolf weore   isunken in þe watere.
     Modred wes i Cornwale   and somnede cnihtes feole;
to Irlonde he sende   aneoste his sonde,
to Sexlonde he sende   aneouste his sonde,
to Scotlonde he sende   aneouste his sonde;   14220
he hehten heom to cume alle anan   þat wolde lond habben
oðer seoluer oðer gold   oðer ahte oðer lond.
On ælchere wisen   he warnede hine seoluen,
swa deð ælc witer mon   þa neode cumeð uuenan.
     Arður þat iherde,   wraðest kinge,   14225
þat Modred wæs i Cornwale   mid muchele mon-weorede,

to perish there utterly. They fought all day, thinking that their leader was still there and was close to them in their great peril.

Then he, the basest of men, took the road which leads to Southampton, made for the harbour and there seized all the ships that were seaworthy and all the steersmen needed for the vessels, and he, the most infamous king of that age, sailed to Cornwall.

And Arthur besieged the town of Winchester very closely and slew all the inhabitants — great was the sorrow there! He killed them all, both young and old. When the people were all dead, the city completely destroyed by fire, then he caused all the walls to be destroyed utterly. Then was it come to pass there as Merlin once prophesied:
'Wretched shall you be, Winchester; the earth shall swallow you up!'
Thus spoke Merlin, who was a true prophet. #

The queen lay at York — never had she been so sorrowful; that was Queen Guenevere, the saddest of women. She was informed by truthful reports how Modred fled repeatedly and how Arthur pursued him; she was sorry then to be alive! She left York by night and made her way as quickly as she could towards Caerleon; two of her knights conducted her there by night. And her head was covered with a holy veil, and she, the most wretched of women, was a nun there. It was not then known what had become of the queen, nor for many years thereafter was it truly known whether she was dead . . . when she was herself submerged in the water. #

Modred was in Cornwall and assembled many warriors; he despatched his messengers to Ireland, he despatched his messengers to Saxony, he despatched his messengers to Scotland, ordering all those who wished to have land or silver or gold or property or estates to come at once. He looked to his defence in all respects, as does every shrewd man in his time of need.

King Arthur, greatly angered, heard that, heard that Modred

and þer wolde abiden   þat Arður come riden.

Arður sende sonde   ȝeond al his kinelonde,

and to cumen alle hehte   þat quic wes on londe

þa to uihte oht weoren   wepnen to beren;   14230

and whaswa hit forsete   þat þe king hete,

þe king hine wolde a folden   quic al forbernen.

Hit læc toward hirede   folc vnimete,

ridinde and ganninde,   swa þe rim falleð adune.

    Arður for to Cornwale   mid unimete ferde;   14235

Modred þat iherde   and him toȝeines heolde

mid vnimete folke   —þer weore monie uæie!

Uppen þere Tambre   heo tuhten togadere;

þe stude hatte Camelford   —euermare ilast þat ilke weorde!

And at Camelforde wes isomned   sixti þusend,   14240

and ma þusend þerto   —Modred wes heore ælder.

þa þiderward gon ride   Arður þe riche

mid unimete folke   —uæie þah hit weore!

    Uppe þere Tambre   heo tuhte tosomne,

heuen here-marken,   halden togadere,   14245

luken sweord longe,   leiden o þe helmen—

fur ut sprengen;   speren brastlien,

sceldes gonnen scanen,   scaftes tobreken.

þer faht al tosomne   folc vnimete;

Tambre wes on flode   mid vnimete blode!   14250

Mon i þan fihte non þer ne mihte   ikenne nenne kempe,

no wha dude wurse no wha bet,   swa þat wiðe wes imenged,

for ælc sloh adunriht,   weore he swein weore he cniht.

    þer wes Modred ofslaȝe   and idon of lif-daȝe,

[and alle his cnihtes   islaȝe] in þan fihte.   14255

þer weoren ofslaȝe   alle þa snelle

Arðures hered-men,   heȝe and lowe,

and þa Bruttes alle   of Arðures borde,

and alle his fosterlinges   of feole kineriches,

and Arður forwunded   mid wal-spere brade;   14260

fiftene he hafde   feondliche wunden—

mon mihte i þare laste   twa glouen iþraste!

þa nas þer namare   i þan fehte to laue

of twa hundred þusend monnen   þa þer leien tohauwen,

buten Arður þe king ane   and of his cnihtes tweien.   14265

    Arður wes forwunded   wunder ane swiðe.

was in Cornwall with a large force, intending to stand his ground there until Arthur approached. Arthur sent messengers throughout his whole kingdom commanding the presence of all those living in the land who were fit to bear weapons in battle; and whoever disregarded the king's command, the king would burn him alive on the spot. Riding and marching, a vast company flocked to the host like the falling snow.

Arthur marched to Cornwall with a vast host; Modred heard of that and advanced to meet him with a vast force — many among them were doomed! At the river Tamar they came together; the place is called Camelford — that name shall endure for ever! And at Camelford were assembled sixty thousand men, and thousands more besides — Modred was their leader. Then the mighty Arthur rode thither with a vast host — yet all were doomed to die! #

They met upon the river Tamar, raised banners, charged together, drew long swords, struck upon helmets — sparks flew; spears clashed, shields shattered, lances splintered. There vast numbers were all embattled; the Tamar was in flood with blood beyond measure! In the battle there no one could distinguish any warrior, nor see who did well nor who ill, so confused was the mêlée, for each, were he squire or knight, fought fiercely.

There Modred was cut down and deprived of life, and all his followers killed in the battle. There were slain all Arthur's valiant retainers, both high and low, and all the Britons of Arthur's Round Table, and all his foster-sons from many kingdoms, and Arthur himself was sorely wounded by a broad and deadly spear; he had fifteen terrible wounds — in the least of them one could have thrust two gloves! Then in the host, of the two hundred thousand men who lay there cut to pieces, there remained alive only Arthur the king and two of his knights. #

Arthur was grievously, mortally wounded. There came to him

þer to him com a cnaue þe wes of his cunne;
he wes Cadores sune, þe eorles of Corwaile;
Constantin hehte þe cnaue —he wes þan kinge deore.
Arður him lokede on, þer he lai on folden, 14270
and þas word seide mid sorhfulle heorte:
"Costæntin, þu art wilcume; þu weore Cadores sone.
Ich þe bitache here mine kineriche;
and wite mine Bruttes a to þines lifes,
and hald heom alle þa laʒen þa habbeoð istonden a mine daʒen, 14275
and alle þa laʒen gode þa bi Vðeres daʒen stode.
And ich wulle uaren to Aualun, to uairest alre maidene,
to Argante þere quene, aluen swiðe sceone;
and heo scal mine wunden makien alle isunde,
al hal me makien mid haleweiʒe drenchen. 14280
And seoðe ich cumen wulle to mine kineriche
and wunien mid Brutten mid muchelere wunne."
Æfne þan worden þer com of se wenden
þat wes an sceort bat liðen, sceouen mid vðen,
and twa wimmen þerinne wunderliche idihte; 14285
and heo nomen Arður anan, and aneouste hine uereden
and softe hine adun leiden, and forð gunnen liðen.
þa wes hit iwurðen þat Merlin seide whilen:
þat weore unimete care of Arðures forðfare.
Bruttes ileueð ʒete þat he bon on liue, 14290
and wunnien in Aualun mid fairest alre aluen;
and lokieð euere Bruttes ʒete whan Arður cumen liðe.
Nis nauer þe mon iboren of nauer nane burde icoren
þe cunne of þan soðe of Arðure sugen mare.
Bute while wes an witeʒe Mærlin ihate; 14295
he bodede mid worde —his quiðes weoren soðe—
þat an Arður sculde ʒete cum Anglen to fulste.

a young man who was one of his kinsmen; he was the son of Cador, Earl of Cornwall; the youth, who was dear to the king, was called Constantin. Arthur, where he lay on the ground, looked at him and, with a sorrowful heart, spoke these words:

'You are welcome, Constantin, you who were Cador's son. I here entrust my realm to you; and you defend my Britons as long as you live, and maintain for them all the laws that have been in force in my day, and all the good laws which existed in Uther's time. And I will go to Avalon, to the loveliest of all women, to the queen Argante, fairest of fairy women; and she shall make well all my wounds, make me all whole with healing draughts. And afterwards I will return to my kingdom and dwell with the Britons in great contentment.' #

With these words there came moving in from the sea a small boat, driven onward by the waves, and therein two women wondrously arrayed; and they at once took Arthur, and quickly bore him up and laid him gently down, and sailed away.

Then was come to pass what Merlin prophesied of yore: that there would be grief beyond measure for Arthur's passing. The Britons yet believe that he is alive, and dwells in Avalon with the fairest of all fairy women; and the Britons still await the time when Arthur will come again. No man ever born of noble lady can tell more of the truth about Arthur. But there was once a seer called Merlin who prophesied — his sayings were true — that an Arthur should come again to aid the people of England. #

LIST OF ABBREVIATIONS

B-H   Blenner-Hassett, R., 'A study of the place-names in Lawman's *Brut*', *Stanford University Publications: Language and Literature*, 9 (Stanford, Calif., 1950)

B&L   *Laʒamon's 'Brut'*, eds G. L. Brook and R. F. Leslie, Early English Text Society, 250, 277 (London, 1963, 1978)

B&S   *Early Middle English Verse and Prose*, eds J. A. W. Bennett and G. V. Smithers (Oxford, 1966, 2nd edn 1968)

BS   *Selections from Laʒamon's 'Brut'*, ed. G. L. Brook, 2nd edn revised J. Levitt (Exeter, 1983)

BT   *An Anglo-Saxon Dictionary*, ed. J. Bosworth and enlarged T. Northcote Toller (Oxford, 1882-1921)

C   MS Cotton Caligula A.ix

Chambers   Chambers, E. K., *Arthur of Britain* (London, 1927), reprinted (Cambridge, 1964)

D&W   *Early Middle English Texts*, eds B. Dickens and R. M. Wilson (London, 1951)

GoM   *The 'Historia Regum Britanniae' of Geoffrey of Monmouth*, ed. N. Wright, Vol. I: Berne, Burgerbibliothek, MS 568 (Cambridge, 1984)

Hall   *Layamon's 'Brut': Selections*, ed. J. Hall (Oxford, 1924)

Lacy   *The Arthurian Encyclopedia*, ed. N. J. Lacy (New York, 1984)

Loomis   *Arthurian Literature in the Middle Ages: A Collaborative History*, ed. R. S. Loomis (Oxford, 1959)

ME   Middle English

MED   *Middle English Dictionary*, eds H. Kurath, S. M. Kuhn and J. Reidy (Ann Arbor, Mich., 1952-)

Mn   *Laʒamon's 'Brut' or 'Chronicle of Britain'*, ed. F. Madden, 3 vols (London, 1847)

O   MS Cotton Otho C.xiii

OE   Old English

OED   *The Oxford English Dictionary*, eds Sir J. A. H. Murray, H. Bradley, Sir W. Craigie and C. T. Onions (Oxford, 1933)

Tatlock   Tatlock, J. S. P., *The Legendary History of Britain: Geoffrey of Monmouth's 'Historia Regum Britanniae' and its Early Vernacular Versions* (Berkeley, Calif., 1950)

Thorpe   *The History of the Kings of Britain*, tr. L. Thorpe, Penguin Books (Harmondsworth, 1966)

Wace   *Le 'Roman de Brut' de Wace*, ed. I. Arnold, 2 vols (Paris, 1938, 1940)

TEXTUAL NOTES

(Indicated by * in the Text)

9320 *þat hatten Tambre is*: MS: *Tambreis*. BS, 1606, emends to *Tambre is* and argues, p.122, that 'the reading of C results from a confusion of two constructions: *þat hatten Tambre* and *þat ihaten Tambre is*, with *hatten* as the old passive form (present or past tense) and *ihaten* as the past participle'. O has *þat Tambre his ihote*. Arthur's final battle, against Modred, takes place at Camelford, *uppe þere Tambre* (14238 and 14244).

9486 *and Vðer þene king*: MS: *and heo Vðer þene king*. *Heo* is emended to *heolden* by B&L, presumably on the assumption that the context needs a verb paralleling that in the preceding line *hædden heo . . . Merlin þer wiðinne*. But *heolden* is not necessary if the sense of the verb *hædden* is felt to continue into the following line. It is very possible that the MS *heo* is a scribal repetition of *heo* in 9485. Cf. O: *þo haden hii mid gynne Merlyn þar wiþine / and Vther þane king wiþhinne hire weldyng*. BS, 1772, omits the MS *heo*.

9489 *his þreo gumen*: clearly an error since only two men, Merlin and Ulfin disguised as Bretel and Jurdan, accompany Uther to Tintagel. Confusion over matters of detail is not infrequent in Laȝamon.

9564 *skenting*: for the meaning and etymology of this Norse word, see under *skentinge* 'entertainment, pleasure' in the glossary of B&S.

9625 *ibalded*: as MS. B&L emend to *unbalded*. But *ibalded* 'emboldened' (MED: *bolden* v. 2) seems more appropriate to the context in that the king's weakness invites contempt for his authority on the part of his subjects. Cf. 9684-90, in which they reject the leadership of his son-in-law Lot out of *muchel mode and vnimete prute*. The form *ibalded* is used in a similar sense in 10674. BS, 1911, retains the MS reading *ibalded* rejected by B&L in 9625.

9731 *bitele*: as MS. B&L emend to *bitere*, as does BS, 2017; but MED cites the adjective *bitel* 'sharp-edged, sharp, cruel'. The form *bitele* is used in a similar sense at 13460, though here again the MS form is emended by B&L to *bitere*.

9826 *na*: as MS. B&L *ma*, apparently in error. Mn, II, p.402, and BS, 2112, *na*.

9958 *richedome*: is usually glossed 'wealth, treasure; splendour, magnificence; abundance' (MED n. (a)). In this context though, where Arthur's vanquishing of other kings seems to rest upon the loyalty of his followers as well as upon his potency, personal and regal (*ræhȝere strengðe*), *richedome* may well refer to the princely largess by which he secured their allegiance.

10062 *þenne his floc is awemmed* 'when his flock is scattered': Mn, II, p.422, translates 'when his flight is impaired'. But *floc* is glossed in MED as 'a flock of birds or domesticated fowl' (*flok* n.¹ 1(b)). D&W, p.169, comment: 'C *floc*, but O *fliht* "power of flight" gives better sense with *awemmed*, since OE *awemman* means "to disfigure, to corrupt"'. In ME, however, the verb can mean 'to ravage, destroy' (MED *awemmen* v. (c)), from which an extended sense for *awemmed* 'cut to pieces, scattered' seems not inappropriate. The comparison between fleeing members of the decimated Saxon army, dispersed and wandering, and the wild crane, separated from his fellows and fleeing in the moorland fen from pursuing hawks and hounds, creates a vivid image, especially when the wild crane is further particularised in reference to the fleeing Colgrim, a Germanic chieftain left without a following. Neither land nor water is safe for either then — 'then the royal bird is doomed in his tracks'. There seems to be a conscious word-play upon *floc* which Laȝamon uses elsewhere in the sense 'a troop of warriors, army, host' (MED 3(a)).

10138 *culde*: Mn, II, p.429, translates *culde* as 'struck (?)', and in his glossarial notes, III, p.496, comments: 'the translation is conjectural, as the word has not been traced elsewhere'. MED, however, cites *culde* as a past tense form of *killen* v. 1(a) 'to strike (sb.), hit; assault'.

10199 *hunger and hæte* 'famine and want': Mn, II, p.434, translates 'hunger and strife (?)', possibly equating *hæte* with ME *hēte* < OE *hete* 'an act growing out of hatred; hostility, an attack, harm, injury' (MED *hēte* n.² (b)). But there is another noun *hēte* in ME < OE *hǣtu*, *hǣte* 'a hot period (of the day, year), hot weather, drought' (MED *hēte* n.¹ (d)). One of the meanings given for *hunger* in MED is 'general scarcity of food, famine', and the phrase *hungere and hæte* in 10199 is cited with the meaning 'a period of famine' (*hunger* n. 1(c)). It seems that the noun *hæte* at 10199, rather than meaning specifically 'drought', acts as an intensifier for *hunger*, referring to a period of famine and general want. The phrase *hunger and hete* occurs again in 10342, and though Mn, II, p.446, translates once again 'hunger and strife (?)', in III, p.497 he comments: '*hete* would here seem to have the sense of *thirst* or *drought*', and he refers the reader to Wace's use of the French word *burent* (9202). *Mid hungere and mid hete* occurs a third time in 10925, and is translated, as before, by Mn, II, p.495, 'with hunger and with strife (?)', but at III, p.497 he concedes that it might mean 'thirst' or 'drought' in this context. Yet in 10925 it does make better sense if one translates *hēte* < OE *hete* 'strife, violence'.

10244 *beorkes*: Mn, II, p.438, translates 'barks (vessels ?)', commenting in III, p.496 that 'the meaning is very doubtful'. BS, 2530, emends to *beornes* 'men, warriors' and states, p.123, that 'the emendation . . . seems necessary as *bark, barque* "vessel" is not found before the fifteenth century'. But the MS *beorkes* could be the plural of *berk* (MED n. 1 'barking (of a dog)'); in the particular context the barking dogs would be the British force as the hunters, intent on pursuing and destroying Childric and his warriors. Childric and his men are the doomed quarry if they remain in Britain and *beorkes abiden* 'face the barking', i.e. 'face the hue and cry'. In 10648 Laȝamon uses the verb *beorkeð* (MED *berken* l(a) 'to bark') in *beorkeð his hundes*.

10253 *wolleȝede*: as MS. Assumed to be a variant spelling for the past tense form of ME *folwen* 'to follow' (MED 3(a)). Cf. O: *folwede*.

10268 *forbæd . . . þat heo liðen stille*: Mn, II, p.440, translates *forbæd* as 'fore-ordered', but to Hall, p.85, this is 'a meaning without parallel'. He argues, on the basis of other occurrences of the word in Laȝamon and on the wording in Wace, that the verb means 'forbade', suggesting that even though there is no negative in the subordinate clause, *liðen stille* implies a negative within the construction. Such a usage seems forced, however, and MED *forbēden* v. lc (a) 'to stop or restrain (someone); to control (someone)' makes better sense in the context.

10342 *hunger and hete*: see under 10199 above.

10397 *al foruaren*: as MS. B&L *ai*, apparently in error. Mn, II, p.451, and BS, 2683, *al*.

fordemen: MS, B&L, BS, 2683, and D&W, 120, *fordemed*. Mn, II, p.451, reads *fordemed* but suggests *fordemen*; Hall, 1052, emends to *fordemen*. The MS *fordemed* breaks the metrical pattern of 10397, and, as a past participle form, is syntactically at variance with the verbs in the other co-ordinate clauses, all of which are in the infinitive.

10512 *adefed*: as MS. B&L and BS, 2798, emend to *adrefed*, but the meaning cited for *adrefen* in MED, 'to drive (sb.) away, expel, banish', does not fit this particular context. Yet the MS reading is also problematic, MED instancing only this one occurrence and querying the form (? *adēven* v.² 'to subdue or annihilate (an enemy)'). It is possible that *adefed* is a scribal error for *adeded*, the past participle of the verb *adēden* 'to deaden, kill' (MED (b)). Cf. O which reads *acwelled*.

10576 *an alre freomeste* 'first and foremost': see MED *firmest* adj.[1]. Instances of metathesis are frequent in C.

10642 *wleoteð*: this word is glossed in Mn as a spelling variant of *fleoteð* 'float'. But we accept the suggestion of J. A. Burrow, *Notes and Queries*, 225 (1980), 2-3, that the source of the verb is OE *wlitigian* 'make beautiful', and that in the immediate context the meaning is 'shine, gleam'. This reading, as Burrow comments, 'provides a much stronger ground of comparison for the first simile'. As he says, 'the gold-plated shields of the warriors lying on the bottom of the Avon can be seen gleaming through the water like the scales of fish'.

10674 *ibalded*: see under 9625 above.

10675 *læʒen*: Mn, II, p.474, translates 'laws (blows)', and glosses the word under *laʒe* 'law, custom, manner'. But see MED *lau* n. 'a stroke, thrust'. In the particular context it makes better sense to translate the phrase *læʒen swiðe stronge* as 'very fierce strokes'. Cf. O: *mid hire stronge mihte*.

10711 *he þencheð mid isunde aʒen cumen liðen* 'hoping to sail home in safety': Mn, II, p.477, translates 'he thinketh with safety again to come [hither]', inserting *hither*, presumably from O *aʒein hider wende*. But the particular context in which these lines occur relates to Arthur's concern that Childric, having fled and 'taken himself off', should not escape across the sea. He commands Cador, therefore, to 'take five thousand men . . . and travel swiftly by night and day so that you reach the sea before Childric does' (10710-14). Arthur's concern is not that Childric might return to Britain, only that, having been defeated in battle, he might escape by reaching the coast and sailing away in safety. Earlier in the narrative, when Childric's army encounters Arthur's forces and is defeated, we are told that 'Childric fled across the river with fifteen hundred warriors, hoping to escape and sail across the sea' (10617-18). For evidence supporting the translation 'to sail home', see MED *lithen* v.[1] 1, and *ayen* adv. 2(a).

10716 *ufele*: Mn, II, p.478, translates *ufele* as 'with evil', and glosses the word under the adverb *ufele*. But it makes better sense to take *ufele* as adjectival (MED *ivel* 1(a)) describing *þene kaisere*, since it is unlikely that Arthur would describe the killing of an enemy as an evil act. The unusual separation of a noun and its post-positioned adjective by the caesura may be due to the demands of the assonance linking the two half-lines.

10833 *þræsten*: Cf. O: *þreaste*. Mn, III, p.499, suggests that the MS *wræsten* is an error for *þræsten*. The senses suggested by BT for *wræsten*, 'wrest, twist', seem inappropriate in this context. *þræsten*, however, not only supplies a suitable alliteration, but also an appropriate sense. BT cite *þræstan* (v. 3) 'to press, constrain', but also comment: 'in later English the word seems mostly used intransitively, *to press* in, on, out'.

10865 *walleð in*: MS *walleð of*. Mn, II, p.490, translates 'falleth in', and at III, p.499 suggests that *walleð of* is an error for *ualleð in*, comparing it with the O reading *falleþ in* and the words in Wace, *dedenz chaeient* (9443). BS, 3151, retains the MS reading but comments, p.125, that the O reading fits the context better. D&W, p.26, emend to *walleð in*. See MED *fallen* v. 6.

10921 *þer heo on sið weoren*: Mn, II, p.495, translates *sið* as 'affliction (?)'. The problem is that the noun *sið* is normally glossed as 'going, journeying, travel'. But see BT *sið* n. 5 'denoting that which occurs to a person, how a person fares, the course of events in the case of a person, lot, condition, fate, experience'. In this passage, the lot of the women is one of great suffering, both physical and mental, and it is on this basis that we suggest the translation 'distress' for *sið*.

10925 *mid hungere and mid hete*: in justification of the translation 'violence' for *hete*, see under 10199 above.

11079 *þe wes his bæd-iþohte* 'who was the object of his prayers': Mn, II, p.509, reading *bæd iþohte* as in the MS, translates 'who was his desire (?) esteemed', and at III, p.500 states: 'I do not understand this line, or the meaning of *bæd*.' BS, p.125, is also puzzled. MED cites *bæd* as a possible variant spelling of *bēde* 'prayer, bead (of a rosary)', and by a figurative extension of meaning 'jewel'. The line might then be translated 'who was considered his jewel', taking *iþohte* as the past participle of *iþenchen* (MED *ithenchen* v. 2(c)). But the meaning 'a bead of a rosary' for *bēde* is first cited in the mid-fourteenth century (MED 3(a)). We tentatively suggest a reading *bæd-iþohte*, a compound word with *bæd* as *bēde* 'prayer', and *iþohte* as the past participle of *iþenchen* 'to remember, bring to mind' (MED 1(b)). The line would then translate 'who was remembered in his prayers', a way of describing the close and loving relationship between Uther and his daughter Anna during Uther's lifetime.

11122 *ruokeden*: Mn, II, p. 512, translates 'got ready', but emends at III, p.500 to 'rocked' or 'rolled', explaining that coats of mail were cleaned by being rolled in sand. See also BS, p.125, and MED *rokken* v. 2(c) 'to burnish (armour) by rolling it back and forth, perhaps by placing it in a barrel of sand and rocking the barrel'.

11127 *beoveden speren* 'prepared spears': MS has *beouweden*, altered by a second hand to *beoveden*. Mn, II, p.513, translates 'bent (?)', and glosses the word as *beoweden* < *buwen* 'to bow'. O, 11125, reads *beoude*. However, the meanings cited in MED for *bouen* v.[1] all relate to bending or curving, and this does not seem applicable to spears. BS, p.126, states: 'it is not easy to identify the word intended by either the scribe or the corrector, though it is clear from the context that the word describes the preparation of armour for battle'. There is a verb in MED, *bounen* 'get (sth.) ready; gather troops' (1(a)) and, although it is not found before the mid-fourteenth century, all examples of the word, with one exception, are from works belonging, like Laȝamon's, to the alliterative tradition. It is possible that, as with the verb *ruokeden* in 11122 which has a specialised sense in relation to the cleaning of coats of mail, so *beoveden* has a specialised sense in relation to the preparation of spears.

>*beonneden*: a variant form of *bonneden*, as in 11122, from the ME verb *bannen* (MED 1(c)).

11265 *þirre*: B&L read *þiire*, but the minim they see as a second '*i*' could equally be read as another '*r*'. Mn, II, p.525, reads *þire*.

11277-8 We have transposed these two lines to allow completion of the reference to the queen in 11276, interrupted in the MS sequence by 11278, a line omitted in O.

11280 *to ȝiueles þingen* 'as a sign of tribute': Mn, II, p.526, translates 'as thing bestowed (?)', and comments: 'a plummet-mark in the margin would seem to indicate some mistake here'. But at III, p.501 he suggests reading *gaueles*, and translates the phrase as 'thing of tribute'. MED cites *gevel/gæfol* as variant forms of *gavel* n.[1] 1(a) 'tribute', and it is also possible that ME *gife* 'gift' may have had an influence on the spelling *ȝiueles*.

11946 *and kept Arður anan* 'and fended Arthur off': Mn, II, p.583, translates 'and observed Arthur anon', though at III, p.502 he suggests 'intercepted' or 'encountered' as preferable to 'observed'. At this point in the narrative Frolle has been thrown from his horse by Arthur who approaches him on horseback, striking at him with his sword. But Frolle grasps his spear in his hand to defend himself (ll1939-45). It makes better tactical sense in this situation that Frolle should use his spear to ward off Arthur's attack. For the meaning 'fended off', see MED *kepen* v. 3b(b), and *an-ōn* adv. & conj. 3.

12232 *bi hire fulle wite* 'upon pain of her extreme displeasure': Mn, II, p.607, translates 'on pain of their paying full penalty', but notes at III, p.503 that in C the plural pronoun is normally represented by *heore* and not *hire* 'her'. It is because of this that we suggest *hire* refers to Guenevere, and tentatively translate *wite* 'displeasure', deriving it from BT *wite* n. 2 'in a general sense: torment, plague, disease, evil, pain'.

12276 *iriuen*: as B&L and Mn, II, p.611. But at III, p.503 Mn states 'for *iriuen* read *irinen*, as in the MS', and derives *irinen* from OE *gehrinan* 'to adorn'. The MS, however, clearly reads *iriuen*, though *irinen* would make better sense in the particular context. MED cites the MS form *iriuen*, but regards it as an erroneous spelling for *irinen* and associates the latter with OE *gehrinan* 'to adorn'.

12287 *þan*: as MS and Mn, II, p.612. B&L emend to *þai*. But the verb *þæinen* 'to serve' takes the dative case (BT *þegnian*), and *þan* is here the dative plural of the demonstrative pronoun *þat*. Cf. *þere quene*, also the object of *þæinen*, where *þere* is the dative singular feminine of the definite article. The verb also occurs in 12274 where both direct objects *þan kingen* and *here-ðringen* are in the dative case.

12471 *ȝe*: MS *ȝet*. Mn, II, p.628, reads *ȝet*, but at III, p.504 notes that *ȝet* is incorrectly used for *ȝe*, required by the sense. BS, 3621, emends to *ȝe*. O reads *ȝe*.

12493 *ah mid strenðe heo eoden an hond and bitahten him al heore lond* 'but they yielded to force and surrendered all their land to him': Mn, II, p.630, translates: 'but with strength they went in hand, and delivered him all their land'. BS, p.126, translates: 'but they resisted him with force and yet they had to hand all their land over to him', supplying a direct object in the first clause and the word 'yet' in the second. However, the phrase *eoden on hond* can be translated as 'yielded' (MED *hōnde* n. 2(a)), and *mid strenðe* as 'through force' (BT *strengðu* n. 2). Cf. *alle heo eoden an honde þan kinge Gurmunde* (14454), translated by Mn, III, p.159, 'all they went in hand (submitted) to the king Gurmund'.

12805 *dreori*: MS and Mn, III, p.17, *reordi*. Mn, III, p.505, is uncertain as to its meaning, but glosses the word as 'loathsome', presumably paralleling it with O's *lopliche*. We, like B&L, accept the emendation *dreori* suggested by O. Arngart, *English Studies*, 36 (1955), 27. He argues that 'the error *reordi* for *dreori* can be readily explained by taking the *d* to have been written above the line in a preceding copy and to have become attached to the wrong *r* when inserted in the word'. For our translation 'cruel', see MED *drēri* adj. 2(c).

12841 *lod-cniht*: as MS and Mn, III, p.21. B&L emend to *lond-cniht*. But see MED *lōd(e)* n. 2, and cf. MED *lōdes-man* n. (b) 'a guide, conductor'.

12882 *irust al mid golde* 'all encrusted with gold': Mn, III, p.506, argues for *ibrust* and not *irust* since the phrase *ibrusted mid gold(e)* occurs three times in the Laȝamon text. MED records both *ibrusted* ppl. 'studded' < OE *gebyrst* 'having bristles, bristling', citing only the three Laȝamon examples, and *irust* ppl. 'ornamented' < OE *gehyrstan* 'to ornament, adorn', giving as the sole example the occurrence in 12882. While the evidence suggests *irust* as an error for *ibrust*, the OE past participle *gehyrsted/gehyrst* < *gehyrstan* relates more closely, with metathesis, to the form *irust*, and we can find no OE form *gebyrst* in BT, only the noun *burst* 'a bristle', or *geberst* 'a bursting, eruption'. It is possible that confusion between the forms developing from OE *gehyrsted/gehyrst* and *iburst* may account for the forms *ibrusted* and *irust* in Laȝamon.

12910 *hore*: MS and B&L *here*. Mn, III, p.26, reads *here* but suggests *hore* and translates 'hoar'. See MED *hōr* adj. 2(b). O reads *ore*.

12952 *hire*: Mn, III, p.30, translates 'serve (?)', and cites the verb *hiren* in his glossary, though at III, p.506 he states: 'I do not understand *hire* in this line, and there appears some deficiency.' But *hiren* 'to obey (sb.), to serve (sb.)' (MED *hēren* v. 6(a)), and thus 'to aid', makes sense in this particular context. The verb *hiren* 'to serve' also occurs in 7062.

13068 *mihte*: MS, Mn, III, p.40, and O read *mihte*; B&L have *minte*, apparently in error.

13075 *hine*: in the MS this word is repeated, unnecessarily, in the second half-line, and we have omitted it. O reads ʒef he f..te wolde.

13253 *grundien*: this verb occurs only once in Laʒamon. Mn, III, p.56, translates 'sink you', supplying an object which is not in the text; and at III, p.508 he comments that the translation is literally 'fell you to the ground'. MED has *grounden* v. 6(b) 'to strike (sb.) down to the ground; to overcome (sb.), defeat', and cites the Laʒamon example, but the only other instance given for this meaning of the verb dates from the early fifteenth century. In addition, the transitive senses require an object, not present in the text. In the particular Laʒamon context, one of the Roman pursuers of the three British earls has taunted them with cowardice for fleeing and not standing up to their Roman pursuers; in response the earls have turned upon their pursuers and killed two of them (l3231-51). Gerin's words (13252-4) are a defiant response to the Roman taunts, and ironic as well in that Roman words have proved empty in the face of British deeds. It is with this context in mind that we take the basic meaning of *grundien* 'to lay a foundation' (BT *gryndan* v.), and assume, by a figurative extension of laying a foundation for words, i.e. by backing them up with deeds, a sense 'to prove oneself worthy' and therefore 'to triumph'.

13311 *and lut þer ofnomen* 'and capturing a few': the MS reads *þer of nomen*, while Mn, III, p.61, has *and lut þer of-nomen*, and translates 'and few there captured', but B&L *and lut þer-of nomen*. If we read *ofnomen* there is a grammatical and metrical parallelism with *ofslogen*, the verb at the end of the second half-line. MED cites the verb *ofnimen* 'to take (hostages)', though only once and from the early fifteenth century.

13460 *bitele*: see under 9731 above.

13478 *hele*: B&L *helþ*, apparently in error for *help*, since they state: 'þ of *help* crowded in by later hand', but they add that Mn (III, p.75) may be right in reading the inserted letter as *e*. See MED *hele* n.¹ for our preferred reading.

13642 *andswarede*: as MS and Mn, III, p.89; B&L have *andswatede*, apparently in error.

13853 In the MS this line begins with an ampersand which B&L retain. The line, however, makes sense without it, and we agree with Mn, III, p.509, that leaving it in results in a mistranslation of 13852-3. Cf. the first half-line of 13887, identical to the first half-line of 13853, but without the initial ampersand.

13867 *com*: as MS. Mn, III, p.108, reads *com* but suggests *gome*, the reading in O, and translates the half-line as 'who was man exceeding stern'. B&L emend to *gome*. But Mn's reading creates a difficult syntactical relationship with the following line, and his suggested sense seems unsuited to the context. In 13866-71 the focus is on the fierce battle between Gawain and Lucius, summed up in *þer wes viht swiðe strong* 'the conflict there was very keen' (13871). It is on this basis that we feel that reference to one of the combatants in 13867 is less likely than a general comment regarding the nature of the combat, to be described in detail in the following lines.

13925 *Modred is mæin* 'the might of Modred': Mn, III, p.113, reads *Modred is mæin*, but suggests *is mæi*, presumably from O *his may*, and translates 'Modred his relative', the *his* referring to Arthur, who is the *he* of 13924. But see MED *main* n. 1, and cf. *Modred is hafd* 'Modred's head' in 13999. For this type of construction in ME, see T. F. Mustanoja, *A Middle English Syntax* (Helsinki, 1960), pp.159-62.

13934 *and he þerto tumbede* 'and he buried him there': B&L have *and he þer-to tumde*, but note that the MS has *tumbede* with the *be* expuncted. Mn, III, p.114, reads *and he þer to tumde*, though he takes note of the MS *tumbede* and translates 'and he thereat was entombed'. At III, p.510, however, he suggests the form *temde* (BT *timan* v. 2(a)) and translates 'and he thereto proceeded'. But although there is no verb in OE meaning 'to bury' which corresponds in form with *tumbede* or *tumde*, the forms in Laȝamon, there is in Anglo-Norman the noun *tumbe* from which the verb *tomb* 'to inter, bury' derives, and which is first cited in English *c.*1330 (OED *tomb* n. and v.). It is possible that *tumbede* is the past tense form of a verb *tumben*, formed from the Anglo-Norman noun.

14017 *furburne*: B&L and Mn, III, p.121, *fur burne*. But see B&S, 47, *furburne*, and MED *forbrennen* v. 3(b).

14084 *þa wile a beoð aliue* 'while they are alive': Mn, III, p.127, reads *a* but suggests *ich*, and at III, p.510 proposes replacing the *a* by *heo* as referring to Guenevere. But B&S, p.346, point out that *beoð* is plural, and that *a* is a miswriting or genuine variant of *ha* 'they'.

14159 *al*: as MS, Mn, III, p.133, and B&S, 189. B&L *il*, apparently in error. BS, 3952, reads *al*.

COMMENTARY

(On points indicated by # in the Translation)

Page 3: The origin of Uther's sobriquet is explained in GoM's *Historia* (§133), where we are told that a celestial portent appears at the death of Aurelius Ambrosius, King of Britain and brother of Uther. It takes the form of a dragon-shaped comet which the prophet Merlin interprets as foretelling the triumphs of Uther and his offspring. On being crowned king, Uther orders two dragons to be fashioned in gold in the likeness of the portent, and uses one of them as his battle-standard, to be borne before him in his wars. Thereafter he is known as Uther Pendragon (§135). GoM says that the name means 'a dragon's head' in the British language, but it has been suggested (Lacy, p.149) that it is more likely to mean 'head dragon', i.e. 'foremost leader'.

Page 3: In GoM, Gorlois, Duke of Cornwall, fights alongside Aurelius Ambrosius in the battle against the Saxon Hengest (§124), gives Uther valuable advice (*erat enim consilii magni atque etatus mature* 'for he was of great experience and mature in years') after Uther's defeat in battle by Hengest's son Octa (§136), and attends Uther's assembly in London where his wife is much admired by Uther (§137). Wace follows Geoffrey's narrative sequence (7807-8, 8461-504), attesting to the valour and courtesy of Gorlois and describing him as a prudent councillor and a man who esteemed honour above life itself. Laȝamon, following Geoffrey and Wace, names Gorlois as a participant in the battle against Hengest (8236-7) but, having perhaps forgotten this earlier mention, seems to reintroduce him in the episode where he gives Uther advice: 'There was an earl, Gorlois, a brave man indeed; he, Earl of Cornwall, was an excellent knight, Uther's man — he was renowned far and wide; he was a very wise man, excellent in every respect' (9159-62). There is no mention of his age or his regard for honour above life itself. According to Tatlock, pp.315-16, the story of Ygerne's seduction by Uther in the likeness of Gorlois, and the subsequent birth of Arthur does not predate its occurrence in GoM.

Page 9: According to GoM (§§106-7), Merlin was born in Carmarthen, begotten upon a nun, daughter of a king of Demetia, by a demon who made love to her in the shape of a handsome young man. It is thought that his name derives from the Welsh form of the place-name, Caermyrddin, 'Myrddin's Town', with *l* being substituted for *d*. Merlin is both magician and prophet, but in Laȝamon the emphasis is on his prophetic role rather than his magical powers.

Page 9: The term 'ploughland', according to MED (*plough-land* n.), was 'a unit of land measure, probably based on the amount of land which could be cultivated with one plough; also, a piece of land having this area'.

Page 11: Merlin's prophecy of the birth of Arthur and his future greatness is reminiscent of the prophetic sayings attributed to him in a section of GoM (§§109-17) originally composed as a separate work. Wace, finding the whole section incomprehensible, omitted it from his translation, and the source of Laȝamon's echoes, here and elsewhere in the narrative, has not been identified. He may have known a version of the Wace text in which passages from the Prophecies section of GoM had been interpolated, or one of the independent copies of the Prophecies which are known to have circulated both in Latin and in French, or he may possibly have had access to them in their original context in the *Historia*. But even where there are vague verbal echoes of Geoffrey's *Prophetie Merlini*, Laȝamon goes far beyond the original. Here, for example, he conflates a reference to the Boar of Cornwall, champion of the oppressed Britons against the invading Saxons (by implication identified with Arthur), a hero whose deeds are to be meat and drink to the tellers of tales (§112.2), with one to the Boar of Commerce whose breast will be food to the hungry while its tongue assuages the thirsty (§115.26). In further extending the imagery to picture the hero as a saviour whose people are to be spiritually nourished upon his body and blood, Laȝamon makes a characteristic leap of the imagination.

Page 17: For the association of a dragon with Uther, and the origin of the dragon as Uther's battle-standard, see above, under Page 3. The royal standard passes from Uther to Arthur; in marshalling his forces for a final battle with Lucius, Emperor of Rome, Arthur (13598-9) 'had the dragon, the matchless standard raised, entrusting it to a king who could protect it well'. Tatlock, p.38, states that the dragon was used as a royal ensign by the Anglo-Saxons and argues, pp.329-30, that GoM derived it, not from any earlier Welsh tradition, but from Harold's dragon at the battle of Hastings. Lacy, p.13, mentions that a Roman cavalry troop which remained in Britain after the withdrawal of the legions had, as a battle-standard, 'a windsock-like dragon on a pole'.

Page 17: Earlier in the narrative, Aldolf, Earl of Gloucester, is appointed by Aurelius Ambrosius as his steward. A man of great valour, Aldolf single-handedly overpowers and captures Hengest, the Saxon enemy of Aurelius who rewards his valour by making him a leader of the people (8102-265). In naming him as the army's choice of leader in Uther's absence, an incident which has no counterpart in Wace, Laʒamon seems to be recalling his earlier role.

Page 23: We are told by Laʒamon (7219-54) that Octa and Ebissa were given land by Vortigern, unlawful king of Britain, when they came there to join their father Hengest, leader of the Saxon invaders. With the defeat and death of both Vortigern and Hengest, Octa and Ebissa, having sought the mercy of Aurelius Ambrosius, are baptised and granted land in the North (8363-432); but hearing of the death of Aurelius and the accession of Uther, Octa and Ebissa *and Osa þe oðer* (9100) lead an unsuccessful uprising against him, are captured and imprisoned in London (9099-221). This is the first mention in Laʒamon of Ossa, though in GoM it is Eosa, Octa's *cognatus* 'kinsman' (§124), who accepts baptism (§126), bands together with Octa against Uther (§136), and is imprisoned with Octa in London (§137). Ebissa is mentioned only twice in GoM: Hengest suggests that Octa, *cum fratruele suo Ebissa* 'with his brother Ebissa', be invited to settle in Britain, and they duly arrive and are given land in the North (§101). Thereafter it is Eosa who aids and abets Octa. The Wace texts confuse the names Ebissa and Eosa, variously spelt, apparently assuming them to be the same person. It is only Laʒamon who distinguishes three different characters, Octa, Ebissa and Ossa, who rebel against Uther, are captured by him and imprisoned in London. See Tatlock, p.146, n.156, for references to these names in historical sources both prior to and contemporary with GoM.

Page 27: According to B-H, s.v. *Verolam*, Laʒamon's *Verolam*, like GoM's *Verolamium* (§141) and Wace's *Verolam* (8891), refers to the old Roman town adjacent to St Albans and known in OE as *Verolamceaster*. Following the foundation there, in the eighth century, of an abbey dedicated to one St Albanus martyred in the town during the Diocletian persecution (GoM, §77), a new settlement developed close to the old town and came to be known as St Albans. Tatlock, p.28, states that by Geoffrey's day the name Verolamium 'was hardly used except historically'.

Page 31: This is the first appearance in the narrative of Colgrim, Laʒamon, like Wace (8913-16), anticipating Geoffrey's first mention of him (§143) as Octa's successor as chief of the invading Saxons. Colgrim's status as the new Saxon leader is confirmed at 9991-8, a passage not in GoM though his succession is briefly mentioned in Wace, 9043-6. According to Tatlock, pp.147-8, there is no reference to a historical Colgrim, though the name, a common Scandinavian one, is recorded in England between the tenth and twelfth centuries.

Page 35: According to GoM (§§127-30), Aurelius Ambrosius, wishing to erect a memorial at the burial site of some four hundred British nobles massacred by Hengest's Saxons (§§103-4), consults Merlin who arranges for the stones of the Giants' Ring to be shipped to Britain from Mount Killaraus in Ireland and re-erected in the same formation near Salisbury. Geoffrey adds that the Giants' Ring is called Stonehenge in English (§180). Merlin tells Aurelius that the stones were originally brought from the remotest regions of Africa by giants who settled in Ireland, and that they have mystical and healing properties. Aurelius is buried within the circle of stones, as are Uther, and Arthur's successor, Constantin. Tatlock, p.42, points to historical parallels of Norman kings being buried in churches which they had founded, and suggests that the account of the origin of Stonehenge is Geoffrey's own invention.

Page 39: Earlier in the narrative, Constantin, the brother of the ruler of Armorica, an earlier name for Brittany, comes to Britain by invitation, and is entrusted with the defence of the realm which, with the departure of the Roman forces, has been left unprotected against foreign invasion (6334-431). Constantin has three sons, Constans, Aurelius Ambrosius, and Uther (6435-46). Constans, a monk, succeeds Constantin who, after reigning for twelve years (GoM §93 has *x. anni;* Wace, 6458 has *duze anz*), is stabbed to death by a Pict (6451-71). Constans himself is assassinated shortly thereafter and Vortigern seizes the throne. Ambrosius and Uther are taken to safety in Brittany, but subsequently return to destroy Vortigern, and Aurelius ascends the throne (6624-8064). According to Lacy, p.117, Constantin is vaguely based on a historical figure, a soldier who was proclaimed emperor as Constantine III in AD 407 by the Roman army in Britain. He may have been British and he had a son, Constans, who was a monk. In AD 411, Constantine surrendered to Honorius, the legitimate Western emperor, and was then murdered. Tatlock, p.159, gives Bede's *Ecclesiastical History*, following Orosius, as the source for this historical figure. Gildas, writing *c*.AD 540, mentions one Ambrosius Aurelianus (*Ambrosius Aurelius* in Bede), a Roman who led the British to victory against the invading Saxons. D. N. Dunville suggests the date *c*.495 for the first successful British battle against the Saxons won by Ambrosius ('The chronology of *De Excidiu Britanniae*, Book I' in *Gildas: New Approaches*, eds M. Lapidge and D. N. Dunville (1984), p.83).

Page 41: According to B-H, s.v. *Duglas*, this is the river Douglas 'which rises near Wigan and flows 15 miles to join the Ribble near the latter's estuary'. The name is of Celtic origin, a compound of *dubo* 'dark, black' and *glais* 'stream'.

Page 45: The place-name York derives from the Scandinavian form *Jorvik* (B-H, s.v. *Euerwich*). The town was called *Eburacum* in the Romano-British period and *Eoforwic* in OE. The form *Eoforwic* was still commonly in use at the time Laȝamon was writing. There is, however, an interesting comment earlier in the narrative when Laȝamon tells of the founding of the city of York, which he says was originally called Kær Ebrauc and subsequently Eborac, but was then settled by 'foreign men' who called it Eoverwic (1332-5). *Kær Ebrauc* and *Ebraucus* are in GoM (§27) and *Kær Ebrac, Eborac* and *Evrewic* in Wace (1517-24); but Laȝamon adds (1336-7): 'and it is not long since that the men of the north wrongfully called it York' (ȝeorc).

Page 45: This is the first mention of Baldolf, brother of Colgrim, leader of the invading Saxon army. Baldolf is encamped by the sea coast, awaiting the arrival of Childric, a powerful Germanic chieftain, who is bringing reinforcements. The only historical Baldolf known is a bishop in north England who died about AD 803 (Tatlock, p.147). The name Childric, *Cheldricus* in GoM (§143) and *Cheldric* in Wace (9061), is associated by Tatlock (p.147) with a Chelric who was king of the West Saxons at the end of the sixth century.

Page 47: Tatlock, pp.346-7, cites parallels to Baldulf's stratagem in William of Malmesbury's *Gesta Regum*, a chronicle completed in 1125 and used by GoM as one of his sources. Alfred, for example, when embattled against the Danes, is said to have disguised himself as a minstrel in order to gain access to the tent of the Danish king and remained there for several days, seeing and hearing everything.

Page 49: Though Laȝamon apparently regards Childric as pre-eminent among the Germanic chieftains warring against Arthur, the title 'emperor' need not associate him with the Roman Empire, and the description of his army as 'the whole might of

Rome' is to be taken metaphorically, expressing his military might.

Page 53: At the corresponding point in GoM (§144), Howel is described as *filius sororis Arturi* 'the son of Arthur's sister', and his father's name is given as Budicius, King of Brittany. Wace, likewise, describes Howel as the son of Arthur's sister (9140-1). But we are also told (GoM §§138-9, Wace 8819-22 and Laȝamon 9616-9, 11073-83) that Arthur's sister, Anna, is married to Lot, King of Lothian, and there is no mention of another sister. Thorpe, p.214, n.1, states that for 'Arthur's sister' we should read 'the sister of Aurelius Ambrosius', and that Howel is, therefore, Arthur's first cousin. But M. Blaess (*The Bibliographical Bulletin of the International Arthurian Society*, 8 (1956), 71-2), regards this as unlikely, since Aurelius and Uther would have been first cousins of Budicius, and such a marriage 'would be well within the prohibited degrees'. She suggests that Howel's mother might have been a half-sister of Arthur, daughter of Ygerne and her first husband. But whatever the explanation for GoM's inconsistency, it is interesting to note that Laȝamon, unlike Wace, consistently describes Howel as Arthur's *mæie* 'kinsman', suggesting either that he is consciously avoiding the confusion in GoM and Wace or that he wishes to stress Howel's kinship with Arthur rather than their precise relationship.

Page 57: Laȝamon's *wude of Calidon* is GoM's (*in nemore*) *Colidonis* (§145) and Wace's *bois de Colidon* (9187). Mn, III, p.375, draws attention to the gloss added to the name Calidon in the fourteenth-century English translation of Wace by Robert Mannyng. Robert, a native of Bourne in Lincolnshire, writes in his *Chronicle* (ed. F. J. Furnivall (1887), Part I, lines 9931-2): *a wod byside hight Calydoun / þat now men calleþ hit ffyskertoun*. According to B-H, s.v. *Calidon*, the reference is to the village of Fiskerton near Lincoln. Tatlock, pp.16-17, however, places the wood of Calidon in Scotland, commenting that '*Calidonia, Caledonia*, and their adjectives, have always been bookish words for Scotland or parts of it'. He also states that 'as to the long chase from Lincoln, it is merely more of Geoffrey's usual prodigality of space in little-known regions'. The point at issue is whether the final showdown between Arthur and his Germanic foes is imagined as taking place within a short distance of Lincoln or after a prolonged flight into Scotland, from where the Germanic forces had originally marched south. All GoM says is that Arthur pursued his foes 'without cease' until they reached Calidon wood; and Wace elaborates upon this only slightly, adding that the Saxons abandoned their armour and horses and that the Britons followed hotly on their heels, striking blows upon the bodies of their adversaries. It could be significant that when we next hear of Arthur he is in Scotland (10500-3), but his punitive campaign in the North is described in Wace (9255-8) as revenge against the Scots for the aid they had given to Childric earlier, and it may not mean therefore that Arthur is in Scotland because the pursuit of his Germanic foes to Calidon wood brought him there.

Page 67: Clud, a shortened form of *Alclud* < *Alt Clud* 'the rock on the Clyde', is the ancient Welsh name for Dumbarton, on the river Clyde below Glasgow. The Gaelic name is *Dūn(m)Bretan* 'the fort of the Britons', whence Dumbarton (B-H, s.v. *Clud*). According to Tatlock, pp.14-15, Dumbarton 'one of the strongest and most ancient towns in Scotland', was the chief city of the British kingdom of Strathclyde, ruled over by British kings until the early eleventh century.

Page 69: Just as the arms and armour of classical heroes were often made for them by gods or demigods, so those of Germanic heroes were often said to be forged by the magical skill of Weland, the famous smith of Germanic mythology. Arthur's corslet, Wygar, is the work of the 'elvish smith' Witeȝe, a name not in GoM or Wace, but identified with the person called Widia and described as the son of Weland in lines 4-10 of the second fragment of the OE poem *Waldere* (*Old English Minor Heroic Poems*, ed. J. Hill (1987), pp.37, 102). The name Wygar is also not in GoM or Wace, and as D&W say (p.170), its derivation from OE *Wīggār* 'battle-spear', makes it a somewhat inappropriate name for a corslet. They suggest *Wigheard* 'tough in battle' would be more appropriate.

The name of Arthur's helmet, Goswhit (Goose-white), is, like Wygar, English in form and not mentioned in GoM or Wace, though the helmet is described in both as having a crest fashioned in the shape of a dragon (§147 and 9286), a detail omitted by Laȝamon. Arthur's sword, spear and shield are named in GoM (§147: *Caliburnus, Priduuen* and *Ron*) and Wace (9279-97: *Chaliburne, Pridwen, Run*), and all three names are from Welsh tradition (Tatlock, p.202). Lacy, p.176, connects the name Caliburnus with Latin *chalyb* 'steel'. One meaning suggested for the name Pridwen is 'blessed form', possibly an allusion, according to Tatlock, to Mary's image on the inner side of the shield, though in early Welsh tradition Prydwen is the name of Arthur's ship (Loomis, pp.16, 33). For Avalon, where Arthur's sword was made, see below, under Page 255.

Page 71: The earl Borel, mentioned here as leader of the Saxon warriors and killed by Arthur, does not appear in GoM or Wace, and is clearly not the earl Borel who is granted Le Mans by Arthur in return for loyal service (see 12067 and below, under Page 145). There may be here, as elsewhere in Laȝamon (see, for example, under Pages 145 and 171), a confusion over matters of detail.

Page 81: The river Teign is in Devon, rising on Dartmoor and flowing into the sea at Teignmouth. The identification of Teinnewic, rendering Wace's *Teignewic* (9393), is uncertain. Teinnewic means 'settlement (OE *wic*) on the Teign', and B-H, s.v. *Teinnewic*, suggests that it might have been the original name for Teignmouth, itself originally referring to the mouth of the river and later superseding Teinnewic as the name for the village.

Page 81: Both GoM (§§148-9) and Wace (9407-8) state that Cador, having killed Childric, restores peace to the land. Laȝamon, however, describes this peace, secure and lasting, in terms reminiscent of those used in *The Peterborough Chronicle* under the year 1135 to praise the peace established by Henry I: *Wua sua bare his byrthen gold and sylure, durste nan man sei to him naht bute god*. The traditional nature of such a comment is suggested by a similar description in the *Chronicle* under the year 1087 of the good peace established by William the Conqueror; and Laȝamon himself uses similar terminology, not in GoM or Wace, twice elsewhere in the narrative, once to describe the reign of Gwendoleine, a formidable early British queen (1255-7), and secondly to praise Uther's re-establishment of peace in the land after his defeat of Octa, Ebissa and Ossa, and subsequent conquest of the North and Scotland (9225-8).

Page 83: The 'expanse of water where marvels abound', is called *(stagnum) Lumonoi* in GoM (§149) and *(l'estanc de) Lumonoï* in Wace (9425), and is thought to refer to Loch Lomond (Tatlock, p.45). Nennius has an account of the lake with its sixty islands and sixty streams but only one outlet, and these details are also in GoM and Wace; but while Nennius describes the lake as the habitation of eagles, he does not mention, as Geoffrey, Wace and Laȝamon do, their prophetic role. The description of water-monsters and the sport of elves 'in that fearsome pool' is, however, original with Laȝamon, and there may be echoes here of the description of the monster Grendel's watery lair in the OE poem *Beowulf*, where there are 'strange sea-dragons exploring the deep, also water-monsters lying on the slopes of the crags' (ed. and trans. M. Swanton (1978), lines 1426-7). For his description of the watery lair and its surroundings, the OE poet is thought to have drawn on details of the Christian hell as described in the *Visio Pauli*, a version of which is found in the OE *Blickling Homily* No.17.

Page 85: Two kings of Ireland, both called Gillomar, appear in the Arthurian section of Laȝamon. The Britons, led by Uther, on crossing to Ireland to fetch the stones of the Giants' Ring, meet resistance from the Irish king Gillomar, but defeat him in battle and put him to flight (8605-65). Subsequently he invades Britain, but Uther defeats and kills him (8980-9023). In the present passage, while Arthur is pursuing the Scots at Loch Lomond, a second Gillomar, King of Ireland, arrives at a Scottish port to aid the Scots but is defeated by Arthur and returns to Ireland. When

Arthur subsequently invades Ireland, Gillomar, vanquished in battle, acknowledges Arthur as overlord and becomes his liegeman (11103-209), and when Arthur holds court at Caerleon, Gillomar is one of several kings in attendance (12166). Laȝamon, with one exception, consistently calls both Irish kings Gillomar where GoM and Wace offer several variant forms of the name. Tatlock, pp.515-22, argues that Laȝamon had personal knowledge of Ireland, reflected in his consistent and historically correct form of this name, and in other details to be discussed below (see under Page 99), a view challenged by Loomis, p.105.

Page 91: The description of the large lake near the seashore is in GoM (§150) and Wace (9537-84), but both place the lake close to the river Severn in Wales. GoM notes that the local people call it *Linliguuam*, taken, according to Tatlock (p.66), from the *Linn Liuan* of Nennius. If, as seems likely, their description refers to the Severn bore, it is odd that Laȝamon chose to omit a reference to his own region. He may have felt that to move from the natural wonders of Moray to those of Wales would disrupt the sequence of his narrative.

Page 93: In GoM (§151), it is *Piramus*, Arthur's own chaplain, who is made Archbishop of York, and in Wace (9605) *Piram, un sage chapelein*. Tatlock, p.244, suggests that the form of the name in GoM is consciously classical, and that Geoffrey is referring to Piranus 'supposed of the early sixth century, the British form (with the usual *p* for *c*) for the Irish bishop Ciaran, reputed to have left Ireland and settled in Cornwall'.

Page 95: Lot, King of Lothian, is married to Anna, daughter of Uther and sister of Arthur (see above, under Page 53), and their two sons are Gawain and Modred. The kingdom of Lothian, at the time Geoffrey was writing, extended from the Tweed to the Forth and the Scottish king did homage for it to the English. There is no historical record for Lot as King of Lothian. Angel, who is entrusted by Arthur with the kingdom of Scotland, is also unhistorical. Urien, King of Moray, is associated by Tatlock (p.153), with the British king Urbgen who appears in Nennius as the enemy of the English kings of Northumbria towards the end of the sixth century.

Page 97: The derivation of the place-name Exeter is 'the fort (OE *ceaster*) on the river Exe' (B-H, s.v. *Excestre*), and this is reflected in the form given by Laȝamon.

Page 97: Gillomar, King of Ireland, is discussed above, under Page 85.

Page 97: The right of sanctuary (*chireche-grið*), of refuge within the precincts of a holy place (OE *cyric-grið*), applied to both persons and goods.

Page 99: Arthur's Irish campaign is touched on only briefly in GoM (§153), though Geoffrey does note that the Irishmen were *nuda et inermis* 'naked and unarmed'. Wace (9659-705) also comments on the fact that the Irish fought naked, lacking armour, but his account of Gillomar rendering homage to Arthur is greatly expanded in Laȝamon. Tatlock, pp.515-18, argues that this expansion reflects a personal knowledge of Ireland but, as mentioned above, under Page 85, this view has since been challenged by Loomis. The holy relic of St Columba, on which Gillomar promises to swear allegiance to Arthur, could refer to either of the two famous relics of the saint: his crozier or half a psalter said to have been copied by him. St Brendan and St Bridget were, like Columba, early Irish saints; but there is no record of Brendan's head or Bridget's foot as holy relics (see Tatlock, p.518).

Page 103: We are told in both GoM (§153) and Wace (9703-7) that Arthur conquered Iceland, but there is no mention of the king of Iceland or his son. No historical source for the names Ælcus and Escol is known. Later in the narrative, where the king of Iceland attends Arthur's plenary court at Caerleon, he is called *Maluasius* in GoM (§156), *Malvaisus* in Wace (10304) and Malverus in Laȝamon (12167).

Page 103: Gonwais, King of Orkney, of whom there is no independent historical record, is called *Gunuasius* in GoM (§153) and *Gonvais* in Wace (9708). When Gonwais attends Arthur's plenary court at Caerleon, he is described as *utlaȝen deorling*: 'beloved of the renegades he ruled' (12170) — *utlaȝen* 'outlaws', echoing Wace's *Ki maint utlage out en baillie* (10310).

Page 105: Doldanin, King of Jutland, another unhistorical figure, is *Doldauius* in GoM (§153), and *Doldani/Doldanied* in Wace (9709 and 10305). At Arthur's plenary court his name is given as Doldanet (12167).

Page 107: The surrender of Rumareth, King of Winetland, does not occur in GoM, but in Wace *Rummaret de Wenelande* is mentioned alongside *Gonvais* and *Doldani* as submitting to Arthur and pledging fealty to him (9708-30). Although no known historical source exists for the name Rumareth, Winetland is thought to be the land of the Wends, a Slavonic tribe living between the Elbe and Vistula in the ninth century. For an argument against the identification of Wace's Wenelande as the land of the Wends, see W. Sayers 'Rummaret de Wenelande: a geographical note to Wace's *Brut*', *Romance Philology*, 18 (1964-5), 46-53. The *Winedas* are mentioned in the OE poem *Widsith* and *Wineda lond* in the Alfredian translation of the universal history by Orosius. When, due to envy over who should have precedence at Arthur's table, a riot breaks out among his followers, an episode not in GoM or Wace, it is a hostage from Winetland, the young son of King Rumareth, who takes action against the instigators of the riot (11371-84).

Page 113: The lengthy and vivid description of the riot at court and the consequent foundation of the Round Table is not in GoM, and is greatly expanded from the brief statement in Wace, the earliest extant reference, that the Round Table was ordained by Arthur so that all his followers sat as equals and no one could boast that he took precedence over another (9747-60). Tatlock, p.472, thinks that the Laȝamon narrative is his own invention, but Laȝamon, like Wace, refers to the stories of many kinds told by the Britons concerning King Arthur (11454-5), and Mn, III, p.383, suggests that Laȝamon was drawing upon popular tradition preserved and still circulating in oral form. According to Lacy, p.463, warriors sitting in circles around their king was an ancient Celtic custom, and certain details in the Laȝamon account, such as the quarrel over precedence, are paralleled in Celtic stories.

Page 115: The Great St Bernard Pass, known in classical times as *Mons Jovis* because of a temple to Jupiter there, was called *Muntȝiof* in OE. Its modern designation derives from the Augustine hospice founded *c*.980 by St Bernard of Menthon (B-H, s.v. *Muntgiu*).

Page 115: It seems that the route to Rome served as a yardstick for long and hazardous journeys. At the end of an early thirteenth-century guide for anchoresses, the author exclaims: 'God knows, I would rather undertake the journey to Rome than begin the writing of it again!' (*The Ancrene Riwle*, trans. M. B. Salu (1955), p.192).

Page 115: For a previous reference to this prophecy of Merlin, see above, under Page 11.

Page 117: For Arthur's departure to Avalon and the mystery of his death or survival, see below, under Page 255.

Page 119: Arthur's plan to put Lot on the Norwegian throne is recounted in GoM (§154) and Wace (9799-862). Sichelin, King of Norway, is *Sichelmus* in GoM and *Sichelins* in Wace, while the name Riculf is *Richulfus* in GoM and *Riculf* in Wace. Tatlock points out that the name Sighelm was well established in England, citing two examples, an official of King Alfred and a bishop of Sherborne in the tenth century, and he also suggests that Geoffrey gave the Norwegian earl Riculf a name current in England (pp.143-4).

Page 121: The name of the pope who instructed Gawain is *Sulpicius* in GoM and *Soplice* in Wace. Geoffrey could be referring to Simplicius, pope in 468-83 or, alternatively, to Silverius, pope in 536-7, sometimes called Severus, and therefore possibly confused with the fourth-century writer Sulpicius Severus (Tatlock, p.251). Gawain's arrival in Norway to join his father is mentioned in Wace but not in GoM; Geoffrey states that at the time of the Norwegian campaign Lot's son, Gawain, was twelve years old and serving in the household of Pope Sulpicius who had dubbed him a knight. Gawain, brought up in the household of the pope, is following the Germanic custom of fostering boys of good birth in other noble households.

Page 125: *Frollo* in GoM (§155) and *Frolle* in Wace (9905-13), an unhistorical character, is a tribune ruling France, the Roman province of Gaul, in the name of the emperor Leo. Wace adds (9914-16) that Frolle is of noble Roman stock, and fearful of no one.

Page 135: For a discussion of Arthur's weapons, see above, under Page 69. The forging of Arthur's lance in Carmarthen by a smith called Griffin is an addition to the details given earlier, and not in GoM or Wace. Tatlock, p.502, attributes this addition to Laȝamon's knowledge of Carmarthen, in his day an important royal fortress and likely to employ skilled armourers.

Page 139: Mn, III, pp.386-7, points to the similarity of this episode to the combat between Roland and Oliver on an island in the middle of the river Rhône near Vienna, but the duel between Arthur and Frolle was probably conceived by Geoffrey in terms of the contemporary form of trial by combat introduced in English legal procedure after the Norman Conquest, most commonly in treason trials. Challenger and defendant fought, not through champions, but in their own persons, armed and mounted, and isolated from the interference of partisans within the lists. Geoffrey seems to be evoking such isolation by placing the combat on an island. Laȝamon's detailed elaboration, stressing the isolation, clearly encompasses the other details of the judicial combat paralleled in contemporary practice. When Henry, Earl of Essex, was appealed of treason in 1163, the combat took place on an island in the Thames at Reading; as late as 1398 when Henry, Duke of Hereford, appealed the duke of Norfolk of treason, the lists prepared for their encounter at Coventry were surrounded by a moat dug for the purpose. GoM, Wace and Laȝamon may all have conceived Frolle's challenge as charging Arthur with treason to their common overlord, the Emperor of Rome.

Page 141: Arthur's intention of marching upon Rome, announced here for the first time, is not mentioned at this point in GoM or Wace. The reference to Belin recalls the telling, much earlier in the narrative, of the capture of Gaul and Rome by this British king and his brother Brenne. Their victory is said to have resulted in many years of British rule over the Roman empire. The prominence given to the reign of Belin in GoM (§§35-44), Wace (2313-3240) and Laȝamon (2140-3035), suggests that Belin held a position of some importance in the record of early British kings, and as a good ruler and successful military leader foreshadows the even more glorious reign and conquests of Arthur. When, at Arthur's plenary court at Caerleon, envoys sent by Lucius, Emperor of Rome, demand that Arthur acknowledge him as overlord, Arthur responds by claiming Rome as rightfully his through his descent from Belin and Brenne (12475-506). The historian Nennius mentions a King Belinus living at the time of Julius Caesar and he is also mentioned in GoM (§56), but there is no historical basis for the later Belin or his conquest of Rome. On the other hand, the Gauls, led by one Brennus, did win a victory over Rome in the fourth century AD, but there is no evidence that this Brennus was a Briton (Tatlock, pp.168-9).

Page 141: Guitard, ruler of Poitou (described later (13488) as also ruling Gascony), is called *Guitardus* in GoM (§155) and *Guitart* in Wace (10117). No historical evidence for this ruler exists, but Tatlock, p.133, thinks there may be an echo here of the name Guichard, borne by the lords of Beaujeu, near Lyons, between the tenth and mid-twelfth centuries. The name Guitard is found in France in the fourteenth and fifteenth centuries, a variant of the tenth-century Withardus and the late-eleventh-century Guitterdus.

Page 145: In GoM (§155), Arthur bestows Neustria upon Bedevere and Anjou upon Kay, but neither Howeldin nor Borel is mentioned. In Wace (10153-66), Kay and Bedevere are rewarded, as is Holdin who receives Flanders, Borel who receives Le Mans, Ligier who is given Boulogne, presumably the Læʒer/Leir, Earl of Boulogne, whom Laʒamon notes among those at Arthur's plenary court (12171-2), and who is grievously wounded in the final battle against the Romans (13807-23), and Richier who is given Puntif (though in nine of the twenty-two MSS consulted by Arnold, lines 10165-6, referring to Ligier and Richier, are omitted). Although Laʒamon has Arthur award Boulogne to Howelden, elsewhere in the narrative (12173, 13610 and 13942) Howeldin is always associated with Flanders. Laʒamon appears to have erred in having Arthur grant Boulogne to Howeldin, but there is also the strong possibility that the name Howeldin is used here in error for Howel, ruler of Brittany and close kinsman of Arthur. When Arthur bestows Boulogne upon Howeldin, he addresses him as 'you who are both my liegeman and my kinsman' (12065), and there is no evidence that Howeldin, ruler of Flanders, is a kinsman of Arthur.

The knight (later called Earl) Borel has a counterpart in GoM, *Borrellus Cenomanensis* 'Borellus of Cenomania' (Thorpe, p.228), who is present at Arthur's plenary court (§156), and like Laʒamon's Earl Borel is slain by King Evander while fighting the Romans in France (§167). Cenomania is thought to be Maine (Thorpe, p.312), and Tatlock, p.135, states that the name Borrel/Borel existed in France, citing among others one Eude Borel, a duke of Burgundy who died in 1102 while on crusade.

Page 147: Cærleon-upon-Usk, by the river Usk in Gwent, the site of Arthur's Whitsun plenary court where he wears his crown in state, was founded, we are told in GoM (§44), by King Belin as his capital city, and was originally called *Kærusc*. The city was subsequently known as *Urbs Legionum* 'the city of the Legions' (Wace, 3194: *Kærlion*) from the Roman legions who wintered there. Historically a Roman military and civil post, *Isca Silurum*, it appears in the Domesday Book as one of the Norman outposts to the west. According to Lacy, p.74, Geoffrey may have chosen this site for Arthur's plenary court simply because of its proximity to his native Monmouth; Geoffey himself (§72) remarks upon the ancient walls and buildings still standing in his day, and there are other witnesses to the impressiveness of the Roman ruins in the twelfth century (see B&S, p.347). In GoM, British kings hold ceremonial crown-wearings at Christmas, Easter and Whitsun, though none is as splendidly described as Arthur's in Cærleon at Whitsun, 'the climax of his reign and of the entire *Historia*' (Tatlock, p.69). Such occasions, however, reflect historical fact in that 'these courts or crown-wearings, at these three great festivals and held in various but sometimes fixed places, are conspicuous in the history of the English kings, ceasing with Henry II' (p.271). In the romance tradition Arthur holds a ceremonial court five times a year, at Easter, Ascension, Whitsun, All Saints and Christmas, and these courts serve as periodic renewals of unity, idealism and loyalty to Arthur. Camelot, the romance counterpart of Cærleon, is not mentioned prior to Chrétien de Troyes, and is identified in Malory with Winchester.

Page 147: The presence of two minsters in Cærleon dedicated to St Aaron and St Julian the Martyr is thought to go back to Gildas and Bede. Bede, Bk.1, Ch.7, tells of Julian and Aaron, *legionum urbis cives* 'citizens of the City of the Legions', martyred during the Diocletian persecution, and this is also mentioned in GoM (§77).

Page 149: The list of noblemen who journey to Arthur's plenary court is also found in GoM (§156) and Wace (10256-67). In GoM, for example, *Arthgal* is Earl of Warwick; in Wace the name is *Argahl*, and in Laʒamon Argal. Geoffrey has *Boso* as Earl of Oxford, while Wace has *Bos* and Laʒamon Beof, the *f* perhaps a misreading of the *s*. But, whereas in both Wace and Laʒamon Gurguint, Earl of Hereford (*Guerguint* in Wace) is listed among the noblemen, this personage is not in GoM. The second list of names, beginning with Dunwald, son of Apries, parallels the names in Wace (10271-82) more closely than those in the extant GoM texts (§156). There is no evidence to suggest that any of the names are historical.

Page 149: The kings listed here all owe allegiance to Arthur and, with one exception, Kailin of Friesland, have already appeared in the narrative (see above, under Pages 85, 103 and 105). Kailin does not appear in GoM or Wace. The earl Cherin from Chartres (spelt Gerin at 13096) is *Gerinus* in GoM (§156) and *Gerin* in Wace (10314), and described as one of the Twelve Peers of France. In early-thirteenth-century historical record these peers are named as the prelates of Rheims, Laon, Langres, Châlons, Beauvais and Noyon, the dukes of Normandy, Guyenne and Burgundy and the counts of Flanders, Toulouse and Champagne, but very little is known of either their history or their function. In the earlier *chansons de geste*, however, the Twelve Peers are the premier nobles of Charlemagne's empire, Roland, Oliver, etc. and Gerin is the only one to figure in both lists.

Page 151: In GoM, Dubricius is appointed to the see of Cærleon by Ambrosius Aurelius (§130), crowns Arthur at Silchester (§143), and addresses the British before the final battle against Colgrim and Baldolf (§147). He is also present at Arthur's crown-wearing in Cærleon, and described by Geoffrey as so extraordinarily pious that he could heal anyone who was ill simply by prayer (§156). We are also told that the 'saintly' archbishop resigns his see because he wishes to become a hermit (§157). The appointment of St Dubriz to the see of Cærleon is also recounted in Wace (8167-9), but his next and final appearance is at Arthur's crown-wearing, at which point his extraordinary piety is commented upon (10292-300), and we are told that he officiates at the religious ceremony (10381-4). Laȝamon follows Wace in limiting his appearance to these two occasions. In the Welsh Annals the date of death of *Dibric episcopi* is noted under the year 612, and twelfth-century accounts associate him with the see of Llandaff as its founder and first archbishop. According to Tatlock, p.245, he seems to have been revered as a local saint at the time Geoffrey was writing, though Geoffrey clearly makes Dubricius the chief ecclesiastic in the country under Ambrosius, Uther and Arthur.

Page 153: The reference to the ancient Trojan custom, carried on by their British descendants, of men and women eating apart on festive occasions, mentioned also in Wace (10452-8), derives from Geoffrey (§157). Tatlock (pp.273-4), while noting that 'this in part recalls contemporary Welsh usage, since it was not usual in Wales for women to join in feasts in the royal hall', also points to Byzantine custom as a possible source for Geoffrey's account (pp.273-4). The ceremonial processions of Arthur and Guenevere described in GoM (§157) have historical parallels in the accounts of coronations of English kings both earlier and later in date than Geoffrey (Tatlock, p.272).

Page 157: Laȝamon's description of the feasting and games at court is found also in GoM (§157) and Wace (10437-620). The references to women's fashions and the need for every knight to prove himself three times in battle before any woman of high birth would accept his suit, occur both in GoM and Wace. Feasting after the solemnities at ceremonial crown-wearings is historically attested (Tatlock, p.272), and in both French and English Arthurian romances feasting, dancing, singing and the playing of games are all part of the rich pageantry of Arthur's seasonal courts.

Page 159: Lucius, Emperor of Rome, entitles himself *rei publice procurator* 'Procurator of the Republic' in GoM (§158). For Wace he is *l'empereür de Rome* (10637), and announces himself as *Luces, ki Rome ad en baillie / E des Romains la seinurie* (10639-40). Laȝamon differs here from Geoffey and Wace in that both the Latin and French texts relay the emperor's challenge in the form of a letter from Lucius read out in court rather than delivered verbally by his envoys. The picture of the Roman Empire given in GoM, and followed by Wace and Laȝamon, is totally unhistorical in its portrayal of a thriving, world-wide empire of the sixth century, but serves rather to heighten Arthur's achievement as conqueror of Rome.

Page 165: For King Belin and his brother Brenne, see above, under Page 141.

Page 167: Geoffrey claims British blood for Constantine the Great through his mother, Helena, daughter of Coel, King of Britain (§78), and relates Constantine's conquest of Rome and subsequent sovereignty *totius mundi* 'of the whole world' (§79). Wace recounts all this in his narrative, adding the story of how Helena found the True Cross in Jerusalem (5719-24), a story repeated in Laȝamon's account of Constantine (5560-72). Maximian, British on his father's side, according to Geoffrey, is another British monarch who conquers Rome, subduing on his way the whole of Gaul (GoM §§81-6, Wace 5824-6115 and Laȝamon 5784-919). It is under Maximian that the Britons conquer the kingdom of the Amorici, known thereafter as Brittany. Elements of the material, sometimes at variance, appear in Gildas, the Latin and OE Bede, and Nennius, but Geoffrey's version of events, in which identities and origins of historical figures are occasionally confused, is deliberately fashioned to emphasise this early phase of British imperialism, providing a distinguished precedent for Arthur's claim to imperial power.

Page 169: 'The Sibyl' is the generic title for an inspired prophetess, a name originating in Hellenistic Greek, but applied to many such women in classical life and literature. Their prophecies were set down in books and came to be known as the Sibylline Prophecies. In GoM (§160), it is the Sibylline Prophecies which testify in verse to Arthur being the third British king who will conquer Rome; in Wace (10927-38) it is the books of the Sibyl and the prophecies she wrote therein which predict Arthur's destiny. According to Tatlock, p.408, 'the classical Sibyl or Sibyls and their utterances . . . were spoken of often by the medievals, and with bated breath', but he can find no evidence to link this particular utterance with any extant Sibylline saying. According to BS, p.127, 'the reference here is simply an appeal to an established and revered poetic authority made in order to give weight to Howel's words'.

Page 171: It is odd to find included in a list of territories which Angel, King of Scotland, exhorts the British to seize after they have taken Rome the names of Brittany, ruled over by Arthur's kinsman Howel, and Normandy, granted to Arthur's cup-bearer, Bedevere, in return for loyal service. We are specificially told that both these territories send troops to aid Arthur in his campaign against Lucius (12693-6). It is likely that Brittany is an error for Burgundy, the name which appears in a list of territories which Lucius's envoys report Arthur as threatening to seize (12631-4), but Normandy is also included in this list. The presence here of Brittany and Normandy appears to be another example of Laȝamon's occasional confusion over matters of detail.

Page 175: The list of oriental kings who, owing allegiance to Rome, come to the aid of Lucius, is paralleled in GoM and Wace (§163 and 11093-112), though in several instances the forms of the names correspond in the Latin and French texts, but differ from those in Laȝamon. The most obvious difference is the name of the king of Spain, *Aliphatima* in GoM and Wace, but Meodras in Laȝamon. For a detailed discussion of the historicity or otherwise of the names in GoM, see Tatlock, 'Certain contemporaneous matters in Geoffrey of Monmouth', *Speculum*, 6 (1931), 206-24. The names of the Roman senators correspond more closely to Wace (11115-16) than Geoffrey (§163), though Wace's *Marcel e Luces Catel, Cocta e Gaius Metel* seem to have been expanded into six separate Romans by Laȝamon. In GoM five senators are named.

Page 175: In GoM (§164), the Roman forces set out *incipientibus Kalendis Augusti* 'with the approach of the first day of August'; in Wace (11124) it is *entrant august*. In England, in Laȝamon's day, the term *heruest* described the season of autumn which could begin as early as August and extend into December (see MED *hervest* n. 1(a)). The term could also apply specifically to the month of August (1(b)). Laȝamon's method of identifying the time of year the Romans set forth is to express it as 'nearest the first day of Autumn', marking the passing of the year through the seasonal cycle.

Page 181: Arthur's dream of the struggle between the bear and the dragon is described in GoM (§164) and interpreted by those around the king as foretelling his struggle with the giant of Mont St Michel in which Arthur, represented by the dragon, will be victorious. But Arthur, Geoffrey tells us, is certain that the dream applies to himself and Lucius. Wace follows Geoffrey in having the dream interpreted as forecasting a struggle between Arthur and the giant, in which Arthur will be victorious, but Arthur declares that his own interpretation of the dream bears upon the issue of the war between himself and the emperor (11239-78). It is odd that Laȝamon with his interest in dreams and prophecy does not provide an interpretation of Arthur's dream, but perhaps he found the dual interpretation in his source unsatisfactory, and so chose to make the comment, reflecting the sternness he constantly attributes to Arthur, that 'no one there dared interpret it as in any way ill-omened, lest he should lose limbs which he valued'.

Page 183: The giant of Mont St Michel is nameless in GoM and Laȝamon, but is given the name *Dinabuc* in Wace (11317), though Tatlock, p.473, n.34, claims that Wace took the name, possibly for the purposes of rhyme, from that of Merlin's playmate in youth, *Dinabuz*, who occurs earlier in his narrative (7369, 7373).

Page 193: In GoM (§165), Arthur compares the contest against the giant of Mont St Michel with that against the giant Ritho on Mount Aravius. Ritho demands Arthur's beard to add to his cloak made of the beards of kings he has slain; if Arthur will not agree to this, then Ritho will face him in single combat, the winner taking the cloak and the beard of the loser. Arthur, of course, is victorious. Wace recounts the same tale (11561-92) which, surprisingly, Laȝamon merely refers to, despite his usual interest in Arthur's personal heroism.

Page 193: In GoM (§165), it is claimed that the mountain peak of Mont St Michel takes its name from Helene's burial place and is called *Tumba Helene . . . in hodiernum diem* 'to this very day'. Wace repeats this, calling the mountain peak *Tumba Eleine* (11604). Tatlock, p.87, suggests that it is the smaller of the two neighbouring islands that Geoffrey is referring to, but he also notes that, prior to the twelfth century, names for the main island included *St Michel au Péril de la Mer*, *Tumbalenia* and *Mons Tumba*, and that the two islands together were sometimes called *Duae Tumbae* (p.88). The association of Mont St Michel with the burial place of Helene is first recorded in Geoffrey.

Page 195: The river Aube, where Arthur encamps, 'rises near Vaillant (Haute-Marne) and flows through Champagne to join the Seine at Marcilly' (B-H, s.v. *Aube*). Laȝamon's spelling, Albe, conforms to the Latin name (*Alba* in GoM (§166), *Albe* in Wace (11640)) which, according to B-H, refers to the clarity of the water.

Page 197: For Gerin, Earl of Chartres, and Beof, Earl of Oxford, see above, under Page 149.

Page 201: For King Belin and his brother Brenne, see above, under Page 141.

Page 201: Quencelin, kinsman of Lucius and 'a leading man in Rome', corresponds to Geoffrey's *Gaius Quintillianus*, nephew of the emperor (§166), and to Wace's *Quintilien* (11741). Both Gaius Quintillianus and Quintilien utter the same sentiments concerning British valour as Laȝamon's Quencelin, and suffer the same fate.

Page 203: Marcel, the second Roman despatched by Gawain, is called *Marcellius Mutius* in GoM (§166), and *Marcel* in Wace (11811).

Page 207: Petreius, 'a noble earl, a Roman of high rank', who comes with six thousand soldiers to the aid of his hard-pressed fellow Romans, is *Petreius Cocta* in

GoM, entitled senator and the leader of ten thousand men (§166). In Wace he becomes *Petreius uns riches ber*, leading ten thousand armed men *tant out en sa cunestablie* (11905-8).

Page 211: Of the four earls ordered to escort the Roman captives to Paris, three are already known to us: Cador, Earl of Cornwall, Borel, Earl of Le Mans, and Bedevere, Earl of Normandy. The fourth, Richer, is mentioned here for the first time. Of the four mentioned in GoM (§166), *Richerius* and *Borrellus* are described as *duos consules* 'two consuls', while in Wace the former is previously mentioned as having received Puntif from Arthur in return for loyal service (see above, under Page 145). Richer disappears again in the fighting when the British force is ambushed by the Romans, and is not mentioned again. We are told that Borel is killed in the ambush (13479), and that Bedevere survives only to die at the hands of the king of Media in the final battle against Lucius (13747-56); Cador is named as one of the commanders in the same battle (13601), but this is the last we hear of him. Arthur, mortally wounded after the battle with Modred, entrusts his kingdom to Constantin 'you who were Cador's son' (14272), implying by the past tense of the verb that Cador is dead.

Page 213: Sextorius and Evander are included in the list of oriental kings who, as allies of Lucius, come to his aid against Arthur (see 12657-70 and above, under Page 175), but Evander, described there as King of Syria is here King of Babylon, seemingly in error as the king of Babylon has previously been named as Mæptisas (12662). The title *of Turkie dux* 'Duke of Turkey', given to Sextorius, King of Libya, is also confusing as it is Irtac who is King of Turkey in the earlier roll-call of names (12659). In both GoM (§167) and Wace (12109-10), Sertorius, King of Libya and Evander, King of Syria, are named as the commanders of the Roman force which sets out to ambush the Britons. Of the three Roman senators accompanying the two kings, only one, Catel, appears among the six Roman senators previously named by Laȝamon (see 12667-70 and above, under Page 175). In GoM (§167) *Wlterius Catellus* and *Carutius Quintus* are the two Roman senators who accompany Evander and Sertorius; in Wace (12111-12) it is *Caricius e Catellus Vulteius*. In view of the names in GoM and Wace, Laȝamon's Catel and Carrius are explainable; the third name, Bal, is not.

Page 215: For Guitard, King of Poitou and ruler of Gascony, see above, under Page 141.

Page 217: For King Evander, see above, under Pages 175 and 213. Catellus is the Latinate form for Catel, the Roman senator mentioned at 12669 and 13429. See also above, under Pages 175 and 213.

Page 217: Merlin's prophecy that, because of Arthur, Rome should fall, is not in Wace, but Mn, III, p.401, suggests that it may refer to one of the Prophecies of Merlin in GoM (§112.2): *Tremebit Romulea domus seuitiam ipsius et exitus eius dubius erit* 'The House of Romulus shall dread the Boar's savagery and the end of that House shall be shrouded in mystery' (Thorpe, p.172). For an earlier reference in Laȝamon to Arthur as the Boar, see above, under Page 11.

Page 219: In GoM (§168), the Emperor Lucius decides to withdraw to Autun (*Augustudunum*), a town in Burgundy, and marches his troops into Langres (*Lengria*) en route. Arthur's stratagem is to waylay Lucius along the route, and the same night *relicta a leua ciuitate* 'the city bypassed on the left' (presumably Langres, but erroneously translated by Thorpe (p.246) as Autun), he enters a valley called *Sessia* (*Siesia/Siessia* in other GoM manuscripts) where he lies in wait for Lucius. Tatlock (pp.102-3) notes that Arthur's forces leaving Langres on the left makes topographical sense for an army marching from the river Aube towards Autun. Wace has Arthur leaving Langres (*Lengres*) on his left, and passing beyond it and bearing to the right, entering the valley of *Soëise* (other Wace manuscript forms include *Suison*, *Soissie* and *Soesie*) which lies on the route between Autun and Langres (12295-304). Laȝamon tells us that 'leaving Langres on his right hand, he [Arthur] advanced along the route which Lucius would take' (13556-7), and that the rightful name of the valley where he halted is Sosie (13560).

Tatlock, p.102, n.83, suggests that Geoffrey's *Sessia* may be Saussy, a little town thirty-five miles south-west of Langres on the way to Autun, but W. Matthews ('Where was Siesia-Sessoyne', *Speculum*, 49 (1974), 680-6) argues for Val-Suzon, thirty-seven miles south-west of Langres on the route to Autun, claiming that 'unlike the nearby Saussy, which fails on various scores, Val-Suzon meets the several requirements of topography, language and familiarity as the true site of that great Arthurian battle that, to speak sober truth, really took place only in the deep valley of Geoffrey of Monmouth's imagination' (p.686). For another argument in favour of Val-Suzon, see H. E. Keller, *Speculum*, 49 (1974), 687-98.

Page 221: For the origin and significance of the dragon as Arthur's battle-standard, see above, under Pages 3 and 17.

Page 221: The mention of two earls of Chester, Gerin and Curselin, is due presumably to confusion; Gerin (see above under Page 149) is Earl of Chartres. Further confusion arises from the fact that in the roll-call of British noblemen at Caerleon (12143-55 and see above, under Page 149), Urgent is Earl of Chester. In the same roll-call of names, Gursal, and not Urgein, is Earl of Bath. The names Curselin and Urgein bear a marked similarity to Wace's *Cursalen* and *Urgen* (12383-4) and Geoffrey's *Cursalem* and *Urgennius* (§168). In GoM (§172) and Wace (12748-54), the names of boths earls are included in a list of those slain in the battle, but Laȝamon omits this particular list, and we are not told of the fate of these two earls.

Page 223: In Wace, though not in Geoffrey, the Romans and their allies are given a strong heathen colouring, the terminology used, for example, *paens et Sarazins* (12625), associating them with the Islamic foes of the Crusaders. The Roman alliance with Islamic potentates and other pagan rulers gives a contemporary Crusader-like tone to Arthur's campaign against Lucius. Laȝamon has Arthur focus upon the paganism of the Romans and their allies in his eve-of-battle speech to his followers, thus emphasising the justness of the war against those who 'deny our Lord and commit themselves to Mahoun'. Laȝamon uses the term Mahoun, from the Old French shortened form of Mahomet (see MED *Mahoun*) much earlier in the narrative to describe the pagan idol which Aeneas brought with him from Troy (117-18), and, in denouncing the Romans and their allies for allegiance to Mahoun, represents the prophet Muhammad as a pagan god.

Page 229: The king of Media, slayer of Bedevere, is Boccus, mentioned by name at 13774 and in the earlier roll-call of those potentates who are allies of Lucius (see 12663 and above, under Page 175).

Page 229: The bold Seftor from Libya is the Sextorius of 12663 and 13427. In GoM (§171), Kay in avenging Bedevere's death encounters the legion of the king of Libya and is wounded. In Wace (12641-50), it is *Sertor, li reis de Libie* who fatally wounds Kay.

Page 229: The name Ridwathelan appears to be original with Laȝamon; Bedevere's nephew is called *Hirelglas* in GoM (§172) and *Hyrelgas* in Wace (12655). Of interest is the description of Ridwathelan as Bedevere's sister's son; both Geoffrey and Wace describe him simply as Bedevere's nephew. In Germanic tradition, as noted by Tacitus in the *Germania*, Ch.20, there was an especially close bond between a man and his sister's son. Old English literary awareness of this is evident in the heroic poem *The Battle of Maldon*, lines 113-16 (ed. D. G. Scragg, 1981), where particular mention is made of the death in battle of Wulfmær, Earl Byrhtnoth's kinsman, *his swustersunu*, and the consequent requital given to the Vikings for his death. The situation is very similar to that described here.

Page 233: For Leir, ruler of Boulogne, see 12171-2 and above, under Page

145. In the battle against Lucius no mention of Leir is found in GoM, and the only reference to the king of Babylon is the inclusion of his name, *Micipsa*, in the list of those on the Roman side who fell in the battle (§172). In Wace (12743-7), *Lygier* engages the king of Babylon and *morz fud li cuens, morz fu li reis*. The incident of Gecron avenging the king his father by slaying Leir is recounted only in Laȝamon.

Page 233: The four brave men of Brittany have their counterparts in GoM (§173): *Chinmarhogus, consul Trigerie* (Thorpe, p.253, 'Duke of Tréguier'), *Richomarcus, Bloccouius* and *Iagwiuius de Bodloano* (Thorpe, p.253, 'of Bodloan'), lords of immense courage who perish on the battlefield. Wace, likewise, lauds the bravery of *Kymar* (*Kinnmarc* as a variant form), *cuens de Triguel, Jaguz de Boldoan, Richomarcus* and *Boclovius* (12787-800), who fall in battle. In the Laȝamon texts, O reads *Iabius* for C's *Labius*. Mn, III, p.404, notes that Strugul, the title of Kinard's earldom in Laȝamon, was an ancient castle situated near the river Ystrigul in Monmouthshire, and gave its name as a title to the earls of Pembroke.

Page 237: After the decisive battle against Lucius, Geoffrey (§176) has Kay carried off *ad Camum* (variant form *Kainum* — see B-H, s.v. *Kinum*), *opidum quod ipse construxerat* 'to Chinon, the town which he himself had built' (Thorpe, p.257). Wace has Kay taken *a Chynon, sun chastel . . . ; / Key cumpassa e fist Chynon / E de Key ot Kynon cest nun* (12996-8). Tatlock, pp.97-8, argues for Chinon as a translation of *Camum/Kainun* rather than Caen (a prior identification) on the grounds that Chinon is geographically more likely as the burial place of Kay, described in GoM as 'Duke of the Angevins' (§176). B-H suggests that Laȝamon, in calling Kay's castle both Kinun and Kain, has identified the latter name as Caen and so confused Chinon with Caen.

Page 239: For reference to Merlin's prophecy about the fall of Rome, see above, under Page 217.

Page 241: As Mn, III, p.406, has noted, Arthur's dream and subsequent conversation with the knight, as well as Arthur's address to his followers and Gawain's speech denouncing his brother Modred, are found neither in GoM nor Wace. Geoffrey says only that news was brought to Arthur of Modred's treachery and his adulterous association with Guenevere, a particular matter about which he, Geoffrey, prefers to keep silent (§§176-7). He then goes on to talk of Arthur's preparations for battle against Modred (§177). Wace covers the news of Modred's treason, Arthur's response to it, and his decision to return to Britain rather briefly (13013-52); Laȝamon goes into much greater detail. The centrepiece of this amplification is Arthur's dream in which the king's hall, a symbol in OE poetry of legitimate royal authority and power, is pulled down by Guenevere and Modred whose perfidy Laȝamon has already referred to (12709-34). Animal imagery is present in the Prophecies of Merlin, and in the dreams of Charlemagne in the *Chanson de Roland*, and the boar and dragon which appear in Arthur's earlier dream are clearly identifiable (see above, under Page 181); the symbolism of the lion and fish in Arthur's second dream is less easy to explain.

Page 243: For the close relationship between a man and his sister's son, see above, under Page 229. The allusion to such a relationship here serves to underline the depth of Modred's perfidy.

Page 245: B&S, p.345, note that, in Laȝamon's day, burning at the stake for treason was a punishment inflicted upon women rather than men.

Page 245: Laȝamon's Whitsond (*Witsant/Witsand* in Wace (13049, 13052)) is identified in B-H, s.v. *Witsond*, as Wissant (Pas-de-Calais).

Page 247: Childric, the Saxon leader, whose aid Modred enlists (*Chelricus* in GoM (§177) and *Cheldric* in Wace (13055)), should not be confused with Childric, the Saxon chieftain and foe of Arthur slain by Cador, Earl of Cornwall, attempting to flee the country after his defeat in battle near Bath (10707-91).   Geoffrey distinguishes between the two, calling the latter *Cheldricus* (§§143, 147, 149); Wace calls both men *Cheldric*. As we have seen with Gillomar (above, under Page 85), Laȝamon calls two kings of Ireland by the same name.

Page 247:   In GoM (§177), Arthur lands *in Rupini Portu*, 'Richborough' (Thorpe, p.258 and Tatlock, pp.34-5).   Wace has *Romenel* (13079).   B-H, s.v. *Romelan*, identifies Wace's Romenel and Laȝamon's Romerel (O reads *Romelan*) as Old Romney.

Page 251:   Though Wace describes Modred's retreat to Winchester and cowardly flight from it (13135-88), he does not mention Arthur's destruction of the city or Merlin's prophecy. The source of the latter is in the Prophecies of Merlin section in GoM (§116.35): 'Kambria [Wales], come here! Bring Cornwall at your side! Say to Winchester: "The earth will swallow you up. . . .   Woe to the perjured people, for their famous city shall come toppling down because of them!"' (Thorpe, p.178).

Page 251:   The last we hear of Guenevere in GoM is of her flight from York to Caerleon where, in the church of Julius the Martyr, she takes the veil (§177). Wace, following Geoffrey, tells us that Guenevere enters a convent of nuns in Caerleon, but then goes on to say (13219-22): *Ne fud oïe ne veüe, / N'i fud trovee ne seüe, / Pur la verguine del mesfait / E del pechié qu'ele aveit fait* 'Never again was she seen nor heard of, never again known of or come upon because of shame for the misdeed and the sin she had committed.' There is, thus, neither in GoM nor Wace, given our present knowledge of the MSS of both, any source for Laȝamon's cryptic allusion to the connection between Guenevere's submersion in water and her death.   The difficulty is twofold: the second half-line of 14215 is missing (see B&L and B&S, 245), and the translation of 14216 itself is therefore problematic. Our translation is an attempt to make as much sense as possible of what, we fear, must in the end remain obscure.   O has, instead of C's 14215-16, the single line *in woche wise ȝeo was dead and ou ȝeo hinne .ende.*! It is of interest to note that Laȝamon, in recounting the story of a much earlier British queen, Judon, who killed her son, relates that she was put to death by drowning (2012: *Gumen heom igadereden and wurpen heo to sa-grunde*), a detail he has added to the account in GoM and Wace.

Page 253:   According to B-H, s.v. *Camelford*, Laȝamon's Tambre is an error for the river Camel, and arises from Wace (13253: *Camble*, with *Cambre/Tamble/Tanbre* as MS variants).   Geoffrey has *ad fluuium Camblani* (§178) 'the river Camblam' (Thorpe, p.259), identified as the river Camel in Cornwall, the river on which Camelford, mentioned in Laȝamon as the site of Arthur's final battle, is situated. The place-name given to Arthur's final battle in the earliest source (The Welsh Annals) is Camlann 'in which Arthur and Medraut fell' (Chambers, p.15).

Page 253:   Laȝamon's statement that only two knights survive the battle contrasts with GoM's roll-call of the many who died (§178), and Wace's description of the battlefield strewn with the dead of both armies and stained red with the blood of the dying (13263-5). In the French prose romance *La Mort Artu*, a source of the fourteenth-century *Stanzaic Morte Arthur* (itself thought to have been used by Malory for his description of Arthur's last battle), two knights are the sole survivors, apart from the dying Arthur, of the battle. Arthur's fifteen terrible wounds is another detail added to GoM and Wace who merely state that Arthur was mortally wounded (§178 and 13276).

Page 255:   In both GoM and Wace (§178 and 13275-9), Arthur, mortally wounded, is borne to Avalon (*insulam Auallonis* and *Avalon*) so that his wounds might be healed.   In Geoffrey's metrical *Vita Merlini*, the island is called *insula pomorum* 'the island of apples', and the connection between the latter name and Avalon is thought to have been made in the twelfth century through the Welsh *aval* 'apple' (see Loomis, pp.65-6).   The idyllic island, an entrancing otherworld in which there is no death and on which apple trees — the apple symbolising immortality — grow, is a feature of both classical and Celtic mythology. Though Glastonbury came to be identified as Arthur's resting-place in the late twelfth century (for the reported discovery of the grave of Arthur and Guenevere in the abbey, see Chambers, pp.112-15 and 268-74), and was thus linked to Avalon, Laȝamon makes no mention of Glastonbury.

The fairy queen Argante appears neither in GoM nor Wace, though in the *Vita Merlini* it is the beautiful Morgan who is the healer of Arthur's wounds in Avalon. J. D. Bruce ('Some proper names in Layamon's *Brut* not represented in Wace or Geoffrey of Monmouth', *Modern Language Notes*, 26 (1911), 65-9) argues that *Argante* is a corruption of *Morgant*, the Old French form of Morgan.

Page 255: In GoM (§178), we are told that Arthur, carried off to Avalon to have his wounds healed, entrusts his kingdom to his kinsman Constantin, the son of Cador, Earl of Cornwall. We are also given the date of this event, AD 542, a rare instance in GoM of a precise date. In the early twelfth century, however, William of Malmesbury in his *Gesta Regum* states: *sed Arturis sepulcrum nusquam visitur, unde antiquitas naeniarum adhuc eum venturum fabulatur* 'But the tomb of Arthur is nowhere beheld, whence ancient ditties fable that he is yet to come' (Chambers, pp.17 and 250). This seemingly widespread popular belief in Arthur's return to the British, reported also by Henry of Huntingdon, *c.*1129 (see Chambers, pp.250-1), is clearly alluded to in Wace (13279-90): 'He is there still, awaited by the Britons, for, as they say and believe, he will return from thence and live again. Master Wace, who made this book, wishes to say no more about his end than was said by Merlin the prophet; Merlin said of Arthur — and rightly so — that his death would remain in doubt. The prophet spoke truth; men have always doubted and, as I believe, always will doubt whether he is dead or whether he lives.'

Laȝamon, while acknowledging that the Britons still await Arthur's return, differs from earlier accounts in interpreting Merlin's prophecy as portending *an Arður sculde ȝete cum Anglen to fulste* 'an Arthur should come again to aid the people of England'. Tatlock, pp.504-5, sees in this reference a supportive allusion to Arthur of Brittany (1187-1203), grandson of Henry II and declared by Richard I his heir should he die without issue. But the reference to the people of England may have more to do with Laȝamon's perception of himself as an English poet.

BIBLIOGRAPHY

Editions, selections and translations

Laȝamon's 'Brut', or 'Chronicle of Britain', ed. F. Madden, 3 vols (London, 1847).

Laȝamon's 'Brut', eds G. L. Brook and R. F. Leslie, Early English Text Society, 250, 277 (London, 1963, 1978).

Laȝamon's 'Brut': Selections, ed. J. Hall (Oxford, 1924).

Selections from Laȝamon's 'Brut', ed. G. L. Brook, 2nd edn revised J. Levitt (Exeter, 1983).

Arthurian Chronicles by Wace and Layamon, tr. E. Mason, Everyman's Library (London, 1912); reprinted, with introduction by G. Jones, 1962; reprinted 1976.

Source studies

Brown, A. C. L., 'Welsh traditions in Laȝamon's *Brut*', *Modern Philology*, 1 (1903-04), 95-103.

Fletcher, R. H., 'Some Arthurian fragments from fourteenth-century chronicles', *PMLA*, 18 (1903), 84-94.

Frankis, P. J., 'Laȝamon's English sources', in *J. R. R. Tolkien, Scholar and Storyteller*, eds M. Salu and R. T. Farrell (Ithaca, NY., 1979), pp.64-75.

Gillespy, F. L., 'Layamon's *Brut*: a comparative study in narrative art', *University of California Publications in Modern Philology*, 3 (1916), 361-510.

Imelmann, R., *Layamon: Versuch über seine Quellen* (Berlin, 1906).

Ringbom, H., *Studies in the Narrative Technique of 'Beowulf' and Lawman's 'Brut'* (Åbo, 1968).

Visser, G. J., *Layamon: An Attempt at Vindication* (Assen, 1935).

Stylistic and metrical studies

Davies, H. S., 'Layamon's similes', *Review of English Studies*, 11 (1960), 129-42.

Friedlander, C. van D., 'Early Middle English accentual verse', *Modern Philology*, 76 (1979), 219-30.

Hamelius, P., 'The rhetorical structure of Layamon's verse', in *Mélanges Godefroid Kurth II* (Lüttich and Paris, 1908), pp.341-9.

Hilker, W., *Der Vers in Layamon's 'Brut'* (Münster, 1965).

Noble, J., 'Variation in Layamon's *Brut*', *Neuphilologische Mitteilungen*, 85 (1984), 92-4.

Sauer, H., 'Laȝamon's compound nouns and their morphology', in *Historical Semantics, Historical Word-Formation*, ed. J. Fisiak (Berlin, 1985), pp.483-532.

Tatlock, J. S. P., 'Epic formulas, especially in Laȝamon', *PMLA*, 38 (1923), 494-529.

Tatlock, J. S. P., 'Laȝamon's poetic style and its relations', *Manly Anniversary Studies* (Chicago, Ill., 1923), pp.3-11.

Wyld, H. C., 'Studies in the diction of Layamon's *Brut*', *Language*, 6 (1930), 1-24; 9 (1933), 47-71, 171-91; 10 (1934), 149-201; 13 (1937), 28-59, 194-237.

General and literary studies

Barron, W. R. J., *English Medieval Romance*, Longman Literature in English Series (London, 1987), pp.132-7.

Bennett, J. A. W. (edited and completed by D. Gray), *Middle English Literature*, The Oxford History of English Literature, Vol.I, Part 2 (Oxford, 1986), pp.68-89.

Blanchet, M-C., 'L'Argante de Layamon', in *Mélanges de language et de littérature du Moyen Age et de la Renaissance offerts à Jean Frappier*, 2 vols (Geneva, 1970), I, pp. 133-44.

Brewer, D. S., *English Gothic Literature*, Macmillan History of Literature (London, 1983), pp.9-14.

Everett, D., 'Layamon and the earliest Middle English alliterative verse', in *Essays on Middle English Literature*, ed. P. Kean (Oxford, 1955), pp.23-45.

Keith, W. J., 'Layamon's *Brut*: the literary difference between the two texts', *Medium Aevum*, 29 (1960), 161-72.

Lewis, C. S., 'The genesis of a medieval book', in *Studies in Medieval and Renaissance Literature*, ed. W. Hooper (Cambridge, 1966), pp.18-33.

Loomis, R. S., 'Layamon's *Brut*', in *Arthurian Literature in the Middle Ages: A Collaborative History*, ed. R. S. Loomis (Oxford, 1959), pp.104-11.

O'Sharkey, E. M., 'King Arthur's prophetic dreams and the role of Modred in Layamon's *Brut* and the alliterative *Morte Arthure*', *Romania*, 99 (1978), 347-62.

Pearsall, D., *Old English and Middle English Poetry*, The Routledge History of English Poetry, I (London, 1977), pp.80-1, 108-13.

Pilch, H., *Laȝamon's 'Brut': Eine Literarische Studie* (Heidelberg, 1960).

Schirmer, W. F., 'Layamon's *Brut*', *Modern Humanities Research Bulletin*, 1957, 15-27.

Swanton, M., *English Literature Before Chaucer*, Longman Literature in English Series (London, 1987), pp.175-87.

Stanley, E. G., 'The date of Layamon's *Brut*', *Notes and Queries*, 213 (1968), 85-8.

Stanley, E. G., 'Layamon's antiquarian sentiments', *Medium Aevum*, 38 (1969), 23-37.

Swart, J., 'Laȝamon's *Brut*', in *Studies in Language and Literature in Honour of Margaret Schlauch*, ed. M. Brahmer *et al.* (Warsaw, 1966), pp.431-5.

Tatlock, J. S. P., *The Legendary History of Britain: Geoffrey of Monmouth's 'Historia Regum Britanniae' and its Early Vernacular Versions* (Berkeley, Calif., 1950).

Wyld, H. C., 'Layamon as an English poet', *Review of English Studies*, 6 (1930), 1-30.